THE ELIZABETHAN HOUSE
OF COMMONS

THE
ELIZABETHAN
HOUSE
OF
COMMONS

J. E. Neale

FONTANA/COLLINS

First published by Jonathan Cape 1949
Revised edition first published in Peregrine Books 1963
First issued in Fontana Books 1976

Copyright © J. E. Neale 1949

Made and printed in Great Britain by
William Collins Sons & Co. Ltd Glasgow

Contents

List of Plates

1 QUEEN ELIZABETH
Part of the embellishment of the Mildmay Charter

2 THE PRESENTATION OF THE SPEAKER, NOVEMBER 1584
From Robert Glover, *Nobilitas politica vel civilis*, 1608. Reproduced by permission of the British Museum.

3 QUEEN ELIZABETH IN PARLIAMENT
A seventeenth-century portrayal of the closing ceremony, from Sir Simonds D'Ewes, *Journals of the Parliaments of Queen Elizabeth*, 1682

4 THE HOUSE OF COMMONS, 1624
This is probably the earliest picture of the House of Commons. The original engraving (a print of which is in Harleian MS. 159, fol. 2) was made for the parliament which met in February 1624. The print reproduced here from the Print Room of the British Museum appears to be from the same engraving, which was re-used probably for the parliament of 1628-9. A copy was inserted by D'Ewes in the manuscript of his *Journals* compiled in 1629-30 (Harleian MS. 73, fol. 8).

Preface

THIS volume has grown out of the first three of the Ford Lectures which I delivered in 1942. I am indebted to the authorities of the University of Oxford, not only for the honour of being Ford's Lecturer, but for the stimulus provided by the occasion, bringing to a head many years of research.

I have been hunting Elizabethan parliamentary documents all my professional life; and as I now reflect on the many friendships and kindly services that this work has brought me, I am conscious how blessed it is to be so rich a debtor. I owe my training and any quality as a scholar to that master of Tudor history, A. F. Pollard. Among friendships I must place first that of Wallace Notestein of Yale University. Since we first met in 1919 we have been Castor and Pollux, he pursuing early-Stuart parliaments and I Elizabethan. Would that in international diplomacy there could be as unshakable a basis for an *entente cordiale*! Conyers Read of Pennsylvania, a great Elizabethan scholar, has been another friend whose encouragement has meant much to me. I think also of those many research students who have given as well as received. In particular I am indebted to two in my Manchester days, Miss Brady and Miss Davey, and two recent London students, Miss Matthews and Miss Trafford, without whose biographical studies of Elizabethan M.P.'s I could not have hoped to write this volume. And they in turn owed much to the late W. D. Pink, whose parliamentary biographies, preserved at the John Rylands Library, Manchester, represent a lifetime of selfless devotion to research. Indeed, no scholar lives to himself, which is the supreme bliss of this happiest of callings.

Owners of manuscripts have been very good to me. I acknowledge with warm gratitude the kindness and hospitality of Lord Braye and of Lady Anstruther-Gough-Calthorpe. I am indebted to the Provost and Fellows of Trinity College, Dublin, to College and University Libraries at Cambridge and Oxford, and of course to the Public Record Office and British Museum, many of whose officials have become my friends. It would require an autobiography to list all the people who directly and indirectly have been helpmates. Though unnamed, I cherish their memory and am thankful. To my wife I owe a debt which far transcends the many hours of labour that she has put into this book; and to Mr R. B. Wernham of Trinity College, Oxford, whom I am proud to number among my former pupils and colleagues, I am indebted for scrutinizing the proofs of the volume.

In my narrative I have had to range over a great deal of local history, where I could not hope to tread with as sure a foot as in the main argument. I only hope that I have not slipped too often or too egregiously. This present volume tells but half my story. I propose to follow it with a parliamentary history of the reign, when the rich quality of the new documents and the vital significance of the Elizabethan period will, I trust, become even more apparent.

University College, London   J. E. NEALE

October 1948

I have taken advantage of the re-setting of the type for this paperback edition to make some corrections, based on later research.

February 1963   J. E. N.

Note on References

THE names and constituencies of members of parliament have usually been taken from the *Return of Members of Parliament* (1878) and the typed list of supplementary returns at the Public Record Office. For the parliament of 1571, which has no returns extant, I have used Browne Willis, *Notitia Parliamentaria*, volume iii, whose list on this occasion is fairly reliable, as are the additional names that he provides for the parliament of 1584-5. In other instances, or where errors or doubts exist, I have given my references. Much of my biographical information has been taken from the *Dictionary of National Biography* or from the four theses to which I have referred in the Preface and elsewhere. I have not thought it necessary to cumber the pages with scores of such references, though other sources of information are cited.

Introduction

In these days of institutional *malaise*, a historical study of our English parliament, though it be of far-off days in the sixteenth century, cannot be entirely remote from our interests. The past explains the present, and the historical process, so far as it emerges from such a study, has its bearing upon our understanding of contemporary life.

With its long and continuous story, it might be said of parliament as of nature, nothing is done by leaps. Evolution and adaptation to a changing society mark its progress, rather than advance from one famous constitutional document to another. It is almost as perilous to speak of something being entirely new in parliamentary history as in the history of thought. Nevertheless, change there was, and trends which in time altered the climate. There are few who would deny novelty to the conditions of the sixteenth century. A hundred years or so before, the legislative character of the institution was submerged under its legal character: in the sixteenth century the reverse was true. Yet a very subtle mind would be needed to trace the change.

Dangerous as the practice is, it helps us in our understanding of history to seize on dates and events as turning points; and Henry VIII's reign, with its religious, social, and political revolution, known to us as the Reformation, has as good a claim as any to serve in this way. Henry VIII has been called, by the master of Tudor history in our time, 'the architect of parliament'. His break from Rome, with all its ramifications, called for legislation on an unprecedented scale. It ushered in the planned state of the Tudors, and it led to a great diffusion of wealth among the landed and legal class. Moreover, with the Church and conservatism entrenched in the House of Lords, the King, for tactical reasons, had to go into partnership with the Commons and use them as the vanguard of his Reformation attack. We enter the period of parity in power and influence, if not in prestige, between the two Houses. By Elizabeth's reign, a balanced history of parliament would be almost as predominantly a history of the House of Commons as it is in early Stuart times. Already, we perceive the shape of things to come.

13

It is at this crucial stage in the history of the House of Commons that our study of its structure and manner of working is placed. Who were these members of parliament? To what classes of society did they belong? How did they come to be elected? How were elections conducted? These are questions which can be very illuminating if one probes into the nature of contemporary society and, so far as is possible, sets the answers in a social and political background. If the narrative sometimes strays a little from strictly parliamentary into social history, this is deliberate. The House of Commons was a reflection of Elizabethan society and offers an approach to social history that it would be a mistake to ignore.

One of the remarkable features in our English parliamentary system — so much taken for granted that we hardly reflect on its incalculable historical importance — is the divorce of the idea of representation from any local ties with the constituency: the ability of anyone from anywhere to contest an election. The very name, 'carpet-bagger', that we have imported from America and given to intruding outsiders, is a term of obloquy; and yet we have reason to thank God that things have turned out so. For how else could the House of Commons have greatly surpassed the average ability of the community; how else have provided room for the nation's best available skill and leadership; how else have secured that parliament should be nationally rather than locally minded? While this practice has a long history, reaching back into the Middle Ages, it was in the sixteenth century that 'carpet-bagging' overwhelmingly and irrevocably established itself; and the reason, as we shall see, was the way society was then constructed.

In addition to a study of the membership of parliament, the book aims at conveying a picture of the House of Commons at work; of its officials, its ceremonies, its procedure, its manners and conventions, even the style of speaking there. And here again there is a singularity about the Elizabethan period. An intimate description of this kind cannot be written of any earlier time. The evidence simply does not exist. It bursts upon us in this reign with a wealth, which, however limited in comparison with the richer age to follow, is remarkable when set against the poverty of the preceding ten years. An efflorescence, though it be in the humdrum sphere of parliamentary sources, harmonizes with our Elizabethan tradition;

and while we must not make the easy mistake of belittling un-recorded times, there are reasons quite sober and cogent enough to interpret the appearance of diaries and speeches and other historical evidence as the reflection of a great parliamentary age.

Except incidentally, this is not a constitutional or parliamentary history. The chronological story of Elizabethan parliaments – a story almost as significant and dramatic in its different medium as that of James I and Charles I's reigns – must be left for a subsequent volume; and there the constitutional theme will find its appropriate place.

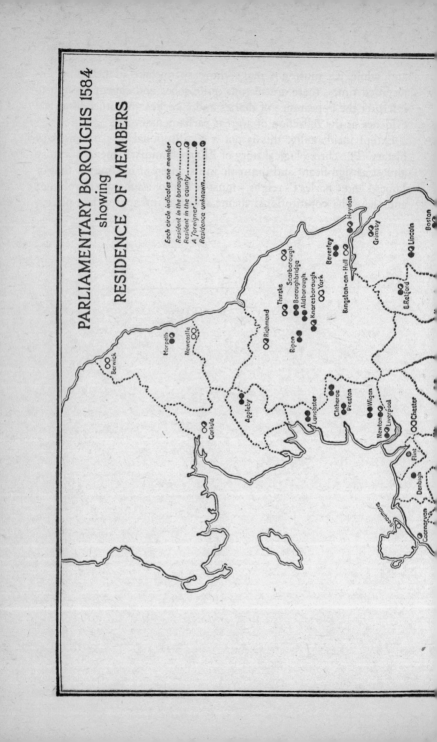

PARLIAMENTARY BOROUGHS 1584
showing
RESIDENCE OF MEMBERS

Each circle indicates one member
Resident in the borough........
Resident in the county........
A "foreigner"........
Residence unknown........

Map compiled by Miss Hazel Matthews

CHAPTER I

The County

ELIZABETHAN England was primarily an agricultural community. Its chief wealth was in land and its ruling class was the landed gentry – the middling and big businessmen of a rural society. To such persons it was the county that really mattered; and this to an extent that we today find hard to appreciate, for though still a reality in our national life, the enormous growth of population, the urbanization of so much of the country, and the centralization of government have all robbed it of its old significance.

To describe the England of those days as a federation of counties would be legally ridiculous, yet such a misnomer conveys a valuable truth. The central government was for its time an active and efficient machine, but it had relatively little direct contact with the individual. The effective unit of government was the shire, with its corps of unsalaried officials: the Justices of Peace, appointed in county commissions, on which it was the ambition of most substantial gentlemen and some less substantial to see their names; and the Sheriff, the chief local executive officer of the Crown, chosen annually from a small number of leading gentry. To this ancient array the Tudors had added a new, gilded head, the Lord Lieutenant, usually the chief nobleman of the county, whose main duty was to hold the annual musters and act as military leader of the shire, though he was used as the head of the county in many other matters. His two or more Deputy-Lieutenants, chosen from the most influential gentlemen, basked in his primacy, and were in consequence pre-eminent among their fellows.

The county was divided into Hundreds – ancient areas that still find a place on our maps. Though their old folk-courts, the Hundred-courts, were sick unto death, most of them being in private hands and all reduced to the pettiest jurisdiction, nevertheless for administrative purposes the Hundred itself remained very much a reality. The Justices were of course appointed for the whole county, but in discharging their innumerable duties – they were the government's 'men-of-all-work' – they often tacitly organized themselves on the basis of the Hundred. Similarly, the Lord Lieutenant and his Deputies carried out their musters Hundred by Hundred. And there were other occasions when this area proved itself the convenient administrative unit. In some counties there was also a tacit division into larger areas, of north and south, or east and west.

These convenient divisions engendered local rivalries but they did not weaken the corporate reality of the county, any more than the 'house-system' in our public schools detracts from the unity of the whole. Justices might often think and act on the basis of the Hundred, but their main and best-known function, the holding of Quarter Sessions, was a county activity. Then there was the Sheriff, whose very name spoke for the whole community. It is customary to talk of 'the decline of the Sheriff' – a sound enough description when applied to some of his ancient powers. But decline was not ease, as the desperate attempts of some gentlemen to escape this office show. His manifold activities were sufficient in themselves to impress unity on the county. And so were the activities of the Lord Lieutenant. Some lieutenancies were spread over more than one county, but when it came to the actual administrative work, at the lower level of the Deputies, the county reasserted itself.

Thus, the country gentleman's world was the county. Here, if prestige mattered at all to him – and being in many respects a childish age, it usually mattered a lot – he cut a figure according to his family's standing and his own wealth and ability. The seventeenth-century antiquary, Gervase Holles, records of his great-grandfather, the Nottinghamshire squire Sir William Holles of Houghton, who died in 1590 a grand old man of eighty-three: 'His retinue was always answerable to his hospitality, very great, and, according to the magnificence of those days, far more than necessary. At King Edward VI his coronation he appeared with fifty followers in their blue coats and badges, and I have heard divers affirm, that knew him, how he would not come to Retford sessions without thirty proper fellows of his own at his heels.'[1]

The country gentleman had his *cursus honorum*, in which Shakespeare advanced Justice Swallow at least two degrees beyond the likely limits of such a nincompoop.

1. *Memorials of the Holles Family*, ed. Wood (Camden Soc.), p. 45.

SHALLOW: He shall not abuse Robert Shallow, esquire,

SLENDER: In the county of Gloucester, Justice of Peace, and 'Coram'.

SHALLOW: Ay, cousin Slender, and 'Cust-alorum'.

SLENDER: Ay, and 'Rato-lorum' too; and a gentleman born, Master Parson, who writes himself 'Armigero', in any bill, warrant, quittance, or obligation, 'Armigero'.

SHALLOW: Ay, that I do; and have done any time these three hundred years.

SLENDER: All his successors gone before him hath done 't; and all his ancestors that come after him may: they may give the dozen white luces in their coat.

SHALLOW: It is an old coat.[1]

Add to Shallow's honours the offices of Sheriff, Deputy-Lieutenant, and knight of the shire in parliament, and we have a table of dignities which the gentry were often forced to covet, either for the sake of prestige, with all its practical consequences, or to prevent neighbours exercising authority over their tenantry. The number of aspirants for the office of Justice must have far exceeded those on the commission: certainly, when government relaxed and honour cheapened, as they did under James I, the roll of Justices increased deplorably.

Rural life, with all its occasions for dispute over the ownership and use of land, has always been full of bickerings. They were exaggerated in a hundred ways in Elizabethan times. The age was litigious, an old failing of the gentry, which, if anything, was on the increase. Various facts suggest this. There was the growing use of the Inns of Court as finishing schools for gentlemen, imparting both a knowledge of law and a taste for it. Half a century later, Fuller wrote of 'The True Gentleman': 'At the Inns of Court he applies himself to learn the laws of the kingdom. Object not, why should a gentleman learn law, who if he needeth it may have it for his money ... Law will help him to keep his own, and bestead his neighbours.'[2] Another reason was the ease with which cases could be begun in the Star Chamber and similar courts. It was a common device to annoy one's enemy in this way, and perhaps impoverish him by the costs of the defence, which the plaintiff could more or less regulate. The number of bills lodged in the Star Chamber and in the Court of Requests – perhaps also in the Chancery, if the figures

1. *Merry Wives of Windsor*, act 1, scene i.
2. FULLER, *Holy and Profane State*.

were known – increased approximately tenfold during Elizabeth's reign. Justice Shallow, it will be remembered, threatened to 'make a Star Chamber matter' of Falstaff's misdemeanours; and well he might. In real life, one Elizabethan gentleman is said to have been involved in no less than twenty-two suits in that court; and another – thrice an M.P., and also a sheriff – is known to have been plaintiff on at least eight occasions.[1] Litigation bred lawyers, and lawyers litigation. Writing at the end of Elizabeth's reign, a well-informed student of such matters commented on the inordinate and dangerous growth in number, wealth, and pride of the lawyer class, and on their propensity to involve young gentlemen, newly come into their livings, in ruinous lawsuits.[2]

In the country gentleman's life there was one convention or institution which must claim a good deal of our attention. We may call it clientage, a vestige of feudalism adapted to new social purposes. Most of the gentry seem to have grouped themselves, in close or loose relationship, round one or other of the few great men of the county, sometimes to the point of accepting their livery and donning it as occasion demanded. Later in our narrative we shall notice George Belgrave esquire, a Leicestershire gentleman of some consequence and independence, putting on the blue coat with bull's head on sleeve of the Earl of Huntingdon to fool the electors of Leicester into believing that he had become the Earl's follower.[3] The younger sons of these dependants might take service in their patron's household, pursuing that 'gentlemanly profession of serving-men' which at the end of the sixteenth century appears to have been on the decline, giving way before the expansion of ordinary domestic service.[4] Their daughters might be placed with the lady of the great house, to be reared as in a school of manners, and perhaps to win her help in the crucial business of marriage.[5] Truth to tell, in a world of

---

1. ELFREDA SKELTON, 'Court of Star Chamber in the Reign of Elizabeth' (University of London M.A. thesis), i, 71.

2. THOMAS WILSON, 'The State of England', ed. Fisher, *Camden Misc.*, xvi, 25.

3. See below, p. 168.

4. Cf. *A Health to the Gentlemanly Profession of Serving-Men* (Shakespeare Assoc. Facsimiles, No. 3).

5. Cf. *Diary of Lady Margaret Hoby*, ed. Meads, introduction.

dependants, independence was a quixotic luxury. The smaller man found friendship, patronage, and protection in the system. The great man gained reputation and power: he made manifest his greatness by the number of gentlemen whom he could on occasion summon to follow him. Francis Bacon has an essay on the subject, entitled 'Of Followers and Friends'. 'There is little friendship in the world', he wrote, 'and least of all between equals ... That that is, is between superior and inferior, whose fortunes may comprehend the one the other.'

Inevitably, this tendency of the gentry to move within the orbit of some magnate provoked or intensified rivalry, which percolated through from the highest to the lowest ranks of the gentry and even to their tenantry. In faction-ridden counties it produced those riots and assaults whose stories we so frequently find in Star Chamber documents. 'There is a great quarrel betwixt two Nottinghamshire gentlemen', wrote Roger Manners to the Earl of Rutland in 1588, 'which I think will revive a faction in the shire.' 'If it fall to banding in the country ...', he went on.[1] In reverse, quarrels from below worked through to the top. 'Factious followers', wrote Bacon, 'which follow, not upon affection to him with whom they range themselves, but upon discontentment conceived against some other', bring about 'that ill intelligence that we many times see between great personages'.[2] Shakespeare's story of Montague and Capulet may have derived its intensity from Italy, but it was not wholly alien to the English scene.

As we should expect, clientage reached its fullest expression at Court. Here was the Mecca of patronage; place and profit incomparable to be had through the favour of the great ones of the land. Ambitious and impecunious young gentlemen strove to find room in their service; and as such servants were not necessarily paid but looked to perquisites for their reward, the households of eminent courtiers and statesmen could grow to astonishing numbers. 'Let thy servants be such as thou mayest command; and entertain none about thee but yeomen, to whom thou givest wages', Raleigh counselled his son; 'for those that will serve thee without thy hire, will cost thee treble as much as they that know thy fare.'[3] Strange doctrine it

1. *H.M.C. Rutland MSS*, i, 240.   2. *Essays*, 'Of Followers and Friends'.
3. *Instructions to his Son*, cap. vi. Cf. my Raleigh Lecture, *The Elizabethan Scene*.

would have sounded in high Elizabethan days. In addition to gentlemen servants, there were many, including the most substantial gentlemen, in various localities, who dubbed themselves followers of eminent men at Court, and, if they lived in any of the several counties in which their patron owned estates, might have taken his livery.

The great ones of England moved about the country like princes. Their followers turned out to escort them when in their county, as the Sheriff and gentlemen of the shire turned out for the Queen on progress; and, like royalty, they entered towns in ceremonial manner to mutual giving of salutations and presents. Sir George Paule, comptroller of Archbishop Whitgift's household, tells us that every third year his master went into Kent, 'where he was so honourably attended upon by his own train, consisting of two hundred persons, and with the gentlemen of the country, that he did sometimes ride into the city of Canterbury and into other towns with eight hundred or a thousand horse.'[1] We hear of the Duke of Norfolk in January 1566 entering London with three hundred horsemen, and in April that year of the Earl of Leicester coming to town 'accompanied with lords, knights, the Pensioners and a great number of gentlemen and others, with the Queen's footmen and his own also, all in their rich coats and to the number of seven hundred'.

At New Year's tide in 1566 the Earl of Leicester arrayed all his followers in blue laces or stripes to display his power, while the Duke of Norfolk, then his opponent, promptly put his men in yellow laces.[2] Thus the rivalries and factions of the Court were communicated to hundreds of followers, and must have penetrated into the counties, aligning with local faction there and strengthening it. As we shall see, this was the situation in Denbighshire and elsewhere in the latter part of the reign.

The grouping and interdependence of the gentry, with its accompanying and constant struggle for prestige and supremacy, permeated English life. It assumed the part played by politics in our modern society, and in the county is a main clue to parliamentary elections. A county election was in fact a mustering of the community. The electoral franchise there was uniform. The voters were the celebrated

1. PAULE, *Life of Whitgift* (1699), p. 104.
2. *Spanish Cal. Eliz.*, i, 511; *Hatfield MSS.* i, 326; *Three Fifteenth-century Chronicles*, ed. Gairdner (Camden Soc.), p. 137.

forty-shilling freeholders – those having 'free tenement to the value of forty shillings by the year at the least, above all charges'; and although there was some argument about the nature of the freehold, to which legal construction permitted a certain elasticity in the sixteenth century as in the eighteenth, this statutory provision remained binding from its enactment in the fifteenth century down to the Reform Bill of 1832.

All the gentry and very many of their tenants and dependants were entitled to vote; and since candidates – more especially when there was prospect of a contest – called on their friends, with dependants and followers, to support them, a county election furnished an opportunity, quite unique in the life of the community, of testing the social standing of an individual or the relative strength of rival groups and parties. Consequently, far more might be at stake than a seat in parliament. Indeed, just as the endeavours of that great faction-leader, the Earl of Essex, to place some nominee in a vacant office at Court in the later years of Elizabeth inevitably transcended the point at issue and became a struggle between Essex and the Cecils for supremacy in the land, so in these county elections it was easy for a contest to become the mere symbol of a vital battle for hegemony in the county, with all its practical consequences. In 1601 Sir John Harington threatened to desert his Rutland house and live on his Warwickshire estates if his will did not prevail in the election: neither his pride nor his prestige could bear the humiliation of defeat. County elections not only fed faction: in their very nature they tended to create it.

The theme can be found in most of the surviving stories of contested elections; but for the moment let us be content with sampling the flavour of an election in Hertfordshire. This county was in a peculiar, though by no means unique situation. Only one of its two seats was really open to competition. In the first half of the reign the other was held by Sir Ralp Sadler, Privy Councillor and Chancellor of the Duchy of Lancaster. His position at Court gave him a social primacy in the county which no inferior – and other than inferiors there were none – would have dreamt of challenging. In 1588, after his death, Lord Burghley, then Lord Lieutenant of the county, seized the opportunity – perhaps a little prematurely, but occasion and person were precocious – to transfer the honour to his son, Robert

Cecil. In this way Hertfordshire had one of its seats foreclosed throughout the whole of the reign. It placed a great strain upon the community, for no two individuals or groups could be satisfied at the same time.

In 1584 the inevitable happened. The county found itself in two minds about the single seat. Sir John Brockett of Brockett Hall, the member in the last and long parliament of 1572, was perhaps disinclined to sit again. At any rate, he and his powerful friend, Charles Moryson of Cashiobury, promised their support to Edward Denny of Bishop Stortford. Then a second candidate appeared. He was Sir Henry Cocke of Broxbourne, an ambitious gentleman, who had already sat in two parliaments, for different boroughs, but since the last election had been Sheriff of his county and evidently thought that the time had arrived to strike for the crowning glory of becoming knight of the shire. He wrote to Charles Moryson explaining that he had tried to persuade a good friend of them both to stand for election; but the friend refused, and along with others urged Cocke to stand. 'I know', Cocke continued, 'my own private credit is not such in the shire (although I account myself very much beholding unto my countrymen) as of myself I can clearly carry away so great a matter as that is.' He asked Moryson out of friendship to support him, or at any rate not to hinder him: he was not deliberately trying 'to encounter or cross any', he added.

Moryson replied that he was already pledged to Mr Denny. He was grieved — as he had already told Cocke — at the prospect of bringing trouble on his county through 'the disgrace of either of you in having the repulse'. All he could say, was: 'Let every man carry himself in his word honestly', and if an open contest were unavoidable, let the result 'be borne with as little dislike of the other side as in honest charity it becomes gentlemen'.

Perhaps the county was not as free from division as Moryson's letter would seem to imply. Cocke was — or became — a protégé of Burghley's, and Denny owed his later knighthood to the Earl of Leicester; which suggests some reflection of Court parties in Hertfordshire. However it be, this election of 1584 certainly split the county. The pitiful quandary in which humble voters found themselves may be illustrated by the men of Watford. These simple townsmen first promised their votes to a powerful neighbour, Harry

Coningsby of North Mimms, one of Cocke's supporters. Then along came Charles Moryson, their 'good neighbour and friend' and – most cogent of all – the lord of their town. Perforce, they withdrew their earlier promise. Coningsby's anger was shattering: 'If your promises', he wrote them, 'be of no better value, and your credits so light, and that you do no better esteem of me, your neighbour, than your letters do purport, but may be drawn to falsify what you have promised; I then must pronounce unto you what I will be to you and the rest that shall so deal with me ... As I will not be injurious to any of you, so will I not be holding unto you in any respect, neither shall you make account of me either as your friend or your neighbour.'

Edward Denny was defeated – by fraud, according to his supporters. Two of these, Sir John Brockett and Brockett's son-in-law, John Cutts, writing to Moryson, reveal how hard it was to follow their own precept of 'honest charity' among gentlemen. 'Such ringing of bells', moaned Brockett, 'as they yet sound in my ears.' He commented bitterly on the 'manifest perjury' of their opponents, and, according to his son-in-law, intended to find out and note down how many unlawful voters they had used, in order to show 'the two great Earls' – Leicester, the Lord Lieutenant, being one – 'how our knight came by his knightship'. 'We all are forthcoming, to abide a new field upon a new occasion', wrote Cutts; a sentiment which his father-in-law echoed. 'We have joined in this together; so by the grace of God we will always, when our success shall be better.'[1]

The rift thus created or widened in the county seems to have continued for many years, and we catch occasional glimpses of it. In 1586 Sir Henry Cocke was again returned to parliament, but in 1588 he gave place to Sir Philip Butler, one of his group, whose mother was a Coningsby. Butler's father shared the deputy-lieutenancy in these later years with Cocke and Brockett, and in 1590 we find Brockett at loggerheads with the other two – significantly enough, over the favour shown to a Coningsby at the expense of Brockett's son. Then in 1593 we hear of another contested election, when Edward – now Sir Edward – Denny once more challenged Cocke and again was beaten. Feelings must have run high, for a gentleman complained that Cocke had lodged a suit against him in the Court of Requests and secured his imprisonment, simply because he had voted

1. Add. MSS. 40629, fol. 33; 40630, fols. 1–8.

for Denny. In the next election fortune turned. Denny, whose
mother and wife were both West-Country women, sat for a Cornish
borough in this parliament, but his friends tried to persuade his
nephew and namesake to contest the Hertfordshire seat. When he
refused, Rowland Lytton of Knebworth took his place, and, against
'great labour' by the other side, carried the election. The contest was
evidently acrimonious, and it may well be that the defeated candidate
was the hitherto triumphant Sir Henry Cocke.[1]

Even in normal counties where both seats were open to competition
and there were only two candidates, an election might engender
bitter feelings, for by Elizabeth's reign custom had come to assign
much additional prestige to the 'first' of the two knightships of the
shire. To secure this place was indeed to win supremacy, and second
place might be only less hard to bear than total defeat. In 1597 Sir
Robert Sidney's servant and agent wrote to his master, then at his
post in the Netherlands: 'I understand that my Lord Cobham' –
whose brother and heir, Sir William Brooke, had with Sidney been
elected for Kent – 'was much grieved to see that you ... had the
chief place given you by the voices of the people, which he would
not have believed.' In the same year, the Countess of Leicester, then
married to Sir Christopher Blount, wrote to her son, the famous
Earl of Essex, complaining of the 'wrong and disgrace' inflicted on
her husband by the Sheriff of Staffordshire in preferring his son-in-
law, John Sutton *alias* Dudley, 'to the first place of knight of the
shire', leaving the inferior seat to Blount. The Sheriff's purse, she
hoped, would pay for it; nor would they forget Sutton's brother,
Lord Dudley, who had a principal hand in the business, in defiance
of a letter from the Earl of Essex.[2]

But conflict is only one thread in our story. Elizabethan society,
for all its restlessness and change, was an ordered aristocracy with
accepted rules of social precedence. To represent the county in
parliament was so coveted an honour that it was normally confined
to a few of the most prominent county families. 'Foreigners' –
'carpet-baggers', as we should say – were quite excluded, unless a
remote and small county such as Westmorland offered an exception
to the rule. The current sentiment was expressed in a letter from

1. *Cal. S.P. Dom., 1581–90*, pp. 654–5; *Hatfield MSS.* xiii, 520; vii, 396.
2. COLLINS, *Sidney Papers*, ii, 62; BIRCH, *Memoirs of Q. Eliz.*, ii, 362.

Christopher Heydon, one of the members for Norfolk in 1588. Writing to Bassingbourne Gawdy, another prominent Norfolk gentleman, early in 1601, when an election seemed imminent, he declared that he did not mean to stand for parliament himself, but wished to oppose the election of a 'stranger'. Therefore he asked Gawdy to hold the votes which he controlled in suspense until the election, when he did not doubt that 'a good Norfolk candidate' could be produced. The 'stranger' to whom he objected was Sir Robert Mansell, who had been settled in Norfolk, on his wife's lands, for close on a decade and become a Justice, as well as Vice-Admiral, in the county. He was a stranger only in an eclectic sense; but as he had recently fought a duel with Heydon's brother, the animosity is understandable.[1]

The restriction of county seats to a few of the most prominent county families could lead to bitter contests. It could equally lead to no contest at all. We must rid our minds of the notion that election generally means a choice of candidates. That is a modern supposition, born of party politics. There were no party politics in the Elizabethan period; and, granted this negative fact and the high valuation set upon a county seat, what really determined the nature of elections was the social structure in each county. Each locality had an electoral pattern of its own, which can be worked out – even when there is little more to guide us than a list of members – as a type of equation between the names of the members and the social hierarchy of the county.

In some counties there might be one, and in others two of the leading gentlemen socially so superior to the rest that no one could either hope or dare to compete with them. They were peerless; and lesser folk, though gentlemen of considerable standing, were forced into the boroughs if they wished to sit in parliament. We have already noticed that one of the Hertfordshire seats was monopolized throughout the reign, first by Sir Ralph Sadler, and then by Robert Cecil. Cecil began his parliamentary career in 1584 at the age of twenty-one, sitting for Westminster, where his father was High Steward. He was re-elected in 1586. He was twenty-five, with this apprenticeship behind him, when in 1588 his father seized the opportunity created by Sadler's death. Writing to Charles Moryson, then Sheriff of Hertfordshire, and maybe also to other influential

1. *H.M.C. Gawdy MSS.*, p. 32.

gentlemen, Lord Burghley pointed out that his son was a Justice of the Peace in the county and would, when he himself died, have 'a reasonable freehold' there. He asked Moryson, if he had not already 'made earnest determination to support others', to grant Robert Cecil the voices of his friends and tenants; though tactfully adding that he wished for no support save with their goodwill.[1] Such a request was tantamount to a command. Who could, or would wish to resist England's foremost statesman and their own Lord Lieutenant, asking favour for a son whose brilliant future few could doubt? The incident may strike us as suspiciously like a government nomination: in Elizabethan practice it was no more than a father securing his son's social heritage.

Oxfordshire presents us with an example of a single family monopolizing both county seats over a period of years. Sir Francis Knollys, whose wife was first cousin to Queen Elizabeth, became Vice-Chamberlain, Privy Councillor, and one of the most notable courtiers on Elizabeth's accession – a man without rival among the commoners in his county. After a long apprenticeship in boroughs, he assumed the senior seat for Oxfordshire in 1563 and retained it till his death in 1596. His eldest son, Henry, sat for the borough of Reading in 1563 and 1571; but in 1572, when he was about thirty-one, he joined his father in representing Oxfordshire.[2] Probably Sir Francis was bent on assuring the succession in the primacy of the county to his heir. At any rate, when Henry died, the eldest surviving son, William, took his place in the next parliament of 1584 and in that of 1593, and after his father's death assumed the senior county seat – as he assumed place at Court and in the Council – for the rest of the reign. Elizabethan Oxfordshire was granted few opportunities for contested elections.

Another county favoured or embarrassed with eminent men was Northamptonshire. Sir Walter Mildmay first represented the county in the last parliament of Mary Tudor, and, being already in government service, took the senior seat against a Spencer. He continued as knight of the shire until his death in 1589, but with fluctuations

1. Add. MS. 40629, fol. 89; draft in Lansdowne MS. 103, fol. 111, which shows that on second thoughts Burghley appealed to Moryson as 'a person of credit' instead of 'as sheriff' – a significant alteration.
2. On the date of his birth, cf. my comments in *Eng. Hist. Rev.* liv, 503.

between the senior and junior seats which illustrate admirably the punctilio of social precedence. He preceded a Montagu in 1559 and Sir Robert Lane in 1571, but retreated to second place when the senior statesman, Sir William Cecil, chose to stand for this county in 1563. In 1572, as Chancellor of the Exchequer and Privy Councillor, he took precedence of the rising courtier, Christopher Hatton, then merely an esquire; but by the next election, in 1584, Hatton had become a knight and Vice-Chamberlain and again Mildmay gave way, as he did when the two represented the county in the following parliament. In his last parliament, 1588, with Hatton removed to the Lord Chancellorship and Sir Richard Knightley as fellow-member, he resumed the senior seat.

Clearly, elections in this county could not have been a source of much strife. Down to 1588 there could have been three occasions only – 1559, 1571, and 1588 – when open competition for a seat was possible, and we can eliminate one of these, for in 1588 Sir Christopher Hatton wrote to the Sheriff, Sir Edward Montagu, recommending Sir Walter Mildmay and also his 'good friend Sir Richard Knightley, a gentleman so well affected to the good of his country as that I doubt not but to find yourself and the rest of our gentlemen very ready'. He asked Montagu to 'move . . . your good friends, freeholders, tenants, and servants for the furtherance of their voices thereunto'.[1] Whatever plans Montagu or others may have had, they thought twice before risking Hatton's displeasure. In 1593 and 1597 Sir Thomas Cecil, Burghley's eldest son, was the senior knight, and in 1601 Sir John Stanhope, Vice-Chamberlain and Privy Councillor. It is unlikely that anyone challenged their election, though whether there was competition for the second seat in these parliaments, we do not know.

In 1624 it was said that 'the ancient course' in Northamptonshire was 'to have a knight on each side' – that is, from the west and the east divisions into which the county was divided for administrative convenience.[2] This arrangement was apparently observed in 1597[3]

1. *H.M.C. Ld. Montagu's MSS.*, p. 21.

2. *H.M.C. Buccleuch MSS.* i, 259; cf. *Montagu Musters Book*, ed. Joan Wake (Northampton Rec. Soc.), p. xxiii.

3. The typed list of supplementary returns at the P.R.O. gives Christopher and Henry Yelverton as the county M.P.s in 1597, in error for Northampton borough. The county M.P.s were Sir Thomas Cecil and Sir Richard Knightley.

and 1601, and curiously enough it coincided with the Hatton-Mildmay partnership, though one cannot believe that anything but social prestige determined the election of these two. It also coincided with the representation of 1571. The practice was calculated to preserve the peace of the county by avoiding contested elections or, at least, reducing their number.

In Herefordshire another Privy Councillor took natural precedence in his own county. This was Sir James Croft of Croft Castle, who had been Lord Deputy of Ireland in Edward VI's reign and under Elizabeth became Comptroller of the Royal Household and a member of the Council. He had sat for Herefordshire as long ago as 1542, resumed the representation and took the senior seat in 1563, and retained this place till his death in 1590. Next in precedence in the county were Thomas Coningsby of Hampton Court, Herefordshire, and John Scudamore of Holme Lacy, Croft's son-in-law and a friend of learning. Both were in due course knighted, and until 1590 were the only two Deputy-Lieutenants of the county, a sure sign of their pre-eminence.[1] Their names, with that of Croft, all but monopolize the parliamentary returns. From 1571 to 1589 Scudamore was junior member to his father-in-law.

In 1593, with Sir James Croft dead, Herbert Croft, his grandson, maintained the Croft tradition, though as junior to Sir Thomas Coningsby; but, having neither age nor the headship of his family behind him, he was ousted by Coningsby and Scudamore and forced to retire to a borough in 1597. By 1601 his father's death had left him head of the family, and from then until his eclipse as a Catholic recusant and refugee about 1615 he managed to retain the junior seat. Significantly enough, having no distinction but that of family, he could not recapture his grandfather's priority in the county. The senior member in 1601 was Sir Thomas Coningsby. He had been reluctant to stand, but perhaps did so to prevent the senior seat going by social superiority to Herbert Croft. 'I am upon my journey to the parliament', he wrote to Sir Robert Cecil, 'whereunto I am elected, as God knows, much against my will; which journey I am to perform in coach, being altogether unable to mount a horse.'[2] And so it may be said of Herefordshire, as of Oxfordshire and Northamptonshire,

---

1. DASENT, *Acts of Privy Council* (hereafter referred to as *A.P.C.*), xx, 38.   2. *Hatfield MSS.* xi, 441.

that the social structure of the county allowed of very little competition in Elizabeth's reign.

In Derbyshire, the key to decode the otherwise uncommunicative list of members of parliament is the story of the notorious Bess of Hardwick. This beautiful, vivacious, vigorous lady, the exemplar of predatory woman in her generation and a shrew and termagant in old age, lived ninety years and buried four husbands. She was the daughter and co-heiress of an undistinguished Derbyshire gentleman, John Hardwick of Hardwick. At fourteen she married a very young squire of that county, Robert Barlow of Barlow, and within a year had lost a husband and gained a second estate. Some sixteen years later, in 1549, she became the third wife of Sir William Cavendish, a Court official. She bore him a family, persuaded him to sell his property in southern England and buy land in Derbyshire, including the famous estate of Chatsworth, and after eight years became an extremely well-endowed widow. Her third husband, Sir William St Loe, Captain of the Guard to Queen Elizabeth, was a Gloucestershire gentleman, but spent his leisure from Court at Chatsworth. There were no children by this marriage; and indeed the surviving three sons and three daughters by Sir William Cavendish remained her only children, on whom she lavished her prodigal ambitions. When St Loe died, he left, it is said, his whole estate to his widow, to the exclusion both of his own daughters by a previous marriage and of his brothers.

Whether it was her rapaciousness over this estate or her mode of life which made her, in her next husband's words, 'defamed and to the world a byword' as St Loe's widow, we do not know.[1] However, money pardons much. Defamed she may have been, and close on fifty – accounted a great age in those days; but she was wealthy enough and vivacious enough to aspire to the highest of marriages – no less than one of England's premier earls. We may be certain that mercenary as well as amorous promptings led the sixth Earl of Shrewsbury, Knight of the Garter and Lord Lieutenant of Yorkshire, Nottinghamshire, and Derbyshire to marry her in 1568. She struck a triumphant bargain. She married her son, Henry Cavendish, to Shrewsbury's youngest daughter, and her youngest daughter to his second son, Gilbert Talbot, afterwards the seventh Earl of Shrews-

1. *Hatfield MSS.* iii, 163.

bury; nuptials which she took care to see celebrated before her own. The manoeuvre was of a piece with the impudent and politically dangerous stroke by which she later married another daughter to Charles Lennox, brother of Lord Darnley, and so procured a granddaughter, Arabella Stuart, with plausible claims to the English throne.

For the first three parliaments of the reign, the county elections in Derbyshire were normal. There may, there may not have been contests: we do not know. In 1563 Sir William St Loe, Bess of Hardwick's husband, was first knight of the shire, but there was nothing odd in that, for his office at Court and his wife's estates in the county gave him priority over other possible candidates. He was dead before 1571, and in this, the third general election, Chatsworth played no very obvious part.

It was in 1572 that the double and irresistible power of Bess and her new husband revealed itself. The Earl of Shrewsbury's second son, Gilbert Talbot, was then only eighteen and a half, and his wife's eldest son, Henry Cavendish, twenty or twenty-one;[1] each, considered in isolation, over young for an Elizabethan parliament, but as a pair of parliamentary knights of a shire probably the most astonishing partnership of youth in the whole reign. The effrontery of it smacks of Bess of Hardwick, and as Gilbert Talbot was married to her daughter and through his masterful wife was very much under her influence, Shrewsbury himself may have had little to do with the plan. As an earl's son, Talbot, though the younger, naturally took precedence of his step-brother. What the staid gentry of Derbyshire thought of it, we cannot say; but, whatever their disgust, they would have been impotent against the freeholders whom the Talbots and the Cavendishes could muster, and in any case would have been loth to incur the enmity of their 'great Earl', not to mention that of his formidable Countess.

Before the next election in 1584 there occurred the famous quarrel between the Earl and his wife,[2] which estranged Gilbert Talbot from his father and Henry Cavendish from his mother, found vent in

1. ibid., p. 162, Shrewsbury is said to have enjoyed Henry Cavendish's living for five years during his minority. If correct, this would make him twenty in 1572.

2. Shrewsbury dated the breach as occurring after his eldest son's death in 1582 (LODGE, *Illustrations of British Hist.*, 1791, ii, 318).

outrageous charges by Bess against her husband, along with bitter comments from him on his rapacious and shrewish wife, employed Burghley, Leicester, and other Councillors in efforts at mediation, and was only patched up in July-August 1586 by the direct and repeated intervention of the Queen herself.[1]

In November 1584 Henry Cavendish again stood for election. Gilbert Talbot was now known as Lord Talbot, a courtesy title, and perhaps for this reason or through sheer disinclination did not seek re-election; though, in any case, as an adherent of his mother-in-law he could scarcely have represented the Talbot interest. That role was played by his younger brother, Henry Talbot. Since Henry Cavendish, who was standing for re-election, was aligned with his father-in-law against his mother in their quarrel, the Countess was likely to be excluded from all influence in the election; and it was evidently this reason which led to the plan of importing the third son, Sir Charles Cavendish of Welbeck, Nottinghamshire, as a candidate — presumably to compete against his brother. One of his household officers warned the Earl of the move, but assured him that he had taken the necessary counter-measures by writing to various gentlemen instructing them to have sufficient freeholders present to secure victory. Unfortunately, we do not know whether the family feud was publicly exposed at the hustings; but if it was, the Earl's authority and power prevailed. Henry Talbot became first knight of the shire, and Henry Cavendish second; and they were re-elected in 1586, no doubt without incident, for the great quarrel was then nominally over.[2]

After 1586 the Talbots withdrew from Derbyshire and indeed from the Elizabethan House of Commons altogether, but Henry Cavendish went on, moving up to the senior county seat. He was elected in 1588 and 1593. There was now an opportunity, as there had been early in the reign, for other county families to share the representation, but not, we may be sure, without Cavendish support. In 1588 the second member was a Zouche, and in 1593 the heir of Haddon Hall, who was married to Bess of Hardwick's granddaughter the same year. In 1601 there was no Cavendish standing, but the senior

1. On the quarrel cf. LODGE, vol. ii, *Hatfield MSS.* vol. iii, *Rutland MSS.* vol. i, and *Cal. S.P. Dom., 1581–90,* especially pp. 450 ff.
2. LODGE, ii, 340; BROWNE WILLIS, *Notitia Parliamentaria,* iii, 100.

member was Francis Leeke, who was related to Bess through her mother, a Leeke.

Derbyshire's story has a quality of its own. In a different setting there is a companion tale from Leicestershire. This county in Elizabethan times was not lacking in substantial gentlemen – Adrian Stokes, married to the Duchess of Suffolk, daughter of Henry VIII's sister, Francis Cave, the Beaumonts, to which family the famous dramatist belonged, the Turpins, the Skeffingtons, and the Skipwiths. All these represented the county when given a chance, and possibly every Elizabethan election would have produced one or more of their names, had not Leicestershire, like Derbyshire, possessed its 'great Earl', with a family, not of children but of brothers.

This magnate was Henry Hastings, third Earl of Huntingdon, who through his mother, a Pole, was in the line of succession to the throne, and, as the hope of ardent protestants, would have been a serious candidate if Elizabeth's attack of smallpox in 1562 had proved fatal. He came into his earldom in 1560, was made Lord Lieutenant of Leicestershire in 1559 and of Rutland in 1569, Knight of the Garter in 1570, and Lord President of the Council in the North in 1572. His wife was a Dudley, sister to the Earl of Leicester. A convinced Puritan and a prominent patron of this surgent party, he displayed the humane and godly virtues of his faith. On his death in 1595 the simple panegyric, *The Crie of the Poor*, told how

> To poor and to needy, to high and to low,
> Lord Hastings was friendly, all people doth know.
> His gates were still open the stranger to feed
> And comfort the succourless always in need. . . .
>
> He built up no palace, nor purchased no town,
> But gave it to scholars to get him renown. . . .
>
> No groves he enclosed nor felled no wood,
> No pastures he paled to do himself good;
> To commons and country he lived a good friend,
> And gave to the needy what God did him send.
>
> Then wail we, then weep we, then mourn we each one,
> The good Earl of Huntingdon from us is gone.[1]

1. Quoted in KNAPPEN, *Tudor Puritanism*, p. 411. Cf. COOPER, *Athenae Cant.*, ii, 202; G. E. C. *Complete Peerage*, vi, 656–7.

The Earl, who was childless, had five brothers, four of whom took a prominent part in the life of the county. Their Puritanism was a family faith, and such was their influence that Leicestershire, with its capital, where the stewardship was held by the family, was a strong puritan area. The situation was unique: an earl and four active brothers, all living in one county, of which the Earl was Lord Lieutenant and two of his brothers the sole Deputy-Lieutenants.[1] Moreover, thanks to their religious faith, they were a united family. Ashby-de-la-Zouch, the family seat, was the symbol of aristocracy at its best.

In the reigns of Edward VI and Mary, sons of the first Earl had sat for the county in five out of the seven parliaments, but never more than one at a time. In Elizabeth's reign the first member of the family to sit was Francis, in 1571. He was the second youngest of the brothers, 'the meanest beagle of the House of Huntingdon', as his literary opponent, the famous Jesuit, Father Parsons, was to call him;[2] but he was probably the most active. He was certainly the keenest parliamentarian of the family, and – token of his qualities – it was he who shared the deputy-lieutenancy with the eldest of the five brothers. He was closely connected with the political leaders of the Puritan party,[3] and attained considerable authority in the House of Commons. It says much for the social gulf – or at least, the disparity in power – between a Hastings and anyone else in the county, that in the election of 1571 he took the senior seat, though he was a younger brother and still possibly in his twenties, while Adrian Stokes, who had been the senior knight in 1559 and had a duchess for wife, was the junior member. He did not sit in the following parliament. Probably something prevented him from standing, since, with his brother Sir George as Sheriff, success would have been doubly assured. Consequently, a Turpin and a Beaumont represented the county in 1572.

The next election, in 1584, brought the first family monopoly, when Sir George Hastings, the eldest brother and heir, decided to sample parliamentary experience, while the politically-minded Francis was anxious to sit again. This was the parliament in which

1. *H.M.C. Foljambe MSS.*, p. 25.   2. *D.N.B.*
3. Cf. SCOTT PEARSON, *Thomas Cartwright*, pp. 69, 72, 384; KNAPPEN, op. cit., pp. 325, 327.

the Puritans launched their first great campaign for reform of the Church. Whether that caused both brothers to stand, we have no means of telling. Nor do we know the reaction of other Leicestershire gentlemen to their exclusion from both county seats. They cannot have liked it, but opposition would have been idle as well as ill-advised. How idle, we can judge from the election of 1621, when in days long distant from the glorious age of the great third Earl, the family harked back to their Elizabethan precedents and were opposed in their bid for a new monopoly by Sir Thomas Beaumont, backed by the Sheriff, a Cave. Against a paltry hundred for Beaumont, they carried the day by the overwhelming acclamation of twelve hundred voters, figures which may be taken to represent the enduring strength of the family in freeholders. But there was a new factor in 1621 – the effrontery of the Sheriff. To practise downright fraud against a Hastings, as this Jacobean official did, would have been inconceivable in the third Earl's days. He shamelessly returned Beaumont; but the House of Commons subsequently reversed his action.[1]

In 1586 Sir George and Francis Hastings again took the two Leicestershire seats, helped, there is reason to think, by the government's general advice to constituencies on this abnormal occasion to re-elect the former members. But between 1586 and the next parliament, Francis Hastings moved his residence to North Cadbury, Somerset, became a Justice of the Peace there, a Deputy-Lieutenant in 1590, and was knighted;[2] and so the prolonged monopoly which threatened Leicestershire through this gentleman's parliamentary enthusiasm was broken. In 1588 and 1593 he was elected first knight for Somerset. In this county, however, the name of Hastings could not work wonders; and he was unable to sustain the seat in every parliament. In 1597, rather surprisingly, we find him back in the junior seat for Leicestershire, while in 1601 he was driven to find a place in a Somerset borough, Bridgwater. In 1604, his last parliament, he regained the senior seat in Somerset.

With the migration of Francis Hastings to Somerset, Leicestershire was left with no Hastings seeking a seat in 1588, and consequently a

1. NICHOLAS, *Debates 1621* (1766), i, 21–3; NOTESTEIN, RELF, and SIMPSON, *Commons Debates 1621*, vi, 360, and refs. in index.
2. *A.P.C.* xviii, 105, xix, 71, xx, 26, xxii, 65, 185; S. W. BATES HARBIN, *M.P.s for Somerset*, pp. 131–2.

Beaumont and a Turpin got their chance. In 1593 there was again a Hastings as candidate – young Francis, eldest son of Sir George; and he was chosen senior knight of the shire. This still left room for another family in the junior seat. But when in 1597 Sir Edward Hastings in his turn decided to sample parliament, and the persistent Sir Francis returned from Somerset, the family monopoly fastened itself on the county for the third time. In 1601 another member of the younger generation, Henry, nephew of the fourth Earl, took the senior seat. However, with Sir Francis out of the way in a Somerset borough – perhaps suggesting that the Leicestershire gentry were opposed, as some were later in 1621, to a monopoly exercised in favour of a non-resident – the junior seat was again free. It did not pass quietly to the second line in the hierarchy of local gentlemen, for Sir John Gray challenged the candidature of a Skipwith, relying on the support of the Earl of Rutland, whose brothers he had befriended when in his custody after the Essex rebellion. He sent the Earl a message, praying 'that those who are yours in that county may stand for him, and that you will give speedy order therein'.[1] The Earl of Rutland was all-powerful in Nottinghamshire, but the gentlemen of Leicestershire, who kotowed to their own great Earl, were not prepared for subservience to any other magnate. They remained true to their traditions, returned William Skipwith, and forced Sir John Gray to make shift with the petty borough seat of Grampound in Cornwall.

How varied all these stories are! How well they blend with that colourful diversity of county life which has so enriched our national history! There is another tale to tell, in quite a different key. It is of Surrey. Here, two families, the Howards of Effingham and the Mores of Loseley, the one noble the other but gentle, shaped the electoral pattern of the county in Elizabeth's days. The Howards scarcely need introduction: their name will survive as long as our island story. On Elizabeth's accession, William, first Lord Howard of Effingham, son of a Duke of Norfolk and great-uncle of the Queen, whose welfare he had protected in the perilous days of Mary Tudor, was made Lord Chamberlain, continued as a Privy Councillor, and became Lord Lieutenant of the county of Surrey.[2] He was among the greatest in the land. His eldest son and heir, Charles, who

1. *Rutland MSS.* i, 380.   2. *V.C.H. Surrey*, i, 377.

was twenty-five when the reign began, succeeded his father in 1573, was in turn made Lord Chamberlain in 1583,[1] and two years later became Lord Admiral, in which capacity he won victory and immortal fame against the Spanish Armada.

In contrast, who has heard of Sir William More of Loseley? Literary historians may know him as the grandfather of the poet Donne's wife and as the medium through which a very valuable collection of manuscripts has descended to us;[2] but he has no place in the *Dictionary of National Biography* and not even a niche in our national histories. Yet he grew to be one of the most experienced parliamentarians of his age; and, twice Sheriff and holding among other offices that of Deputy-Lieutenant from 1569, he became a local administrator of unrivalled efficiency and influence in the county.

More began his parliamentary career in 1547 at the age of twenty-seven as member for the Surrey borough of Reigate. In the six subsequent parliaments of Edward VI and Mary's reigns he sat three times, on each occasion for Guildford, close to the Loseley estate, which became a sort of family borough. He was Sheriff of the county at the time of the election to Elizabeth's first parliament, and so was precluded from returning himself to parliament; but as Sheriff, and no doubt also as the director of many humbler freeholders' votes, he became the focus of much preliminary negotiation.

More's support in this election was evidently pledged to his friend, Sir Thomas Cawarden of Bletchingley Castle, Master of the Revels, of whose will he was soon to be joint-executor.[3] Cawarden had already represented the county twice – in 1553 and 1554 – as first knight of the shire, and before that had sat twice for his borough of Bletchingley. As candidate for the senior seat in the new parliament, he had linked his fortunes, or, as later centuries put it, paired with Thomas Browne of Betchworth Castle, whose principal attribute at this time seems to have been that he was the son-in-law of Sir William Fitzwilliam. Some three weeks before the election two other would-be candidates appeared, both of whom sought More's support. The one was Sir Henry Weston of Sutton, who had sat for Petersfield

---

1. CHAMBERS, *Elizabethan Stage*, i, 40. The *D.N.B.* erroneously gives 1574 instead of 1583.
2. The Loseley MSS. Cf. *H.M.C. Rep.* vii, 596 ff.; KEMPE, *Loseley MSS.*
3. ibid., pp. 15 ff.

four times, and was to sit for that borough, of which he was the lord, twice more before he achieved his ambition of representing the county in 1571. The other was Thomas Copley, lord of Gatton, for which borough he had already sat three times and was to sit again in this parliament and the next. Obviously, for these two gentlemen, with safe borough seats at their disposal, it was not a mere question of getting into parliament. They wanted the prestige of being chosen by the county.[1]

Browne, a diffident young man, was being thrust into the front rank of the county by his father-in-law, not by his own ambition and determination. A fortnight before the election he wrote to More, declining nomination 'in consideration of inexperience and ill-health' and asking him to transfer his influence to 'my cousin Copley, who is a warm friend to Mr Cawarden'. At once the father-in-law stepped in, begged More to delay his answer, and then screwed up his son-in-law's courage so that he withdrew his resignation.[2]

Two days later came a new shock, which incidentally seems to have made the weak Mr Browne waver again. This was no less than the decision of the Lord Chamberlain, Howard of Effingham, to run his eldest son, Charles, for the county. He wrote to More asking for his support, and had the freeholders around Kingston canvassed, only to find that their voices were already promised. Sir William Fitzwilliam hastily sent to Cawarden, who, to his relief, replied that he would 'take no knowledge' of the Howard move and thought Browne should do the same; but if Browne withdrew his candidature, then he for his part would not stand. No doubt Cawarden realized that if young Charles Howard were elected, he would, as a peer's heir, be given the senior seat; and while prepared, in combination with Browne's voters and supported by William More, to defy the Howards, Cawarden would not face the ignominy of taking second place. 'Thus have I satisfied my said son [-in-law] of Mr Cawarden his mind', wrote Sir William Fitzwilliam to More, 'and of mine own also ...; and I hope, with the good help of you and other good friends, the matter will go well enough on our side.'[3]

Unfortunately, we know nothing about the election itself. It is of

1. *H.M.C. Rep.* vii, 614b, 615b.   2. ibid., p. 614b.
3. ibid.; ELLIS, *Original Letters*, 2nd ser. ii, 261–3 (also printed in WRIGHT, *Queen Eliz. and Her Times*, i, 3–5).

course possible that Lord Howard withdrew his son's candidature after discovering that he was too late in the field. Incidentally, he had a perfectly safe seat at his disposal in Reigate, where his second son[1] sat for every parliament except one between 1559 and 1597. But the heir of the Howards was too great a man for a borough. It was a case of a county seat or nothing. Probably Thomas Copley contested the election,[2] and it may even be that all five prospective candidates stood. We only know that Sir Thomas Cawarden and Thomas Browne were elected, while Copley and Weston were forced back into their boroughs. It was a remarkable victory for William More, and an unpleasant check for the Howards.

At the next election, in 1563, the Lord Chamberlain made amends for his previous failure. Charles Howard was elected first knight of the shire. The second seat went to William More – his first entry into a county seat and a sign of his increasing stature. The election may have been contested: at any rate, More received three letters about candidates.[3] In 1571 More was again chosen for the junior seat, the senior on this occasion going to Sir Henry Weston. Probably Charles Howard was unable to stand,[4] but in the following year he was once more elected to the senior seat, while More was compelled to retreat on his borough of Guildford, leaving the junior place to another gentleman.

Before the next parliament, the whole situation changed, for in 1573 Charles Howard succeeded his father in the peerage, and Sir Francis Walsingham, back from his embassy in France and appointed to the Secretaryship and the Privy Council, took Howard's place as senior knight at a by-election. Henceforth, while Walsingham lived, Surrey was virtually reduced to a one-seat constituency, for there was no contending with so important an official. In consequence, the Howard and the More interests could no longer be served at one and the same time, as they had been in 1563. The dilemma revealed itself without any delay, for at the next election, in 1584, the Earl

1. William (afterwards Sir Wm.) Howard of Lingfield. He should not be confused with his nephew, also William, M.P. for the county in 1588, 1597, and 1601.

2. A letter from Richard Bydon states that he and his friends intended to vote for Copley and Browne (*H.M.C. Rep.* vii, 614b).

3. ibid., p. 618a.

4. He was at sea with the fleet in the autumn of 1570 (cf. *D.N.B.*).

of Lincoln and Lord Howard of Effingham, a socially formidable combination, wrote to More, now a knight, recommending Walsingham and William Howard – presumably Lord Howard's heir, aged about nineteen – as the county representatives.[1] The letter was dated two days before the election, and was in effect an invitation to More from his social superiors to efface himself. Most Elizabethans would have done so; but More stood for the county, was elected, and in the next parliament of 1586 was re-elected. The bare facts, which are all we know, are eloquent enough: here indeed was a great commoner. But the riposte came in 1588, when the Howards prevailed and back went More to Guildford; whether as the result of a contest or by mutual arrangement, we do not know.

When the next election came round, in 1593, Walsingham was dead, his seat was free, and Lord Howard and Sir William More were found working together in irresistible partnership. More's daughter was married to Sir John Wolley, Latin Secretary to the Queen and from 1586 a Privy Councillor, who had sat in every parliament since 1571, always representing boroughs except in the last parliament of 1588 when he sat for the county of Dorset. It was Lord Howard himself who, influenced no doubt by friendship with Wolley and his wife at Court, suggested that both Sir William More and his son-in-law should stand for Surrey.[2] They did, and were elected, Wolley, as a Privy Councillor taking the senior seat. In 1597 Howard and More again appear to have collaborated: at any rate, Howard wrote to More in good time, announcing his design to run his eldest son, now Sir William Howard, for the county.[3] As for More, at seventy-seven years of age he probably realized that this would be his last parliament, and was bent on establishing the succession of his own heir, George More, who since 1584 had been sitting for the family borough of Guildford. Accordingly, Sir William took the humble borough seat himself and put his son into the junior county seat, thus establishing a further family lien on the county, which, except for retreats to Guildford in 1604 and 1624, lasted till 1626.

After this election, but two days before the parliament met, Lord Howard was created Earl of Nottingham, so devolving on his heir the courtesy title of Lord Howard of Effingham. By a curious error

1. *H.M.C. Rep.* vii, 640a.   2. ibid., p. 650a.   3. ibid., p. 657a.

the new Earl thought that his son was thereby incapacitated to sit in the House of Commons, and therefore promptly wrote to Sir William More recommending the substitution of his second son, Charles. On the day parliament met, Charles was elected, 'vice William Howard, a peer'.[1] It was quick work, and it was also a gross blunder. One wonders how it could have happened and how it was done. By the next parliament they realized their mistake, and William, though Lord Howard of Effingham, was elected as first knight, while Sir George More, now owner of Loseley and a knight, was the second county member. And so ends a story of commoner and peer, in harmony unchallengeable and in rivalry not ill-matched.

Once more the electoral pattern changes when we look at Huntingdonshire, a county in Elizabethan days without men of noble rank. Even the lieutenancy was in the hands of commoners until the latter part of the reign, and the peer then appointed, Lord St John of Bletsoe, was not a local landowner with much electoral influence.

In this county there were three great houses or estates, Leighton Bromswold, Kimbolton, and Hinchingbrooke, the owners of which for long determined the county elections. At the beginning of the reign Sir Robert Tyrwhitt of Leighton Bromswold, the last male of his line, and one of the two Lord Lieutenants, enjoyed complete supremacy. There was nobody to dispute his election as first knight of the shire in Elizabeth's first parliament. A possible rival, Kimbolton, was temporarily under his control, its owner, Thomas Wingfield, being a minor, aged nineteen or twenty. This young man had for uncle the influential councillor and courtier Sir Francis Knollys, and had he been normally responsible and efficient, would soon have become a power in the county. Instead, he was a wild character, a mere wastrel; and it was not until his son Edward came of an age to represent the county that Kimbolton began to play its natural part in elections. The son too showed prodigal tendencies like his father, but he apparently sobered down, earned the name of 'the great warrior', and was knighted in 1588.[2]

Hinchingbrooke, like Kimbolton, at the opening of the reign was

1. ibid.; list of supplementary returns at P.R.O.
2. V.C.H. Huntingdonshire, ii, 23, 26 ff., iii, 80.

not ready to exert its influence. Its owner, Henry Cromwell alias Williams, was twenty-one and had only just emerged from a fourteen-years' wardship.[1] The family were fairly recent intruders into the county, offering glaring testimony to that flexibility in the English aristocratic system which permitted new families to spring suddenly from obscurity to wealth and position. They had been raised from the lowly estate of a Putney ale-brewer and innkeeper through the patronage of Henry VIII's notorious minister, Thomas Cromwell, whose sister Henry Cromwell's grandfather had married, and whose name, in gratitude or by calculation, his father had adopted. Appropriately enough, their fortunes were based on monastic spoils, for Sir Richard Williams alias Cromwell had purchased most of the lands of Ramsey Abbey.[2] It was this gentleman's son and heir, Henry, who, after his emergence from wardship, consolidated the family's position in the county by building the great house at Hinchingbrooke, and drew the veil a little further over his family's origin by reversing his alias, calling himself Cromwell alias Williams.[3] At Hinchingbrooke he entertained Queen Elizabeth in 1564, and was knighted by her during the visit.[4] His liberality was profuse, his magnificence almost princely. The story goes that he scattered largesses to the people as he moved past admiring country folk gathered to witness his progresses from Hinchingbrooke to his summer residence at Ramsey Abbey.[5] He was known in his days as 'the Golden Knight'. His son followed his example; but two generations of exotic splendour impoverished the family. Hinchingbrooke was sold in 1627, and the fame of the Cromwells was preserved, not by pomp and circumstance but by the genius of a junior member of the family, the great Protector Oliver.

It was not until the second parliament of the reign, in 1563, that Henry Cromwell ventured to put his social standing to the test of a county election. He was chosen first knight of the shire. But, though he sustained his eminence in the sphere of local administration, and

1. *Cal. Pat. Rolls, Ed. VI*, i, 167, *Ph. & Mary*, iv. 469.
2. *V.C.H. Hunts.*, ii, 13, 23.
3. In October 1558 he is *alias* Cromwell (*Cal. Pat. Rolls, Ph. & Mary*, iv, 469), and in the parliamentary return of December 1562 he is *alias* Williams (*Return of M.P.s*, i, 404).
4. CHAMBERS, *Eliz. Stage*, iv, 81; SHAW'S *Knights*, ii, 71.
5. *V.C.H. Hunts.*, ii, 135.

was four times Sheriff of Cambridgeshire and Huntingdonshire[1] — quite exceptional for an office shared with the gentry of another county — he presumably found experience of a single parliament sufficient for a lifetime. His interests were local, not national; he was a stay-at-home.

Sir Henry Cromwell — as he now was — had no perceptible influence over the election of 1571, though as likely as not he acquiesced in the choice; but in the following year, when Sheriff, he secured the election of his younger brother, Francis, as junior member. Francis was again a candidate in 1584. On this occasion, however, he had the Sheriff — Sir Henry Darcy, owner, through his wife, of Leighton Bromswold — against him. By the familiar trick of deferring the election beyond the legal day, and also — if a fragment of a case in the Star Chamber is reliable evidence — by perjured voters, he was defeated. Complaint was made to the House of Commons, but that body quite properly decided that the issue lay outside its jurisdiction. Behind the brief evidence we possess must lie a good election story, lost to posterity.[2]

In 1586 young Edward Wingfield was of age to stand for the county, and in this and the two following parliaments was first knight of the shire. The Cromwell interests in 1586 were represented by a friend of the family, whose heir married a Cromwell;[3] and the faction which defrauded and defeated them in 1584 was presumably put to rout. Then at last, in 1588, the young heir to Hinchingbrooke, Oliver Cromwell, aged about twenty-five and unencumbered by the tell-tale alias of Williams — whose quaint recessional now reached its end — was ready to take that continuous place in the county representation which his father had renounced. With one intermission, he sat from 1588 to 1625. In 1588 and 1593 he was junior to Edward Wingfield, the heir to Kimbolton and then in 1590 its owner; while in 1597 and 1601 he was subordinated to the other rival house of Leighton Bromswold, when Sir Gervase Clifton, its owner through marriage, became first knight of the shire. By 1604 all this was changed. Now a knight — Sir Oliver Cromwell — and newly entered

1. *P.R.O. Lists & Indexes*, no. ix (List of Sheriffs), p. 14.
2. D'Ewes, *Journals*, pp. 337a, 344–5; Trinity Coll. Dublin, MS. N2, no. 12; Star Chamber 5, A 41/32, A 42/30.
3. George Walton. Cf. *V.C.H. Hunts.*, ii, 26.

upon his inheritance[1] and upon a splendour of living that rivalled his father's, he stood a tip-toe in his county as its senior member of parliament. And so he did in 1614. But when he reappeared in parliament in 1624 and 1625, the portents were dark. The little day of the *parvenu* Cromwells – 'the Golden Knight' and the grand Sir Oliver – was ending. A younger son of the Montagus of Boughton in Northamptonshire – to a still younger son of which prolific family Hinchingbrooke itself was to be sold in 1627 – had bought Kimbolton. Becoming a Viscount, he introduced the peerage into county affairs; and his son, Edward Montagu, as a peer's heir, thrust Sir Oliver back into the junior knightship of the shire.

With its three dominating estates, Elizabethan Huntingdonshire in normal circumstances ought to have had a fairly simple electoral history, but owing to a triple accident – the lack of male heirs at Leighton Bromswold, a minority and a ne'er-do-well owner at Kimbolton, and the failure of Sir Henry Cromwell to interest himself in parliament – its story is confused and blurred. Had conditions been otherwise, there might have been a constant tussle between the great three for the two parliamentary seats, or alternatively a working arrangement on the lines of Northamptonshire, dividing the four Hundreds of the county into their two natural divisions of north and south. In the latter event Hinchingbrooke would have controlled one seat, and Leighton Bromswold and Kimbolton shared control of the other. As a matter of fact, a rough division of this sort, though not invariable and perhaps accidental rather than deliberate, can be seen in the returns for Elizabeth's reign.[2]

Studying these county elections, their intimate relationship to the prevailing conditions of the locality becomes clearer and clearer. In all the county returns the names were those of the leading families and individuals, but the frequency with which they recurred obviously depended partly on personal inclination and partly on the feasibility and intensity of competition. Let us take Warwickshire as another illustration. This county at the beginning of Elizabeth's reign had as its senior knight a Privy Councillor, Sir Ambrose Cave of Dudeston, Warwickshire, Chancellor of the Duchy of Lancaster. In

1. His father died in January 1604. Cf. *Visitation of Huntingdon*, ed. Ellis (Camden Soc.), p. 80.
2. Cf. *V.C.H.* Hunts., ii, 26.

the last parliament of Mary's reign he had transferred from representing Leicestershire to Warwickshire, and continued to sit for this shire till his death in 1568.[1] There was no resisting such a person; but otherwise – and with one further exception later in the reign – the gentry of Warwickshire seem to have been insistent on sharing the honour of their county seats as widely as possible. Only two men – Sir Thomas Lucy of Shakespearian fame or myth, and Clement Throckmorton, member of an eminent county family – attained the honour twice. It was not that they regarded membership of parliament as a burden. Clement Throckmorton was an inveterate parliamentarian. Since 1542 he had sat four times for the borough of Warwick, once for Devizes, and once for Sudbury, before being elected for the county in 1563. He reached country rank only to lose it in the following parliament, when the Cornish borough of West Looe gave him refuge. In 1572, his last parliament, the county again elected him.

The exception in this pattern of constant change was Sir Philip Sidney's intimate friend Fulke Greville, later Lord Brooke, himself a famous Court and literary figure, who, in the words of a contemporary, 'came to the Court in his youth and prime . . ., backed with a plentiful fortune'. He 'neither sought for, or obtained, any great place or preferment'; yet – or should one say 'therefore'? – he 'had the longest lease, and the smoothest time, without rub' of any of Queen Elizabeth's favourites.[2] His mother was a Neville, daughter of Ralph, Earl of Westmorland; his father, established at the great family seat of Beauchamp Court, was one of the largest landholders in Warwickshire, a man noted 'for the sweetness of his temper' and 'much given to hospitality'.[3] The heir to so much, himself endowed with exceptional qualities and the favour of his prince, was indeed a person of such social eminence that the monopoly of a county seat seemed a natural right.

Greville first entered the House of Commons in 1580 at the age of twenty-six through a by-election for Southampton, which the House subsequently declared invalid.[4] In 1584 he sat for Heydon in York-

1. The names of the Warwickshire M.P.s for 1559 depend on Browne Willis. He may have guessed them, but was probably right about Cave.
2. NAUNTON, Fragmenta Regalia.   3. D.N.B. sub Greville, Sir Fulke.
4. Commons Journals, i, 135–6.

shire along with his cousin, Henry Constable, who no doubt was responsible for his nomination to this family borough. Then, in 1586, he began the representation of his home county, Warwickshire. On that occasion he was junior knight, but in 1588, 1593, 1597, 1601, and 1621, though only the eldest son and heir of a commoner till his father's death in 1606, and not even knighted till 1603, he secured and retained the senior seat.[1] Quality, not its trappings, mattered in this instance. It seems as if a faction, aided by Sir Thomas Lucy, then Sheriff, plotted to break the monopoly in 1601, At any rate, the Privy Council severely reprimanded the Sheriff for illegally postponing the election, summoned the Under-Sheriff to appear before them, and only refrained from ordering the immediate attendance of Lucy himself because of his health. Sending a new writ, they commanded him to conduct himself in an upright and impartial manner: 'We are not ignorant', they wrote, 'of the train and course intended to ... divert the ... election from some person who both in respect of his blood and quality, his sufficiency to do service to the State, and estimation in her Majesty's gracious opinion, deserveth to be preferred before others.'[2] Greville was the intended victim. Of that there can be little doubt; and the Council's heavy hand discomfited his adversaries.

In the western counties of Cornwall, Devon, and Dorset a sustained monopoly was apparently out of the question; and, with few exceptions, twice was as often as the more influential gentry could hope to represent the county. In Cornwall, Peter Edgcumbe of Mount Edgcumbe came as near a monopoly as anyone. He began his parliamentary career in 1555, at the age of approximately nineteen, in a Devon borough, sat for a Cornish borough in 1559, when his father sat for the county,[3] and did not attain the county seat until 1563, when he was about twenty-seven and had succeeded to his father's estates. Even then, he could not hold the place consecutively, but sat for Devon – in which county part of his estate was situated – in 1571, Cornwall again in 1572, and a Cornish borough, Liskeard, in 1584.

1. The *D.N.B.* errs in making his father M.P. for Warwickshire in 1586 and 1588. The member was an 'esquire', and therefore the son.

2. *A.P.C.* xxxii, 247–8.

3. We are dependent for both names on Browne Willis, where the county member, Richard, should be given as 'knight'.

He then had a final run for Cornwall in 1586, 1588, and 1593. It is hard to believe that so prominent a man – he was a Deputy-Lieutenant in Cornwall[1] – and so keen a parliamentarian would have been content with a borough seat in 1584 if he had been able to secure election for either of his two counties, Cornwall or Devon. Another Cornish gentleman, William Mohun – later knighted, and made Deputy-Lieutenant – might have run Peter Edgcumbe close, if he had not been excluded, as Sheriff, from election in 1572, and death had not stopped his progress towards the record. He sat three times for the county after entering parliament through a Cornish borough.

In Devon, Sir William Courtney alone managed to secure a county seat three times during Elizabeth's reign, while in Dorset no one exceeded twice and only three gentlemen attained that number. One of these, Ralph Horsey, clearly owed his election in 1586 to his cousin, Sir John Horsey of Clifton Maubank, who was then Sheriff and whose heir he was. When next he was elected, in 1597, he was owner of Clifton Maubank, knighted, a Justice of the Peace, and an ex-Sheriff, a man of sufficient importance to secure his own election.

These shires were of course far-distant from Westminster, and it is just possible that reluctance to take on the burden of a long journey may have had some part in shaping their electoral pattern. However, all things considered, this hardly seems likely; and if, in the absence of direct evidence, our inference be judged sound, then it may shed some light on the rather odd parliamentary career of Sir Walter Raleigh.

This great Elizabethan was a Devon man, with roots or interests in all three counties. In 1585 he was made Warden of the Stanneries – an office controlling mining in both Devon and Cornwall – Lord Lieutenant of Cornwall, and Vice-Admiral of Cornwall and Devon. He also became a Deputy-Lieutenant in Devon, and in 1592 secured from the Queen a lease of the Sherborne estate in Dorset, which became his well-loved home.[2] One might have supposed that so eminent a courtier and local official, though not a Privy Councillor, could readily have secured election for Cornwall or Devon at any time after 1585, and for Dorset after 1592. He was a persistent parliamentarian from 1584 on, and with his notorious pride cannot have

1. *Foljambe MSS.*, p. 26.
2. STEBBING, *Sir Walter Ralegh*, pp. 34, 102; *Foljambe MSS.*, p. 25.

been insensitive to the vital social distinction between a knight of the shire and a mere parliamentary burgess.

Raleigh entered parliament in 1584 as the junior knight for Devon, his native county, where apparently he intended to fix his country residence at this time.[1] He attained the senior seat in the next parliament of 1586, by which time the Wardenship of the Stanneries and other local offices had made him eminent in the west. When the 1588 elections were held, he was in Ireland on royal service, and did not sit in that parliament.[2] In 1593 when he again sought election, and, having settled at Sherborne, had three counties to choose from, most surprisingly he was unable to find a county seat and had to be content with representing a petty Cornish borough, St Michael. It was the time of his disgrace at Court owing to his relations with Elizabeth Throckmorton. If this was a factor in barring him from a county seat, it suggests that the gentry were ready to seize any excuse to oppose him. In the next parliament of 1597 he was the senior knight for Dorset; but he was apparently unable to retain the place, and in 1601 used his Cornish influence to secure the senior seat there.

It is difficult to avoid the conclusion that these western counties would not tolerate parliamentary monopolies. In all probability, Raleigh did not possess sufficient tenants himself or sufficient influence over other local gentry to maintain a stable place. He was not of the soil, a true territorial magnate. He was an adventurer and interloper, and his 'bloody pride', which prompted a description of him in 1587 as 'the best-hated man of the world in Court, city, and country',[3] was calculated to arouse opposition, not devotion. His peripatetic career as a parliament-man savours of the 'carpet-bagger' and cannot be likened to the careers of such rare personages as Sir Ambrose Cave and Sir William Cecil, or, in the later part of the reign, Sir Thomas Cecil and Sir John Harington, who also moved from a seat in one county to a seat in another. These men were indigenous in two shires and welcome as knights in either. Once past the probationary borough stage of early youth, they were never forced back to the junior status of burgess.

1. STEBBING, pp. 100–1.   2. *Cal. S.P. Ireland, 1588–92*, p. 37.
3. STEBBING, p. 61.

CHAPTER 2

County Elections: Preliminary Moves

THE preliminary moves in a county election were usually made as soon as news got abroad that a parliament was to be summoned. The initiative might be taken by various people. In some instances it was would-be candidates, anxious to rally their friends and obtain sufficient promises of support to justify standing. Here, for example, is a letter, which is a model of its kind, received by a Norfolk gentleman, Bassingbourne Gawdy senior, who possessed estates in Suffolk in his wife's right. The letter was written by his brother just before the Suffolk election of 1584, in which Sir William Drury won the senior seat. In slightly conflated form, it reads: 'I am to desire you in Sir William Drury's behalf as well as at my entreaty that you will procure all your freeholders in Suffolk and your friends with yourself to be at Ipswich the 2nd November, where he desires your company and to have your voices.'[1]

Alternatively, the names put to the electors might be determined, not by the aspirants themselves but by the leading gentlemen of the county, or by some group or groups, or even by a single individual whose wishes few were inclined to cross.

The process could be very simple; equally it could be very complicated. Much depended on the social background in the county. How much, we can illustrate by considering the Norfolk election of 1601. Norfolk then was a county with one nobleman, Lord Cromwell, and he an impoverished baron of no consequence.[2] But it possessed a number of substantial gentlemen, more or less each other's peers. Faction was apparently never far beneath the surface. In October 1600 two of the leading gentlemen, who had both represented the county in parliament, were brought before the Privy Council for threatening a breach of the peace. One was Sir John Townshend, who two or three years later lost his life in a duel, and the other Sir Christopher Heydon, a restless man though a prominent

1. Egerton MS. 2713, fol. 61; *Gawdy MSS.*, pp. 4, 15, 22, 27.
2. Cf. *Hatfield MSS.* vi, 294.

Justice of the Peace. It was Heydon who actually challenged his opponent to fight, but both shared the blame for the quarrel.[1]

The fact that Edward Coke, the great lawyer, who had thwarted Heydon by marrying the Suffolk heiress, Bridget Paston, offered to go bail for Townshend suggests that the quarrel was embedded in county faction. What is more, while the Privy Council was detaining these two contentious gentlemen in London, thus preventing one private battle, another Norfolk quarrel reached its climax in a famous duel. The protagonists in this second affair were Sir John Heydon, Sir Christopher's younger brother, and Sir Robert Mansell or Mansfield, a young Norfolk sea-captain and Vice-Admiral. The Lord Chief Justice, showing commendable anxiety to forestall this duel as the other had been forestalled, wrote to warn Sir Robert Cecil of an imminent 'outrage' between the two men, adding that the feud had made and would make a breach in the whole county, which, he feared, was 'already too much wrought into faction'.[2] The warning came too late. Heydon and Mansell fought a desperate duel outside Norwich in October 1600, and Heydon fell, grievously wounded, losing a hand, which subsequently found its way as a curious relic into Canterbury Museum.[3]

The county was 'too much wrought into faction'. These were troublous times. The clouds of the Essex Rising were already gathering; and here in Norfolk, as elsewhere in the country, one can detect local parties aligning themselves for or against England's romantic Earl, whose overweening nature blended private feuds into the poisonous decoction of rebellion. Both the Heydons were the Earl's followers. Sir Christopher was one of his knights of Cadiz:

> A gentleman of Wales, with a knight of Cales
> And a laird of the North Countree,
> A yeoman of Kent upon a racked rent
> Will buy them out all three.

1. ibid., x, 367, 458; *A.P.C.* xxx, 731.
2. *Hatfield MSS.* x, 432–3. The date of the letter (31 December) is puzzling. News of the duel was in London by 10 October (cf. *John Chamberlain's Letters*, ed. McClure, i, 107). Therefore, either the letter is misdated, or a second affray was feared. The antagonists were before the Council in January (cf. *A.P.C.* xxxi, 89, 95; *Gawdy MSS.*, p. 72).
3. *Gawdy MSS.*, pp. 69–71; *Gentleman's Magazine* (1853), new ser. xxxix, 481–8, xl, 54.

Sir John was with the Earl on his fatal Irish campaign in 1599, and returned with the dubious honour of an Essex knighthood. Both took part in the Rising, when in February 1601 the storm-clouds burst, while their enemy, Sir Robert Mansell, was active against them, on the Queen's and Cecil's side.

But before the rebellion broke out, in the preceding months of December and January, the Norfolk gentry were busy taking soundings for the parliamentary election that was then expected. The most prominent of those wishing to stand was Sir Bassingbourne Gawdy of West Harling, son of our previous Bassingbourne and member for Thetford in the 1593 parliament. He was born in 1560, was great-nephew to two judges, and was one of a family which through its several branches had five members in the parliament of 1597. Aiming now at the highest honour, the county seat, he received advice from a friend, who counselled him to write to various people: to two of his uncle's servants, through whom he could secure the support of certain areas, and to the local Bailiff of the Duchy of Lancaster, who presumably commanded the votes of Duchy tenants. Further, he should procure the Bishop of Norwich's favour, thus making sure of his tenants, and Sir John Townshend's favour, to obtain his friends and tenants. Finally, through his great-uncle, the judge, he should make sure of Attorney General Coke's friends. Let him secure all these, and none could stand against him for the senior seat – 'for the first voice', as his friend put it.[1]

The Duchy, amenable to Cecil's influence, Sir John Townshend, Edward Coke: what were these, if not elements of an anti-Essex, anti-Heydon group in Norfolk? And to strengthen the list, Sir Robert Mansell, the duellist. Gawdy was a close friend of Mansell, whose wife – a daughter of Lord Keeper Bacon – was aunt to his wife. Though thirteen years younger than Gawdy, Mansell, on the strength of their marital relationship, was wont to sign his letters, 'Your most assured loving friend and affectionate uncle'! Notwithstanding the scandal of his recent duel, he resolved to stand for parliament along with his friend Gawdy – a decision in which Edward Coke encouraged him to persevere. Nor was Gawdy dissuaded from linking his fortunes to those of his friend, when his cousin, Henry Gawdy of Claxton – who, incidentally, had ends of his own to serve – wrote

1. *Gawdy MSS.*, p. 72.

to tell him that Mansell was not liked and that it would be fatal to pair with him.[1]

The Essex rebellion postponed the parliament, and it was not summoned until September 1601, by which time the Heydons had been broken through their share in the Rising. Once more Sir Bassingbourne Gawdy announced his intention to stand, and still was faithful to his partnership with Mansell. We possess a document of his, headed 'Copy of my letters which I writ unto divers gentlemen for Sir Robert Mansfeld and myself'. Announcing his determination to use his friends and try the love of his country for being knight of the shire, he went on to ask for 'your first voice with all your tenants and other such friends', adding the like request for Mansell, 'we being determined to join, myself to have the first voice and he the second'. Lord William Howard – perhaps the son of the Lord High Admiral – seems also to have written to his friends in Norfolk, presumably on Mansell's behalf.[2]

Among Sir Bassingbourne's supporters were his great-uncle, the judge, who wrote telling his nephew that he had moved many to do as he wished, but some desired to be at liberty for their second voice – that is, not to be bound to Mansell. The duel may have had something to do with their reluctance; but also there were other candidates in the field. Henry Gawdy of Claxton, who had represented the county in the last parliament – against his will, so he said – wrote to his cousin, Sir Bassingbourne, to announce that he and his brother-in-law, Nathaniel Bacon, Francis Bacon's half-brother and M.P. for Norfolk in 1584 and 1593, were both determined to stand. Though he must have known of Sir Bassingbourne's plans, he coolly asked him to use his influence with Sir Nicholas Bacon and others on their behalf, adding that the electors, so he heard, would have no young and inexperienced men, 'but mean to have their free election' – a comment directed both against Mansell, who was only twenty-eight and had not yet sat in parliament, and against the device of pairing.[3]

In the previous December, Clippesby Gawdy, Henry's younger brother, had told Sir Bassingbourne that he intended to stand for the junior seat himself.[4] No doubt he had since withdrawn in his brother's favour, and therefore the election which took place on

1. ibid., pp. 71, 72.   2. Add. MS. 36989, fol. 11; *Gawdy MSS.*, p. 74.
3. *Gawdy MSS.*, pp. 71, 74.   4. Add. MS. 36989, fol. 12.

5 October 1601, was probably a contest between two sets of paired candidates, Bassingbourne Gawdy and Mansell on the one side, and Henry Gawdy and Nathaniel Bacon on the other – all of them relatives. The good sense of the county or of the Sheriff must have resolved the dilemma created by this pairing. They chose Sir Bassingbourne Gawdy for senior knight and Henry Gawdy for junior, leaving Sir Robert Mansell to find a borough seat for himself at King's Lynn four days later, and Nathaniel Bacon to await his solace at the next county election.

As we have seen, in some counties noblemen interfered in the choice of candidates. If this caused no resentment on what we might term constitutional grounds, it was because elections were essentially community affairs, and the territorial nobility were the natural leaders of their communities – a role enhanced by the system of clientage. It was not an affront to liberty for their help to be sought, though to be effective it had either to be reasonable or else be backed by overwhelming voting power. As an example of lordly prestige – very great prestige, but not overwhelming power – failing to get its way, we may cite the intervention of the Earl of Essex in the Staffordshire election of 1593.

This unique peer showed the same fatal lack of moderation in parliamentary elections as in the more dramatic incidents of his whirlwind career. In 1593 he wrote to a follower of his, Richard Bagot, one of the Deputy-Lieutenants of Staffordshire: 'I cannot write several [i.e. separate] letters to all those that have interest in the choice of the knights of that shire ..., to which place I do exceedingly desire that my very good friend, Sir Christopher Blount, may be elected. I do therefore commend the matter to your friendly solicitations, praying you to move the gentlemen, my good friends and yours, in that country, particularly in my name, that they will give their voice with him for my sake.'[1]

Blount, a military man, was Essex's step-father. He had been attached to the Earl of Leicester's service in the Netherlands, and within a year or two of her husband's death the Countess of Leicester, formerly Countess of Essex, had made this surprising marriage – an adventure which, with other traits of character obnoxious to the Queen, excluded her from the Court. Blount became the devoted

1. DEVEREUX, *Lives of the Earls of Essex*, i, 281.

follower of his step-son, and was later to lose his life on the scaffold as one of the principals in the Rising of 1601. He lived with his Countess at Drayton Basset in Staffordshire, and therefore had claims, very strong claims, as a candidate for a county seat. His intrusion left as rivals for the remaining seat two gentlemen who had represented Staffordshire in 1588, Sir Walter Harcourt of Stanton Harcourt in Oxfordshire and Ellenhall, Staffordshire, and Sir Thomas Gerard, son of the Master of the Rolls, both knighted by the Earl of Essex at Rouen in 1591.[1]

It was characteristic of Essex that he could not remain content with backing his step-father. A week after his first letter to Bagot, he wrote again: 'I do, with no less affection and earnestness, entreat your like favour towards my very good friend, Sir Thomas Gerard, for the other place, praying you that you will employ your credit and use my name to my good friends and yours there, that they will stand fast to me in this request ... They cannot give me better testimony of their love and affection ...; and you may assure all such as shall join with you in election that I will most thankfully requite their readiness, and furtherance them by any good office I can.' Then in a postscript, giving rein to his supreme folly, he engaged his credit in the result : 'I should think my credit little in my own country if it should not afford so small a matter as this, especially the men being so fit.' He had added a similar postscript to his first letter, but with a precautionary injunction: 'Yet I pray you, use me so kindly in it, as to have no repulse.'[2]

His megalomania met with the repulse it deserved. Blount obtained the senior seat, but the other was won by Sir Walter Harcourt, the older and more influential of the two remaining candidates.

Another nobleman, the Earl of Rutland, had considerable influence in the selection of the county members for Nottinghamshire: at least, this was so during the heyday of Edward Manners, the third Earl — 'that magnificent Earl, who kept an house like a prince's Court', and journeyed to London with his Countess accompanied by forty-one servants, including a chaplain, trumpeter, gardener, and apothecary.[3] He held many offices and honours, including the lieu-

---

1. WEDGWOOD, *Staffs. Parliamentary History*, i, 388–90.
2. DEVEREUX, i, 282.
3. *Memorials of the Holles Family*, ed. Wood (Camden Soc.), p. 215; *D.N.B.*

tenancy of Nottinghamshire and Lincolnshire, and the Order of the Garter. He was supreme in the affairs of the county, for his only possible rival, the sixth Earl of Shrewsbury, a greater man than he, had his attention absorbed elsewhere.

It seems fairly evident that both in 1584 and 1586 the Earl of Rutland determined the choice of the county's representatives. In 1584 they were Sir Thomas Manners, his uncle, and Sir Robert Constable who had a double tie with his patron, for his mother was a Manners and his brother apparently a member of the Earl's household. Constable was the Earl's nominee at the borough of Nottingham in 1586. Sir Thomas Manners was re-elected for the county in 1586, and along with him, on this occasion, a Nottinghamshire gentleman, Sir Thomas Stanhope, who later becomes a principal in our story. Stanhope was a man of substance and power, well able, one would have said, to stand on his own feet; but, as is shown by a letter from Sir George Chaworth, one of Rutland's followers, whose uncle was Sheriff at the time, it was as a client of the Earl that he chose to appear at the election. 'I lie at your disposition concerning the election of knights for this shire', wrote Sir George to the Earl. 'Sir Thomas Stanhope would willingly supply one place, as associate with Sir Thomas Manners or any other.'[1]

But there came a hiatus in Rutland power. The lustrous third Earl died in 1587, and within a year his brother, who succeeded him, was dead, leaving a young heir only eleven years old. A long minority reduced the family's influence. There is no trace of the Rutland hand in the election of 1588, and even Sir Thomas Stanhope, who might have stood on his own power and prestige, was excluded through being Sheriff at the time.

Then in 1590 the sixth Earl of Shrewsbury died, and his son and heir Gilbert chose Worksop as his principal residence, thus importing a new, a disturbing power into the affairs of Nottinghamshire. This Earl, who filled the vacuum created by the Rutland minority, was a hot-tempered man, whose natural disposition had not been tempered by marriage to Bess of Hardwick's daughter, a lady only less masterful than her mother. The marriage had drawn him to his mother-in-law's side in her notorious quarrels with his father, thus causing his father to keep him in a state of financial stringency. More-

1. *Rutland MSS.* i, 109, 174, 183, 208, 244.

over, he succeeded to a shorn fortune, a further reason for irascibility. His early years as Earl were a succession of violent quarrels. He quarrelled with his mother-in-law over the administration of his father's estates; with his second brother Edward, whom he accused of conspiring against his life and whom he challenged to a duel, giving him 'the lie in his throat' over a question of a forged deed. He quarrelled also with his youngest brother, Henry, with his mother's relatives, the Manners family, and with his neighbours, the Wortleys and the Stanhopes.[1]

This head of an illustrious house, one of England's premier earls and Knight of the Garter, set the county of Nottingham by the ears. Some of the gentry, unable to preserve neutrality while faction raged, and deprived of their customary protection owing to the Rutland minority, transferred their allegiance to the Earl of Shrewsbury. Or so John Holles implied when in a letter to the Dowager Countess of Rutland in June 1593 he assured her of Sir Thomas Stanhope's constancy to herself and her house: 'neither hath he, with the Gentiles of this country', he added, 'bestowed his honouring elsewhere'.[2]

In 1593, the year of the next parliamentary election, there was a tremendous quarrel going on between the Earl of Shrewsbury and Sir Thomas Stanhope over a weir that Stanhope had erected on the river Trent on his property at Shelford. The quarrel is a minor history in itself. It left a trail of Star Chamber cases, and for more than a year kept the Privy Council busy trying to assuage it.[3] There were reverberations even in the streets of London, where John Stanhope, son and heir of Sir Thomas, after being committed for a week to the Marshalsea prison for breaking a Council order against provoking Sir Charles Cavendish, Shrewsbury's brother-in-law, to a duel, was set upon by Cavendish and his servants in Fleet Street, a few days after his release, and had one of his servants seriously injured.[4]

The feud drew many people into it. Gervase Holles in his

1. LODGE, *Illustrations of British Hist.* (1791), ii, 342 ff., iii, 41, 50 ff., 61; *D.N.B.*
2. *H.M.C. Portland MSS.* ix, 161.
3. Cf. Star Chamber 5, S19/34, 24/30, 74/34, 77/36, 25/16, 70/28; *A.P.C.* vols. xxiii, xxiv, passim.
4. ibid., xxiv, 125, 135, 143, 181–2, 206.

Memorials of the Holles Family tells how his kinsman and patron, John Holles of Houghton, afterwards first Earl of Clare, came to be involved through his marriage with Sir Thomas Stanhope's daughter. The Earl of Shrewsbury, he says, took the marriage 'as the greatest affront in the world', for Holles had renounced a kinswoman of the Earl's to marry into the house of his great enemy.

Like master, like man. As became their gentlemanly profession, servants pursued their masters' quarrels. One of Holles's servants slew the Earl's Gentleman of the Horse in a duel; and out of this affray arose a quarrel between the Countess of Shrewsbury's 'gallant' or 'champion', Gervase Markham, and John Holles, which landed the two of them in the Marshalsea, at the same time as John Stanhope, for attempting a duel in London. This particular episode ended five years later in a real fight in Sherwood Forest in which Markham was worsted and grievously wounded. The Earl of Shrewsbury, so Gervase Holles says, raised six score of his servants, ready to apprehend Holles should Markham die of his injuries; on news of which, Lord Sheffield at once repaired to Houghton with three score of his retinue out of Lincolnshire, ready to aid Holles, who was his kinsman.[1]

Little wonder that the Privy Council was angry and perturbed at the breeding of 'troubles, division, and quarrels', already, as they declared, 'kindled too far in that county'.[2] The Countess of Shrewsbury showed herself a true daughter of Bess of Hardwick. She sent her messenger, like a royal herald, bearing defiance to Sir Thomas Stanhope: 'My Lady', he announced, 'hath commanded me to say thus much to you. That though you be more wretched, vile, and miserable than any creature living; and for your wickedness become more ugly in shape than the vilest toad in the world; and one to whom none of reputation would vouchsafe to send any message; yet she hath thought good to send thus much to you: that she be contented you should live (and doth noways wish your death) but to this end – that all the plagues and miseries that may befall any man may light upon such a caitiff as you are; and that you should live to have all your friends forsake you; and, without your great repentence

1. *Memorials of Holles Family*, pp. 90–2; *Portland MSS.* ix, 2, 84–91; *A.P.C.* xxiv, 125, 135.
2. ibid., p. 128.

(which she looketh not for, because your life hath been so bad) you will be damned perpetually in Hell Fire.' All this, the messenger assured Sir Thomas, was but a mild version of the Countess's original text![1]

In the midst of this quarrel came the summons of the parliament of 1593. Though we could wish for full details of what evidently was a dramatic election story, there are a few rays of light. The two great antagonists, Shrewsbury and Stanhope, were both involved, the first as sponsor of his brother-in-law, Sir Charles Cavendish, and the second on his own behalf. Already, four weeks before the election, and before the writs were issued in London, the canvassers were at work. 'I understand that Mr Pierrepoint has sent two of his men to Orston', wrote the Dowager Countess of Rutland's legal agent to her on 11 January 1593, 'and procured the consent of most of the free-holders in the county hereabouts to give their voices as he shall appoint . . ., in the same way as others have done in other parts of the shire for Lord Shrewsbury.' Mr Pierrepoint was the Earl of Shrewsbury's brother-in-law, who, a few weeks before, had been ordered by Stanhope and other Justices to relinquish his office of Justice of the Peace, as a recusant. Stanhope evidently suspected that his election-eering activities betokened an intention to stand for parliament; but this was later denied by the Earl, and presumably it was merely as his agent that Pierrepoint canvassed.[2]

It seems as if the reckless Shrewsbury at first intended to make an unadulterated faction-fight of the election. 'His Lordship will nominate Sir Charles Cavendish and Mr Robert Markham', the Countess of Rutland was told. This Markham was father of John Holles's opponent, and was related to the Cavendishes through his wife. But prudence, or local opinion, led the Earl to ally with Philip Strelley esquire, son and heir of Sir Anthony Strelley, a family which appears to have belonged to the Rutland entourage. It was an astute move, lending a slight air of respectability to proceedings otherwise shameless. Sir Thomas Stanhope, for his part, paired with a certain Thomas Markham. Their chances were slender, for the Sheriff – the sort of man who later that year just ignored orders from the Privy Council in

1. LODGE, i, intro., p. xix.
2. *Rutland MSS.* i, 306; LODGE, op. cit. (ed. 1838), iii, app. pp. 71–2; Heralds' Coll. Talbot MS. I, fol. 164.

Stanhope's favour and had to be summoned to London to be disciplined – belonged to the opposite faction.[1]

The election was held at Nottingham on Monday, January 29th. We have only the Earl of Shrewsbury's account of it, in a letter to Lord Burghley; and a deceptive tale it is. The Earl told how he came to Nottingham on the Sunday night, accompanied by his servants, numbering about eighty. On the way he was met by the Sheriff and by gentlemen whom he described as 'most of the Justices of Peace', though they were doubtless merely his own faction : Stanhope had his rival group of Justices. He was told 'that Sir Thomas Stanhope had gathered thither all his servants and many of his tenants, who were to be in readiness with extraordinary weapons, whereupon it was supposed that some great breach of the peace would be offered'. On alighting at his lodging, he required the Sheriff and Justices to take special care for the preservation of the peace and sent messengers to the Mayor ordering him to have a guard of townsmen ready to suppress any disorder. Into this charged atmosphere early next morning came a Privy Council letter, the purpose of which was to prevent a duel between John Holles and Gervase Markham. It was a timely warning, for the news was going round that both these gentlemen, straining to get at each other, intended to be present at a hunting-match at Newark the following Sunday, when a pitched battle was likely.

The Earl glossed over the actual election proceedings, but our knowledge of the tricks of the trade leaves little doubt as to what happened. As 'the freeholders were very many', he wrote, and the Shire Hall, where elections were customarily held, 'would not have contained the fifth man who had a voice in the election', the Sheriff, 'upon good advice', decided 'to adjourn the county court from the Shire Hall within the town to her Majesty's Castle', which was outside the town. 'So in the Castle court', this disingenous statement continues, 'the election was made, at the time limited by the statute, of Sir Charles Cavendish and Mr Philip Strelley, with one voice of all, without contradition of any one man.' It must have been the same trick that we shall later see practised at Monmouth and Wrexham, where the Sheriff bamboozled his opponents by holding the election surreptitiously in another part of the town. Presumably, Stanhope

1. *Rutland MSS.* i, 306; *A.P.C.* xxiv, 201, 261, 267.

and his followers were kept in ignorance of the change of venue and were thus hopelessly fooled. As the Earl, with suspicious economy, told Burghley: 'At the same time, as I heard, Sir Thomas Stanhope and Mr Thomas Markham, accompanied with none but their sons and servants, unless they procured the two Coroners to stay with them, did sit in the Shire Hall.'[1]

It was a gross fraud. The most curious feature of the story is the absence of any violence or even of quarrelling. 'We, after our election and dinner done', wrote the Earl, 'departed the same night in as peaceable and quiet manner as could be imagined.' Perhaps the letter which arrived from the Council that morning put the fear of dire consequences into men's minds; perhaps the two leaders were men of too great consequence to let civil strife break out in their presence; or more likely, Shrewsbury told too innocent a tale. On this or some other occasion in the next week or two, some 'lewd persons did deface the coach of Sir Thomas Stanhope', and others 'did set up certain vile pictures of the Talbot'.[2]

By way of contrast to the turbulent scene in Nottinghamshire, let us look at Sussex in 1584, where again noblemen exercised electoral influence. One of them, Thomas Sackville, Lord Buckhurst, was running his son and heir, Robert, who was then twenty-three years old and ready to commence his parliamentary career. 'Cousin Calvert', he wrote to the Sheriff, 'I hear that Mr Herbert Pelham and Mr G. Goring do stand to be knights of the shire; and as you friendly offered me your furtherance if need were, so now, though I doubt not of any great need, yet would I be glad to use the help of my friends in this cause for Sir Thomas Shirley and my son.' Four days later, this letter was reinforced by one from Viscount Montague of Cowdray. 'I have thought good to signify unto you', he wrote to the Sheriff, 'that both sundry noblemen and gentlemen, with myself, have thought Mr Robert Sackville and Sir Thomas Shirley most fit ... if the country shall like so to make choice ... I pray you to make my wish and desire to be known to the freeholders there.'[3]

Against so influential a group of sponsors, the opposition's chances

---

1. Talbot MS. I, fol. 164.   2. *A.P.C.* xxiv, 78.
3. Harleian MS., 703, fols. 18b, 19b. Modern copies in Add. MS. 5702, fols. 88–9. Printed in Horsfield's *Hist. of Sussex*, ii, app., p. 23.

– if, indeed, Pelham and Goring persisted in their candidature – were slender. Robert Sackville, in virtue of his noble parentage and despite his youth, was elected to the senior place, while Sir Thomas Shirley, nineteen years older than he, was given the junior seat.[1] But it is perhaps symptomatic of the limitations to noble persuasion – even the persuasion of a Privy Councillor, for by 1586 Lord Buckhurst had attained this office – that Sackville was forced to choose the borough of Lewes when next he sat in parliament in 1588. Not until he was thirty-one or -two was he able to maintain that continuous representation of the shire to which his distinguished parentage, and no less his own intellectual qualities, bade him aspire; and then he sat for the county from 1593 until his father's death in 1608 transferred him to the peerage.

If Viscount Montague was not exaggerating, a number of Sussex gentlemen had joined with him and Lord Buckhurst in selecting Sackville and Shirley as candidates for the 1584 election. Such preliminary soundings among the leading gentry were common, and must have averted many contests. 'Averted' is the appropriate word. Contemporaries do not seem to have regarded contests as normal, and certainly they cannot have thought them desirable. They intensified faction, and were too great a threat to the peace of the county. Writing to Lord Spencer in January 1624, Lord Montagu of Northamptonshire expressed a sentiment that responsible Elizabethans would have applauded: 'I am driven into a strait for this business of the knightship of the shire; but ... myself and other knights hereabouts have entreated Sir John Isham to acquaint your Lordship with our desires for the ancient course observed, to have a knight on each side – from the western and eastern divisions of the county – for the better service of the country, without any opposition.' And in 1625 he again hoped for preliminary agreement, in order that the business might be 'carried in love and with small charge, which otherwise may breed new distractions'. Charles Moryson said much the same in Hertfordshire in 1584; and in Essex in 1604 Sir Thomas Mildmay deplored the active preparations for a contest, fearing that

1. The returns for this county are missing for 1584, but BROWNE WILLIS (iii, 105) gives the names from a MS. of Le Neve. The *D.N.B.* sub Sir Thomas Shirley (1542–1612) erroneously gives him as M.P. for Steyning. His eldest son sat for this borough and he for the county.

a county hitherto 'peaceable' would become 'factious', an evil that both contestants 'as good patriots' should shun, setting aside all private interests.[1]

We cannot hope to know the precise proportion of contested to uncontested elections. There were ten general elections during Elizabeth's reign, with thirty-nine English and twelve Welsh county elections at each. Some contests led to lawsuits, some to intervention by the Privy Council, some find a memorial in surviving letters, and we might guess at others; but the total would not carry us very far, nor would it have any validity. In the absence of any figures, we must fall back on general considerations. Elizabethan gentlemen were so sensitive about their honour that they did not lightly court defeat. When, as a result of pressure from the Privy Council and after a meeting of the Justices, one of the candidates in the Essex election of 1604 was asked to retire from the campaign and thus preserve the peace of the county, his consent was coupled with the reflection, 'though unhappily I may hereby expose my credit to divers misconstructions'; and the Justices took care to assure him that his 'reputation and credit' was 'tendered by us all as it well deserveth'.[2] The result of an Elizabethan election must often – one might even say usually – have been predictable. Unless a candidate had previously obtained, or knew that he could rely upon, the support of sufficient substantial gentlemen, or alternatively, unless he had the backing of an unscrupulous Sheriff, it was hopeless for him to stand. Failing one or the other, we may be sure that the average gentleman would not have exposed himself to the humiliation of 'having the repulse'. And so we may conclude that the majority, perhaps the great majority, of Elizabethan county elections went uncontested.

When no contest was anticipated and the election, to employ a phrase from Northamptonshire in 1604, was to be with 'no repugnant voices', there was probably little canvassing of the ordinary freeholders and nothing like a full muster of voters. Doubtless, those gentlemen attended who conveniently could; doubtless, they brought a body of tenants proportionate to their dignity to do honour to the friend or patron who was to be elected. But it might not even be in the candidate's interest – and certainly was not in the common free-

1. *Buccleuch MSS.* i, 259, iii, 257; *Eng. Hist. Rev.* xlviii, 401.
2. *Eng. Hist. Rev.* xlviii, 408-9.

holder's who might have to trudge miles to the county town – to have an overlarge assembly; for in some counties it was the custom to entertain the freeholders at an election. 'Small charge' as well as peace entered into Lord Montagu's argument for an arranged election in Northamptonshire in 1625. In the Essex election of 1604 – which had at first threatened to bring an exceptional crowd to Chelmsford – after the reduction of candidates to two and the casting of lots for first and second place, there followed a prompt cancellation of instructions to the freeholders, partly to save them the trouble of journeying to the election, but equally and perhaps more urgently to avoid the extraordinary charges of entertainment into which the contestants were sorrowfully drifting.[1]

Thus we should picture the average Elizabethan county election as a tame affair; a small and friendly gathering of the gentry, a somewhat formal meeting. We shall need to remember this through the pages that follow.

When a contest was expected, the scene was quite different. Candidates or their lieutenants made every effort to secure promissory votes from the gentry, and, through them or by direct canvassing, from their tenantry and other freeholders. Canvassing was a general practice on such occasions; and to us, with our organized parties and our conception of representing individuals, not communities, this may seem both natural and inevitable. But the official Elizabethan convention – closer to Rousseau's 'general will' than to our 'one vote, one value' – was hostile to it. It had been condemned in the middle of the fifteenth century, and was regarded as infringing that 'free election' enjoined by a statute of 1406.[2] The old prejudice lingered. Plaintiffs in Star Chamber cases, stressing and exaggerating any canvassing that had taken place, were wont to make it a charge against the other side, partly no doubt as evidence of conspiracy – a recognized offence for this court's jurisdiction – but also as illegal in itself. For their part, defendants did their best to minimize or deny their activities while turning the charge against the plaintiff. The Privy Council, also, on more than one occasion, frowned on the practice, though in the role of country gentlemen some at least of its members must have indulged in it. The oddity of all this diminishes if we re-

1. *Lord Montagu's MSS.*, p. 32; *Eng. Hist. Rev.* xlviii 410, 412.
2. 7 Hen. IV, c. 15.

flect that contested elections were abnormal, that, unavoidable as canvassing might be on such occasions, the occasion itself was to be deplored, and that the more intense the practice the deeper the rift created in county society.

How thorough canvassing could be, we may judge from an illuminating letter written to Sir Robert Sidney of Penshurst, Kent, about the election for that country in 1601. Sidney was away in Flushing, where he was Governor of that Dutch cautionary town; but he had sent orders to one of his servants to back the candidature of Sir Henry Neville, Lord Treasurer Buckhurst's son-in-law.[1] We do not know the full tale of candidates, though as Sidney's servant anticipated, Francis Fane, who was backed by Lord Cobham, proved to be one. He was, in the words of the diarist Manningham, 'a young gent. of great hope and forwardness, very well affected in the country already'. The 'great hope' was his wife, who was the daughter and heiress of Sir Anthony Mildmay, reputed to be worth £3000 per annum; and there were further expectations of £1200 per annum from his mother-in-law.[2] In addition to Fane and Neville it seems that Sir John Scott of Scot's Hall, Kent, a successful candidate in the county election of 1604, was also a candidate; and for all we know there may have been others.

This was no ordinary election. It gave vent to at least one, and possibly two major feuds. Fane's mother was rival claimant against Sir Henry Neville's father for the barony of Bergavenny;[3] and it would be strange if the contention between parents did not extend to the sons. About the other feud – that between their respective backers, Lord Cobham and Sir Robert Sidney – no reservation is required. It was as deep-seated as any in the country. On the death of Cobham's father, who had been Lord Warden of the Cinque Ports and Lord Lieutenant of Kent, both Sidney and he, the former supported by the Earl of Essex and the latter by the Cecils, had stood for

1. The *D.N.B.* sub Neville, Sir Henry, wrongly identifies the M.P. with the ambassador of this name, who was a Berkshire man and moreover was at this time in the Tower for his part in the Essex conspiracy (cf. *Chamberlain's Letters*, i, 122–3, 127, 145, 192; *Hatfield MSS.* xi and xii, passim). *Arch. Cant.* xxi, 230 confuses the M.P. with the 4th Baron Bergavenny, who died in 1586.

2. *Manningham's Diary* (Camden Soc.), p. 13.

3. Cf. *D.N.B.* sub Fane, Sir Thomas.

the succession to these offices, which carried with them the primacy of the county. The Court had rung with the noise of the contest, and Sidney felt his defeat deeply. It made him only of secondary social consequence in his own county; and therefore such an occasion as a parliamentary election offered the opportunity, and may even have imposed the necessity, of flaunting his power in face of that of Cobham – of showing the Sidney flag in Kent, as we might say. Once engaged in the demonstration, though *in absentia* and not on his own behalf, no half-measures would do. His prestige in the county was as fully involved as it had been in the previous election of 1597, when he wrested the senior seat for himself from his rival, Cobham's, nephew and heir.

'Finding your Lordship's great desire to advance the party for Sir Henry Neville', wrote Sidney's servant, 'I did presently practise in all places near about Penshurst, and the next day sent farther off. I am in good hope that you shall be very well satisfied, and shall carry with you a very good troop, if it so fall out that your Lordship do come over before the day of election . . . If your Lordship could be here, it would give great encouragement to many that otherwise will be afraid to show themselves against the other competitors. If Mr Francis Fane do stand (as I hear he will, being thereunto encouraged by my Lord Cobham) we shall be out of all hope of those about Hadlow, Tunbridge, Tudely, Goudhurst, and most of all that quarter, for thereabouts lies his own strength. Mr Rivers is not in the country . . ., but at his return I know he will do his best amongst his selected band: your Lordship may do well to write unto him. Mr Willoughby, both Kelham and Thomas, can raise a good company of Mr Percival's tenants and followers, and I have their promise to do it effectually; and therefore they will look for thanks from your Lordship. I am assured of Penshurst, Leigh, Chiddingstone, Cowden, Hever, and some out of Bidborough. They that belong unto Mr Smythe have warning to go with Sir John Scott. I have written to Edward Petley to practise with the tenants belonging to Otford, and will be amongst them myself upon Friday and Saturday; likewise to Mr Beswick and Mr Whitton about Lamberhurst, I have written; and I know they will do their best, although it be in the heart of the adversary . . . I hear not of Sir Henry Neville, although I should know the day and place of the election. I pray God he follows his business effectually and speedily, for in this race there is nothing can do more good than expedition, to take hold of the first promises. Hitherto I know I am the first that hath moved in all these quarters, and therefore do assure myself of them wholly.

'I would gladly know your Lordship's pleasure, if it chance your Lordship be not here yourself ..., whether you would have that company I can raise, to go to Sir Harry Neville by ourselves or in the company of any other ... I hope by the next to send you the names and number of all such as will go for your Lordship out of every quarter. If your Lordship do write to Sir Henry Lindley for those about Tenterden and those parts, it would do some good; although being not many, yet it may cause many to tarry at home, which I likewise practise with such as fain would, but dare not go against Mr Fane. This is all I have done as yet, but will never rest until I have done my uttermost.'[1]

Alongside this letter may be set a brief catalogue entry of one of Francis Fane's papers: 'The names of such gentlemen as my master wrote unto for their voices, when he was chosen one of the knights of this shire of Kent at Penenden Heath (near Maidstone) 21 September 1601.' The list, says the cataloguer, is a very full one.[2]

Francis Fane won the senior seat, and Sir Henry Neville the junior.[3] The partial rebuff, which to Sidney must have appeared as another triumph for his great enemy, was doubtless hard to bear. Curiously enough, when the Clerk of the Crown came to make up his list of members, he reversed the order of the names. Why, we do not know. Perhaps the Sheriff played a trick; perhaps it was a mere clerical slip.

When canvassing, it was usual to compile lists of the freeholders who promised their voices or votes. They were embryonic poll-lists, and were in fact used by candidates if the election proceeded as far as a poll. Perhaps, as the 1604 Essex election suggests, they were sometimes used in making arrangements for entertaining the electors. It was a nice point of honour that no one, however humble, should go back on a promise once given, even when given in ignorance that friend, patron, or lord was to be a candidate or was supporting the

1. COLLINS, Sidney Papers, ii, 231–2.
2. H.M.C. Rep. X, iv, 6. ('Pickendon hothe' must be an error.)
3. ibid.; Manningham's Diary, p. 13.

other side. The convention gives point to the flaming anger and contempt poured on the wretched men of Watford who, in the expressive term used in those days, 'revolted' at the Hertfordshire election of 1584.[1]

Most forty-shilling freeholders were the tenants or dependants of some squire. They were a measure of his standing in the county, his solid phalanx in trials of strength. When Sir Robert Sidney's man was pressing him to acquire Otford in Kent from the Queen, he argued: 'for by it you shall be ever able to have many freeholders at your command, which in a man's own country is specially to be regarded'.[2] Their duty in an election was clear: it was to line up behind their master and vote as he directed. And on occasions, their promises were exacted in this blind manner.

At its crudest and most blatant, this dependence prompted the following remarkable letter in 1604 from the Earl of Suffolk to 'the Treasurer and Chamberlains of Walden and to all my servants, tenants, and townsmen there'. 'I understand that you have been laboured unto to give your voices in the election of the knights of the shire to Sir Francis Barrington, knight. Whereat I cannot but wonder that he would either solicit any of you to that purpose without my privity, or you so slightly to regard me as to pass your voices before you know my pleasure; which I take very ill at your hands, especially of the better sort that should have had more discretion in advising the rest ... Howsoever you have engaged yourselves, I have thought good to signify unto you my mind therein, that I do expect and challenge at your hands, as I am lord of the town and most of you my tenants (if there were no other respect), that you give your free consents and voices to my good friend Sir Edward Denny, knight; which if you shall not regard what I now make known unto you, I will make the proudest of you all repent it, be you well assured.'[3]

The letter rings like the echo of an earlier one from Queen Elizabeth's Earl of Leicester to the men of Denbigh,[4] though the occasion then was a borough election. In the face of such downright coercion, how very remote the statutory right of 'free election' seems! But, as Suffolk's reference to 'free consents and voices' suggests, it was one

1. *Eng. Hist. Rev.* xlviii, 402; above, p. 27.
2. COLLINS, op. cit., ii, 157.   3. *Eng. Hist. Rev.* xlviii, 405.
4. See below, p. 146.

of those anomalies which every age tolerates and only posterity finds baffling.

Such letters were exceptional. A milder quotation – they 'did persuade some ... by fair and plausible speaches ... and threatened others' – conveys a more normal impression.[1] When the gentry of a county were at cross purposes, humble folk might well be between hammer and anvil. One Denbighshire gentleman, it was said, swore that he would turn out of their lands any of his freeholders who refused to vote for his candidate; and there are many stories of victimization, from inclusion in the levies for Ireland to demotion from superior to petty jury service. A Justice of the Peace or a Sheriff had a hundred ways of persecuting the simple freeholder; and no doubt the readiness of some voters – 'such as fain would, but durst not, go against Mr Faine' – to seek the precarious harbour of neutrality, explains why canvassers often thought it worth while to urge them to stay away from the election.

1. See below, p. 127.

CHAPTER 3

County Elections: At the County Court

COUNTY elections were held at the county court, an assembly which met every fourth week on a fixed weekday. The Sheriff or, if he were absent, his deputy presided, and in contested elections was usually the key man. He conducted the proceedings, which he could manipulate in a surprising variety of ways; he declared the result; and he made the return to Chancery – the official evidence of election. Being one of the leading gentlemen of the county, he frequently had special ties of relationship or friendship with particular candidates, and in faction-ridden counties as likely as not belonged to one of the factions. He was rarely impartial. Fulke Greville, who was once threatened by the tricks of a Sheriff, wrote an inelegant couplet on the subject in his *Treatise of Monarchy*:[1]

> The large times, strength-like, kept elections free.
> Sheriffs used no self-art in their county-days.

Greville was a shade too innocent: the game was older than he thought, and his 'large times' as mythical as the golden age. As long ago as 1429 there had been a statute which made Sheriffs liable to a fine of one hundred pounds and a year's imprisonment for misconduct of an election. But it evidently proved ineffective, and when confirmed in 1445, parliament added what promised to be a more efficient check, by giving a defrauded candidate, or, should he fail to sue, any other person an action of debt for one hundred pounds against a fraudulent Sheriff.[2] Plowden's *Reports*[3] record a successful action of this kind as late as Mary Tudor's reign, and for all we know there may have been later cases.

By Elizabeth's reign, however, inflation had seriously reduced the value of the monetary penalty, and for this and other reasons it was

1. Sec. vii, 'Of Laws', stanza 297.
2. 8 Hen. VI, c. 7; 23 Hen. VI, c. 14 (*Statutes of the Realm*, ii, 243, 340–2).
3. Ed. 1816, i, 118 ff. (Trinity Term, 1 & 2 Ph. & Mary).

no longer an adequate deterrent. Though still far from the state described by Prynne in 1663, when some gentlemen were 'so ambitious, vainglorious, indiscreet, as to spend one or more thousands of pounds to procure an election in any county',[1] candidates and their supporters were on occasions ready enough in the heat of a faction-fight to enter into bonds with a compliant Sheriff to save him harmless, as the phrase went, from the legal consequences of his trickery – in other words, to pay his fine. As one Elizabethan shamelessly put it: the Sheriff 'might return whom he would ..., notwithstanding he were never elected, for ... he knew the Sheriff did for such offence incur but the penalty of one hundred pounds', which he 'was well able to pay'.[2] As we shall see, it was no idle boast.

No doubt one of the reasons why actions under the statute of 1445 proved discouraging was the uncertainties, technicalities, and delays of common-law suits; but if this form of remedy virtually passed out of use, as one suspects, it was because, at the beginning of Elizabeth's reign, lawyers discovered more appropriate remedy, and incidentally a better tribunal, in the Court of Star Chamber. At Common Law, under the statute, an aggrieved candidate could only take action against the Sheriff, whereas in the Star Chamber there was no limit to the defendants he could name. He could proceed against the successful candidate and his leading supporters, who as a rule were no less responsible for the fraud. Conspiracy, or the wrongful use of force, were typical Star Chamber offences; and one or both were elements in many Elizabethan elections. The court possessed another advantage. It could make the punishment fit the crime. For while due regard was paid to the statutory penalties provided for an offence, it was not confined to them.

Apparently, it was the Attorney General, soon followed by candidates' own lawyers, who, at the opening of Elizabeth's reign, first realized that the Star Chamber could serve as a tribunal for election cases.[3] And what a stroke of fortune for the historian! In this, as in other conciliar courts, all the proceedings, prior to the final hearing and judgement, were in writing; so that, when the complete *dossier* of an informative case has survived, with the plantiff's bill, de-

1. *Parliamentary Writs*, iv, 610.
2. My article, 'Three Elizabethan Elections', *Eng. Hist. Rev.* xlvi, 209.
3. In Attorney General *v.* Bronker, 1 Eliz. (Star Chamber 5, A 14/14, 14/15).

fendants' answers, and the examinations on detailed interrogatories
both of the defendants and of the witnesses on each side, we command as good a substitute for the witch of Endor as heart could
desire. In one case, local commissioners spent seven days examining
one hundred and twenty-two witnesses, and in another case, fourteen days examining one hundred and twenty-seven. Questions and
answers all survive. The past lives again.[1]

Though the most flexible of courts, the Star Chamber could not
give what we today should regard as the obvious and appropriate
remedy: it could not unseat a fraudulently elected member. If there
had been no other reason, the time that necessarily elapsed between
complaint and judgement would have made this impracticable. In
the sixteenth century there was only one tribunal that possessed
the requisite authority and expedition – the Privy Council; but it
had little time or inclination to bother itself with such disputes.
The proper remedy did not come until James I's House of Commons, lacking all historical or constitutional warrant, and yet with
sound sense behind its action, usurped jurisdiction over election
questions. In that reign, what with the inducement now offered to
disgruntled candidates and the jealous watch kept over their new
monopoly by the Commons, Star Chamber election cases fade out.
They did little more than outlast the reign in which they began, but
they have provided us with an astonishingly detailed knowledge of
the way parliamentary elections were conducted.

Although in some shires, as a rule Welsh, the county court was
held alternately at two places – for example, in Denbighshire at
Denbigh and Wrexham, and in Sussex at Chichester and Lewes[2]
– normally its meetings were at the county town. We have no actual
knowledge on the point, but one would imagine that in a large
county like Yorkshire this resulted in the absence – disfranchisement would seem too modern a word – of the more distant small
freeholder. In any case, many voters were faced with long journeys
on foot; and it was on this fact that the first trick in a Sheriff's
repertoire turned.

By statute the Sheriff was obliged to hold an election at the first
county court after the receipt of the parliamentary writ, whether

1. *Eng. Hist. Rev.* xlvi, 210
2. T. W. Horsfield, *Hist. of Sussex*, ii, app., p. 23.

it gave him adequate time to warn the county or not. Consequently, candidates had often to act on general knowledge or rumour that the writ was on its way and would be executed at an imminent meeting of the county court. To an unscrupulous Sheriff, bent on securing the triumph of a minority party, the temptation to take advantage of such a situation was strong. While no Elizabethan instance is known of a writ being sprung on an assembly before it was expected, the opposite device of concealing the receipt of the writ, either to give one's side further time for preparation, or to inveigle one's opponents into assembling all their voters in vain – a labour they were unlikely to repeat with the same success four weeks later – was evidently known in the mid-fifteenth century [1] and was practised in Elizabethan times.

The best illustration – it is in a Star Chamber bill [2] – comes from the Radnorshire election of 1597. Being a Welsh county, it had only one seat. There were two competitors, Roger Vaughan of Clyro and James Price of Monachty. Possibly, there had been a long-standing rivalry between these two families. At any rate, a blind but equitable fate had arranged that in 1572, when Vaughan was opposed by a candidate married to a Price of Monachty, the Sheriff had been a kinsman of his, and – if another Star Chamber bill is moderately truthful [3] – had first tried to rig the election and then blatantly returned Vaughan in the face of an opposing majority. Now, in 1597, the Sheriff – by name, Richard Fowler – was just as flagrantly on the other side.

On this occasion, the task of delivering the parliamentary writs in the six shires of Radnor, Brecon, Glamorgan, Pembroke, Carmarthan, and Cardigan was committed to a certain Pierce Maddox, a messenger or pursuivant. Perhaps he was a native of those parts and therefore a partisan; perhaps he had been bribed; certainly he was in collusion with the Sheriff and with Vaughan's opponents. He travelled *via* Radnor, where he stayed the night and spoke with the Sheriff, who lived within half a mile of the town. Had he done his duty he should then have delivered the writ. Instead, he retained it and went on to the other five counties. He was actually back in

1. *Paston Letters*, ed. Gairdner, ii, 36.
2. Roger Vaughan *v.* James & Clement Price (Star Chamber 5, V 7/9).
3. Thomas Lewis of Harpton *v.* Edward Price (ibid., L 24/21).

Radnor and in the Sheriff's company on the night before the county-court day, 20 September. Yet he still did not deliver the writ, the reason being – so Vaughan alleged – that there was 'a very great appearance of freeholders', bent on electing Vaughan. Consequently, the freeholders who had come to the county court, expecting an election, 'lost their labour and returned home', Though we have only one side of the story, a comparison of dates leaves little or no doubt that the writ must have been fraudulently delayed.[1]

When the next county-day arrived, on 18 October, there was only 'a small appearance of freeholders', many staying away, 'grieved and mocked' by their fruitless journey a month before. Nevertheless, Vaughan – so he claimed – still had a majority, but, 'by fraud and corruption and for rewards given unto him', the Sheriff returned James Price, arguing that Vaughan, who in fact was a Deputy-Lieutenant of Radnorshire, who had been born at Clyro in that county, and who had always kept a house there, was ineligible because he lived in Herefordshire. Who can doubt, after such a tale, that a Sheriff could 'return whom he would'?

Election proceedings were supposed to begin between the hours of eight and nine in the morning. In the Elizabethan period this was unquestioned law; though law, be it added, made by a printer and not by parliament. It is a quaint story. The act of 23 Henry VI, in which the hours were specified, gave them as between eight and eleven; but the printer of Rastell's edition of the statutes in 1557, using Roman numerals, transposed his type and printed 'ix' instead of 'xi'. Subsequent editions of the statutes copied Rastall, and for half a century or more the electoral law of England reposed on a misprint![2]

The early hour, especially in winter, must have brought many freeholders to the county town the day before, thus raising problems of accommodation. It was important for candidates to take up inns and houses for their own supporters and deny them to their

1. The writ was dated 23 August (cf. *Interim Report of the Committee on House of Commons Personnel*, Cmd. 4130, 1932, p. 92). The elections in the other counties visited by Maddox were held between 20 September and 5 October, and the writs were probably delivered within about a week from 8 September.

2. Cf. my article in *Eng. Hist. Rev.* xlvi, 215 n. 5.

opponents. This aspect of a campaign emerges in clearest detail in the Essex election of 1604, when Sir Thomas Mildmay, who was all-powerful in the town of Chelmsford, caused concern to a candidate by going over to the other side along with the inns he had bespoken. 'I know not who hath any authority to except against me' – he wrote – for taking up inns 'in mine own town, being lawfully required for myself and friends.' But even Mildmay could not establish a monopoly in Chelmsford, and Lord Rich, who was the most active supporter of the opposition, not only arranged for stores of his own food to be taken there, but got hold of the New Inn and the Dolphin. 'I also sent to the Lion', he wrote, 'but his answer was, he knew not whether his landlord would serve for you or no.' Lord Rich's grandfather, it seems, had been active in much the same way in the first Essex election of Elizabeth's reign, for the Privy Council had then intervened, presumably in the interests of peace, asking Sir John Rainsforth to forgo a house which had first been hired by Lord Rich for the election, and afterwards commandeered by Rainsforth.[1]

In the Montgomeryshire election of 1588, in which Edward Herbert, lord of the town of Montgomery, was a candidate, the victuallers were ordered only to lodge men brought to them by certain followers of his. And in the Denbighshire election of 1601, Sir John Salusbury, who rode to Wrexham the day before the election accompanied by his friends and a company of followers, with 'thousands' more due that night, attempted to get hold of the church as a place of shelter for his men, only to find himself forestalled by his rival, within whose sphere of influence the town lay. A great man such as Salusbury did not lack lodging for himself, even in Wrexham, nor probably did the gentry on his side, but his humbler followers must have fared worse than their opponents.[2]

A county town was often an extraordinary spectacle when a contest was in prospect. Every forty-shilling freeholder who could be got there by persuasion or threat was present. So were many others: they 'scant left a boy at home to drive the plough'.[3] Those who were

1. BOHANNON, 'The Essex Election of 1604', *Eng. Hist. Rev.* xlviii, 401–2; *A.P.C.* vii, 38–9.
2. My article in *Eng. Hist. Rev.* xlvi, 223 ff., 236.
3. ibid., p. 214.

unqualified to vote or were aliens from neighbouring shires, and attended out of friendship, duress, or sheer love of fun, swelled the chorus bawling their candidate's name. They might even, with the Sheriff's connivance, influence the course of the election.

There were between a thousand and two thousand freeholders at Wrexham in the Denbighshire election of 1588. In Montgomeryshire, where the number of qualified voters was authoritatively estimated at sixteen to seventeen hundred, one side in 1588 claimed eleven hundred or slightly more legitimate votes, and the other side just over the thousand, while in the Norfolk election of 1586, according to the Sheriff's estimate, there were three thousand people present.[1] The record, as one might expect, comes from Yorkshire. After the 1597 election, fifteen of the Justices of that county wrote to Sir John Stanhope, a defeated candidate: 'The love that the gentlemen of this county bear to you, brought us with eighty-six knights, Justices, and esquires, and many more gentlemen and freeholders, numbering about three thousand, to choose you at the election to be our first knight of the shire'. Opposing Stanhope was Sir John Savile, with – the estimate is that of opponents – 'only eight other gentlemen of any reckoning, but with a great number of clothiers and artificers, among them above three hundred that had no freehold and many more that had not even copyhold'. 'Citizens and inhabitants of York, women and children and other strangers not having lawful voices, to the number of five hundred or six hundred' were also said to have been present; and though a healthy scepticism is called for when assessing partisan figures, it is clear that the crowd at the election must have numbered close on six thousand.[2]

While the law did not specify the actual place within the county town where the election should be held, custom normally did. The point is not trivial. On it turned another of the tricks at the service of a Sheriff.

We cannot do better than take for our illustration the story of the Monmouthshire election of 1572.[3] Though brought into the parliamentary system along with the Welsh shires in Henry VIII's reign,

1. ibid., pp. 214–15, 238; D'Ewes, *Journals*, p. 396.
2. *Hatfield MSS.* vii, 414, 416.
3. The references will be found in my article, 'More Elizabethan Elections', *Eng. Hist. Rev.* lxi, 27 ff.

this county was granted two members on the plan of the English shires. In 1572 no doubt existed about the candidate for the first place. Charles Somerset, a younger son of the second Earl of Worcester, who had sat for the county in the previous year, was again seeking election; and when a scion of the lords of Raglan desired to enter parliament, a Monmouthshire seat was his for the asking. This left only one seat to meet the conflicting claims of the two other outstanding families, the Herberts and the Morgans, who, though related by marriage, seem to have been prone to quarrel. The bar sinister was in the lineage of some of the Herberts, but they sprang from an earl and esteemed themselves the social superiors of a Morgan.

The wealthiest member of the Morgan family at this time was William Morgan of Llantarnam, richly endowed with monastic property and, as impecunious bards hopefully described him, 'generous, gold-gifted'. He had been Sheriff in 1557–8, and had represented the county three times in parliament, the last being in the previous year, 1571. He was again a candidate in 1572. The Sheriff in this year was Thomas Herbert of Wonastow, an estate close to the town of Monmouth. He had been Sheriff before, in 1559–60, and had twice represented the county in parliament. In any case, it is likely that he would have conspired to prevent William Morgan establishing a monopoly of the second county seat; but, as it happened, he was also anxious to establish his eldest son, Henry, in the leadership of the county, and this was his opportunity.

Between 6 a.m. and 7 a.m. on 1 May 1572, the day of the election, Thomas Herbert met his supporters by arrangement at St Thomas's Church on the outskirts of Monmouth by the river Monnow. At the same time – if the figures can be trusted – some nine hundred freeholders, most of them Morgan's supporters, gathered in and about Monmouth Castle, in the Common Hall of which, by long custom, the county court was invariably held. There was no apparent reason to suspect that the court would not be held at the Castle on this occasion: indeed, the Sheriff's officers were busy preparing the Hall with furniture and cushions. While the voters waited here, there was a little rough play, as will happen with a crowd, and it is possible, though not certain, that the hall door and some windows were damaged. The Sheriff was brought the news, whereupon, without further inquiry or notification of his intention, he made it the excuse for carrying out a plan that had either been in his mind from the beginning or had been devised as soon as he realized that Morgan's followers greatly outnumbered his own. That plan was to hold the election elsewhere.

The Sheriff went to the house of one, Hopkin Richard, 'a simple ale-house' in the suburbs at 'the town's end'; close, in fact, to where he had met his supporters, and as distant a place from the Castle as was possible within the town's limits. Here he stayed awhile, pretending to prepare himself for coming to the county court. On Morgan's side the leaders, who were evidently suspicious of being tricked, sent to ask when he intended to come to the Castle – a move which the Sheriff countered by sending twice to Morgan, ostensibly to negotiate. He included among his messengers the chief candidate, Charles Somerset, who was allied with him. It was a subtle choice. Who could have suspected that the election would be held in this man's absence?

The manoeuvre succeeded. While the deputation was acting as a decoy, the Sheriff dispatched his business. He himself walked in the street outside Hopkin Richard's house, so that no one should guess what was afoot, while, inside, his Under-Sheriff got through the formal agenda of the county court, with no Coroners present and a mere pretence of suitors. This preliminary business lasted about a quarter of an hour. Then, being told that it was ended, the Sheriff scampered through the election in the open street, in the presence of about one hundred and fifty voters, perhaps less, perhaps more. He first declared the contents of the election writ, and then seems to have asked, 'Are you content that Mr Charles Somerset and my son, Henry Herbert, shall be knights of the shire?' Those present cried, 'A Somerset! A Somerset!' for one of the knights, and for the other, some cried 'A Herbert!' and others, 'William Morgan!'

When the nine hundred freeholders at the Castle heard the cries and realized what was happening, they attempted to join in the election by calling out 'William Morgan! William Morgan!', and came running down to Hopkin Richard's house. Before they could reach it, the Sheriff declared his son elected, went off to his horses, and rode away. Some of Morgan's leaders pursued and overtook him. They demanded that he return and hold a poll, but though they spoke as Justices and in the Queen's name, their importunities were of no avail. Contemptuously he answered that so much of the election as he would or meant to do was done, and he would do no more that day. It only remains to add that the election – if it be graced by that name – was held before the statutory hour of 8 a.m., and the indenture or certificate of election included the names of at least three gentlemen who were not present that day.

It was a blatant trick. For sheer impudence and crudity it had a parallel in the Denbighshire election of 1588, the story of which will be told later; and it is obvious that something along the same lines happened in the Nottinghamshire election of 1593.

As the Monmouthshire election indicates, the initial proceedings at an election were those of a county court. The court was 'set', then proclaimed, and a few cases called *pro forma*. After this, the election writ was read and the nomination of candidates followed. If procedure was decorous, the Justices and leading gentlemen, sitting on the bench with the Sheriff, usually proposed the candidates. If indecorous, the Sheriff took the nomination on himself, or the body of freeholders, like a noisy football crowd, bawled out the names. In the Yorkshire election of 1597, 'Sir John Stanhope and Sir Thomas Hoby and Sir John Savile being first nominated – in more or less formal manner, one supposes – Sir John Savile caused the Sheriff to read certain statutes ... purporting that none should be chosen ... but such as were resident in the county at the *teste* of the writ; and hereupon Sir John Savile took upon him, forthwith rising, to propound unto the people, "Will you have a Mauleverer or a Fairfax?" – as second knight to himself – meaning to make knights at his will as is thought, or otherwise by several nominations to distract the voices of freeholders from others before named. After which, the cries and voices of the people continued confused and divers, by the space of two hours and more, for Sir John Stanhope, Sir Thomas Hoby, Sir John Savile, and Sir William Fairfax.'[1]

In this Yorkshire account, the nomination appears to merge, with no clear distinction, into the second stage of the proceedings, the election by voices, or, as it was sometimes called, 'the general election'. For this, everyone shouted his lustiest, calling the name of his man. 'Your friends must not be spare-voiced, but with their voices

1. *Hatfield MSS.* vii, 413–14.

pronounce it roundly and fully', wrote an anxious parent, coaching his son in election tactics in 1614; and, according to a witness of the result, 'the cry "A Phelips! A Phelips!" was so great and violent for three-quarters of an hour at least, that at the Cross and all about it, I heard no other noise nor sound but "A Phelips!" ' During the pandemonium, the Sheriff was supposed to discern who had the greatest number of voices.[1]

When there was no contest, the vote by voices terminated the election, and even in contested elections might suffice for the senior seat, if this was not challenged. In addition, there was always the chance that an unscrupulous Sheriff might give a partisan verdict and brazen it out. But when competition was close, mere noise was no measure of numbers, nor could the ear distinguish 'forty-shilling' voices from unqualified ones. If the Sheriff ventured a verdict, one side was certain to challenge it, and the election was then supposed to proceed either to 'the view' or directly to the poll.

The view was a device to avoid the time-consuming procedure of the poll. It was taken by separating candidates' supporters into district companies, which the Sheriff or a party of gentlemen could survey, and guess at the relative size of each. Some elections must have been terminated in this way: otherwise it would be hard to explain why the procedure survived. But in the more acrimonious contests – which are those that have left evidence – this rough and ready device was bound to be unsatisfying, and a poll was usually demanded. In a post-Elizabethan dictum, the great lawyer, Sir Edward Coke, declared that 'if the party or the freeholders demand the poll, the Sheriff cannot deny the scrutiny, for he cannot discern who be freeholders by the view'. While there was no precise statutory authority for his assertion, it was both common sense and accepted practice, and by 1624, if not earlier, was recognized as good law by the House of Commons.[2]

When a poll was conceded, the freeholders had to pass before the Sheriff or his officer, assisted by representatives of the competing candidates. The lists compiled during the canvassing seem now to have come in useful both for marshalling the voters and recording

1. FARNHAM, 'The Somerset Election of 1614', *Eng. Hist. Rev.* xlvi, 592.
2. COKE, *Fourth Institute* (1669), p. 48; JOHN GLANVILLE, *Reports* (1775), pp. 82–3.

their names and their votes. Each side had the right to challenge a man's qualifications, and when challenged he had to declare on a corporal oath that he possessed the statutory value of freehold and perhaps that he was resident in the county. A mark was usually set against his name to record that he had been sworn, thus providing evidence of perjury should the declaration be false. There is a Star Chamber case in which the Attorney General prosecuted twelve Huntingdonshire voters for alleged perjury in the county election of 1584.[1]

For one reason or another, there was sometimes great reluctance to proceed to a poll. In the Yorkshire election of 1597,[2] the prolonged pandemonium of the election by voices apparently eliminated Sir Richard Mauleverer from the contest, leaving a clear issue between Sir John Savile paired with Sir William Fairfax and Sir John Stanhope paired with Sir Thomas Hoby. The latter, according to their own reckoning, had six or seven hundred more voices at the beginning of the hubbub, after which 'the greater number seemed doubtful'. It was then agreed that each side should appoint a gentleman to accompany the Under-Sheriff and view the rival companies from an upper window of the Castle. The verdict was unanimous: Savile and Fairfax had a majority of two to three hundred. All the same, Stanhope's supporters demanded a poll, on the ground that five or six hundred of the voters in the opposing company were unqualified. Savile and Fairfax, for their part, seem to have suggested as an alternative that their rivals should appoint sixteen or twenty of 'the best men of knowledge of the country' to take another view and pick out any they suspected of being unqualified, to whom an oath would be administered. The Under-Sheriff, who was in charge of the election, was also averse to a poll, and one can readily sympathize with him, for by this time the morning was far spent and the number of voters was 'exceedingly great'. Stanhope and Hoby, however, insisted, and the Under-Sheriff gave way.

It was agreed that the Castle gate should be shut and no more people let in, that 'two of the gentlemen triers on either side should note or nick every score' of voters – a device to speed up the scrutiny – 'and that all should be sworn and examined against whom any exceptions should be taken'. Preparations were accordingly made,

1. Star Chamber 5, A 41/32, 42/30.   2. *Hatfield MSS.* vii, 411 ff.

and one of Stanhope's leaders was ready with 'a knife and stick to nick on the scores on the one side', when Sir John Savile came up on horseback and demanded of the Under-Sheriff what he was about. 'To proceed to trial by poll, according to agreement and law', he answered. 'Though they would make you an ass', retorted Savile, 'they shall not make me a fool'; and vowing that he would have no such trial, and would 'hold that he had', he commanded the gate to be opened and roughly forced his way out, taking the Under-Sheriff with him.

For two hours or more Stanhope and Hoby's supporters remained at the Castle, awaiting the Under-Sheriff's return to proceed with the poll. They probably expected some trick. But he was merely at dinner with Savile and Fairfax. Three hours elapsed before he returned, and then, having proclaimed silence, without more ado he pronounced Savile and Fairfax elected and adjourned the county court. In an official report to the Privy Council, the Archbishop of York and other members of the Council in the North declared with justice that he had 'dealt very affectionately against Sir John Stanhope and Sir Thomas Hoby'. They also reported that Savile had shown contempt for their authority, for which offence – but not for his behaviour at the election – the Privy Council ordered his imprisonment, taking care, however, to limit its duration so that he should not be prevented from taking his seat in parliament.[1]

Sir John Stanhope, who was about fifty-two years old at the time of this election, was Master of the Posts and Treasurer of the Chamber, a Court official close to the Queen. He was born in Yorkshire, was *Custos Rotulorum* of the North Riding, and was 'a large landowner' there. He had a brother who was a member of the Council in the North.[2] But against these local ties must be set the fact that he spent most of his time at Court, while his territorial affiliations were with Northamptonshire rather than Yorkshire. His opponents were not simply captious when they got the Under-Sheriff to quote the law on the residential qualifications for candidates.

As for Sir Thomas Postumous Hoby, he was a younger man, aged thirty-one, the son of an ambassador and a nephew of Lord Burghley.

1. *Hatfield MSS.* vii, 436–7; *A.P.C.* xxviii, 46, 114.
2. *D.N.B.*; *Hatfield MSS.* vii, 417; REID, *Council in the North*, pp. 227, 495.

As a child, he had been undersized and difficult. His mother, one of the most learned, remarkable, and forceful women of the age, on one occasion angrily described him to Burghley as 'both most ungodly and monstrous'. He outgrew the ungodliness, which was perhaps but a touch of his mother's stubbornness, and became a serious-minded Puritan. But he remained diminutive: 'the little knight that useth to draw up his breeches with a shoeing-horn'. He came to Yorkshire by marrying an heiress of that county, Margaret Dakin, who had previously married in turn brothers of Robert, Earl of Essex, and of Sir Philip Sidney. At the age of twenty-four she had been twice widowed. Hoby's pursuit of her, begun after her first widowhood and renewed after her second, was irresistible. His own persistence, his mother's imperative mustering of support from Lord Burghley and other great ones of the land, left the young widow little option. However, she had been brought up in the keen puritan household of the Countess of Huntingdon, who, in her own words, knew 'how to breed and govern young gentlewomen'; and Hoby's puritan zeal, if not his person, proved a sound basis for marital happiness. They were married in August 1596, and settled down – she to run an efficient, godly household and keep a diary, and he to help run the North Riding of Yorkshire, with no less efficiency, though with little humour and much friction. To his enemies he was the 'scurvy urchin', 'spindle-shanked ape', 'the busiest saucy little Jack in all the country', who 'would have an oar in anybody's boat'; 'he came over the water with his coach and three horses, but all scant worth sixpence, or sixpence apiece'.[1]

Thus, at the time of the 1597 election Stanhope was an absentee landowner and J.P., and Hoby an interloper of one year's standing. Need we wonder that Sir John Savile chided the voters? 'Fie, Fie!' he said, 'you shame your country to choose strangers. Turn to us.'[2]

In their letter to the Privy Council, the Archbishop of York and his fellow-members of the Council in the North explained, perhaps a little disingenuously, that Stanhope and Hoby were first named for the two Yorkshire seats 'some time' after the county was notified of the coming parliament, and because 'no gentleman of this country seemed to wish to be elected'. The Archbishop, they declared, actually

1. *Diary of Lady Margaret Hoby*, ed. D. M. Meads, introduction, passim.
2. *Hatfield MSS*. vii, 416.

asked Sir John Savile if he wished to stand, but was answered no; and it was not until a fortnight before the county day that he changed his mind.[1]

The change can probably be explained, at any rate in part, as a revolt of the West Riding – where the Savile family was closely connected with the clothing interest and where the clothing towns yielded 'the greatest number of freeholders' – against a northern and eastern monopoly. Moreover, Savile, a lawyer, was at the time fighting the Council in the North in defence of the clothing interests; and both Stanhope, a Court official and dependant of the Cecils, and Hoby, a cousin of Sir Robert Cecil, were patently countenanced by the Archbishop and his colleagues for official rather than local reasons.[2]

However, according to Stanhope's leading supporters, the chief reason for Savile's opposition was the notorious feud which had raged between Stanhope's recently deceased elder brother, Sir Thomas, of Shelford, Nottinghamshire, and the seventh Earl of Shrewsbury – a feud which, as we have seen, had set that county ablaze. 'Sir John Savile', they told Stanhope, 'a little before the election, instigated by the Earl of Shrewsbury's followers in this county, Nottinghamshire, and Derbyshire, opposed himself to you, and drew over Sir William Fairfax on the morning of the election to stand for the other place, although only the night before he had promised you his vote and interest.' And they quoted Savile's racy boast that the Stanhope 'pied horse nor no devices could carry' the election to Sir John, 'nor to never a Stanhope in England'. Significantly enough, one of Stanhope's lieutenants in this election was Edward Talbot, the Earl of Shrewsbury's brother – he whom the Earl had challenged to a duel. Thus, through the wide dispersal of their estates and interests, did the feuds of the great spread over the land.[3]

The Archbishop of York thought Stanhope's partnership with Hoby a blunder. He had to be careful with his words, for he was writing to Sir Robert Cecil, Hoby's cousin. If only, he wrote, the Under-Sheriff had followed his advice and held separate elections for

1. ibid., p. 417.
2. ibid., p. 436; REID, op cit., p. 221; BIRCH, Memoirs of Queen Elizabeth, ii, 61.
3. Hatfield MSS. vii, 416.

each of the two seats, then no doubt Sir John Stanhope would have secured one, 'for he is generally well thought on in all this country. Sir Thomas Hoby, a gentleman of very great hope is not as yet so well known, and was hindered especially by a rumour (true or false, I know not) spread abroad in the clothing towns in the West Riding ... that in the last parliament his brother, Sir Edward Hoby, did prefer a bill against northern cloths, which they thought did very much concern them.' [1]

After this failure at York, Sir John Stanhope was hastily provided with a seat at Preston, a Duchy of Lancaster borough, while Sir Thomas Hoby provided himself with a seat at Scarborough, six miles from his and his wife's estate in the picturesque dales at Hackness.

We cannot leave this Yorkshire election without reflecting that if the poll, with its thousands of voters to be scrutinized, had really proceeded, there is no telling how long it would have lasted: certainly into the dark evening and almost certainly into the next day. The Commons' Committee of Privileges and Elections in 1624 spoke of there being so many freeholders in some counties 'as cannot be polled or numbered in one or divers days'. Yet we have no evidence, even in James I's reign, of a poll extending over several days, and perhaps the Committeee was expounding theory rather than practice. In Elizabeth's reign elections were one-day affairs, and even to spend the whole day over the business raised problems of feeding, accommodation, or a night-trudge home that might defy satisfactory solution and cause the freeholders to melt away before the poll ended. One of the most prolonged elections of which we know was in Montgomeryshire in 1588. It lasted from the statutory hour on a Saturday morning, throughout the day and night, until four or five on the Sunday morning, when the poll was abandoned in disgust by a weary Sheriff.[2]

Sheriffs might dislike polls, but they found scope in them for more of their tricks. Much might turn on the order in which the scrutiny was made. If one candidate's supporters were numbered before another's, it was an advantage to be first. If the scrutiny was by Hundreds, taking all the voters from one district at a time, the Sheriff might give priority to the Hundreds in which his own party had an overwhelming majority, and defer the rival's strong suit until

1. ibid., pp. 435–6.   2. GLANVILLE, *Reports* p. 105; below, p. 101.

87

the end of the game, by which time some of his voters would probably have started back home. Furthermore, by brow-beating at the poll; by confusing ignorant folk over the technicalities of their qualifications; by frightening those on the margin of 'forty shillings' – small men who had hitherto kept off the Sheriff's list of 'sufficient freeholders', thus evading jury service and subsidy payments – threatening to enrol them and thus raise them to the respectable but onerous level of 'the good yeoman' who made 'a whole line in the subsidy book';[1] or perhaps by gross partiality in accepting or refusing their oaths; by these and kindred methods the Sheriff might turn a minority into a majority.

It was a moot question – on which an authoritative, but not necessarily sound ruling was given in 1624 – whether freeholders, arriving on the scene after the election by voices but before the end of the poll, had the right to vote. The phraseology used by parties and witnesses in Elizabethan Star Chamber cases often suggests that the poll was a scrutiny of those who had given their voices in the election by voices, making the latter the true election: hence the opposition to late-comers. But in 1624, the Commons' Elections Committee, on the general principle that 'all favour is to be afforded in allowing voices to as many freeholders as reasonably may be had', held that the whole election, however long it lasted, was 'but one continued act in law', and therefore anyone coming while the election remained uncompleted, 'cometh time enough to give his voice'.[2]

The Radnorshire election, which was held at Presteign on 6 May 1572, illustrates some of these points.[3] The Sheriff was determined to secure the election of a kinsman, Roger Vaughan of Clyro, and thwart an enemy, Thomas Lewis of Harpton, an older and more influential gentleman. He had openly declared – so it was said – that 'if Lewis should fortune to obtain the greater number of voices, yet he would not return him; no, not although he should incur the danger of the law and loss of five hundred pounds'.

In the election by voices, Lewis appears to have had a clear majority of the 'three hundred or more' freeholders. The Sheriff refrained from making out his return, but otherwise acted as if the election were ended, and went to dinner, expecting, as indeed happened,

1. FULLER, *Holy and Profane State*, 'The Good Yeoman'.
2. GLANVILLE, *Reports*, pp. 102–3.   3. Star Chamber 5, L 24/21.

that many of Lewis's supporters would depart home in the belief that all was over. Meanwhile, Vaughan, who had either not yet arrived at Presteign or had gone off to hurry up reinforcements, came to the town with three hundred 'very light, lewd, and dis-ordered persons ..., gathered out of several shires' – probably from Hereford and Brecon, as well as Radnor, in all of which he was, or was to be, a Justice – 'half not resident in the county, nor yet suffi-cient freeholders'. In this advantageous position, but with utter irregularity, another assembly was summoned at 3 p.m.

From the contradictory evidence it is difficult to deduce the pro-cedure then followed. Apparently, the Sheriff attempted to declare Vaughan elected at about 5 p.m., but was forced to hold a poll. He had not yet, however, run through all his tricks. It happened that he and his two sons-in-law and others of his party held a royal com-mission to assess the subsidy, and when, after numbering Vaughan's voters, he came to scrutinize Lewis's men, he attempted to frighten them with the threat that if they voted for Lewis they 'should be taxed and assessed in payment of the subsidy as pleased him and the other commissioners'. Quarrelling ensued, for which each side blamed the other; weapons were flourished – swords, glaives, long-bills, and main-pikes; and bloodshed was only averted by the inter-vention of the Justices. At this point, the Sheriff withdrew, ordering the freeholders to move to the church, ostensibly to keep better order, but perhaps – as was said – in the hope that some of Lewis's sup-porters, reflecting on the threat to mulct them in the subsidy, would quietly disappear *en route* to the new voting place.

By now, the hour was growing late. If the Sheriff can be believed, Lewis had not been idle, but, taking a leaf out of his opponent's book, had sent to a fair at Knighton, a few miles distant, for rein-forcements, which arrived about 10 p.m., clamouring to give their voices. There was much bickering, and progress with the poll was necessarily slow, though it is likely that the Sheriff had no intention of completing his task and dilly-dallied on purpose. According to his own account, he was busy 'all the afternoon and almost all night and until it was nigh day'. Said Lewis, 'the night drew on'; and with this for excuse the Sheriff refused to finish the poll. He was asked 'to come into some quiet place where the electors for both sides might be indifferently numbered and tried'; but he refused and departed to his lodging, and next morning once more refused to hold a proper poll, saying that he would spend no more time on the business.

He returned his kinsman, Roger Vaughan, as knight of the shire, and subsequently, when framing his answer in the Star Chamber, made his proceedings seem quite regular and the poll complete, putting Vaughan's majority at one hundred. We have no check on the two rival stories, but it seems very unlikely that Vaughan, who was a newcomer in Radnor elections and managed to capture the seat only on this occasion, honestly beat Lewis, who had already been Sheriff, had represented the county in 1559 and 1563, and was to win the next election in 1584, and the following one in 1586.[1] Either plaintiff or defendant in this case was an egregious liar, and the presumption is strongly against the defendant.

Some reflections, written by one of the defeated side after the Hertfordshire election of 1584, throw interesting light on polling. If only our voters had been scrutinized first! this gentleman lamented; 'I think it would have furthered us greatly'. He complained because the Sheriff refused to accept the votes of their copyholders, 'the most substantialest men of the country'; a complaint which reflected his chagrin at the loss of many supporters, but which he must have known had no basis in law. There were thirty or more of their freeholders, he went on to say, who, seeing the contest lost, 'desired not to appear, for that they were not in the suitors' books' – that is, in the lists of freeholders on whom fell jury service. 'Their appearance', these humble men had argued, 'could do us no good; which I agreed unto.' But his greatest grief, he declared, was that they 'suffered such manifest perjury'. Evidently, no note had been taken of the name and residence of voters who were put to the oath. If only this had been done, 'they durst not have afforded their oaths so liberally to their knight'. 'Of my own knowledge I do know perjury committed of many, and besides I fear there was many ... which escaped' any challenge. 'In my very conscience, two hundred of them were not sufficient of freehold. But now it is too late.'[2]

The last word in an election was necessarily with the Sheriff. It was he who drew up the indenture, sealed by a selection of free-

1. Cf. W. R. WILLIAMS, *Parliamentary History of Wales*, p. 172; JONATHAN WILLIAMS, *History of Radnor*, p. 83.
2. Add. MSS. 40630, fol. 6.

holders, and made the official return to Chancery. If prepared to face the legal consequences, he could do exactly as he pleased. He could conclude the election after the initial acclamation, or refuse to proceed beyond 'the view', or break off the poll, or falsify its manifest verdict. In 1624 there was a case of a Sheriff omitting to take a poll, though it had been demanded and promised: the House of Commons dealt firmly with the offence, annulled the election, and brought the Sheriff before the House for reprimand. There was also a case – a Norfolk election – where the same House and Committee, but by majority votes, ignored a similar offence. We happen to know, from other, if rather confused evidence, that their decision was just, if illogical.[1]

The first election case that came into the Star Chamber, which was that of Wiltshire in 1559, shows a Sheriff deliberately reversing the clear result of a poll.[2] On this occasion there was no dispute over the first seat, but the second was contested by George Penruddock and Sir John Thynne. Penruddock was Steward to the Earl of Pembroke, whose chief residence was at Wilton, while Sir John Thynne was a fairly recent settler in this county, who had bought Longleat in 1541 and was soon to build the famous house of that name. Thynne had once been Steward to Protector Somerset, and his loyalty to his unfortunate master probably explains the bad terms on which he stood with the Earl of Pembroke. In other words, there were the elements of a feud, and not simply rival parliamentary aspirations, behind this election story.

The poll appears to have been dispatched with expedition, the Sheriff sitting in one place to take the votes for Sir John Thynne, and his Deputy in another to take those for Penruddock. Agents of each side watched the proceedings and challenged any voters they wished sworn. In the result, Penruddock had a large majority. Thereupon Thynne's party not only proceeded to question the qualifications of Penruddock's voters – an objection that was utterly invalid in view of the right of challenge they had exercised during the poll; they also disputed the election on the grounds that Penruddock was

1. Glanville, *Reports*, pp. 3–6, 80 ff.; *Stiffkey Papers*, ed. Saunders (Camden Soc.), pp. 39–41.
2. C. G. Bayne, 'The First House of Commons of Queen Eliz.', *Eng. Hist. Rev.* xxiii, 470 ff.; Star Chamber 5, A 14/14, 14/15.

not resident in the county, and that his social status was not exalted enough to be a knight of the shire. Neither of these latter arguments was unique. In this election game it was a recognized gambit to maintain that the law demanded residence at the time of the *teste* of the writ.[1] As for the other contention, in the Somerset election of 1614, six lawyers, with more ingenuity than substance, were to argue that an untitled candidate was ineligible when opposed by a knight.[2] Both objections were in fact preposterous. Penruddock had been senior knight of the shire in the last parliament, and either at the time of this election, or certainly a few months later, was Provost Marshal and Justice of the Peace.[3]

To counter these quibbles, Penruddock undertook to enter into recognizances with the Sheriff to hold him harmless if the election should be questioned; whereupon, after a solemn *Oyez!*, the Sheriff declared him elected. Penruddock returned thanks to the voters, invited everyone to dinner at the Earl of Pembroke's house, and there made merry. The Sheriff promised to have the indenture ready next day for sealing.

Afterwards, Thynne's supporters once more tackled the Sheriff, whose sympathies, one imagines, were with their side. He decided to send up to London for legal advice, but then, without waiting, drew up an indenture and returned Sir John Thynne, incidentally making him the senior knight. One of Thynne's friends gave the Sheriff a bond for three hundred pounds to save him harmless from the consequences of his action. It is consoling to know that the Attorney General, probably at the instigation of the Earl of Pembroke, prosecuted the Sheriff in the Star Chamber, where he was fined two hundred pounds, with a year's imprisonment, while Penruddock was given sureties for the hundred pounds damages due to him.[4] The bond from Thynne's friend presumably covered the monetary loss, but not the imprisonment.

1. *Eng. Hist. Rev.* xlvi, 592 n. 4, to which add references to the Leicestershire election of 1621 in NOTESTEIN, *Commons Debates 1621.*
2. *Eng. Hist. Rev.* xlvi, 595.
3. *Cal. S.P. Dom., 1547–80*, p. 140 (September 1559).
4. DYER, *Reports* (1585), fol. 168b.

CHAPTER 4

County Elections:
The Montgomeryshire Election of 1588

THE Court of Star Chamber has already served us well. In a few instances the surviving documents come so near to recreating the whole scene of a contested election with its background of county society, that they must be treated as narratives in their own right. For three of them we go to Wales, a country where feuds were apt to be more exuberant than in the average English county, and where parliamentary elections more readily provoked a contest since Welsh counties each returned only one knight of the shire.

Our first story concerns the Montgomeryshire election of 1588, which led to a Star Chamber suit by the unsuccessful candidate, Arthur Price of Vaynor, against the Sheriff, Jenkin Lloyd of Berthlloid.[1] Hitherto, the electoral history of this county had been peaceful. It was dominated by one person, Edward Herbert, whose principal house was Blackhall, just outside the borough of Montgomery. He was High Steward and Constable of Montgomery Castle, Deputy-Lieutenant to his powerful relative, the Earl of Pembroke, Justice of the Peace, and *Custos Rotulorum*.[2] The famous Lord Herbert of Cherbury, his grandson, wrote of him in his *Autobiography*: 'My grandfather's power was so great in the country that divers ancestors of the better families now in Montgomeryshire were his servants, and raised by him. He delighted also much in hospitality; as having a very long table twice covered every meal with the best meats that could be gotten, and a very great family. It was an ordinary saying in the country at that time, when they saw any fowl rise, "Fly where thou wilt, thou wilt light at Blackhall"; which was a low

1. References will be found in my article, 'Three Elizabethan Elections', *Eng. Hist. Rev.* xlvi, 227 ff.

2. *Autobiography of Lord Herbert of Cherbury*, ed. Sidney Lee, pp. 4–5; LEWIS DWNN, *Heraldic Visitations*, i, 312.

building, but of great capacity, my grandfather erected in his age.'[1]
As our Star Chamber documents describe him in 1588, he was an
'ancient, grave gentleman' of seventy-five, 'a man of great wealth',
'reputed to be the best man of living and government in the shire'.

For forty years past, say these documents, he had at all times
carried the voices of the freeholders in the county for himself or for
such others as he thought convenient. No less complete was his control of the borough seat. He himself had sat for the county in every
parliament from March 1553 to 1571, while the members in 1572,
1584, and 1586, one of whom was his son, had been elected on his
nomination or at least with his approval. And so it continued with
the Herbert family. With the exception of 1593, the year in which
Edward Herbert died, a Herbert sat for the county until the Long
Parliament.

The other Deputy-Lieutenant was John Price of Newtown,[2] elder
brother of Arthur Price, one of the candidates in 1588, and his right-
hand man in that election. The family were second only to the Herberts, and in the important Hundred of Newtown were all-powerful.
They, if anyone, might have broken the electoral peace of the county.
But their sister, Elizabeth Price, was married to Edward Herbert,
and both John and Arthur Price took their turns in parliament with
the goodwill of their brother-in-law. The former represented the
borough of Montgomery in 1563 and the county in 1572, while the
latter sat for the borough in 1571.

So long as Elizabeth Price lived there was peace, but her death in
May 1588,[3] and Herbert's old age, seem to have allowed minor factions to effect a breach between the two great families of the county.
There is a degree of mystery about the initial events of the 1588
election. It looks as if at the outset Edward Herbert had no intention
of standing. Had John Price coveted the seat, he could have secured
it without opposition; for, if a Herbert was not available, who more
inevitable than the head of the Price family? But it was quite a
different matter for a younger brother to aim at representing the
county. Though Arthur Price's first wife was a Bourchier, daughter
of the second Earl of Bath, and though he had his elder brother's
backing, in the opinion of his opponents he was 'not so fit' to be

1. *Autobiography*, p. 7. 2. *Foljambe MSS.*, p. 26.
3. LORD HERBERT'S *Autobiography*, p. 9 n.

knight of the shire. It was this weakness in his candidature that gave the enemies of the Price family their chance.

When talk of an election first began, it seems that a certain Roland Pugh, who belonged to a hostile group of gentry, intended to stand in opposition. Certainly Price began his electoral campaign with this story, and appears to have had no inkling that Edward Herbert, who was an old man, a very old man by Elizabethan standards, might wish to stand. After all, he had not sat in parliament since 1571. Consequently, Price's friends and servants canvassed Herbert's kinsmen and followers, telling them that Price had secured the goodwill of the Herbert clan – of Sir Edward Herbert, lord of Powis, of Edward Herbert himself, and of his son, Richard; and many of these people promised him their voices. Indeed, when the day of election arrived, some felt so constrained by their promise, that they actually voted against their natural allegiance.

Then, suddenly, the prospect changed. Roland Pugh was obviously no match for the marshalled might of the Price family. Realizing this, their enemies, led by the Sheriff, Jenkin Lloyd, gathered to themselves all the Herbert forces by the simple and sure device of persuading the aged and perhaps senile Edward Herbert to stand himself. Jenkin Lloyd was Herbert's son-in-law, and, with Elizabeth Price dead, was probably able to make the old man his tool. The ineffective Pugh offered no difficulty. He was induced to efface himself by the gift of the borough seat, the nomination to which belonged to Herbert.

Once Edward Herbert entered the contest, its whole nature was transformed. Play fair, play foul, in Montgomeryshire a Herbert had to win. On the one side, Price was too far involved to withdraw with dignity, while on the other, the unchallenged primacy of the Herberts was at stake. This explains the tricks and ill humour of the election. It also explains – if the charge be true – Herbert's promise to save the Sheriff from all troubles and harms that might follow his behaviour.

The Sheriff made no pretence of neutrality, and took open part in the canvassing of the electorate. This was carried out in an elaborate and methodical manner. Both sides prepared careful lists, Hundred by Hundred, of the freeholders whose promises they secured. Morgan Glynn of Glynn, cousin-german to the Sheriff, a rather muddle-headed, garrulous, and therefore useful witness, told how he, together with Richard Herbert of Park and others, prepared such a list for the Hundred of Llanidlos. Sir Edward Herbert, lord of Powis, lent his support by ordering the bailiffs of his manors to canvass their freeholders. On Price's side, Oliver Lloyd of Leighton, through his servants, canvassed the most part of three hundred and eighty freeholders in three Hundreds, while a second supporter secured ninety freeholders in one of these Hundreds and one hundred and twenty in another.

They may have gone further, anticipating a notorious eighteenth-century practice by the creation of forty-shilling freeholders to swell their numbers. At any rate, one of the Sheriff's witnesses in our Star Chamber case named four voters living in his Hundred who, so far as he knew, did not possess forty-shilling freeholds, 'saving that he heard it reported that some of them had leases of John Vaughan esquire, for term of lives, colourably the day next before the election'. As we shall see, this was not the only election when such an allegation was made; but the practice was not general, nor ever on a large scale. It was a striking curiosity; little more.

The county court was to be held at Montgomery on 26 October; and as the day drew near, tension grew. Hearing of armed preparations by the other side, the Sheriff took the advice of two lawyers on the expediency of going armed to the election. He probably also consulted them about the devices open to him to secure a victory for his side. Certainly, he was prepared to resort to tricks. Several of Price's witnesses testified to hearing servants and followers of Herbert – one, for example, who wore a 'mandilion' or loose coat bestowed on him by his patron as livery – prophesy that their master would carry the election, whatever his votes and whatever it cost. If Price had a majority of a thousand, said a brother-in-law of Herbert's, still Herbert would be returned; and Herbert himself was overheard reassuring a servant who told him that his freeholders were outnumbered. Some of Price's followers, on their way to the election, were bade 'get them home like fools, seeing that they should not carry the knight-ship of the shire': a deposition which the witness or his examiner thought too homely and forthright, for in the manuscript 'fools' is crossed out and 'unwise men' inserted in its place!

Such reports put Price on his guard. Evidently he feared that the

Sheriff might try to overreach him by holding the county court at the Castle of Montgomery instead of the Shire Hall, or alternatively might seize the Shire Hall, exclude opponents, and carry the election by the acclamation of the voters within the Hall, ignoring those without. He took precautions against both possibilities. As the Sheriff and his party rode into Montgomery along the Newtown road on the eve of the election, they saw about a hundred 'light and desperate persons', armed with swords, bucklers, forest-bills, long staves, and glaives. They were under the leadership of a captain and other officers, and paid by Price, and were stationed between the road and the Castle. There they remained all night and part of the next day, and broke down the bridge leading to the Castle in order to prevent access to it. In the town itself another group, armed with 'divers kinds of monstrous weapons', guarded the Shire Hall all night, ready, so an opponent said, to quarrel with any of Herbert's followers who passed amongst them.

Morgan Glynn described how that night he and the Sheriff went to bed together. He rose before daylight, and, leaving the Sheriff in his lodging in company with Richard Herbert and other gentlemen, repaired to Edward Herbert's house, Blackhall. There he found Herbert and other friends, who, accompanied by the main body of their supporters, moved off towards the Booth or Shire Hall. As they were coming down from the churchyard, they met the Sheriff's party by the Market House and halted while he made a proclamation for keeping the peace. He had just made a similar proclamation by the Shire Hall where Price and his followers were. During the halt, Richard Herbert of Llyssen, one of Edward Herbert's supporters, took a 'view' of the rival companies and reported that, although there were some three to four hundred of their men among Price's supporters at the Shire Hall, yet the company gathered round Edward Herbert was greater than that at the Hall. It so happened that at this very time one of Price's men was also taking a preliminary 'view'. He arrived at the opposite conclusion; and we may let one optimist cancel out the other.

The Sheriff returned to a hasty breakfast, after which he came to the Shire Hall, and, finding some of Price's followers standing guard over the door, armed with weapons, bade them begone and allow free entrance. He then entered the Hall, went to the bench, and caused the county court to be set and proclaimed. There were about two thousand persons present, overflowing into the streets on all sides. After certain actions had been called, the Sheriff's clerk read the election writ, whereupon the Sheriff declared its effect in English and required the freeholders to nominate and choose a knight. Some shouted 'Herbert!' others 'Price!'; and the cries were taken up by those without. Men knocked and beat the Hall with their feet, and there was such confusion, contention, and hurly-burly that the people were in great uproar and tumult. Some light and unruly persons, says Glynn, imagining that the company within had fallen to violence, rushed upon the doors, while others began to quarrel and brawl, being desperately bent and more desirous of brabblement and contention than of any civil government.

Price's side claimed that in this 'general election' – their own phrase – they easily had a preponderance of voices. They 'did in a manner clean drown the voices that cried "Herbert! Herbert!"' Price himself put his majority at between five and six hundred. Nevertheless, the Sheriff, because, as he told the Star Chamber, the number of people was great, and being dispersedly placed, some above the Shire Hall, some below, and some on each side thereof, together with the sounding of their voices all at or about an instant, bred such confusion that he could not judge; for this reason, and because many were not forty-shilling freeholders and many were from foreign counties, he decided upon a poll. 'Gentlemen', he said, 'I do take these voices to be equal or indifferent, and therefore I will make trial by the polls, and the readiest way I think to be thus (and so I am advised by counsel); to call the Hundreds of the shire in order, and so to make trial of the greater number.'

He can scarcely be blamed. On each side there were many un-qualified persons, who for good will, as one witness put it, did cry or make voice with their friends. According to one of Price's fol-lowers, there were forty such men in Herbert's company from the parish of Montgomery alone, while a witness actually named fifty-four on Price's side from a single parish in the Hundred of Newtown, and it was implicitly admitted that there were sixty – though no more – from this Hundred. Richard Herbert of Park put the grand total of 'insufficient freeholders' and 'foreigners' present for Price at two to three hundred – an exaggeration, no doubt.

Price does not seem to have objected seriously, if at all, to a poll. For a time, owing to the disturbance outside the Hall, it was doubtful whether the election would proceed. From one of the windows the Sheriff made a proclamation for keeping the peace, and sent certain Justices out to quell the brawl. But it increased rather than diminished, and order was only restored when the most eminent men from each side went out.

Now came the arrangements for taking the poll. The Hall was cleared of all but twelve to sixteen chosen on each side to see fair play. Two gentlemen, John Price and Roland Pugh, the latter acting for Herbert, were assigned to keep the outer door of the Hall at the stair-foot, and two others, Lewis Blayney and Morgan Glynn, to keep the door at the top of the stair. Another four, chosen two from each side, with the Sheriff's clerks acting for Herbert, were appointed to register the names of the voters and compile duplicate lists. The freeholders themselves were called one at a time on the instruction of the Sheriff, their names being taken from lists prepared by each candidate and handed to the Sheriff. Each Hundred had its separate list, drawn up during the canvassing and checked on the election day; each also had its party manager or managers, and it was no doubt through them that the gentlemen at the door worked. They saw that the men were forthcoming when their names were called. The voters were merely 'perused' by the Sheriff and their names registered, unless the other side challenged their qualifications, when they were sworn on the Holy Evangelist touching the yearly value of their freehold in the county, and a note set against their names to show that they had been put to the oath.

The order of calling the freeholders was a crucial question. Several suggestions were made on Price's side. One old gentleman of seventy-six, Thomas Williams of Great Wollaston in Shropshire, who had been a Justice of the Peace and High Sheriff in the county of Montgomery and had stood for parliament there, urged the Sheriff to divide the voters into two companies and so peruse and examine them by the polls — presumably taking one from each alternately or, possibly, conducting a simultaneous, double scrutiny as was done in Wiltshire in 1559.[1] This course he had seen used at divisions in Shropshire. Price and his leading supporters, no doubt with the idea

1. See above, p. 91.

of saving the time and trouble of a poll, offered to deduct three hundred from their number, take their company aside, and if it were still not greater than Herbert's then to pay him one hundred pounds. On the other hand, if there was to be a poll, they suggested that the Sheriff should call the electors from the Hundreds of Machynlleth and Newtown, one from each Hundred alternately; and so on throughout the county, balancing a 'Price' Hundred against a 'Herbert' Hundred. The Sheriff rejected all their proposals. It was his court, he declared, and he would proceed as pleased himself, but would do justice or else the law was open to take remedy against him.

The Sheriff justified his refusal to divide the electors into two rival companies by asserting that it would have been dangerous. Whether he entertained any such fear, is in fact quite irrelevant. His intentions, or rather, his tactics, were already decided: he was determined to call the Hundred of Machynlleth first. For excuse, he maintained that, being the furthest Hundred from the town of Montgomery, it was customary when county courts were held at that town to call actions from there first. Maybe it was; though the custom was not such common knowledge that all his own witnesses could confirm it. But parliamentary elections were not the same as legal actions. His motive was only too manifest. Machynlleth was Herbert country, where Herbert himself dwelt, and where his greatest strength in voters lay. Price's strong suit was the Hundred of Newtown. The principle of selection adopted by the Sheriff enabled him to postpone calling the Newtown freeholders until, as we shall see, he gave up calling at all.

The Sheriff's intention was first to call all the freeholders on Herbert's side from Machynlleth, and then, for anything we know to the contrary, to call Price's supporters in the same Hundred. But Price by now was in a state of revolt. Naturally, he wanted to play his best card against his opponent's; and therefore, after the first of Herbert's voters had been perused and a second called, John Price at the outer door let in a man from Newtown, whose name the clerks for his party proceeded to record. This he continued to do, letting in one from Newtown for every one from Machynlleth, until, on complaint being made, the Sheriff demanded to know what warrant Price's clerks had to keep a court there while he kept another where he sat. He ordered them to cease. For a time they persisted, but after arguments and cross-speeches the Sheriff promised to peruse Price's supporters in Machynlleth immediately after Herbert's, before going on to another Hundred; and to this Price at last yielded.

After all the names had been registered for Machynlleth, another attempt was made to have the Hundred of Newtown called; but the Sheriff insisted on calling the two adjoing Hundreds of Mathravall and Llanvilling. In one of these, Mathravall, Edward Herbert's son, Richard, lived. In the other, says Price, the number voting for him exceeded the number for Herbert by sixty. The tide was turning.

But it was now four or five o'clock on the Sunday morning, and the Sheriff had continued in the Hall, without meat, sleep, or rest, since before nine o'clock the previous morning. He had already decided to finish after the third Hundred. Seeing the day approached, he says, and being wearied by his long toil and disappointed in what he had believed to be the best course, he thought out another way of deciding the election. His 'other way' was a purely arbitrary verdict. John Price tried to dissuade him. If there were not a majority of three hundred sufficient freeholders on their side, he and all his friends, he said, would give their voices with Herbert. And when the Sheriff finished, he made a last offer, suggesting that he choose any one from five of the six remaining Hundreds, and this Hundred should end the election. The Sheriff would not yield.

A great demonstration followed. The men of Newtown, waiting with many others in the lower part of the Hall, shouted the name of their candidate, and others in the town, hearing the cry, assembled round the Hall and called out for Price. The voices for Herbert, said old Thomas Williams, were scarcely heard at all; and Price, his mortification playing havoc with his numbers, declared that there were at least fourteen hundred of his supporters there from the uncalled Hundreds, among them the greatest number of gentlemen and people of substance and valour. To these, it was a bitter humiliation that the mountain people of Machynlleth and the other two Hundreds should have such privilege and they be utterly rejected. Asked to make an indenture for Price's election, the Sheriff refused. In the Hall – 'in court and at the bar' – were a group of gentlemen and others belonging to both parties, with divers weapons, such as swords, bucklers, halberts, etc., ready, as it seemed, 'to fall by the ears and do mischief'. There were cross-speeches and provocations. Making proclamation that every man should put away his weapons and depart, the Sheriff adjourned the court. Later he returned Herbert as knight of the shire. Price, perhaps, would have been prepared to swallow his pride and forgo his remedy at law, but the best gentlemen among his followers told him that if he took this wrong quietly at the Sheriff's hands, they, the freeholders, would never again vote for him.

One of the reasons afterwards given for discontinuing the poll was the scarcity of food. The argument was in the nature of a boomerang, for in a town controlled by Herbert it was 'the common sort of electors' on the other side who 'felt the smart'. Victuallers were ordered only to lodge men brought by certain followers of Herbert's, and Price's voters had access to only four houses. One of Price's witnesses told how he and a friend offered to pay sixpence apiece to have a stable for their geldings and pay for their meat besides, but were informed that on Herbert's command only his supporters could be accommodated. As a matter of fact, there is no proof that many freeholders were driven home by want of food.

The Sheriff justified his return of Herbert by transparent sophistry. According to his story, he estimated the total number of freeholders who had given their voices at the acclamation as about sixteen or seventeen hundred. In the three Hundreds polled, there were, he said, four hundred and twenty allowable votes for Herbert. In addition, at the end of the poll Herbert had handed in a list of about six hundred names of supporters in the uncalled Hundreds. From these figures he drew the inference that Herbert had a majority.

What he so conveniently forgot was to control his arithmetic by making the calculations for Price's side. If we do this for him, we have three hundred and forty registered voters in the polled Hundreds, plus – according to Price's witnesses – two hundred and sixty in the Hundred of Newtown and three hundred and eighty in three of the uncalled Hundreds. There are no corresponding figures for the Hundreds of Montgomery and Llanidlos; but a conservative allowance will bring Price's total to a minimum of eleven hundred, against – to make Herbert's figure precise – ten hundred and sixteen.

Both calculations are of course partisan and unreliable. But from them emerges a very interesting point. A weight of official experience – of past and present Sheriffs, of a Sheriff's clerk, and of Bailiffs of

Hundreds – put the grand total of forty-shilling freeholders in the county at sixteen or seventeen hundred. One Bailiff, giving his figures, declared that he never could find above that number to serve the Queen on juries in the Great Sessions, Quarter Sessions, and other courts. Assuming that this evidence, though all from Herbert's side, is substantially correct, it will obviously not square with the figures of voters given by the rival candidates, which indicate an electorate of over two thousand; and if any appreciable number of freeholders stayed away from the election through illness, intimidation, or other cause, as some almost certainly did, then the disparity would be greater. The dilemma disappears if we assume that in Montgomeryshire as in other counties there was a fair number of marginal forty-shilling freeholders, who regarded themselves as 'insufficient freeholders' when it was a question of serving on juries or paying subsidies, and 'sufficient' when it came to parliamentary elections.

We are ignorant of the Star Chamber's judgement in this election dispute. The decree books of the court have been missing since the seventeenth century. If we ourselves pass judgement, the number of voters claimed by each side cannot decide the issue, if only because we have no coefficient for exaggeration or downright lies. A surer guide is the Sheriff's behaviour. It is difficult to believe that he ever intended to complete the poll. True, he was not entirely responsible for the waste of time. In the early stages, Price's door-keepers were obstructive, and there was rough play due to the intrusion of their supporters into the Hall. A witness declared that he and another of Herbert's voters were not allowed to pass until they had been called three or four times, while his companion was violently rushed and cast to the ground. Price's men lingered in the Hall, crowding and hindering their opponents, though when their own voters were called they stood back to the walls to allow free access. But such incidents must have happened when the Newtown voters were being irregularly registered. Once agreement had been reached on this point, Price's side, apart from an altercation or two, had every reason to expedite the poll. And yet, throughout a day and a night, only seven hundred and sixty votes were registered. Surely, as Price alleged – though in different language – there was ca' canny.

The plain facts are that the Sheriff canvassed for Herbert, that his clerks acted for him in the election, that he perused Herbert's voters before those of Price, that he called the Hundred where Herbert's greatest strength lay, and that he abandoned the poll before reaching Price's principal Hundred. It was the behaviour neither of an impartial official nor of a partisan confident of victory.

CHAPTER 5

County Elections:
The Denbighshire Elections of 1588 and 1601

IN Elizabethan Denbighshire there was no pre-eminent person or family to dwarf and control faction, as in Montgomeryshire.[1] The county was split into two halves: east was east, and west was west. Each had a different historical pedigree, and administrative convenience confirmed the division by grouping the three eastern Hundreds together and the three western ones. The county had two Deputy-Lieutenants. One was selected from the eastern gentry, one from the western; and it was the same with the two Coroners.[2] Finally, the county court was held alternately at Denbigh and Wrexham, the capital towns of each area.

This dualism had to adapt itself to the Welsh system of a single county seat in parliament, thus, one might have thought, creating the conditions for factional contests. Before our story is ended we shall see east and west at feud; but prior to 1588 there is no evidence of any contested election, and even in that year the county did not split along its natural line of fission. Whether we should infer from this that the county elections were quiet before the latter part of Elizabeth's reign, it is impossible in the present state of our knowledge to say, and it would be rash to guess. Perhaps peace was preserved by some vague understanding to share the representation between east and west; but if so, the understanding was elastic enough to permit the great man of the west, Sir John Salusbury of Llewenny, to occupy the seat in three consecutive parliaments of Mary's reign, and three easterners to follow one another in Elizabeth's reign.[3]

1. Most of the references for this chapter will be found in my article, *Eng. Hist. Rev.* xlvi, 212 ff. Also see A. H. DODD, 'North Wales in the Essex Revolt of 1601', ibid. lix, 348 ff.
2. *Register of Council in Marches of Wales*, ed. R. FLENLEY, pp. 132–3.
3. *Return of M.P.s*, i, 384, 388, 392, 412, 416; BROWNE WILLIS, op. cit.,

In 1588, the year of our first story, east was not ranged against west. The west had enjoyed the representation in the previous parliament, and was clearly content to leave the seat to an easterner. The east's own feuds caused the trouble. Officially, the most important gentleman in this half of Denbighshire was William Almer of Pantyokyn. He was the Deputy-Lieutenant in that area,[1] and had represented the county in 1572. He was again seeking election in 1588, and seems to have been first in the field. Later, in the Star Chamber, he employed the conventional way of explaining how he came to stand. The commonalty of the shire, he declared, had discussed among themselves whom they thought most meet to be elected, whereupon it was generally bruited throughout the county that the greatest number of gentlemen and freeholders of the best understanding, power, and sufficiency were disposed to elect him. It was a naïve statement. In fact, he wrote round to his friends and prominent gentlemen about a fortnight before the election, and scored what ought to have been a decisive success when he secured promise of support from the young owner of Llewenny, John Salusbury.

The house of Llewenny was *primus inter pares* among the gentry of Denbighshire, and more or less carried with it the hosts of the three western Hundreds, where a majority of the freeholders lived. But in 1588 it was under a cloud. The grandson of the great Sir John Salusbury, after succeeding his grandfather as head of the family in 1578, had become involved in Babington's Plot and had been executed in 1586 as one of those famous, execrated traitors. His younger brother, John, succeeded him. But it is indicative of the gloom cast on Llewenny by this catastrophe that when a new Deputy-Lieutenant was appointed from western Denbighshire, the office went to a kinsman, Robert Salusbury, two years younger than John and head of a cadet branch of the family, whose principal residence was at Rûg, over the Merioneth border.[2] Moreover, it was this same Robert Salusbury, then aged twenty, who had represented Denbighshire in the 1586 parliament. Incidentally, in 1588 he sat for Merioneth.

---

iii, 86. W. R. WILLIAMS, *Parliamentary History of Wales*, omits some of Mary's parliaments, and is an unsafe guide.

1. *Foljambe MSS.*, p. 26; Star Chamber 5, A 31/30, Owen Brereton's examination.

2. *Foljambe MSS.*, p. 26; *A.P.C.* xxv, 17.

John Salusbury might be under an official cloud, but he could still muster his freeholders for an election; and since his kinsman of Rûg, who held lands in Denbighshire as well as Merionethshire, was also on Almer's side, as was Edward Thelwall of Plas-y-ward – head of a western family second only to the Salusburys – the west was marshalled in almost solid array.

With this backing and his own friends and dependants, William Almer was by arithmetical calculation irresistible. The election ought to have been peaceful. But there was a strong party in his own half of the county opposed to him. Perhaps they were jealous of the seniority conferred by his deputy-lieutenancy. Perhaps the office created friction. Certainly there were personal feuds. About two years earlier, Almer's servants had fallen foul of the servants of a member of the Edwards family, the chief family in Chirkland, who held the office of Constable of Chirk Castle. The feud had raged ever since: 'they and their followers had often fought', and 'sundry hurts and wounds' had been inflicted. Probably it was this feud that brought the Pulestons into the quarrel, a family whose chief seat was at Emral in Flintshire, though they were also established in Denbighshire and bore comparison for wealth and standing with the Salusburys. Roger Puleston, the head of the family, was father-in-law of John Edwards, a young man of twenty-five or -six, the head of the Chirkland family. Almer was also at feud with the Breretons of Borras, with whose servants he and his men had an affray in Wrexham in the May preceding the election. Edwards, Puleston, Brereton constituted an anti-Almer faction, and with them was another of Roger Puleston's sons-in-law, Richard Trevor of Trevalyn, whose name will be prominent in our later election story. These gentlemen, complained Almer, had long envied him and sought his and his friends' blood. Witness their boast: 'There will be a Puleston in Emral, a Brereton in Borras, and a Trevor in Trevalyn, when there will be no Almer in Pantyokyn.'

Feeling as they did, this group of gentlemen could not stomach the idea of Almer as their knight of the shire. 'His conditions and behaviour were so lewd and unseemly for his calling, being a Justice of the Peace, and he himself [so] given to quarrels and contentions, . . . that he was like to set all the gentlemen in the shire together by the ears.' He was reported to be involved, as plaintiff or defendant, in seven suits in the Court of Star Chamber at the one time, and was thought to desire election merely 'to have the country's money to maintain his brabbling causes in London'.

At the outset, two of the anti-Almer group, John Edwards and Richard Trevor, thought of becoming candidates and embarked on independent election campaigns. On his own initiative Edwards wrote to Salusbury — as to others — asking for support, only to be told that his promise was already given to Almer. At the same time, Richard Trevor, with the backing of Roger Puleston, Owen Brereton, and others, made his preliminary approaches. It was quickly realized that they must all combine to resist Almer, and accordingly some half-dozen constituted themselves a committee of management, meeting at the house of John Owen, a confederate, in Wrexham.

Their tactics were dictated by the fact that John Salusbury held the balance of power. If possible, he and his westerners had to be detached from Almer. Roger Puleston, John Edwards, and Trevor accordingly visited him, tried first to persuade him to transfer his support to Edwards, and failing in this, urged him to choose any candidate other than Almer — or, as Puleston said, choose someone 'not misliked by either party', east or west. It was tantamount to a confession that hostility to Almer was their governing impulse, and that Salusbury held the whip hand. Their mission failed. As a last resort, they decided to approach Salusbury's father-in-law, the Earl of Derby, in the hope that he might intervene and secure support for Trevor, in which event Edwards was to stand down. Otherwise, all were to back Edwards; which, ultimately, they did.

Canvassing went ahead. In at least one section of the county, and probably in others, it was systematic. John Wynn Edwards of Chirk, so it was said, threatened to turn out of their lands any of his freeholders who would not vote his way. Nor were freeholders alone pressed. Owen Banbury, a yeoman of Chirkland, aged thirty-two, told how his father called him from his bed on the morning of the election and bade him come with him to Wrexham and give their elections with Mr John Edwards. When he objected that neither of them possessed any freehold, his father replied that they were desired by Mr Edwards to go with him and do as occasion should serve. Both went, and both cried 'Edwards! Edwards!' A great number, similarly situated, did the same: one Lawrence a tailor, and his brother Edward Goghe a fuller, and some thirty of Mr Edwards's tenants.

Men were procured from adjoining counties to pose as Denbigh free-holders: Roger Puleston, for example, brought several from Flintshire. It was further alleged that they created forty-shilling freeholders for the occasion – a stratagem we have already met in Montgomeryshire; and this time we know that there was substance behind the charge.

On the mere counting of heads, their position was hopeless. Almer put his voters at sixteen hundred, and the long tale of one hundred and twenty-eight witnesses whom he summoned in his Star Chamber case virtually recreated his following, for most told how many supporters came from their parish. We can safely accept the figure as something over the thousand. Men of long experience in the shire observed that they had never seen so great a number of freeholders joining in election one way; and making every allowance for what his opponents said – namely, that Almer's friends 'had scant left a boy at home to drive the plough' but had brought them all to Wrexham 'to make a show and also to give their voices . . . if they might be suffered and go unsworn' – still, Almer is left a liberal majority over the six or seven hundred which was John Edwards's own, rather dubious, estimate of his following.

But the opposition were not disheartened. They were holding the trump card, for the Sheriff was Owen Brereton, one of themselves. Three days before the election, Roger Puleston was prepared to lay five hundred pounds that his side would carry the day, and a young gentleman of Wrexham, infected by his confidence, took on two bets at four to one against Almer.

The election day was 8 October 1588, and on this occasion it was the turn of Wrexham, where, as one old gentleman of eighty-six testified, who had known all the county courts held at the town since the division of Wales into shires, it had been the invariable rule to hold the court in the Shire Hall. Knowing that they could not be beaten by fair means, Almer's side was on the alert for trickery. They anticipated that their opponents might put all their men beforehand into the Shire Hall, which was not large, and then return Edwards as elected by the majority of voters in sight. Accordingly, they placed a number of their own men in the Hall before daybreak and filled it before 8 a.m., maintaining an entrance and space clear for the Sheriff and his officers.

Their next precaution was to keep the Sheriff in sight during the crucial hour of eight to nine o'clock, when the election had to be held. While Edward Thelwall remained in command at the Shire Hall, from which, as time passed and the Sheriff did not appear, he sent messenger after messenger, the Salusburys and others met the Sheriff at the town's end, intending to bring him to the Hall. He seemed willing enough to accompany them, but on the plea of having some business to transact first, entered his lodging at John Owen's house, along with Roger Puleston. John Salusbury noticed the two in conference, and then saw Puleston go into the Under-Sheriff's room and presently leave the house, followed by this official. Salusbury himself stayed with the Sheriff, waiting for him to set out for the Shire Hall; waiting, until news arrived of the trick that had been played on them.

Early that morning men had been going about, telling opposition supporters to repair to the house of William Edwards, uncle to the candidate and an especial enemy to Almer, whose blood he had threatened to have. His house was on the outskirts of Wrexham: indeed, according to the best testimony it was technically not within the town. A Chirkland man stopped a gentleman of Almer's side on his way past the house and asked if he were a friend of John Edwards. He had the wit to say yes, and was told that the election was to be there. Similar resource was shown by a group of Almer's supporters who, noticing a troop of their opponents making for this place, and suspecting some guile, followed and managed to press into the courtyard. Another group, detailed to follow Puleston and the Under-Sheriff when they went off mysteriously from the Sheriff's lodging, also arrived at the house. In fact, if, as seems likely, only eighty to one hundred of Edwards's men managed to get there in time, it is probable that they were outnumbered by their opponents. But most of the latter were outside the house, the gates of which had been closed on them; and perhaps more than one who had got into the courtyard thought it too dangerous to remain within, and, by leaping on a brick wall, joined their friends on an adjoining green. One of William Edwards's servants confessed that he was set to guard the doors and walls of the house, armed with a double musket ready charged with powder and one round bullet, which he was told to discharge upon any of Almer's party trying to break in. There were probably other armed guards.

Roger Puleston and the Under-Sheriff brought the election writ to this house. There, after a warning had been shouted from a window, 'Chirkland men, draw near!' they prepared to hold the election in the hall of the house, with door and windows to the courtyard open. A crier proclaimed the keeping of the county court, a few cases were called, and then the Under-Sheriff read the election writ. Thereupon, those present cried 'Edwards! Edwards!' and outside, Almer's company shouted 'Almer! Almer!' The cry was taken up by many running down from the Shire Hall, and echoed again by those remaining at the Hall. Almer's supporters called for trial by the poll; but shouts and protestations had no effect.

As we know, the leaders of Edwards's party had discussed this and other possible manoeuvres at their meetings before the election. Some believed that the Sheriff might keep his court in William Edwards's house or in any other, provided it were in Wrexham. Puleston had no such illusion. He had taken legal advice, and was told that it would be against law and orderly proceeding to hold the county court elsewhere than in the common and usual hall.

When news reached the Sheriff that the election was accomplished, he left his lodging and proceeded to the Shire Hall. It was still before nine o'clock, and both on the way and formally at the Hall he was urged to hold a valid court and election, Almer's supporters crying 'Almer! Almer!' to declare their nomination. Edwards's leaders, on the other hand, asked him to proceed with the Quarter Sessions which they had arranged for that day at Wrexham, and which, if not summoned for the purpose, certainly served as colour for their action in holding the county court elsewhere. The time passed in discussion until, it being nine o'clock, further persuasion was useless. As a final gesture, John Salusbury tendered the Sheriff an indenture for the election of Almer, with the names and seals of the gentlemen who chose him. It was rejected. Nothing remained but for Almer's host to withdraw to a field adjoining the churchyard, where they were numbered and thanks offered them for their pains and goodwill.

Sure of financial backing from his fellow-conspirators, who agreed to save him harmless from the legal consequences of his act – entering, it was said, into a bond for three hundred pounds – the Sheriff nonchalantly declared that he would 'stand to' the election and answer in law to it; which in due course he and nine of his companions were compelled to do. But the Under-Sheriff was less easy in mind. In the Star Chamber he confessed that in his conscience he thought the county court was held in William Edwards's house in order that John Edwards might be chosen knight. He confessed the obvious.

For all we know to the contrary, after this scandalous episode Denbigh elections settled down to quiet methods for a time. In 1593 Roger Puleston, one of the leaders against Almer, was elected. He was an easterner succeeding an easterner. As the Sheriff at the time [1] was friendly to John Salusbury, it seems that the disgrace brought on Llewenny by the traitor-brother may still have prevented the leader of western Denbighshire from aspiring to public honours. Who represented the Shire in 1597 we do not know; but by then the eastern faction was linked to the Earl of Essex, who was at the height of his fame and power, and in these circumstances it may be doubted whether the west could have reasserted itself.

Faction was conjured back into this Welsh county by the magnetic name and career of Robert Devereux, Earl of Essex. The Devereux were a border family, possessing estates and a great house in Pembrokeshire, where the young Earl spent much of his boyhood.[2] A turbulent land, rich in impecunious gentry, Wales was renowned for its breed of soldiers; and with England at war and the siren of military greatness enticing this restless nobleman on to fortune and to fame, there was every inducement, territorial, sentimental, and material, for him to maintain and develop his Welsh connexions. Through his Welsh steward, Sir Gelly Meyrick, a malign influence in his career, he exercised irresistible power in Pembrokeshire and the neighbouring counties. In the north he may have established ties as the spiritual heir of his step-father, the Earl of Leicester, who had been Baron of Denbigh and Ranger of Snowdon Forest; also, Gelly Meyrick, organizer of his Welsh clientele, came of Anglesey stock. 'Men of action' gravitated naturally to the matchless leader of their

1. Henry ap Evan Lloyd. He was one of Almer's commissioners for witnesses' evidence in his Star Chamber suit. After the 1601 election, he was a fellow-defendant with Salusbury in Trevor's suit.

2. Cf. DAVID MATHEW, *The Celtic People and Renaissance Europe*, pp. 336 ff.

fraternity; and Denbighshire, close to Ireland and on the route to that land of incessant warfare, was inevitably infected with the military spirit of the time. In the years 1594–7 Robert Salusbury of Rûg and Richard Trevor of Trevalyn were both serving in Ireland. Both returned with a knighthood; doubtless also with the profits that captains made out of their companies.[1] Two scions of the house of Rûg, Captains John and Owen Salusbury, were with Essex on the Cadiz expedition of 1596; and when, as 'Great England's Glory', he went to Ireland in 1599 on his last, ill-fated adventure, he took with him these two Welsh captains, their brother-in-law, John Lloyd of Bodidris in east Denbighshire, and one of Sir Richard Trevor's brothers.[2]

John Salusbury held aloof from this investment of spirit and fortune in Essex's career. Perhaps already he was attached to the rival party of the Cecils. Apparently he had been an Esquire of the Body to the Queen since 1595, a service involving attendance at Court.[3] True it is, the Earl of Essex never mended faction, he created it; and the mere fact that the gentry of eastern Denbighshire joined his military following was calculated to open the fissures between east and west. It was not simply an army but a band of brothers that the Earl was fashioning. 'I love them for my own sake', he wrote of his 'men of action'; 'for I find sweetness in their conversation, strong assistance in their employments with me, and happiness in their friendship.'[4] In the late nineties, with the glory of Cadiz about their leader and the adoration of the people, his followers were on top of the world.

By contrast, how ill had fortune treated John Salusbury! At the time of the Irish campaign he was thirty-four, and though head of the premier Denbigh family was neither knighted nor a Deputy-Lieutenant, but a mere Justice of the Peace. His rival, Sir Richard Trevor, was a knight, a Deputy-Lieutenant, a commissioner of Oyer and Terminer and a member of the Council in the Marches of Wales. What is more, John Lloyd of Bodidris, who was already, or soon was to be allied by marriage to Trevor, brought back an Essex knighthood from Ireland. There were thus two knights in the east of the county, none in the west.

1. *Cal. S.P. Ireland, 1592–6*, passim; *Cal. Carew MSS. 1589–1600*, passim.
2. *Eng. Hist. Rev.* lix, 359, 361.   3. ibid., p. 366.
4. DEVEREUX, *Earls of Essex*, i, 487.

Friction was inevitable. It rose in crescendo until it reached its climax in the election of 1601. In 1593 Owen Salusbury fought a duel with John Salusbury. It was an early omen of the breach between the younger members of the Rûg family, followers of the Earl of Essex, and the senior branch of the Salusburys at Llewenny.[1] Then came the repeated pressing of men for Essex's expeditions and the Irish wars, offering opportunities to those in the ascendant to line their pockets and vent their spite on dependants of their enemies. As Deputy-Lieutenant Trevor had prime responsibility for these levies, and when at last the downfall of his patron, the Earl of Essex, exposed him to retribution, he was prosecuted in the Star Chamber for various offences – extorting coat and conduct money from the county and diverting it to his and his friends' use, and levying men either through malice or to extract the price of their release. The occasions ranged from the Cadiz expedition of 1596 to reinforcements for Ireland in August 1600; and the documents in the case would serve as admirable illustrative pieces for the muster scene in Shakespeare's *Henry IV*.

That adherents of the house of Llewenny were victims of this petty tyranny, there can be little doubt. When Sir John Lloyd lodged a bill against John Salusbury in the Star Chamber for truculently discharging a number of pressed men, Salusbury answered that he and Edward Thelwall, his fellow-westerner in the commission, had simply taken the law into their own hands to rescue a number of men – in all likelihood their own followers – chosen for the Irish wars through the malice of Captain John Salusbury and other members of the Trevor-Lloyd faction.

But the ascendancy of the east did not endure. They had hitched their fortunes to the Earl of Essex, and fell with him. Captains John and Owen Salusbury and Captain Peter Wynn, all of this faction, were directly involved in the Essex Rising in February 1601; and Sir John Lloyd, to whom these three were said to be 'the greatest friends and the inwardest that the said knight had', came under suspicion of being privy to the conspiracy.[2] Owen Salusbury was slain in defence of Essex House; Captain John Salusbury got off with a moderate fine and brief imprisonment. The government, in its policy of mercy and calculated blindness, might not desire to pry too deeply

1. *Eng. Hist. Rev.* lix, 357–8; *H.M.C. Rep.* VIII, i, 375–6.
2. *Hatfield MSS.* xi, 96.

into the plot; nevertheless, the Trevor-Lloyd faction was besmirched by its association with traitors.

Here at last was Llewenny's opportunity. John Salusbury had, it seems, been in London at the time of the Rising and had taken part in its suppression. He returned to his county with a knighthood conferred by the Queen herself for this service, determined to restore the primacy of his house in Denbighshire, and ready, as he showed, to use aggressive tactics. He was soon at loggerheads with Sir Richard Trevor and Sir John Lloyd. The question of precedence, so intimate a point of honour with Elizabethans, seems to have been the ostensible cause of the quarrel. Since the recent death of their Lord Lieutenant, the Earl of Pembroke, in January 1601, there had been no Deputy-Lieutenants in the county. Consequently, priority on the local bench depended on the title of knight. Both Trevor and Lloyd were knights of longer standing than Salusbury, but the latter claimed that the royal creation gave him precedence. Lloyd, he scornfully declared, had been knighted by a traitor – Essex; Trevor by a subject, no better than Salusbury himself.

In the autumn, while this quarrel raged, came the parliamentary election. Nothing could have suited Salusbury better. By standing for election he could demonstrate beyond a shadow of doubt his supremacy in the county. Not only that. Here was the occasion, the unique occasion, for forcing Trevor and Lloyd, in the face of the whole county, to yield him the higher place on the bench of Justices. He possessed the bigger battalions, and after long and humiliating years of subordination was not disposed to compromise. Twice in the campaign, it seems that he might have secured an unopposed return, had he been willing to ask courteously for the other side's support and give way to his two rivals on the question of precedence. He would make no terms. Why should he? Though the Sheriff, Owen Vaughan, was on his opponents' side, and Owen Brereton, the Pulestons, and the rest of the eastern faction were ready to back them, their electoral outlook was desperate.

Tricks might be tried, but in such a situation they were likely to avail little. According to Salusbury, the election writ reached the Sheriff in time for the county court held on 23 September 1601, but because the meeting was then at Denbigh, which was in the Salusbury sphere of influence, and because the Trevor-Lloyd party needed time for their preparations, the Sheriff illegally concealed its receipt, thus postponing the election to 21 October at Wrexham. The allegation may or may not be true. Certainly the opposition needed time. They had to find a candidate.

Their initial move was clever. They chose William Middleton, a near kinsman of the Sheriff and a gentleman of great kindred and alliance in the county, one who stood aloof from the factions. It was said that they promised him fifty pounds towards his expenses as member, over and above his parliamentary wages. Middleton agreed to stand; but about four days before the election, doubtless realizing that he had become the instrument of faction, he withdrew and advised his friends to vote for Salusbury. In desperation the party turned to Sir Richard Trevor. Not that he wished to stand; but Salusbury's contemptuous refusal to make any overtures left no alternative.

Much canvassing had been going on, though little was said about it subsequently in the Star Chamber. A novel factor was the providential arrival of Council orders to levy sixty men for the Irish wars. According to Salusbury, Trevor saw the letters immediately on their arrival, and, perceiving their electioneering value, kept them secret from his fellow-commissioners in Salusbury's ranks, some of whom ought to have been associated with him in pressing men from his section of the shire. Moreover, by keeping the letters secret he delayed others in making the levies elsewhere in the county, thus preventing them from playing his own game. Presuming on his authority, he proclaimed a general muster of all the inhabitants in his area, which was the Hundred of Bromfield, and, between the proclamation and muster, sent round to canvass the freeholders there. In two parishes, Gresford and Holt, close to his estate, most of the voters, through fear of his displeasure, were ready to yield their voices as he directed. He therefore dispensed with their appearance at the muster, though when they asked for whom they were to vote, he brusquely answered that he scorned to tell them. 'Ere long', said he, 'they should know and feel his authority, and such as refused to yield their voices ... should suffer his indignation and be compelled to serve in the wars in Ireland, whosoever should be against it.'

Trevor held his muster at Wrexham two days before the election, accompanied by only one other Justice, a member of his faction. He had with him a list of names compiled by his canvassers. Consulting this, and finding out from his servants any who were friends either of Salusbury himself or of his prominent supporter in those parts, David Lloyd of Ruabon, he pressed for the Irish service only those who had refused him their voices, or whose masters had declined to support him. Twelve men and no more were to be taken out of of the whole Hundred; but he gave press money to fourteen from David Lloyd's parish of Ruabon alone, one of the least of six parishes in that area. Most of the men he pressed were freeholders worth thirty pounds per annum, and therefore immune from compulsory service; some were aged, impotent, and unfit for the wars; the rest were household servants or tenants of gentlemen pledged to Salusbury. In all, he pressed forty, and kept them from the election by a command to be at a distant place that day, on pain of death. The forty, however, did not all go to Ireland. Bribery or a pledge of service bought release. Of the fourteen from Ruabon only six went to the port of embarkation, Chester. One man paid twenty shillings for his discharge. He was able-bodied. Poor John ap John, lame, impotent, and maimed, had no money. With a truly Shakespearian touch, he was sent to the wars. Of course it would be foolish to believe every detail of this partisan story, but there is good reason to regard much of it as substantially true.

Salusbury, too, was in the commission, with an area in which to levy men. Thanks to Trevor, his orders probably reached him late; but, if Trevor told the truth – which is doubtful – he was not without resource. Contrary to instructions – so this story goes – he delayed his levy until the day after the election, meanwhile letting it be known that he would send to Ireland any freeholders who refused him their voices or any who were servants, kinsmen, or friends of his opponents.

The preparations made for the election were more befitting a civil war. Salusbury gave his description of events. Trevor and his friends – he said – seeing that they could not carry the election by voices, vowed that they would win it with blades, terrifying and daunting any that dared stand in opposition. As a commissioner of Oyer and Terminer, Trevor argued that he might require his followers to assemble with arms. He therefore had two wagon-loads of pikes and other weapons brought from Chester, and at his muster ordered the trained soldiers to leave their armour and weapons behind in certain friends' houses in Wrexham.

Thus prepared – the story continues – they gathered together from Denbighshire and adjoining counties several troops of wilful and disorderly persons, most of them no freeholders either in Denbighshire or elsewhere, but vagrant and idle men, meet to commit any villainy. Who or what they were, their leaders cared not, so long as they had weapons and were resolute fellows. Trevor himself assembled some two hundred from the counties of Denbigh, Flint, Shropshire and Cheshire; Sir John Lloyd one hundred from Denbigh and Flint; Thomas Price forty. They marched in troops twenty miles through the county, armed with pikes, forest-bills, and other unlawful weapons, to the great terror of the inhabitants. A Justice named Trafford brought eighty persons from his coal-pits and other places; the notorious Captain John Salusbury of Rûg, released from prison and ebullient once more, brought another fifty from Carnarvon, Merioneth, and Denbigh; the Sheriff contributed some hundred from Montgomery and elsewhere; John Eaton and Piers Wynn, gentlemen of Flint, came with about forty. What element of romance is concealed in all this, who can say?

In reverse, Trevor's side accused Salusbury of openly boasting that he would be chosen knight of the parliament, or it would cost five hundred lives. He and his, they declared, used many threatening speeches to terrify voters; and in vaunting manner he declared that he would take precedence of Trevor and Lloyd at the county court or die for it.

Salusbury's way to Wrexham, as he rode there on the day before the election, lay through Ruthin, where he was joined by friends and their followers from the surrounding country. As Trevor describes them, they were a warlike company, armed with swords and daggers, bucklers, targets, pistols, two-handed swords, horsemen's pieces, gauntlets, long piked staves, long Welsh hooks, privy coats, petronels, and quilted caps. Drawing near to Wrexham, Salusbury sent one of his company in advance to get the key of the church, perhaps, as Trevor thought, to hide a posse of men there; more probably, as he himself explained, to provide his rank and file with shelter, since Trevor, who dwelt nearby, had taken up most of the lodgings in the town. Whatever the purpose, Trevor's precautions thwarted it. The company entered Wrexham with trumpets sounding, Salusbury riding, truncheon in hand, wearing sword and dagger, his boy by his side carrying a sword and target. They rode through the town to the house of one David Jones, where they alighted, giving out that there were thousands behind who would come to Wrexham that night.

In the evening, the Sheriff and two Justices went to Salusbury's lodging to demand an explanation of his conduct and take order for avoiding a conflict the next day. They seem to have suggested a compromise by which Trevor and Lloyd would not oppose his election if he, in turn, would not dispute their right to precedence in the county court. Nothing came of it. Salusbury was set on gaining all. In any case, these mediators were partisans and untrustworthy. The next morning – 21 October – the Sheriff led another deputation. Salusbury now promised to stay away from the election, on condition, it seems, that Trevor and Lloyd also stayed away. Two persons from each side were chosen to see fair play at the proceedings.

Wrexham that morning was a strange sight. William Lloyd of Ruthin, a kinsman of Salusbury's, tells how he went to the Shire Hall, where the county court was usually held, but finding it shut, walked towards the churchyard. There he saw a great company of pikemen and other armed forces standing before Trevor's lodging. Presently, they came marching along the street, Trevor at their head with a coloured scarf about his neck. They stopped in the High Street, by John Owen's house, making a show as though they would quarrel with somebody, and then returned to the churchyard. Another armed company was standing in the open street near a house where Sir John Lloyd and other leaders were said to be lodged. Salusbury's troops were gathered outside his lodging, and here he and the Justices with him caused at least two open proclamations to be made for keeping the peace, bidding all persons lay aside their weapons, freeholders repair to the county court, and those without vote to depart. Trevor had a similar proclamation made in the churchyard, ordering all who were not electors to remain there. It was move and countermove, void of substance.

Because of the numbers and the danger of a riot, the Sheriff decided to hold his county court in the open, at the High Cross, instead of in the Shire Hall. At the time the court was being set, Trevor was in the churchyard, where he is said to have had some three hundred armed men, apart from a number, equipped with muskets, calivers, and similar weapons, placed in the church, where the county's store of powder was kept. Others were stationed in the neighbouring house of John Owen.

It was usual at such meetings as this for the gentry to walk in the church, as their kind did in London in St Paul's; and Salusbury, who may or may not have been under pledge to remain in his lodging, perhaps felt that he would pass for a coward if he let his enemies keep him away. Whatever his motive – whether to brave Trevor, or, as he argued, to make his devotions – he walked to the church, accompanied by some friends, baring his head as he went by the county court. At the churchyard, he and Trevor passed each other, one going out as the other came in. Trevor quickly turned back. Soon they were bidding each other keep the peace, Salusbury doffing his hat and crying 'God save the Queen!'; until, by repeated and mutual injunctions to peace, they warmed themselves into drawing their swords. Then, says Salusbury, a warning piece was shot off, which brought Trevor's men pouring into the churchyard. Among them was Captain John Salusbury who demanded where the villain was, 'swearing outrageously that he would shoot him through'. Sir John's boy managed to worm his way through the crowd and hand his master the gilded Spanish target or shield that he carried for him. The situation looked ugly. But the Sheriff, being warned, left his court, where as yet he had called neither action nor plaint, hastened to the churchyard, and interposing himself and his company between the combatants, in the end persuaded Salusbury to depart.

No election took place. Salusbury blamed the Sheriff, for, said he, after this disturbance he himself returned to his lodging and all on his side was quiet, while the Sheriff went to the county court and dispatched other business. He might quite well have proceeded with the election, but 'most partially took that colour to dissolve the county, and elected no knight or burgess'. On the other hand, the Sheriff, in his report to the Privy Council, gave for excuse his fear of bloodshed. It is difficult to blame him.

Trevor left Wrexham that afternoon about four o'clock, accompanied and guarded by his troops as far as the town's end, where he thanked them for their kindness and rode away. The day's story ends on an anti-climax; so many threats, alarms, and warlike forces, yet no blood shed! Owing to delays at Westminster, a new election did not take place until 16 December 1601, three days before the parliament ended. Sir John Salusbury was then elected – a solace to his pride, a tribute to his power, but, so far as parliament was concerned, an empty victory.

Warned by the Chief Justice of Chester of the dangerous situation in Denbighshire, 'where the people are factious and ready to follow those they do affect in all actions without respect to the lawfulness or unlawfulness thereof',[1] the Privy Council summoned the three quarrelsome leaders, Salusbury, Trevor, and Lloyd, to London. Nevertheless the feud went on. Salusbury started a suit in the Star Chamber against Trevor, Lloyd, the Sheriff, and forty-seven other persons arrayed against him at the election; Trevor countered with a rival suit against Salusbury and forty-eight of his supporters.

From time to time in the next year or two, Salusbury called on Sir Robert Cecil to prevent his enemies, who were not without friends in high places, from carrying affairs in the county their way. He successfully stayed the appointment of Trevor as Sheriff in 1601–2; and in July 1602 wrote in alarm at a report that Trevor and Lloyd were to be the two new Deputy-Lieutenants. The correspondence fades away with a long-drawn out effort to secure justice against one of his adversaries whose servants and followers had deliberately and in cold blood murdered a kinsman and servant of his.[2]

1. *Hatfield MSS*, xi, 460.   2. ibid., vols. xi, xii, xvi, passim.

CHAPTER 6

County Elections:
The Rutland Election of 1601

ELIZABETHAN Rutland was a small, peaceful county, with three outstanding families, the Haringtons of Exton, the Digbys of Stoke Dry, and the Noels of Brooke.[1] Save in the election of 1563, which remains a puzzle, these three families monopolized the representation of the county throughout the reign.

One might have expected trouble with two seats and three great families to share them. But the county was fortunate. At the beginning of the reign, the Noels were relatively newcomers to Rutland, while the head of the family was accounted a Leicestershire man. He died in 1563, and a long minority of thirteen years left the Haringtons and Digbys in undisputed supremacy. Then, as the new squire of Brooke, Andrew Noel, came of age and emerged into the front rank of the gentry, the Digbys, afflicted in their turn by a minority, and discredited by conversion to Catholicism, faded out.

By 1592, when Sir John Harington succeeded his father at Exton, he and Sir Andrew Noel were unquestionably the two greatest men in the county, and appropriately enough were the two Deputy-Lieutenants. The primacy of the Haringtons was equally unquestionable. Sir John's mother was a daughter of Sir William Sidney, allied to the greatest in the land, while his father had been five times Sheriff of Rutland and once of Leicestershire, and on the seven occasions when he represented his county in parliament had invariably taken the senior seat. The family's fortune and reputation continued to expand. Sir John – born about 1540 – married the rich heiress to Combe Abbey, Warwickshire, thus acquiring wealth before inheriting it. In a passage written about 1600 a commentator on the state of England mentions him as one of several knights, 'thought to be able to dispend yearly betwixt £5000 and £7000 of

1. References will be found in my article, *Eng. Hist. Rev.* lxi, 32 ff.

good land', whose wealth equalled that of 'the best barons' and came 'not much behind many earls'.[1] Sir John married his elder daughter Lucy, a patron of letters,[2] to the Earl of Bedford, while he himself, in favour at the Courts of both Queen Elizabeth and her successor, was made a baron after the accession of James I and entrusted with the upbringing of the Princess Elizabeth. He was a devout and charitable man. 'He relieves many poor and sets them to work; he builds not only his own houses, but colleges and hospitals', wrote his cousin, John Harington of Kelston.[3] And the same writer described Lord Burghley and Sir John Harington together at Bath, afflicted with gout: 'It gave me some comfort to hear their religious discourse and how each did despise his own malady and hold death in derision, because both did not despair of life eternal.'[4]

Sir John first entered parliament in 1571 when his father was Sheriff of Leicestershire and a Rutland seat was therefore vacant. He sat as junior member to Kenelm Digby; quite correctly, for he was not the head of a family. His next parliament was that of 1586. On this occasion, his father sat for Rutland and therefore he himself had to turn to Warwickshire, where his wife's estate of Combe Abbey had already brought him the office of Sheriff. He was returned as the senior member. By 1593 he had succeeded his father at Exton, and in the election of that year was duly returned as the senior knight for Rutland. In 1597 he was perhaps in bad health, for it was a few months after the election that his witty cousin met him with Lord Burghley at Bath. 'My lord,' he wrote, 'doth seem dead on one side, and my cousin on the other, though both in their health were ever *on one side*.'[5] Whatever the cause, Sir John's place in the Rutland representation in 1597 was taken by his brother, James Harington of Ridlington.

Andrew Noel, who was knighted in 1585, first entered parliament in 1584 as the junior colleague of Kenelm Digby, being probably the Harington nominee. Thereafter he continued to sit for the county — in 1586, 1588, 1593, and 1597 — as junior to one or other of the three members of the Harington family.

---

1. ed. F. J. Fisher, *Camden Misc.* xvi, 23.
2. Cf. B. H. NEWDIGATE, *Michael Drayton and his Circle*, pp. 60 ff.
3. Quoted ibid., p. 60.   4. HARINGTON, *Nugae Antiquae* (1804), i, 236.
5. ibid.

In all likelihood the Rutland elections of Elizabeth's reign were made on the nomination or advice of two families – the Haringtons and the Digbys down to 1584, and the Haringtons and the Noels from 1586 on; and we may perhaps assume that with the possible exception of the mysterious election in 1563, when two new names appear in the return, there was not a single contested election before 1601. Certainly, after the eclipse of the Digbys there was nothing to disturb the harmony of the county. Sir Andrew Noel was married to Sir John Harington's sister – a happy alliance, which, reinforced by Sir John's devout, puritan temperament, must have made Rutland a model county. No adventitious circumstance caused friction. Honours were always double. There were two deputy-lieutenancies, two seats in parliament; and the seniority of the Haringtons was so far beyond question that the order of priority created no difficulties.

This state of bliss might have continued but for a regrettable accident. At the time of the 1601 election, it happened that Sir Andrew Noel was Sheriff, and so was precluded by law from returning himself to parliament. But if he let slip his hold on the second county seat, it would mean the intrusion of a new person, break a long-standing monopoly, and conceivably imperil his family's position in the county. This was the kind of opportunity often taken by a father to introduce his son and heir to his future heritage. However, Sir Andrew's eldest son, Edward Noel, was unfortunately a mere youth of nineteen, a student at the Inner Temple and recently down from Cambridge, where he had graduated B.A. He was under age, possessed no freehold in the county, and technically was incapable of election. There was also the consideration that if the great Sir John Harington stood for parliament, he might by the sensitive conventions of the age regard himself as touched in honour and dignity by having a stripling, though his nephew, for colleague. It was a dilemma.

Sir John Harington apparently was still in poor health and not at all eager to stand for parliament. When first invited to do so by his friends, he suggested that he should be 'passed over' and that Sir Edward Cecil, the great Lord Burghley's grandson, who had married Sir Andrew Noel's daughter a few months before, should be chosen instead – a sign, surely, of goodwill towards the Noel family. Subsequently, he must have changed his mind. Sir Andrew Noel was similarly approached by friends. That he had already resolved to put up his son, despite the law and despite the awkward possibility of a breach with his brother-in-law, there can be little doubt, though he later told a naïve and improbable story, saying that his son was suggested by these friends, on learning that he himself could not legally stand.

About a month before the election, following, one imagines, the customary way of arranging elections in this county, Noel wrote offering to support either Harington himself or any nominee of his. At the same time he asked for reciprocal support for his own nominee, though who this was to be he did not disclose until the morning of the election. He merely promised that Harington would like him. It certainly looks as if he was playing a subtle game; as if, while conscious that he would give offence, he hoped to keep his plan secret and thus avoid organized opposition.

The election took place on 22 October. Though the Haringtons later on accused Noel and his servants of active plotting and canvassing, attendance at the county court was probably not abnormal. In all likelihood the gentry did not anticipate a contest, but, recognizing that, as in the past, one seat was at the disposal of Sir John Harington and the other of Sir Andrew Noel, were only concerned to please both magnates. When Sir Andrew told his brother-in-law that he intended to nominate his son, arguing that others as young as he were likely to be elected in other counties, Sir John replied that he was too young. Noel must then have realized, if he had not done so before, that he was jeopardizing the harmony of the county.

When the time came, Sir Andrew Noel, presiding over the assembly as Sheriff, first nominated Sir John Harington for the senior seat and then announced his desire to have his son elected, in accordance, so he said, with the suggestion of some of the freeholders. Thereupon, Harington told the company bluntly that he did not consider Edward Noel a fit person to be elected. He suggested choosing Sir Edward Cecil, Noel's son-in-law, instead. To this, Sir Andrew, who did not conceal his annoyance, retorted that Cecil would not accept nomination. He can hardly have been telling the truth, for Cecil accepted the far less estimable honour of a Yorkshire borough seat.

This open breach between their leaders embarrassed the gentry. Anxious above everything to preserve peace, they pressed Sir Andrew to accept nomination himself, though he warned them that the House of Commons might fine him for acting illegally. Whether he yielded because he was unable to resist the pressure, or whether he already saw how to turn the situation to his own ends – 'sustaining the name of the place but for a time, until he should find opportunity to have his son elected', as his opponents declared – we cannot say; but yield he did, returning Sir John Harington and himself as the two representatives. The meeting ended in seeming goodwill. Noel appeared satisfied, said Harington, and shared with him the cost of entertaining the freeholders, 'as the usual manner hath been'.

Sir John Harington went up to Westminster, and, with this formidable opponent and other leading gentlemen out of the county, Noel set to work to get his son into parliament. Instead of appearing at Westminster himself, he engaged a distinguished lawyer and member of parliament to procure the annulment of his election by the House of Commons. When the matter came before the House, there was a suggestion that Noel should be fined or otherwise punished, but Sir John Harington at once rose in defence and with essential honesty and fairness assured the House that Noel had been an unwilling party to the election. The election was annulled and a new writ issued in time for the next county court on 19 November.

Preparations in Rutland did not wait for the arrival of the writ. Noel, it was said, vowed that he would either have his son elected or 'lie in the dust'. His servants rode up and down the country, canvassing and enrolling the voters. They got some of them to sign their names, as a surer means of binding them to their promise, and were said to have entered certain names falsely on their rolls in order to delude neighbours into following the lead. The arguments they employed are not without interest. One canvasser urged freeholders to vote for Edward Noel because he had 'always lived among them with his father', whereas his opponent – Sir John Harington's brother, James – had for the most part been 'a dweller in another county'; arguing also that the election of a second Harington would make the county dependent on one family. Another canvasser pointed out that this was a splendid opportunity for Edward Noel – 'being a young gentleman and likely to succeed in his father's place' – to gain 'better experience' under the guidance of his uncle.

The problem confronting Sir John Harington's friends was to find a candidate. They decided to run his brother, James, who had sat for the county in 1597. It would of course be a violation of the convention by which the Haringtons and the Noels had hitherto shared the representation; but Noel's stubborn insistence on his son's candidature, not any desire of theirs for a monopoly, was the cause. When Sir John broached the subject – both he and his brother being in London in early November – James was reluctant to stand. He had been of the parliament before, he said, and hoped his countrymen would not lay the same burden on him again, against his will. Though he did become their candidate, his reluctance probably introduced an element of uncertainty into their campaign, emphasizing its negative but true purpose – to keep out Edward Noel. One of Sir John Harington's servants told how he and others canvassed freeholders to choose James Harington, or Mr Bodenden, a kinsman of Sir John's, or any other sufficient gentleman, but not Edward Noel.

Sir John Harington made his emphatic opposition to his nephew clear in letters from London; but the election campaign was planned by a group of his friends and servants who met several times at Exton, his Rutland house, under the leadership of Sir William Bulstrode of Ridlington Parva, a kinsman, who at the time was living at Exton. They toured the county, compiling lists of supporters. Where freeholders were already bound to the other side, they sometimes tried to persuade them to stay away from the election: 'If you can do us no good, do us no harm.' They 'did persuade some ... by fair and plausible speeches', said Noel, 'and threatened others'. On the Sunday before the election there was an attempt to restore peace, apparently on the basis of withdrawing James Harington's candidature, while Sir Andrew Noel was to satisfy the county that his proceedings did not tend to the disgrace of Sir John Harington. It failed. Sir William Bulstrode and Sir Andrew Noel, the two leaders, could not be brought to agreement.

The election was held in the Castle hall at Okeham on 19 November 1601. The thorough canvassing by both sides must have brought most of the forty-shilling freeholders and many others to the county court. According to their opponents, Noel's side had got together the majority of the recusants or Catholics, who usually did not show themselves at these assemblies. Certainly, James Digby was there.

George Butler, a gentleman dependant of Sir John Harington's and a rather hot-headed leader of the party, jostled him, told him that as a recusant he had no voice and might be gone, and complained openly that Sir Andrew Noel would carry the election with papists. To this Digby replied, 'Though I be a recusant, yet I have a voice here, and will have a voice, for I pay subsidy and fifteenth and have more freehold to lose than you.' We can readily believe that the recusants were willing to support Noel: not that he was a Catholic, but they hated the puritanically inclined Sir John Harington.

In the Castle hall, James Harington and Sir William Bulstrode – though the latter was not a Justice or freeholder in Rutland – sat on the bench with Sir Andrew Noel. After reading the writ, Noel announced that he was a suitor on behalf of his son. He also inveighed against those servants of Sir John Harington who had laboured and practised against him. James Harington then spoke: Edward Noel, he said, was his nephew, 'one whom he loved', and a youth of very good parts; but his tenderness in years made him unfit for election, especially to be joined with Sir John Harington who was in years and so sickly that he might be unable to fulfil the county's interests in parliament. A man of gravity and experience ought to be elected; and this, he declared, was Sir John's wish. Sir William Bulstrode also spoke, answering Noel's attack on Sir John's servants. He too urged the choice of a grave person. James Harington seems still to have been reluctant to stand, but cries of 'A Harington! A Harington!' and the importunities of friends prevailed. He left the bench and went down into the Castle yard to show himself to the freeholders and take a note of the names of his supporters to deliver to the Sheriff.

Such was the mild story that James Harington and his friends told. True, they indicated that there was a little bickering. Noel supplied the embellishments. He depicted Harington as 'countenancing, fronting, and facing' him, and terrifying the freeholders with 'great threatening words' if they ignored the express desire of Sir John Harington. George Butler and another of Sir John's servants leapt on the bench and like men distracted of their wits railed at Edward Noel's supporters. Then, says Noel, perceiving that the greater number were against them – an assertion we need not believe – they followed James Harington and Bulstrode down from the bench, called on 'all that loved a Harington' to follow them, and went into the Castle yard where they 'trooped and banded themselves' with their followers and 'marched up and down' the yard. They quarrelled with their opponents, so that Noel was compelled to come down to them and make a proclamation for keeping the Queen's peace.

It all reads like an overcoloured account of the second stage in an election, when the two sides usually marshalled themselves preparatory either to the 'view' or the 'poll'. Indeed, one witness described Sir Andrew Noel as coming down from the bench, not to preserve the peace but to rally his supporters, bidding 'all that would give their voices with a Noel to follow him'; and another told how the freeholders divided themselves in the Castle yard, James Harington going out at one door with his followers and Sir Andrew at the other with his. Doubtless the scene was rowdy, and there was some horseplay. It was often thus. Proclaiming the peace need not be taken very seriously. Apparently there was no pretence at an election by 'the view', though James Harington seems to have suggested it.

The poll followed. Sir Andrew Noel played fair enough in polling Harington's supporters first; but there, if we believe his opponents, fairness ended. The scrutiny was carried out in the Castle Hall and was probably controlled by the list of freeholders prepared by each side. Pursuing normal procedure, an oath was administered to any voter whose qualifications were challenged; and it was this on which Noel seems to have counted to whittle down the opposition's numbers. With stern countenance and reiteration, says Harington, he demanded whether their lands were worth forty shillings 'over and above all charges'. The emphasis was on 'charges', a term that the Sheriff refused to explain. Technically he was quite in order, but if it be true that no contested election had taken place in Rutland for decades, we can understand that 'ignorant people' were nonplussed, imagining that charges extended to the cost of housekeeping. According to Harington, some of his supporters, though known to be very sufficient freeholders, were rejected for hesitating to swear to Noel's formula, and then were refused a second chance when they grasped its limited meaning. In addition, one voter who declared that he had a parsonage impropriate for three lives, and others who were 'freeholders by lease for the term of three lives', were rejected, though the votes of some leaseholders for twenty years were accepted on the other side. In fairness we must cite Noel's claim that he accepted from Harington's side the oaths and votes of certain 'cottiers of cottages', some of whom were so mean that they worked for twopence a day at threshing and fourpence a day at other daily work.

We cannot assess the degree of truth in these accusations or the extent of any damage done to Harington's cause. Harington named twenty persons whose votes were refused on the ground of insufficiency. Since Noel admitted that not a single voter on his son's side was rejected for this reason, we can hardly avoid inferring that the conduct of the poll was not impartial. In addition, it is clear that Noel's servants – and possibly Noel himself – tried to deter some of their opponent's marginal forty-shilling freeholders from recording their votes by threatening them with liability to pay taxes. 'They had made a good precedent for themselves', the threat ran: 'since they had sworn their lands to be worth forty shillings a year, Sir Andrew Noel would set them forty shillings apiece in the subsidy book.'

According to Harington, three of Noel's servants – one of whom virtually admitted the charge – induced some of their own voters to take the oath, who otherwise would not have done so, by offering them forty shillings or more for their freeholds, thus easing their path to perjury. And, as is so often the case, the same accusation was made by the other side. Indeed, one of Sir John Harington's servants who took the oath and voted, deposed that his 'ancestors' had purchased his land for ten pounds about sixteen years previously, and that before the election he had been offered forty shillings a year for it, while on the day of the election – though he denied that the offer was fraudulent – one of Sir John's servants bid forty shillings for it. Some of Harington's voters, said Noel, wanted to take the oath in the form that they had been offered forty shillings a year for their freehold.

The voting must have been very close. We may hazard a guess that at the election by voices Harington had a majority. At this stage in the proceedings, one of Noel's servants – who more or less confessed to the charge – called out to Noel to return his son, since as Sheriff he 'could but answer it'. At the poll, however, the scales were probably turned by a certain amount of trickery. Whatever the facts, Sir Andrew Noel gave the victory to his son.

Compared with our Welsh elections or the Yorkshire election of

1597, this had been a gentlemanly contest. James Harington was probably annoyed at being wrongfully deprived of votes, but relieved at escaping an honour which he did not covet and which – he is supposed to have said – would have cost him two hundred pounds. He and Sir Andrew parted on friendly terms: in fact, on his initiative they and others dined together. In all likelihood we should have known nothing about the election if the reputation of so great a man as Sir John Harington had not been engaged. According to Noel, it was Sir John or some other person who caused a Star Chamber suit to be started against him in James Harington's name, and paid the fees. This was followed by a second suit against eight of Noel's servants, and countered by a bill of Noel's against the two Haringtons and sixteen of their supporters.

But the interest of the election does not end here. 'A man', wrote Francis Bacon, whose precepts were so much wiser than his actions, 'is an ill husband of his honour that entereth into any action, the failing wherein may disgrace him more than the carrying of it through can honour him.'[1] Measured against this sage reflection, Sir John Harington had proved fallible; and his ruffled honour brought the bane of faction into a peaceful county. In his Star Chamber bill Noel complained of his 'greatness' in Rutland, where he, along with James Harington who succeeded Sir Andrew as Sheriff, endeavoured 'to bear the whole sway, direction of causes, and government'. John Presgrave, who had been Sheriff's Bailiff under Noel and was probably a relative of one of his servants, told that when he made the proclamation for keeping the peace at the election, James Harington had threatened to 'sit upon his skirts', and subsequently, when he became Sheriff, turned him out of office. Another witness told of James Harington putting six or seven of Noel's servants off the grand inquest, on which they were wont to serve, replacing them by four of Sir John's men – one under age; and to complete their discomfiture, he returned them for service on petty juries.

The Harington faction set itself to frustrate and insult Sir Andrew. Once, when he was on official business at Okeham Castle, some of Sir John's servants played a practical joke on him, closing the Castle gate except for the wicket door, across which they fastened a chain. 'We will now cause Sir Andrew Noel to stoop', they boasted; and

1. *Essays*, 'Of Honour and Reputation'.

stoop he did. On another occasion when he was sitting as a commissioner for rating the subsidy and had a tenant of Sir John's before him, one of the same men exclaimed, 'What dost thou, calling on Sir Andrew Noel? He will not hear thee. But call on Mr Bodenden, my master's kinsman: he will hear thee.' Another of Sir John's servants, whose rating assessment for the town of Ashwell had been raised, told one of Noel's servants who was an assessor, that 'he would not be raised by him nor his master . . . nor by any of his partakers'; and he went on, in language much too homely for quotation, to rail at Noel and his party. There were other incidents; all petty matters, no doubt, but they convey a picture of faction-strife in its milder manifestations, and are part of the texture of Elizabethan country life.

CHAPTER 7

The Gentry and the Boroughs

ONE of the most arresting and puzzling facts in our parliamentary history is the remarkable growth in the membership of the House of Commons during the sixteenth century. The number of members at the beginning of the century was two hundred and ninety-six,[1] at the end it was four hundred and sixty-two; an increase of one hundred and sixty-six, or fifty-six per cent.

Thirty-one of these seats were added when Wales, Monmouthshire, and Cheshire were brought into the representative system by Henry VIII. There is nothing perplexing about this. But the rest — they were the result of an apparently haphazard creation or restoration of parliamentary boroughs, excusable by no argument that would be valid today, and certainly having little connexion with population. During the next two centuries, from the death of Elizabeth to the eve of the Great Reform Bill of 1832, the number of additional English seats was only fifty-one, and of these as many as forty-five were added during the reigns of James I and Charles I. Clearly, this astonishing expansion was a Tudor phenomenon which persisted into the early Stuart period.

In addition to his Welsh and Cheshire seats and to two transient seats at Calais, Henry VIII had a small share in the expansion. He added seven boroughs, each sending two representatives.[2] Under Edward VI the process gathered great impetus, especially in the second of his two parliaments, when the creations included a batch of seven Cornish boroughs. In all, seventeen boroughs and thirty-four members were added in this brief reign.[3] Under Mary the pace

---

1. *Inst. Hist. Res. Bulletin* iii, 175; WEDGWOOD, *Hist. of Parlt. Register of M.P.s 1439–1509.*
2. Berwick-on-Tweed, Buckingham, Lancaster, Newport (Cornwall, cf. ROWSE, *Tudor Cornwall*, p. 92), Orford, Preston, and Thetford.
3. Boston, Bossiney, Brackley, Camelford, Grampound, Heydon, Lichfield, Liverpool, Michael (Cornwall), Penryn, Peterborough, Petersfield,

slackened a little. Fourteen boroughs were added, but as three were single-member constituencies, they returned only twenty-five members.[1] The most prolific of all borough-makers, whether Tudor or Stuart, was Queen Elizabeth. She created or restored thirty-one parliamentary boroughs, sending sixty-two members.[2] But if length of days be brought into the sinful reckoning, the record does not look so black. In four times the number of years she exceeded the combined score of her brother and sister by only three.

It used to be thought that the motive for creating these additional seats was to pack parliament. Had it been so, we might expect to find the new constituencies more or less consistently returning royal nominees or out-and-out government supporters. In fact, they did not. By this obvious test the theory breaks down, sometimes quite ludicrously; and as our narrative proceeds its essential fallacy will become increasingly clear.

To turn our thoughts the right way, we need to understand the process by which these boroughs came to acquire their new rights. A minority were enfranchised by a clause in letters patent of incorporation. Now the business of incorporation began with a petition from the borough, drafted by its legal advisers and as a rule sponsored by the lord and owner of the borough if it was a proprietary borough, or by some influential patron attached to the Court. Whether the letters patent contained a clause granting representation depended on two conditions: that the petition included such a clause, and that the sovereign left it in the grant. In other words, the initiative was local, not central. In 1579 the Earl of Rutland was seeking the incorporation and enfranchisement of his borough of Newark. He received a

Saltash, Thirsk, West Looe, Westminster, Wigan. Maidstone elected M.P.s in March 1553, but I have assumed that they were disallowed, and have therefore debited Elizabeth with this borough (cf. my remarks in *Eng. Hist. Rev.* lvi, 495–6).

1. Abingdon, Aldborough (Yorks.), Aylesbury, Banbury, Boroughbridge, Castle Rising, Droitwich, Higham Ferrers, Knaresborough, Morpeth, Ripon, St Albans, St Ives, Woodstock.

2. Aldeburgh (Suffolk), Andover, Berealston, Beverley, Bishop's Castle, Callington, Christchurch, Cirencester, Clitheroe, Corfe Castle, East Looe, East Retford, Eye, Fowey, Haslemere, Lymington, Maidstone, Minehead, Newport (I. of W.), Newton (Lancs.), Newtown (I. of W.), Queenborough, Richmond (Yorks.), St Germains, St Mawes, Stockbridge, Sudbury, Tamworth, Tregony, Whitchurch, Yarmouth (I. of W.).

letter from the Queen's Secretary informing him that he had obtained Elizabeth's consent to all the articles of the letters patent, 'save the nomination of two burgesses', which clause the Queen refused to sanction. It was not until Charles II's reign that this borough was enfranchised.[1]

However, the majority of new parliamentary boroughs were not enfranchised by letters patent. A few were 'restored' boroughs: that is to say, they had sent representatives to parliament on one or more occasions in the past, but had discontinued sending. The rest lacked even this excuse. There appears to be no direct evidence to indicate exactly how they were authorized to make their first elections; but it seems reasonable to assume that like established boroughs they received a precept from the Sheriff.[2] Now, although the writ to the Sheriff did not name the parliamentary boroughs within his jurisdiction to which he was to send his precept, long-established custom did; and one can hardly imagine a sixteenth-century Sheriff adding a new constituency without explicit warrant from the Chancery.

Supposing that a Sheriff chanced his arm, or supposing that a new borough, by-passing the Sheriff, attempted to send representatives without receiving a precept, the election return had still to be accepted by the Clerk of the Crown in Chancery, who compiled the official list of members. And of all the administrative departments, the Chancery was perhaps the most insistent on having proper warrant for its actions. We are therefore driven to the conclusion – which indeed is common sense – that these new constituencies were called into being by a precept from the Sheriff, who must have received a special writ from the Chancery, which in turn would have required a warrant from the Crown. The only conceivable exception might be the 'restored' borough. The Clerk of the Crown might have been induced to accept such a return on the strength of old precedents; but one can hardly believe that he ever did.

There happens to be one piece of evidence from Stuart times which bears out our inference that the process began with the Crown.

1. *Rutland MSS.* i, 117.
2. We know that Newport (I. of W.) received a precept for its first election in 1584 (T. CAREW, *Hist. Account of Elections*, 1755, ii, 13), and that Aldeburgh (Suffolk) made its first election indenture in 1571 with the Sub-Sheriff (*H.M.C. Various Coll.* iv, 303).

Secretary Coke conveniently preserved a note relating to some petitions that he presented to the King in May 1625. One item refers to an attempt by the borough of Blandford in Dorset to secure representation. It reads: 'Bailiff and burgesses of Blandford, where no beggar was ever suffered, to have two burgesses in parliament (refused).'[1]

This Blandford episode throws light on our further, and crucial question: How was the Crown moved to take action? There can be little doubt about the answer. As with newly incorporated boroughs, the initiative came from the locality – from the boroughs themselves, or to speak more realistically, usually from their lords or patrons. The Isle of Wight furnishes us with the clearest evidence on this point. Here, in 1584, the boroughs of Newport and Yarmouth, which had jointly sent two burgesses to parliament in Edward I's reign, were each enfranchised, as also was a third island borough, Newtown. Since this striking extension of borough representation to the island coincided with the first general election after the appointment of the Queen's relative, Sir George Carey, as its Captain-General or Governor, we might have guessed the riddle. But luckily we are not left to guess. In its borough records Newport noted that 'at the special instance of Sir George Carey ... two burgesses were admitted into the High Court of Parliament'; and as a token of thanks he was granted for life the right to nominate one of the burgesses. It was clearly the reward he expected and the motive for his suit to the Queen. He probably exercised the same, or a more extensive, right in the other two boroughs. In 1601 he wrote to the Mayor and burgesses of Yarmouth: 'Send up unto me (as heretofore you have done) your writ, with a blank wherein I may insert the names of such persons as I shall think fittest to discharge that duty for your behoof.'[2]

In 1584 there were also two new members from Berealston in Devon. As the return states, they were elected 'at the request' of William, Marquis of Winchester, and William, Lord Mountjoy, chief lords of the town and borough. Can there be any reasonable doubt that this borough owed its enfranchisement to these noblemen?

1. *H.M.C. Cowper MSS.* i, 197.

2. CAREW, op. cit., ii, 13; F. BLACK, *Parliamentary History of the Isle of Wight* (Newport, 1929), pp. 3, 5; W. S. WEEKS, *Clitheroe in the 17th Century* (Clitheroe, n.d.), p. 223.

or any doubt of their motive? At an earlier date, in 1571, the borough of Christchurch in Hampshire was enfranchised. The person responsible was almost certainly the powerful Earl of Huntingdon, for in 1584 – the borough's third election – we find the Mayor writing that the Earl 'hath and of ancient right ought to have the nomination of one of our burgesses'. On this occasion they carried subservience even further by electing as their second member – their own nominee – a lawyer, 'one in counsel with our aforesaid good Lord'.[1]

The Earl of Leicester seems to have had a hand in the game. In 1584 he was looking round to increase the number of his parliamentary seats, and, with this in view, wrote to the borough of Andover in Hampshire: 'Being Steward of your town, I make bold heartily to pray you that you would give me the nomination of one of your burgesses ...; and if, minding to avoid the charges of allowance for the other burgess, you mean to name any that is not of your town, if you will bestow the nomination of the other burgess also on me, I will thank you for it.' Then, in a postscript: 'If you will send me your election [return] with a blank, I will put in the names.' According to our evidence, which seems quite conclusive, Andover, not yet a parliamentary borough, sent no representatives in 1584; but it did in 1586. Very likely, the Bailiffs, in reply to their Earl, explained that they were not entitled to elect members, whereupon Leicester persuaded the Queen to remedy the deficiency in time for the following parliament.[2]

This statesman got his way with Elizabeth. Others did not. In 1597 Sir Robert Cecil received a curious letter from his follower, Edward Stanhope, Recorder of Doncaster. Cecil, who had recently become High Steward of the borough in succession to Lord Hunsdon, cousin to the Queen and Lord Chamberlain, had evidently been presented by Stanhope with a blank election return for Doncaster and presumably had written in two names, only to have them refused by the Clerk of the Crown. The borough, wrote Stanhope in explanation, had told him that they had made burgesses 'anciently' – a claim which appears unwarranted – and that Lord Hunsdon, on some occasion – perhaps in 1588 – had nominated two members. Moreover, in 1593 the borough had sent an official with the town seal

1. *Return of M.P.s*, i, 413 n.; S. P. Dom. Eliz. 173 no. 89.
2. MEREWEATHER and STEPHEN, *Hist. of Boroughs* (1835), ii, 1393.

to Stanhope, offering him one seat as Recorder and leaving the other at Lord Hunsdon's disposal. Being unable to accept for himself – Stanhope explained to Cecil – he had passed on both nominations to Lord Hunsdon, who named two representatives, and, for anything he knew to the contrary, they had sat in parliament. Stanhope could not understand why now in 1597 Cecil's nominees should not be accepted as Lord Hunsdon's had been; and he promised to call on the Clerk of the Crown next morning and send to 'the clerk of the parliament' – presumably the Commons' clerk – to demand an explanation.[1]

It is an odd tale. We notice the omission of any reference to a precept from the Sheriff. Apparently, the borough by-passed this official and attempted to bluff its way into the House of Commons with the bogus argument of being an ancient parliamentary borough; all, of course, to please its powerful patrons. The manoeuvre must have failed every time. Neither Lord Hunsdon nor Sir Robert Cecil got his nominees past the Clerk of the Crown; and if, as may have happened, either of these two influential courtiers tried to persuade Elizabeth to enfranchise Doncaster, as she had enfranchised Andover, he met with no success. Borough-making was finished for the reign.

Though few, these illustrations – as, indeed, will become increasingly apparent – must be typical of what happened. They leave little room for the old-fashioned theory of packed parliaments; they even render superfluous any curiosity about the geographical distribution of the new boroughs. The monarch was obviously a mere agent, yielding to pressure for more seats. It would be mistaken to think him a free agent. If it was his prerogative to dispense privileges, it was also his function; and with Court life exquisitely organized for powerful begging, the most alert and self-willed of monarchs had often to yield when discretion whispered refuse. Elizabeth exercised great care in her grants and favours. She scrutinized, she applied a strong brake. No trait in her character is more conspicuous. Nevertheless, the pressure for new parliamentary boroughs was too strong for her. For twenty-seven years she gave way at every parliament. In 1559 it was three new boroughs, in 1563 eight,[2] in 1571 eight, in

1. *Hatfield MSS.* vi, 317, vii, 442.

2. I have included Tregony and Minehead in the 1563 figure. There are no earlier returns extant, and an entry in the *Commons Journals* for 1563

1572 one. And then came the first indication that she was beginning to cry Hold!; for when the Earl of Rutland tried to have Newark enfranchised in 1579, the Secretary, telling him of the Queen's veto, added: 'It is thought that there are over many [burgesses] already, and there will be a device hereafter to lessen the number of divers decayed towns.'[1] Alas, for good resolutions! The next parliament brought the record creation of the reign – ten boroughs. But with that, the Queen did revolt; except – and how human a touch if she saw the incident in this light! – a final and unique favour was granted to her peerless favourite, the Earl of Leicester, whose borough of Andover was enfranchised in 1586, the only new borough that parliament, and the last of the reign.

Such lordly patrons of boroughs as Hunsdon, Huntingdon, Leicester, Mountjoy, Rutland, and Winchester, and eminent commoners like Sir Robert Cecil, did not want the seats for themselves. Their pressure on the Queen was simply a transmission of the pressure that was being put upon them. It was the country gentry from whom the demand came. This is a point that we shall appreciate much better if for a moment we turn aside to glance at the composition of the House of Commons.

Fifteenth-century statutes and the writs sent to the Sheriffs imposed both social and residential qualifications for membership. Knights of the shire were to be knights, girt with a sword, the most suitable and discreet of the county. Borough members were to be chosen from the more discreet and suitable of the resident citizens or burgesses. Substituting the word 'gentlemen' for 'knights' – as we have statutory authority to do – then the House of Commons in Elizabeth's later years ought to have been composed of ninety country gentlemen, representing the counties, and three hundred and seventy-two resident citizens and burgesses, representing the cities and boroughs.

This was the law. Had it been observed, had Tudor and Stuart parliaments really contained four townsmen, many quite petty and

---

(i, 63) seems clearly to imply that they first returned members to that parliament. However, BROWNE WILLIS (iii, 63, 66) gives them M.P.s for 1559. His names for Tregony are the same as in 1563, which suggests guessing, but one Minehead name differs, which normally is a sign of reliability.

1. *Rutland MSS.* i, 117.

most of them timorous, for every gentleman, how different would have been our history! That acute seventeenth-century thinker, James Harrington, commenting in his *Oceana* on the changes brought about by the Tudor period, observed: 'By these degrees came the House of Commons to raise that head which since has been so high and formidable to their princes that they have looked pale upon those assemblies.' If the House of Commons had been as the law required, how could this have happened? How could parliament have displayed the spirit and tenacity needed to challenge and overthrow the monarchy?

We know the law. What of the facts? Out of a total membership of 460 in the parliament of 1584–5, it has been possible to classify 447. The number whose primary occupation was associated with a borough – that is, those who were merchants or borough officials and cannot be described as belonging primarily to the gentry or professional classes – was 53. A similar analysis of 435 members out of a total of 462 in the 1593 parliament gives us the same figure; and less reliable calculations for the parliament of 1597 do not differ materially. To this figure of 53 we might on legalistic grounds be constrained to add a few more members – Recorders and gentlemen who held borough offices, although occupationally they belonged to a different class. In the 1584 parliament they raise our total from 53 to 77. Even allowing in addition for a few country gentlemen who possessed houses in the towns they represented and were technically qualified to be burgesses of parliament according to the law, the theoretical proportion of ninety country gentlemen to three hundred and seventy-two resident citizens and burgesses would be reversed. Instead of one gentleman to four townsmen, Elizabeth's later parliaments contained four gentlemen to every townsman. The country gentleman and his cousin, the lawyer, had captured the House of Commons. It is a fact of quite fundamental importance in our history.[1]

This invasion of the boroughs by the country gentleman reaches back a long way. The faction struggles of the fifteenth century were

1. The figures are derived from two London M.A. theses – HAZEL MATTHEWS, 'Personnel of the Parliament of 1584–5', and EVELYN E. TRAFFORD, 'Personnel of the Parliament of 1593'; and from a Manchester M.A. thesis, CONSTANCE M. DAVEY, 'The Personnel of Parliament, 1597'.

largely responsible for its first impressive phase; and it has been calculated that in the parliament of 1478 at least half of the borough
representatives were not true burgesses.[1] However, the total number
of borough members was then only two hundred and two. It is a far
cry to the three hundred and seventy-two of late Elizabethan days,
of whom nearly three hundred were gentry. Moreover, the whole
complexion of the story had changed. The Wars of the Roses were
past history. It was not faction, but a rapidly expanding desire to sit
in parliament that explains the new surge into the boroughs.

The Reformation, with its subtle, far-reaching consequences, probably marks a significant stage in the new phase of the movement.
We might speak of infiltration before, and of invasion afterwards.
To express the question as one of supply and demand can be quite
illuminating. It seems clear that for a long time the existing parliamentary boroughs were more or less adequate to meet the needs of
the gentry; but by the end of Henry VIII's reign demand was pressing on supply, and thereafter exceeded it. The enfranchising of new
boroughs was the response; and even the strong personality of Queen
Elizabeth could not stem the demand or deny it substantial satisfaction.

Social habit may prove an amorphous subject under analysis.
Reasons are complex; cause and effect chase one another in circles.
If we ask why the Elizabethan gentry were so desirous of a seat in
parliament, we might answer, as we should answer for more recent
times – ambition, dignity, curiosity, a desire to be at the centre of
things, or even business reasons. We have seen how social rivalry
and the peculiar test of social status afforded by county elections
enhanced the prestige of a county seat. Many a gentleman who fain
would have sat for his county found solace in a borough seat instead;
and who can say whether the motive was a simple desire to be in
parliament, or an illogical impulse not to be kept out? In any case,
as the gentry swarmed into borough seats, mere emulation increased
the demand; and the keener the competition, the more attractive and
interesting an assembly the House of Commons became.

In post-Reformation England, as a result of peaceful conditions,
economic expansion, and a remarkable unifying of national life,

1. M. McKisack, *Parliamentary Representation of Boroughs during the
Middle Ages*, pp. 106 ff.

London and the Court became increasingly the social centre of the kingdom. Not only noblemen, but a surprising number of gentlemen acquired London houses or lodgings; and many others came to town on business or pleasure. The unique centralization of the law in the capital, where virtually all civil cases were tried and where a vast equity and conciliar jurisdiction was concentrated in Chancery, Star Chamber, and Court of Requests, brought hither a litigious breed of gentry. 'In term-time', wrote London's Mayor in 1583, '... all the houses in Fleet Street and the streets and lanes adjoining, as also without Temple Bar, do use lodgings, victualling, or letting out chambers.' Clearing the City of its temporary visitors at the end of the law-term was a royal concern. From time to time – usually the day after the end of Hilary or Trinity term – 'every Justice of the Peace and gentleman of sort and quality, in or near the City', was summoned to a ceremonial sitting at the Court of Star Chamber, where the Lord Chancellor delivered 'the Queen's commandment' in an hortatory address, which, though varying in its contents with the political circumstance of the moment, generally enjoined 'gentlemen of what sort or quality soever, which have left or forsaken their country dwellings', to return home and attend to their public and social duties. It was the break-up of the London season; and indeed, the pattern of this modern institution can be foreseen in Elizabethan days. By the end of the reign, even the prototype of the 'man-about-town' had appeared in John Chamberlain, a gentleman of wealth, leisure, and culture, who had no country estates to manage but walked and talked in St Paul's, knew Court and county society, and wrote his news and gossip in weekly or fortnightly letters over a period of twenty-nine years to his intimate friend, the diplomat Dudley Carleton.[1]

Every legal term brought society to London; but when there was also a meeting of parliament, it was the season of seasons. As Dudley Carleton wrote to Chamberlain at parliament time in 1601: 'Hoping that the term, the parliament, or good company ... has brought you to London.'[2] In Elizabethan days, the Court was in residence locally; noblemen with their retinues, and gentlemen with their servants,

1. WRIGHT, *Queen Elizabeth and her Times*, ii, 183; HAWARDE, *Reportes del Cases in Camera Stellata*, ed. Baildon, p. 56.
2. *Cal. S.P. Dom., 1601–3*, p. 111.

thronged Westminster and the City; printers and propagandists timed their publications for the occasion. A matchless attraction it was to be in London at this time; to be 'of the parliament'; to move on the fringe of the Court, marvelling at its fashions and splendours; to see and hear the Queen; perchance to kiss her hand; to be at the heart of politics, and listen to famous men speaking in the House; to gather news from all quarters of the kingdom and the world. Such a one stood a tip-toe among his neighbours on his return home.

'I am one that loves to see fashions, and desires to know wonders; therefore, if I be elected, I will not refuse it', wrote Thomas Bulkeley, Recorder of Beaumaris, when the great John Wynn of Gwydir sought to persuade him to forgo the seat in favour of a friend. Recollect, also, the argument used in the Rutland election of 1601: what excellent experience parliament would be for young Edward Noel, heir to a great house! 'Son', says a father in a tract by the Elizabethan, Arthur Hall, 'forasmuch as I now have obtained for you my place in the Common House of parliament, for the increase of your knowledge, you growing to the world, and I from it ...' Later, in 1626, Sir George Chudleigh, who held the nomination for a seat at East Looe but did not intend to take it himself, expressed the same sentiment: 'I should now gladly be a spectator and give my son a little breeding there.'[1]

It would be folly to doubt the eager wish of gentlemen to be in parliament. An anonymous and dateless letter shows a suppliant tackling Sir James Croft, Herefordshire magnate and Privy Councillor: 'Whereas I have of long heretofore served in parliament, moved in duty to her Majesty and the Commonwealth ... so am I at this present, led by the same affection as also for some other particular respects of a case of mine own, desirous to be one of the number ... I am bold to become a humble suitor unto you to help to place me a burgess in your country, where it shall seem to you best. Your Honour shall command me and my service.' In 1586, Sir Henry Bagenall – then thirty-two – wrote to the Earl of Rutland, his relative by marriage: 'If you have any borough left whereof you may prefer a burgess, I pray you to have me in remembrance, "for that I am

1. N. L. W. Wynn of Gwydir Papers, Panton group, 9051 E, no. 99; above, p. 126; ARTHUR HALL, *Account of a Quarrel* (1815 reprint), p. 51; *Cowper MSS.* i, 252–3.

very desirous for my learning's sake to be made a parliament man".
Perhaps I shall be elected a knight for a shire in Wales.' The Earl
placed him at Grantham, but he had no need for the seat since he
was elected knight for Anglesey, where he possessed an estate. 'Good
brother', wrote William Slingsby in 1597, being then thirty-five years
old, 'put my father in mind to make me a burgess of the parliament,
for it is [a] thing I do exceedingly desire.' His father placed him in
the family seat of Knaresborough. There must have been many
similar letters, long since perished.[1]

As for lawyers, membership held many attractions for them. It
offered a means of widening their circle of acquaintances and adding
to their clients; it provided a stage whereon to display their talents.
For those bent on an official career it brought them to the notice of
statesmen and courtiers, or maybe to the notice of the sovereign
herself. Of the lawyers sitting in the parliament of 1597, twenty were
subsequently promoted to legal office.[2] As a rule, parliament met during the legal term, when the lawyers were gathered in London, and it
was easy enough for them to slip out of St Stephen's into Westminster
Hall, where the chief law-courts were conveniently situated.

This invasion of the boroughs was facilitated by the relationship
of urban communities to the aristocracy. Some boroughs were still, in
varying degree, in private ownership – the property of 'lords'; some
were royal boroughs, subject to a High Steward appointed by the
Crown; some were part of the widely scattered property of the Duchy
of Lancaster, subject to the Chancellor of the Duchy; some were
part of the Duchy of Cornwall; and even those that were independent
usually had their patron, whom they appointed as High Steward or
to similar office. Most boroughs had business of one sort or another –
ticklish lawsuits, bills to promote or oppose, charters or favours to
seek – which needed the interest and advice of the upper class; and
complete independence was a luxury few could afford. Peers, statesmen, courtiers, distinguished lawyers, neighbouring gentry, are all
found in official or merely benevolent relationship with urban communities, much as they were with monasteries on the eve of the
Dissolution.

1. Inner Temple, Petyt MSS. 538, vol. x; *Rutland MSS.* i, 207; *Diary of
Sir Henry Slingsby*, ed. Parsons, p. 253.
2. DAVEY, 'Personnel of Parliament 1597'.

These men, with their influence in boroughs, were the obvious road to parliamentary seats. They were willing accomplices of the gentry, not for political reasons but to gratify friends and followers. The arrangement fitted perfectly into the contemporary system of clientage, since it endowed magnates, who preened themselves on their following, with highly esteemed favours to bestow on supporters; and nothing tied the gentry more firmly to their patrons – as Francis Bacon demonstrated by deserting Lord Burghley for the more generous Earl of Essex – than an assured flow of favours. For this reason, if no other, rival courtiers and Councillors, no less than other magnates, were impelled to covet and seek nominations to borough seats.

The relationship of patron and client appears in a letter written by a certain Edward Lenton to Sir Robert Cecil in 1601. 'My name has been given by Sir John Fortescue – a Buckinghamshire gentleman and Privy Councillor – to the corporation of Wycombe to elect me one of their burgesses, but my Lord Windsor, their Steward, to whom they were wont to grant the nomination of one [burgess], hath written for both. Wherefore, my humble suit is that you would vouchsafe by your letters to give that corporation some encouragement in electing me, for though my Lord Windsor objects in his letters that I am one that doth but follow my Lord Norris (in whose business I now am), yet I hope your Honour knoweth that I have given myself as a servant to none but you.' Lenton was not elected.[1]

As our narrative proceeds, we shall have much to say about the intervention of patrons in borough elections, but an example or two at this point may not be out of place. In 1586 the Earl of Rutland wrote to the borough of East Retford – to which the right of representation had been restored in 1571, probably at his request – asking for the nomination of one or both burgesses. 'Having considered the matter', came the answer, we 'consider ourselves bound to satisfy you in that and any other much weightier thing. May it please you, therefore, to make choice and nominate and we will ratify it. If it pleased you to think well of Mr Denzil Holles we should be very glad, but if not, as your Lordship pleases.' Denzil Holles, who had been their member in the previous parliament – as likely as not on the Earl's nomination – was the eldest son of Sir William Holles of

1. *Hatfield MSS.* xi, 400.

Houghton near East Retford, a friend of the Earl's and a fine old English gentleman, beloved and respected by all. The Earl approved of the choice. Holles and another nominee were returned to parliament.[1]

Not all towns were so considerate or obsequious. In 1572 the Earl of Leicester had occasion to write a scarifying letter to his borough of Denbigh for making an election that displeased him. 'I have been lately advertised how small consideration you have had of the letter I wrote unto you for the nomination of your burgess; whereat, as I cannot but greatly marvel (in respect I am your Lord and you my tenants, as also the many good turns and commodities which I have been always willing to procure you ...), so do I take the same ..., as, if you do not upon receipt hereof presently revoke the same and appoint such one as I shall nominate, namely, Henry Dynne, be ye well assured never to look for any friendship or favour at my hands in any your affairs hereafter.' Perhaps – he went on – it would be argued that the choice had been made before they received his letter. 'I would little have thought that you would have been so forgetful, or rather careless, of me as, before your decision, not to make me privy thereto, or at the least to have some desire of mine advice therein ...; but as you have yourselves thus rashly proceeded herein without mine assent, ... I signify unto you that I mean not to take it in any wise at your hands.' By the time this letter was received, it was too late for Denbigh to rescind its return of a Cavendish, but not, we may be sure, to repent of its hasty action.[2]

In 1563 Liverpool, a Duchy of Lancaster borough, landed itself in a similar predicament. Saddled with a Molyneux – son of the Crown lessee of the lordship of the town – as one member of parliament, and anxious to elect as the other their own popular alderman, 'merry' Ralph Sekerston – a remarkable man, merchant, alderman, and sometime Mayor of Liverpool, whose local patriotism was legendary a century later – the town authorities were embarrassed by a demand from the Chancellor of the Duchy to nominate a member. Their escape from the dilemma was ingenious, if rash. They avoided a definite answer by declaring that the second seat was reserved for the Earl of Derby, whose pleasure they were awaiting. Then, afraid of

1. *Rutland MSS.* i, 208, 242; *Memorials of the Holles Family*, pp. 37–47.
2. JOHN WILLIAMS, *Ancient and Modern Denbigh*, pp. 98–9.

being outreached by Sheriff and Chancellor, they sent Sekerston riding 'almost post' to London, where he saw the Earl and secured for himself his Lordship's nomination. As a last resort, the Chancellor tried to prevent him taking his seat in the House, probably taking advantage of the Sheriff's refusal to handle the town's indenture. But Sekerston was a bold, indomitable man. As the Town Books proudly record, 'he [did] stick to the matter still, and obtained his room'.

What these townsmen had yet to learn was the sombre sixteenth-century truth that it was perilous to offend so great a man. The Chancellor retaliated by issuing a *quo warranto* writ to inquire into the town's privileges – a formidable threat to any borough. But, 'as God would', and by the skilful diplomacy of Master Sekerston, the Earl of Derby was persuaded to talk with the Chancellor, and the writ was recalled, 'which, if it had not, the town had been put to a great charge'.[1]

A desire to please, or a healthy fear to offend: both caused boroughs to succumb to patrons. But there was also a financial motive. Parliamentary constituencies were under legal obligation to pay their representatives wages. For cities and boroughs the rate was two shillings a day. Any member of parliament could sue out his writ *de expensis* from the Chancery and so compel the electors to pay the statutory wage. Large boroughs had no occasion to quail. Even Liverpool, only a middling-sized community, preferred its own Ralph Sekerston at a cost of two shillings a day, rather than a nominee of the Duchy of Lancaster *gratis*. But for small boroughs the cost was serious, or even prohibitive. Take the Suffolk borough of Dunwich. Here is its budget for the year 1598–9: receipts £41 12s. 10d., with £5 still owing; payments £41 10s. 3d.; result, as Mr Micawber would have said, happiness. But what if there had been a bill for £20 for its members' wages in the parliament of 1597–8? The borough just had to have free service; and free service it got. The Earl of Essex, its High Steward, received one of the nominations in 1597; the other went to Attorney General Coke, 'in respect of his former and continual favour and friendship many ways'.[2]

1. *Liverpool Town Books*, ed. Twemlow, i, 216–19.
2. ibid. p. 219; *H.M.C. Various Coll.* vii, 82, 85–6, 87.

The Reformation Parliament, with its eight sessions and unprecedented duration from 1529 to 1536, must have caused many a borough to groan under the burden of wages. At Lincoln the total wage bill for both members in the previous parliament of 1523 had been £12; but by 1535, before this extraordinary parliament had inflicted its full costs, the city was faced with two bills of £45 4s. od. each, and rejoiced when one of its members, 'out of his zeal and love to the city', accepted a final payment of £7 instead of the £11 3s. 4d. still owing him. Salisbury, a year earlier, evaded a debt of about £30 to one member by granting him a discharge from the office of Mayor for the ensuing year; but the other member, in 1535, presented a writ *de expensis* for £43 8s. od., and although 'of his goodness' he remitted the odd £3 8s. od., payment of the rest had to be spread over three annual instalments. Canterbury rejoiced when one of its members cut short his attendance in 1532, thus 'saving of the wage that he should have of the city', and expressed its gratitude by contributing to a new bonnet for him. When he played truant again the next year, they gave him a gratuity towards another bonnet. It would be interesting to know whether the financial strain of this exceptionally long parliament speeded the intrusion of the gentry by making them welcome in many more boroughs.[1]

Patron and borough were both conscious of the money factor. Many magnates employed the two-pronged persuasion of Sir Thomas Heneage, who, as Steward of Salisbury, asked that city for the nomination of a member in 1593: 'so shall you ease the town of half your charge, and make [me] beholding unto you for this courtesy'. Heneage failed, but the Bishop of Winchester succeeded with a similar, if more tactful, plea to his city of Winchester in 1572. He asked them to elect his friend, John Caplin of Southampton, 'your own countryman and well known to the more part of you, who can, I am assured, do that city and country such service ... as is required ..., and also will ease you of such trouble and charge as usually you have been at in that behalf; so that therein you shall further yourselves and also pleasure me; which your doing to requite, you shall find me both mindful and ready'.[2]

1. *H.M.C. Rep.* XIV, viii, 31, 34; *Various Coll.* iv, 217–18; *Rep.* IX, i, 152b.

2. *Various Coll.* iv, 230; HOARE'S *Wiltshire*, iv, 296; *H.M.C. Rep.* vi, 605a.

Normally, either patron or nominee promised that service would be free, but some boroughs made assurance doubly sure by taking bonds from their members to indemnify themselves against any claims. Grimsby, which had been gratifying patrons since the middle of the fifteenth century, took these bonds as early as Henry VIII's reign and as late as 1625.[1] Such boroughs were prudent, for nothing could prevent a member obtaining a writ for his wages, if he so wished. In 1577 Nicholas St John esquire, a Wiltshire gentleman, who was member for Marlborough in the parliament that met in 1572, 1576, and 1581, and in all likelihood had agreed to serve for nothing, obtained a writ and then sued the borough in Chancery. Ultimately, the borough had to pay him £8 8s. od., which sum the Earl of Hertford – who may have nominated St John and so bore moral responsibility – refunded in 1584.[2] Another member, the irascible and unbalanced Arthur Hall of Grantham, who was expelled from the House of Commons in 1581, played the same scurvy trick. He was member for Grantham from 1571 to 1585 and had promised to serve without wages, but in 1585 or 1586 he obtained a writ and then commenced a suit in Chancery to enforce payment for these parliaments. On this occasion the House of Commons itself intervened and persuaded Hall to forgo his claim.[3] A third member, Richard Edgcumbe, placed in a Totnes seat in 1563 by his brother, the lord of the borough, jibbed at the prospect of serving a second session without proper remuneration. The borough had paid him forty shillings – a token figure – in 1563, but membership, so he claimed, had cost him an additional twenty marks and more. In 1565, expecting a call to a new session and having no personal business to take him to London, he wrote to the borough asking them either to elect someone else – which of course they could not do – or allow him 'the bare fee' of two shillings a day. What happened, we do not hear.[4]

It would be a mistake to judge Elizabethan borough elections by modern democratic standards. They could only appear shocking, whereas they were a true reflection of contemporary society and were

1. ibid., XIV, viii, 250 ff., especially pp. 274, 279.
2. CECIL MUNRO, *Acta Cancellariae* (1847), pp. 448 ff.; B. H. CUNNINGTON, *Hist. Records of Marlborough* (reprinted from Wilts., Berks., and Hants. County Paper, October 1928).
3. D'EWES, *Journals*, pp. 403–4, 406–7, 417–18.
4. WM. HONE, *The Year Book* (1832), p. 755.

not essentially vicious. Bribery was practically unknown. There was no cash nexus either between patron and borough or patron and nominee. The bond was social. Those gentlemen who wished to enter parliament but lacked the requisite influence in any borough – the situation of very many – were inevitably compelled to seek out some patron; and their way to the patron lay through clientage or else friendship, at first or second hand. True, there were boroughs that had one or both of their seats free from patronage and were approached directly by candidates. Here, one might suppose, was a chink through which bribery could creep in.

There was a case of bribery in Elizabeth's reign. It is well known – too well known, for it appears in our text-books with no hint of its singularity. It was the case of Thomas Long, a Wiltshire gentleman who lived near Westbury, owned property in that parish, and was elected for the borough in 1571. He openly confessed in the House of Commons that he had given the Mayor and someone else four pounds for his seat. But Mr Long, as the Journals record, was 'a very simple man and of small capacity to serve in that place': that is to say, he was scarcely *compos mentis*, unequal to his posthumous fame. The House ordered repayment of the four pounds, imposed a fine of twenty pounds on the borough 'for their ... lewd and slanderous attempt', and sent a pursuivant to bring the two recipients of the bribe to Westminster to answer before the House.[1]

The virtuous wrath of the Commons may not impress the cynic; nevertheless, it remains a fact that amidst so much evidence on Elizabethan borough elections, this case of bribery is unique. That the system was susceptible to corruption is obvious: we know that it went that way. The House of Commons was itself an unwitting instrument of vice, for by usurping jurisdiction over disputed elections in James I's reign and introducing the novel remedy of unseating members, it undermined the natural working of the Elizabethan system, prompted disputes and election petitions, and so stimulated the growth of corruption.

In medieval theory the Commons were attorneys for their constituencies: as the election writs enjoined, they were to be given 'full and sufficient power' to consent to the business of parliament for themselves and the communities they represented. This conception

1. *Commons Journals*, i, 88, 89.

was still alive in the sixteenth century. It made the representation of boroughs by alien gentry, though formally illegal, less objectionable than we might imagine. There was no incongruity in employing a stranger as attorney.

What Elizabethans themselves thought of the practice can be gathered from a debate in the parliament of 1571 on a bill 'for the validity of burgesses not resiant', which reversed the prevailing law about residence. According to Thomas Norton, member for London, who may, indeed, have had a hand in framing the bill, it had a double purpose: to avoid the choice by decayed or small boroughs of unfit members, 'which is too often seen'; and to legalize the current practice of electing strangers, lest the validity of any parliament should be challenged. In the debate on the second reading there was apparently little or no criticism until a lawyer, who was both Mayor and member for Hereford – a city that resolutely withstood election patronage – uttered a brief warning to genuine burgesses, pointing out that it might 'touch and overreach their whole liberties'. 'Lords' letters', he prophesied, 'shall from henceforth bear all the sway.' Norton, a member of great persuasive authority, answered him, whereupon a majority of the House cried 'Yea!' for the penultimate stage of ingrossing the bill. At this juncture, when all seemed set fair for passing the bill, an anonymous member reopened the debate and changed its fate.

He began his speech with a comment on decayed, or as we should say, rotten boroughs. A sharp reminder it is that our ideas are not those of the sixteenth century. Any thought of disfranchisement was no more in his mind than in the bill. On the contrary, the very decay of a borough might be reason for its representation. The bill pretended to ease the burden of such communities by permitting the election of strangers. This he thought doubtful policy. Better local members, who, 'feeling the smart, can best make relation of their estate, and ... devise and advise of such helps as ... may restore the old ruins. All things are in change, and nothing so suppressed but by God's grace the same may in time by policy be raised up.'

'What sort of men are to come to this court?' he asked. 'Whether from every quarter, country, and town there should come, as I might say, home-dwellers, or ... men chosen by direction, it forceth not whom?' He preferred home-dwellers. 'How may her Majesty, or how may this court know the estate of her frontiers? ... We who never have seen Berwick or St Michael's Mount can but blindly guess of them, albeit we look on the maps.' 'Since we deal universally for all sorts and all places', there should 'be here [men] of all sorts and all countries.'

Questioning whether it was 'liberty' to allow towns and boroughs to 'choose at liberty whom they would', he cited the example of 'a Duke of this realm', who, a hundred years ago, 'wrote his letters to a city which I know', asking them to elect two members from four names that he sent. 'The letter under the Duke's seal is still preserved. But hear you the answer. He was written to with due humbleness that they were prohibited by law' and might 'choose none of them'. Venturing a little nearer his own days, he told how 'in Queen Mary's time a Council of this realm (not the Queen's Privy Council) did write to a town to choose a Bishop's brother, and a great Bishop's brother it was indeed, whom they assured to be a good catholic man ... The Council was answered with law. And if all the towns in England had done the like', the evils of that reign had been the less.

'What hath been, may be,' he added. It will be said that the bill's purpose is merely to leave towns at liberty to choose whom they list. 'I say, that liberty is the loss of liberty; for when by law they may do what they will, they may not well deny what shall be required. It is too truly said, *Rogando cogit, qui rogat potentior*. And I have known one that to avoid a great man's displeasure that dwelt near him, that was desirous (as he knew) to buy his land, did ... bind himself not to alienate his land from his true heirs. This being known ... the great man was contented to let him keep his own quietly, which otherwise he would not have done. Surely, law is the only fortress of the inferior sort of people.'

But the speaker was no extremist. Acknowledging that some towns did not possess men of fit discretion, he went on: 'I can never be persuaded but that either the lord, whose the town is (be the town never so little), or the Steward if it be the Queen's, or some good gentleman of the country adjoinant, will either assign them who know the town and can be content to be free among them and to serve by their appointment, for their country and for them; or else, for some reasonable fee, such as be of their learned counsel, and who know them and the country will deal for them. I mean it not so strictly that those who should be chosen should of necessity be dwellers in the town, but to be either of the town or towards the town, borderers and near neighbours at the least.'

He concluded by urging the House to stand upon the ancient usage, 'which is the only warrant and sole stay of freedom in parliament'.

Robert Bell, an eminent lawyer, who was to be Speaker in the next parliament, and later Chief Baron of the Exchequer, answered this speech. Some boroughs, he argued, had neither the wealth nor the men of their own to provide fit members. Admitting the danger of noblemen's letters – Bell was member for King's Lynn and a Norfolk man, in which county the princely power of the Duke of Norfolk had been felt in every parliamentary borough – he suggested that a penalty of forty pounds be imposed on every borough electing anyone on the nomination of a nobleman.

Another prominent member, Francis Alford, added more suggestions. He noted that many young and inexperienced men, 'for learning's sake, were often chosen – through whose default he knew not; whether letters of noblemen, love or affection in the country, their own ambition, or the careless account of the electors'. He proposed an age qualification of thirty for membership. On the main issue, he was of opinion that 'Moses and Aaron should be conjoined together'. Towns should elect 'one of their own, or some gentleman near them, who had knowledge of the state of the country; and the other, a man learned and able to utter his mind and opinion'. In brief, 'the law should be in force for the one burgess, and at liberty for the other'.

The intervention of our anonymous member – with whose sentiments the diarist-reporter of the debate clearly sympathized – had made the appropriate question now to be put to the House one of committing, not ingrossing the bill. It was committed. No doubt, when the committee met, in the sobriety of a small group of nine, they perceived the difficulties and dangers inherent in such a measure, and with bad logic but practical wisdom let it sleep in their hands.[1] The law remained unchanged. Fifteenth-century statutes and

1. *Commons Journals*, i, 84, 85; D'EWES, pp. 168–71; Cotton MS. Titus F 1, fols. 157 ff.

the election writs continued to demand residence, while townsmen and gentry, peers and Privy Councillors, all went their own way, not a whit disturbed by a general conspiracy to defeat the law. With its phalanx of law-breakers, the House of Commons aided and abetted this victory of social forces over its own legislation.

CHAPTER 8

Borough Types

NOT all boroughs surrendered to the gentry. In each parliament a few managed to preserve complete independence; others elected one local member, thus adopting Francis Alford's ideal that 'the law should be in force for the one burgess, and at liberty for the other'; the rest gave up both seats to outsiders. Sometimes the outsiders were local gentlemen of the same county – 'borderers and near neighbours', in the words of our 1571 debate; sometimes, to use the expressive contemporary description, they were 'foreigners' – from strange, perhaps distant counties.

Excluding single-member constituencies from our calculations, as also London, with its four members who were always citizens, and construing residence in the borough broadly enough to include the Recorder, who was often an absentee-official, we can give the residential figures for 166 of the 175 normal two-member constituencies represented in the parliament of 1584–5, and for 158 of the 176 constituencies in 1593. Set out in tabular form, their significance will be clearer.

	1584	1593
Both members resident in the borough	22	19
One resident in the borough, one in the county	18	16
One resident in the borough, one 'foreigner'	21	20
Both resident in the county	32	22
One resident in the county, one 'foreigner'	34	45
Both 'foreigners'	39	36

The number of boroughs complying fully with the law – 22 in 1584 and 19 in 1593 – is strikingly small; and even had the residence of every member been known and our figures therefore been complete, it is highly unlikely that this group would have numbered more.

The other conspicuous feature of the table is the number of boroughs returning two outsiders, whether resident in the county or 'foreigners' – 105 in 1584 and 103 in 1593. Here again, without fear of appreciable error, we can bring in the missing boroughs, thus arriving at a probable total of 109 for the parliament of 1584 and 118 for that of 1593. The preponderance of such boroughs over those which returned at least one of their own residents is remarkable. By 1593 the proportion was two to one. In the nature of things there must have been a saturation point. This was probably it. Though figures are not yet available to substantiate the statement, there is reason to think that the movement had been progressive and that in the earlier parliaments of the reign fewer boroughs succumbed completely to the gentry.[1]

As one would expect, it was the larger boroughs that tended to elect two of their own community. They could afford to pay parliamentary wages, or alternatively could find well-to-do burgesses ready enough to bear their own expenses. Also, they were better able to resist the blandishments of the great. All the same, the number that succeeded in avoiding a single lapse was astonishingly small. Apart from London, the only boroughs which seem to have sustained unswerving independence throughout Elizabeth's reign were Bath, Bristol, Ludlow, and Worcester.

Bristol's place among the élite was indeed meritorious, for its successive High Stewards – the Earl of Pembroke, the Earl of Leicester, Lord Burghley, the Earl of Essex, and Lord Buckhurst – were all election-patrons, though the most importunate, the Earl of Essex, was denied the opportunity of testing its resistance. If any of these great lords asked for a nomination, none was granted; if they refrained, their reticence bespoke futility. Consistently the city returned its Recorder and one of its aldermen.[2]

Ludlow's record was nearly spoilt when in 1597 the Sheriff of Shropshire, perhaps deliberately, misdirected his precept to the borough, with the result that a nominee of the Earl of Pembroke, who was Lord President of the Council in the Marches of Wales and whose headquarters were at this borough, was returned. However, the proper authorities sent in a rival return, and this, with the assistance of the House of Commons, prevailed. Later, in 1609, when Robert Cecil, then Earl of Salisbury and the most powerful man in

1. The figures are based on the theses of Miss Matthews and Miss Trafford.
2. Cf. A. B. BEAVEN, *Bristol Lists: Municipal and Miscellaneous* (Bristol, 1899), pp. 165 ff., 231.

England, asked them to choose a nominee of his at a by-election, they declined, answering that they could elect none but a resident and had already refused the then Lord President, Lord Eure's request to elect his brother.[1]

A most striking absentee from the roll of the impeccable is the city of York. Technically it should probably be included, but it did have one lapse from grace. This was in 1601 when, after electing city officials and aldermen throughout the reign, it returned the Archbishop of York's Chancellor, Dr Bennett. And thereby hangs a tale. Dr Bennet had sat for Ripon in the previous parliament. At that time his master, the Archbishop, had been Lord President of the Council in the North, and apparently in each of his capacities held the nomination to a seat in this borough. He could therefore afford to ingratiate himself with Sir Robert Cecil by passing on to him, at his request, one of the two nominations. In 1601 Cecil renewed his request, and in the moment of his triumph over the Earl of Essex, when his power was undisputed, could scarcely be refused. But, alas for Dr Bennett! there was now a new Lord President – Cecil's brother. Consequently, the Cecils monopolized both Ripon seats, leaving the Archbishop's Chancellor unprovided. It was presumably this situation which caused the York authorities, under pressure, to break their long record of independence.[2]

Dr Bennett, we may presume, was a resident citizen of York,[3] and therefore only the fairly obvious element of patronage in his election deprives the city of a place in the highest rank of parliamentary boroughs. The same is true of Salisbury, which consistently restricted its choice to members of the city council and the Recorder, except in 1572 when the Earl of Pembroke, their local magnate, wrote in favour of a certain Hugh Tucker. Very likely Tucker was a citizen, but he was not a councillor. The city authorities sanctioned a breach of their 'ancient orders and privileges' on this occasion, though they

1. D'EWES, op. cit., pp. 556a, 593b; *I.H.R. Bulletin* xii, 15 n.; *Cal. S.P. Dom., 1603–10*, p. 566; H. T. WEYMAN, 'M.P.s for Ludlow', *Trans. Shrops. Arch. Soc.* 2nd ser. vii, 3 ff.; MEREWEATHER and STEPHEN, op. cit. ii, 1431.

2. G. R. PARK, *Parliamentary Representation of Yorkshire* (Hull, 1886), pp. 50 ff.; *Hatfield MSS.*, vii, 404, xi, 390, 409, 442.

3. He was made a freeman in 42 Eliz. Cf. *Reg. of Freemen of York* (Surtees Soc.), ii, 45.

made their feelings clear in a rider which stated that from henceforth they alone were to nominate and elect their burgesses, and only members of their assembly were to be eligible. What is more, in spite of eminent High Stewards, they kept to their resolution. When that practised patron, Sir Thomas Heneage, who succeeded Sir Christopher Hatton as High Steward in 1591, proceeded to ask for a nomination in 1593, they had the courage to say no, and elected two former Mayors.[1]

A number of boroughs tried to safeguard their freedom by local ordinance, but, as is the way with good resolutions, the time too often arrived when they failed to live up to them. At Cambridge there was an ordinance, dating back to 1460, which laid down that no one should be elected unless he were 'inhabitant and resident within the town'. In virtue of this 'statute' they refused the request of their High Steward, the Duke of Norfolk, to elect a gentleman-servant of his to Mary Tudor's last parliament; and in 1566, in a letter to Sir William Cecil, they cited it to justify the strange plea that their two members, elected in 1563, should be unseated for the second session of this parliament on the ground of non-residence: as though a Cambridge by-law had any validity in such matters! In 1571 the ordinance was solemnly confirmed, with the addition of a proviso making their Recorder eligible for election; and in 1601 a new ordinance of a similar nature was passed, this time defining residence as having dwelt within the town with wife or family one whole year before the election. Mayor and electors were all to be sworn to observe it. One might ask, could good intentions be more clearly advertised?[2]

Nevertheless, the Elizabethan record of Cambridge was not unspotted. The first lapse occurred when at a by-election in 1581 they elected John North esquire,[3] the eldest son of their High Steward, Roger, Lord North, Lord Lieutenant of the county. Probably it did not seem a heinous sin, for in 1572 they had paid this young aristocrat the compliment of making him a free burgess and alderman.[4] But at the general election in 1584 John North took his appropriate

1. HOARE'S *Wiltshire*, iv, 282, 296, 593, 696, 708, 711, 812; *H.M.C. Various Coll.* iv, 226, 230, 232.

2. COOPER, *Annals of Cambridge*, i, 211, ii, 140, 270, 613; S.P. Dom. Eliz. 40, no. 65.

3. Typed list of supplementary returns at P.R.O.

4. *D.N.B.* sub North, Sir John.

place as knight of the shire, and the borough authorities evidently found themselves unable to resist a request to elect his brother, Henry North, as his successor. However, with this display of weakness, compliance stopped; and although they were soon to expose themselves to double pressure by initiating a new policy of choosing eminent statesmen or courtiers, instead of lawyers, for the office of Recorder – selecting in 1590 no less a person than Lord Hunsdon, the Lord Chamberlain – they managed to re-establish and retain their independence. It seems as if both Lord North, their High Steward, and Lord Hundson, their Recorder, asked for nominations in 1593; but the borough, to its notable credit, elected two aldermen.[1]

Like Cambridge, Oxford had laudable aspirations. Throughout Mary Tudor's reign it regularly elected two of the leading citizens, and though the identification of one member in Elizabeth's first parliament is obscure, probably the same policy prevailed on that occasion. Then, in October 1559, the corporation appointed the Earl of Bedford as High Steward, a magnate who cultivated election patronage. They thus found themselves at the next election being asked for a nomination that they were unable to refuse.[2] The Earl nominated one of his gentlemen-servants,[3] and the city authorities insisted on him coming to Oxford to take the oath as a burgess and freeman before election. It was a condition that many boroughs exacted, perhaps as lip-service to the principle of electing only burgesses, perhaps to give a semblance of legality to the election, but also because the oath and status of burgess was some guarantee that their members would be bound to the interests of the community should any business crop up in parliament affecting them. Quite a number of boroughs must have found themselves, as presumably did Oxford, balancing the risks of less efficient service from a stranger, against the desire to gratify a powerful patron.

Oxford disliked the novelty. Of that there can be no doubt. At the beginning of 1564 the Earl resigned his High Stewardship, and the city appointed in his place Sir Francis Knollys, the Queen's relative,

1. COOPER, ii, 483–4, 521.
2. *Records of Oxford, 1509–83*, ed. Turner, pp. 277, 301, 302.
3. William Page. He appears in the Earl's will, among the bailiffs and stewards, as the Earl's 'very faithful servant', and was left £10 (I owe this information to Miss G. Scott Thomson).

courtier, official, Privy Councillor, and an Oxfordshire gentleman. In November 1568, more than two years before the next election, the Common Council, under a penalty of forty shillings for disobedience, enacted that no freeman should give his voice in parliamentary elections to anyone who had not been resident in the city and a freeman for the last three years, and was not of the status of Bailiff; an obvious attempt to nullify the precedent of 1563 and return to the choice of senior citizens. Alas! they were as the children of Israel under Rehoboam, who complained of a heavy yoke, only to be subject to one more grievous. For their new High Steward had a great brood of sons. There were three of them to be placed in the parliament of 1571, and naturally he looked to Oxford for one seat. Thus the city authorities had to eat their fine words at the first election after enacting them. They passed a formal resolution suspending the regulation for that parliament, with the optimistic rider that it was still to 'remain in full force' for the future. But Edward Knollys was re-elected in the following year, and when his death created a by-election in 1575 there was yet another son ready to be launched on a parliamentary career. He held the seat until 1588–9.[1]

By this time the memory of their declarations of independence, or at least the will to reassert them, had gone. Oxford had sunk in the hierarchy from a constituency returning two local members to one returning a single local member and an outsider. In 1592 Sir Francis Knollys resigned his office and was succeeded by another election-patron, Lord Hunsdon. In 1593 the city meekly surrendered its senior seat to him and he, like Knollys, placed a son there. Hunsdon died in 1596, and Oxford again chose high, and chose fatally, in selecting the Earl of Essex. In 1597 the city Council resolved that one parliamentary seat should 'be at the disposition of my Lord of Essex, our Steward, to certify such one as he shall name'; and the person he named was his devoted follower, Francis Bacon's brilliant but invalid brother, Anthony. Essex was succeeded by Sir Thomas Egerton, Lord Keeper of the Great Seal. In the last parliament of the reign he nominated his son-in-law, a Warwickshire gentleman.[2]

At Shrewsbury, a borough with a relatively wide franchise, all

1. TURNER, op. cit., pp. 306, 325, 336; *Oxford Council Acts, 1583–1616*, ed. Salter (Oxford Hist. Soc.), p. 14.
2. *Oxford Council Acts, 1583–1616*, pp. 68, 76, 102, 113, 139, 141–2.

burgesses living within the town and contributing to its charges were entitled to vote; and to prevent disorderly scenes the town Council attempted to lay down rules about the conduct of elections. In January 1558, for example, they forbade preliminary canvassing – one more indication of contemporary prejudice against what seems to us an essential element in parliamentary elections.[1] In the first half of Elizabeth's reign the community was consistent in choosing members of the corporation.[2] But then came a change. The local gentleman appeared, as did the patron; and there were contested elections. Perhaps a desire to ease the burden of wages had something to do with it. In 1557 the borough was two and a half years late in paying one member's wages; and the situation grew worse. In 1563 an assessment was made in order to pay a member for four parliaments, ranging from 1553 to 1559, and seemingly the obligation had not been discharged when this person sat for a fifth time in 1571. At any rate, he went to the trouble and expense of taking out five writs for his wages – proof, one imagines, that he had failed to secure payment in a less formal way.[3] In 1581 we find the borough settling the even longer-standing claims of another member for service in 1559, 1563–6, and 1571; and again there was at least one writ, sued out five years after the parliament, when presumably he had tired of waiting.[4]

In these circumstances, the town drifted from its earlier, independent practice. In 1588 they seem to have asked their Recorder, Thomas Owen, an eminent lawyer of Lincoln's Inn and Condover, Shropshire, who had been their member in 1584, whether they were compelled to choose a resident as their representative in the forthcoming election. The answer was no.[5] In 1593 there were at least two approaches from outside. The Earl of Essex, whose interests in Wales and its borderland presumably furnished him with his opening, wrote

1. *H.M.C. Rep.* XV, x, 13, 14.

2. Compare the names of M.P.s with the lists of Bailiffs, etc. in OWEN and BLAKENEY, *Hist. of Shrewsbury*, vol. i. The M.P.s in 1559 were Robert Ireland and George Leygh (cf. payments cited in *H.M.C. Rep.* XV, x, 15, 22, 37). BROWNE WILLIS (iii, 66) has clearly just reinserted the two names from Mary's last parliament.

3. *H.M.C. Rep.* XV, x, 15, 37. The date on p. 37, namely 1562–3, is presumably wrong, or alternatively payment could not have been for five parliaments. Leygh's fifth parliament was 1571.

4. ibid., p. 22.

5. *H.M.C. Rep.* v, 342b. The date of the letter must be 1588, not 1589.

asking them to elect one of his stewards, while a Shropshire gentleman, at the instance, so he said, of friends in the corporation, proffered his own candidature, as one who conceived a special good liking of their town and good government, and whose ancestors had been near inhabitants to the town. The Earl succeeded, the gentleman failed. In a characteristic letter, Essex thanked them very heartily for their friendly readiness in electing his servant, 'notwithstanding earnest suit made for others'; and as a token of gratitude waived his claim against the Bailiffs for some geldings, and further, promised them his favour in the future. He was their 'very loving friend'. But his seductive pen wrote in vain when, in 1597, being at Plymouth on the eve of sailing on the Islands Voyage, he asked for both nominations in the forthcoming election. He got neither. Not that Shrewsbury was repenting its loss of independence. One seat went to a Shropshire gentleman who sat for the borough in every parliament from 1586 to 1601. With the other, the electors evidently preferred to please their late Recorder, Thomas Owen, now a judge. At his request they elected his son.[1]

Repentance did at last come to the town authorities. In 1604 they attempted to reverse recent tendencies by an order that, in future, choice was to be made of burgesses residing within the town or suburbs and 'known to be men fearing God, of sound religion, lovers of the estate of this town, and able to speak in that place [the House of Commons] as occasion may require'. Oh, admirable sentiments! Had there been resolute wills! If, as one supposes, this order preceded the election of that year, it was violated at once by the choice of a Northamptonshire lawyer and antiquary, Francis Tate.[2]

With boroughs such as Nottingham and Leicester the pattern changes. Of middling size, they were not incapable of independence, but there were powerful patrons at hand, whose wishes it was politic, and no doubt agreeable, to meet. Nottingham was the capital of the Earl of Rutland's county, and the third Earl, perhaps the second also, was High Steward of the borough. In the first parliament of Eliza-

---

1. ibid. XV, x, 56; OWEN and BLAKENEY, op. cit., i, 550 n. 16; 'Early Chronicles of Shrewsbury', *Trans. Shrops. Arch. Soc.* 1st ser. iii, 325–6; *H.M.C. Rep.* v, 342b.

2. 'Orders of the Corporation of Shrewsbury, 1511–1735', *Trans. Shrops. Arch. Soc.* 1st ser. xi, 165.

beth's reign, the Rutland influence seems to have determined the choice of both representatives, either directly or indirectly, for one was a local gentleman of note, reared in the second Earl's household, and the other a secretary of his.[1] In 1563 the secretary was re-elected, along with Nottingham's Mayor. And then, momentarily, the Rutland influence vanished, probably owing to the youth of the new Earl. The third Earl began his interest in elections in 1572, when his uncle and the secretary monopolized both seats. In 1584 – when the secretary sat again – and in 1586 we have direct evidence of intervention:[2] on each occasion a Rutland nominee shared the representation with the borough's Recorder.

The third Earl died in 1587, but a member of his family was elected along with the Recorder in 1588. After this, owing to a long minority, Nottingham was left to its own devices. For the last three parliaments of the reign and the first of James I, two members of the corporation were elected. As the authorities soon realized, however, independence could be a costly state. In 1606 they were confronted with writs from their two members for expenses in the first session of the 1604 parliament; and although, by a majority vote of the town Council, they compromised with their creditors for twenty pounds, the memory of this experience endured. In December 1620, on the eve of the elections to James I's third parliament, the borough frankly abandoned its high estate, paying unambiguous testimony to the deterrent effect of parliamentary wages. 'The greater part of this company', states a minute of the town Council, 'do hold it convenient that two foreigners be chosen for the town to serve in this parliament, for the easing of the town's charges.' In the division on the question, seventeen councillors voted for two foreigners, six for two townsmen, and three for one foreigner and one townsman.[3]

Leicester differed from Nottingham in owing a double allegiance. It was part of the Duchy of Lancaster, and therefore within the jurisdiction of the Chancellor of the Duchy. It also had its great Earl, the

---

1. Thomas Markham, gent., and John Bateman, gent. (cf. list of supplementary returns in P.R.O.). BROWNE WILLIS (iii, 65) has one name wrong. Cf. *Rutland MSS.* iv, 362–3.

2. *Rutland MSS.* i, 208.

3. STEVENSON and RAINER, *Nottingham Records*, iv, 278, 373; T. BAILEY, *Annals of Notts.* ii, 600.

Earl of Huntingdon, in whose family for most of the reign was lodged the stewardship of the borough. The Earl possessed a town house there — 'the Lord's Place' or 'the Great House' purchased in 1569; and not far away was Ashby-de-la-Zouch, the family seat. In its records the town has the appearance of a family borough: nor could it have been otherwise with a family that was great and active enough to dominate the county. Elizabethan Leicester owed much to the patronage and generous interest of the Hastings family, especially to the devout and altruistic third Earl, who, for example, gave six pounds yearly for seven years to provide fuel for the poor.[1]

Elections to parliament were made by the Mayor, aldermen, and councillors — the Twenty-four and the Forty-eight — assembled in Common Hall. The part played by their noble patron was rather wordily described in a Star Chamber bill at the end of Elizabeth's reign: 'Of their love to the Earls of Huntingdon' they 'have from time to time, for the better and more judicial direction of their choice of burgesses ... taken the advice of the same right honourable Earls, and conferred their election upon such persons as the Mayor and burgesses have by the aid of such advice thought good to choose.' It is by no means clear how often this description agreed with the practice in the first half of the reign: not often, one suspects.

When evidence first reaches us, in 1584, the Mayor and some of his 'brethren' or fellow-aldermen were obviously intending to act quite independently. As soon as they received news of the impending election, they decided to choose their Recorder — a Nottinghamshire gentleman and lawyer, who was also Recorder of Nottingham — along with a townsman. Meanwhile, would-be candidates were putting themselves forward, including Mr Tamworth, an embarrassment and a bore, in dealing with whom the Mayor invoked the aid of a certain Mr Dixon in a comedy of deceit: 'There is a gentleman, our neighbour, one Mr Tamworth, which hath married a kinswoman of mine, that is an earnest suitor to me to be one of our burgesses, and by no way can doff him off; so that I am fain to tell him we have chosen you to be one, and will not choose any other before we hear from you.' Also, there was a local gentleman, Thomas Johnson

---

1. Jas. Thompson, *Hist. of Leicester*, p. 256; *H.M.C. Rep.* VIII, i, 416–17, 430 ff.; Bateson, *Leicester Records*, vol. iii.

esquire, one of the Queen's Serjeants-at-Arms. To him the Mayor tactfully replied that his letter came too late: their choice was already made.[1]

So far there was nothing singular or difficult. But then came a double intervention to ruffle the arrangements. The Chancellor of the Duchy of Lancaster, Sir Ralph Sadler, wrote asking for the nomination of both members; to whom the Mayor replied that they were committed to the Recorder and a townsman, but if the former declined to serve they would be ready to grant one nomination. The final embarrassment was a letter from Sir George Hastings, brother and heir to the Earl of Huntingdon, on behalf of Serjeant Johnson, whose candidature they had already rejected. Luck came to their rescue, for their Recorder chose to sit for Nottingham, and by jettisoning their prospective townsman-member they were able to grant one seat to Sir Ralph Sadler and at the same time please Sir George Hastings by electing Serjeant Johnson.[2]

At the next election the Earl of Huntingdon himself asked for a nomination. Perhaps he had in mind to use the seat as an insurance lest his brother, Francis, should fail to secure re-election for the county. At any rate, when the gentry of the shire decided to follow the Privy Council's recommendation and re-elect their former members, the Earl was content that the same principle should be adopted by the borough.[3]

In 1593 the town was exposed to a serious menace from a new Chancellor of the Duchy, that aggressive seat-hunter Sir Thomas Heneage. Possibly he had turned up in the files of the Duchy a copy of Sir Ralph Sadler's 1584 letter, asking for both nominations, and was genuinely ignorant of what actually happened on that occasion. On the other hand, it would be in keeping with the man if he was relying on bluff and effrontery. Whatever the explanation, he wrote to the borough, in virtue of his office, asking them to leave 'the choice of both your burgesses to me as heretofore it hath been to my predecessors'. True, in order 'not to take any liberty of free election from

---

1. Star Chamber 5, A 54/2; BATESON, op. cit., iii, 208, 209, 210.

2. ibid. pp. 209–10; THOMPSON, op. cit., pp. 274, 275; H.M.C. Rep. VIII, i, 431.

3. BATESON, iii, 227, 228; THOMPSON, p. 277; NICHOLS, Leicestershire, I, ii, 404b.

you', he expressed his willingness to accept 'one of your own town'; but the tone of the letter was perilous in the extreme. Compliance would probably have meant permanent subjection to the Duchy. Fortunately, the Mayor, who had been one of the borough's M.P.s in 1572, saw the danger.

When the Common Hall met for the election, Heneage's letter was before them, as also were letters from two local gentlemen, including the irrepressible Mr Tamworth who had badgered the Mayor in 1584. Five or six of the aldermen were for compromising with Heneage, granting him one nomination. But the only sound strategy, as the Mayor and the majority perceived, was to elect two townsmen, thus erecting the safe fortress of the law between them and the Chancellor's wrath. They 'agreed to have no stranger', and elected the Mayor himself along with an alderman, the former to bear his own charges and the latter to be paid. After the election the Mayor wrote to the Chancellor declaring that the eight-year-old concession to Sir Ralph Sadler was unique and had been made because he nominated a Leicestershire gentleman, well-known to them. He informed Heneage that he had read his letter to the inhabitants, who, however, would have no stranger.[1]

By a firm stand the borough had rid itself of peril from one direction; but the more congenial power of the Hastings family remained to trouble them. In 1597 the new Earl of Huntingdon, Sir George Hastings, wished to nominate a Leicestershire gentleman, Thomas Beaumont. Someone – not the Mayor and not the Town Clerk – seems to have replied favourably to his letter. Very likely the body of aldermen did decide to choose his nominee; but when it came to the election, with the Forty-eight – the commoners – present, the company would not have Beaumont, since, as they said, he was 'an encloser himself and unlikely to redress that wrong in others'. Such a political judgement in Elizabethan elections was extremely rare. The electors chose their Recorder's son and the son of their former Mayor and representative in 1593. To the Earl it appeared a singularly vile affront, and naturally he suspected the Recorder of crossing him. In a letter to the Mayor he poured out his indignation. 'I write not this', he added, quite forgetful of his intervention in the 1584

---

1. BATESON, iii, 289–90; THOMPSON, p. 294; NICHOLS, I, ii, 407a; H.M.C. Rep. VIII, i, 432b.

election, 'in regard that I would be a placer of burgesses, for I never before writ to any [for] place for any.' In an explanatory reply, the Mayor did his best to placate his Lordship. The incident revealed that even an Earl of Huntingdon in his own borough could exceed the limits of his influence by backing an unpopular candidate.[1]

The smart remained. In 1601, anxious to avoid a second breach with the Earl, the Mayor wrote three or four weeks before the election to warn him that already 'complotters ... design beforehand the election of our burgesses'. 'Contrariety of factious heads and minds and voices hinder our good wills': in brief, trouble was brewing. Their 'good will' – the plan that the Mayor and his party had in mind – was, subject to the Earl's approval, to elect two particular men, one of whom was the Recorder's son, their member in 1597, now become 'the Queen's man'. In his reply, the Earl urged the Mayor to substitute a Mr Bromley,[2] a follower of the house of Huntingdon, for the Recorder's son; but he laid main stress on opposing an unofficial candidate, a Leicestershire gentleman, George Belgrave esquire. He hoped that all, from the best to the meanest, knowing his dislike of this man, would oppose his candidature; and he asked for the names of those who yielded to 'Belgrave's proud and saucy enterprise'. 'If ever you account of my love and friendship towards you and all your brethren', he added, displaying a rancour surely never present in his mild and pious brother, the third Earl, 'let Belgrave have no place, who, if chosen, I will [never] shake hands with the choosers.' In a later Star Chamber bill this gentleman, who was described as 'a noted enemy' to the Earl and 'a daily detractor' of his service as Lord Lieutenant of the county, was said to have made great and urgent suit to the Mayor and burgesses, seeking election for the sake of parliamentary privilege, that 'he might in the parliament time freely walk up and down without fear to be arrested by his creditors, being indeed greatly indebted to many'.

The majority of the electors – the independent commoners, one suspects – evidently favoured his candidature: 'they had given their voices and desired Mr Belgrave to undertake it'. But would they

1. BATESON, iii, 336–7; THOMPSON, pp. 300–1.
2. Presumably the Roger Bromley of Bagworth Park who wrote on the Earl's behalf in 1586 (cf. H.M.C. Rep. VIII, i, 431b).

openly defy their patron? That was the question. Belgrave tried to resolve the dilemma by writing a placatory letter to the Earl, offering to follow him – to become his dependant – 'in that sort as is fitting for a gentleman of his worth'. If, as seems likely, the letter is rightly placed at this stage of the story, it drew a reply but not reconciliation. Thereupon, Belgrave resorted to deceit. At the election he appeared before the Mayor and burgesses in the Huntingdon livery – a blue coat with the family cognizance, a bull's head, on the sleeve – and announced that he was the Earl's servant. Offering to confirm his pack of lies by a corporal oath, he told them that very late the night before, too late for the Earl to confirm it in writing, Sir Henry Harrington had procured his Lordship's support for him: and he 'much bemoaned his former undutiful carriage' towards his Lordship. The electors, who, as a Leicestershire member afterwards told the House of Commons, 'were both willing and worthy to be deceived', after a prudent show of doubtfulness, elected him, along with their own candidate – a Leicester boy turned prosperous London goldsmith.

Then the storm burst. In an endeavour to pacify the irate Earl and turn his wrath from the town to the imposter, the unhappy Mayor poured out the whole story of deception. Thereupon, the Earl induced the Attorney General to lodge a bill against Belgrave in the Star Chamber. In order to deprive the defendant of any benefit under an act of general pardon, it was filed during the sitting of parliament, thus creating a question of privilege and bringing the story before the House of Commons. The case was debated on several days, and members showed manifest sympathy with their colleague. 'If we should punish him for coming indirectly to this place', said one member, 'we should punish three parts of the House, for none ought to be chosen but those that be resident and sworn burgesses of the town.' In the end, they resolved that Belgrave had not abused the House, nor was he to be molested on any such imputation. By this formal 'act of the House', duly entered in their Journal, they drew one sting from the Star Chamber bill and hoped that the court would treat him lightly in consequence.[1] What became of the case, we do

---

1. Star Chamber 5, A 54/2; BATESON, iii, 435, 436; TOWNSHEND, *Historical Collections*, pp. 289, 295–6, 330; D'EWES, op. cit., p. 688a.

not know. Perhaps the Privy Council, after report from the borough, intervened to stop it.[1]

As the Leicester elections suggest, the county functioned as a social hinterland for the more important inland borough. Country gentlemen sometimes had town houses in the local metropolis, just as noblemen, courtiers, and wealthy gentlemen of wider outlook and interests had town houses in the national metropolis. Many interests and activities, economic, administrative, and social, took gentlemen to town, and if we had lists of borough freemen we should probably find that some of our members, though rightly classed as country gentlemen, were also burgesses and not so alien in the role of parliamentary burgess as might appear. The poet Michael Drayton's patron, Henry Goodere esquire, a typical country gentleman, who was Sheriff of Warwickshire in 1570, possessed a house in Much Park Street, Coventry – a city which with only two or three exceptions returned its own local citizens to parliament; and there, probably in 1571, the very year in which he represened Coventry in parliament, his younger daughter Anne, Drayton's 'sweet nymph of Anker', was born:

> Happy Much-Park ev'ry year,
> On the fourth of August there,
> Let thy maids from Flora's bowers ...
> Deck thee up ...[2]

Occasionally these boroughs might let in the foreign world through a High Steward or a Recorder, but their natural tendency was to be circumscribed by their own and the county boundaries.

Not so the ports; or, at least, the southern ports with their continental traffic and naval activity. These were more cosmopolitan. Strangers frequently passed through, and both Portsmouth and Southampton had impressive numbers of noblemen, courtiers, officials, and gentry on their burgess-rolls; distinguished visitors or

1. On 10 February 1602, Belgrave entered a demurrer to the bill, quoting the resolution of the Commons, and demurring to the jurisdiction of the Star Chamber. On 1 May 1602, the borough of Leicester sent the Privy Council an account of his conduct, presumably at the Council's request (cf. BATESON, iii, 448). Only the bill and demurrer are extant in Star Chamber documents, which may indicate that the case proceeded no further.
2. NEWDIGATE, *Michael Drayton and his Circle*, pp. 26, 41; T. W. WHITLEY, *Parliamentary Representation of Coventry* (Coventry, 1894) pp. 53 ff.

people having official or other relations with the port, to whom they granted the freedom of their borough.[1] They were in consequence more exposed and susceptible to the intrusion of outsiders into their parliamentary seats.

From 1559 to 1571 Portsmouth appears to have followed the policy of electing one local burgess and one outsider. Then began an association with the Radcliffe family, when Sir Henry Radcliffe – heir apparent to the earldom of Sussex and a Hampshire gentleman who represented his county in 1571 – was made Captain of the town and isle of Portsmouth. In 1572, perhaps because competition precluded him from seeking re-election for the county, he was chosen as one of Portsmouth's members. For its other seat the port elected a second outsider, one of the Queen's Gentlemen Pensioners, who was a friend and follower of the rising favourite, Sir Christopher Hatton. Since Hatton was made an honorary burgess of the town three years later, it is just possible that he was responsible for this nomination.[2] In any case, like the pettiest of boroughs Portsmouth left its parliamentary fortunes entirely in the hands of gentry. It did the same in 1584, by which date Sir Henry Radcliffe had succeeded to his earldom. One seat went to his nephew, the other to an intruder from the Court, Thomas Bodley, the scholar-diplomat. In 1586 the town returned to its earlier policy of one local member, to which it kept true for the rest of the reign. Probably it left the second seat to the nomination of the Earl of Sussex, who in 1590 became High Steward of the borough. When on his death Lord Mountjoy succeeded to the office, he in turn was granted a nomination in 1597.[3]

Southampton also declined from grace during the Elizabethan period. It opened the reign completely independent, choosing two aldermen in 1559 and an alderman along with the Recorder in 1563.[4] Then it began to let in an outsider: in 1571 the Captain of the Isle of Wight, who a few months before had been made an honorary bur-

1. R. EAST, *Portsmouth Records* (1884) pp. 337–8; *H.M.C. Rep.* XI, iii, 20–2.

2. ST JOHN BROOKS, *Sir Christopher Hatton*, p. 68; EAST, op. cit., p. 337.

3. EAST, op. cit., pp. 199, 205, 211–12.

4. Compare the names of M.P.s with the list of Mayors and Sheriffs in SPEED'S *Hist. of Southampton*, ed. Aubrey (Southampton Rec. Soc.), pp. 185 ff.

gess; in 1572 a prominent Hampshire gentleman, Sir Henry Wallop. Wallop possessed a house in the town and had been placed on the roll of burgesses in 1569; but the local connexion can scarcely have been a decisive principle, for when his absence in Ireland occasioned a by-election in 1581, the town replaced him by the Warwickshire squire and courtier, Fulke Greville. Perhaps Greville was the Earl of Leicester's nominee, for this Earl was given a nomination for the next parliament in 1584.[1] The Court connexion reappeared in 1586 when the Mayor and aldermen intended to elect one of the Clerks of the Privy Council, Thomas Wilkes, to whom they had granted the freedom of the borough six and a half years before. Very likely no patron was involved, and the borough merely wished to pay a compliment and save wages. Wilkes refused the nomination on the ground that the Queen was sending him on a mission to the Netherlands, though, oddly enough, he was re-elected for the Bishop of Winchester's borough of Downton in this parliament. When refusing the seat, he suggested substituting his brother-in-law; and at much the same time the London attorney or agent of the town wrote urging them, if they intended to elect 'a burgess that is no townsman', to choose his friend Sampson Lennard, a Kentish gentleman and inveterate 'carpet bagger'.[2] Both suggestions were ignored. Instead, they chose their Recorder along with one who was possibly a townsman. But the return to two local members was only momentary. In 1588 and 1593 they elected Wilkes, and in 1597 the famous Francis Bacon, a complete stranger, whose patron, or link with Southampton, quite eludes us.

A third southern port, Plymouth, must at least be granted excellent intentions. In 1570 its Council resolved that 'only such men as be town dwellers and of the Council of the town' should be chosen. In 1601 the qualification was extended to freemen, and in that year was observed.[3] Otherwise, their list of Elizabethan members never seems to accord with their good intentions, but includes Devonshire gentlemen and even rank outsiders. In 1584 and 1586 they elected the

---

1. J. S. DAVIES, *Hist. of Southampton*, p. 203; *H.M.C. Rep.* XI, iii, 20; D'EWES, op. cit., p. 308a.

2. R. C. ANDERSON, *Letters of the 15th & 16th Centuries* (Southampton. Rec. Soc.), pp. 98, 99.

3. R. N. WORTH, *Plymouth Records* (Plymouth, 1893), pp. 54, 60.

Lord Chancellor's son and heir, Henry Bromley esquire, a gentleman of Worcestershire and Shropshire, who was later to be knight of the shire for these two counties, and in 1588 they returned Miles Sandys esquire, a Buckinghamshire gentleman who was Clerk of the Crown. Someone must have nominated these two men. Bromley may have been sponsored by his father; Sandys probably owed his seat to the Earl of Leicester.

Turning from these pliable southern ports to the Norfolk port of Great Yarmouth, what a contrast! Here there was a succession of High Stewards, unsurpassed in their greatness: the Duke of Norfolk, the Earl of Leicester, Lord Burghley, the Earl of Essex, and the Armada hero, the Earl of Nottingham. One might have anticipated a tale of constant patronage. Understandably, there was a poor start under the princely Duke of Norfolk; but after his fall and execution, unlike most other boroughs, Great Yarmouth successfully withstood the trend of the times and consistently elected true townsmen, if in that category one includes their Under-Steward or Recorder. In 1583 they resolved that no one was to be elected who was not an alderman.[1]

The Suffolk port of Ipswich was more flexible. It was large enough, it was rich enough, to elect its own townsmen, and doubtless it would have preferred to do so. But it was a county town as well as a port, and being closely linked with the local gentry could not resist their appeal for seats. At the beginning of Elizabeth's reign, a local gentleman, Thomas Seckford esquire, heir to an estate at Great Bealings, not far from Ipswich, established a hold on one seat. He was made a freeman of the borough in 1559 at the time of his first election; but he was no stranger there, and after succeeding his father in 1575 built 'a very fair house' for himself in the town.[2] Probably Ipswich valued the association because he was one of the Masters of Requests, a Court appointment that gave him access to the Queen. One of the many contemporary stories about Queen Elizabeth – whether genuine or apocryphal, who can say? – records his ready wit when, after many vain efforts to secure audience and present the petitions or bills which it was his duty to bring before her, he came at last into her presence during a progress, wearing a new pair of boots. 'Fie, sloven!' said Elizabeth, who disliked the smell of new leather, 'thy new boots

1. C. J. PALMER, *Contin.*, *Manship's Hist. of Gt Yarmouth*, pp. 200, 320 ff.
2. NATH. BACON, *Annals of Ipswich*, p. 252; *D.N.B.*

stink.' 'Madam,' answered Seckford, 'it is not my new boots that stink, but it is the stale bills that I have kept so long.' Any borough would have been glad of a friend at Court in so privileged a position.[1]

Seckford represented Ipswich in 1559 and 1563. Then in 1571 he secured election as knight of the shire, but being unable, while only heir to the family estates, to sustain this high dignity, he returned to his Ipswich seat in the next parliament. His colleague in 1559 was a townsman, who was paid £31 4s. 0d. for his services – treble the statutory wage and a sure sign that economy was not the town's motive in choosing outsiders.[2] In 1563 the second member was another Suffolk gentleman, Edward Grimston esquire. He was re-elected in 1571, when he had a townsman for colleague, and again in 1572 when he and Seckford once more monopolized the representation. Seckford sat in no more parliaments, while Grimston moved to Eye in 1588, and in 1593 as 'Old Grimston' – the Nestor of his times – was member for the minor Suffolk borough of Orford. Meanwhile, Ipswich in 1584 adopted the principle of one Suffolk gentleman and one townsman, soaring high for its gentleman – Sir John Heigham, an ex-Sheriff of the county and son of a former Ipswich member who had been a Privy Councillor and Speaker of the House of Commons in Mary Tudor's reign. After this, for two parliaments the electors chose townsmen only.[3]

Their preference for local members, evident in 1586 and 1588, met with a set-back in 1593 when their new High Steward, Lord Hunsdon, secured a seat for one of his servants. But in December 1596, a few months after Hunsdon's death, they showed their dislike for the innovation in a resolution of the Bailiffs, portmen or aldermen, and common councillors, restricting election to resident freemen. No sooner was it passed than they realized that it was too rigid, and a new resolution laid down that none 'shall be chosen ... except some of the portmen, or such as are freemen of this town and inhabiting within the same, or such knights as be resident within this county of Suffolk'.[4]

1. Cf. my article, 'The Sayings of Queen Elizabeth', *History*, x, 223. The same story is told of Walter Haddon (cf. *D.N.B.*).

2. *Notes & Queries*, 2nd ser. iv, 275. One of the M.P.s in 1593, Zachariah Locke, was paid £5 (ibid.).

3. BACON, *Annals of Ipswich*, pp. 252, 264, 290, 294, 340, 355, 372.

4. ibid., p. 387.

Alas! they cannot have known the nature of their new High
Steward, the Earl of Essex, whom they had just chosen as Hunsdon's
successor. Nor did they foresee another consequence of that appointment. In choosing Essex they had rebuffed his political rival, Sir
Robert Cecil, who, with strange obtuseness, seeing that the borough
was selecting a successor to a most eminent peer, had written to them
urging the choice of a supporter of his, Michael Stanhope esquire of
Sudborne, Suffolk, a Groom of the Privy Chamber. It was characteristic of Essex to exploit any chance of patronage; and Ipswich did
not escape. In 1597 the Earl was granted a nomination and chose
Francis Bacon, who, on taking the freeman's oath, administered
to him in London, was duly elected. He probably preferred
Ipswich to Southampton, where he had been elected three weeks
before.[1]

For their other member in this parliament the town authorities
intended to elect Sir William Waldegrave, who as a Suffolk knight,
was, unlike Francis Bacon, eligible under their recent resolution. He
had written for the place, doubtless as an insurance against the risks
of the county election. When he was chosen first knight of the shire
a month before the Ipswich election, the authorities offered the seat
to Michael Stanhope, perhaps as a conciliatory if belated gesture to
the Cecil faction. Before the next election, Essex had died as a traitor,
Francis Bacon had gone over to the Cecilians, and Ipswich, consciously or unconsciously, reflected the political monopoly of the time,
and incidentally violated its own resolutions a second time, by re-
electing Stanhope and Bacon. Both were mere esquires, and Bacon
a rank outsider.[2]

At the other end of the scale from these large or middling boroughs,
which all exercised a measure of independence and elected a proportion of local townsmen, were boroughs so petty that neither finan-
cially nor socially could they do otherwise than return outsiders. The
small Suffolk borough of Dunwich has already been mentioned.
Here, from the borough of Aylesbury in Buckinghamshire, is an
election return which, though notorious for two and a half centuries,

1. BACON, *Annals of Ipswich*, pp. 384, 389, 390, 391; *Hatfield MSS.* vi,
332-3; *H.M.C. Rep.* IX, i, 255b.
2. BACON, op. cit., pp. 389, 390, 408; *H.M.C. Rep.* IX, i, 256a.

still retains its arresting qualities. It was made by a woman in 1572, shortly after her husband's death had left her lord of the borough.[1]

'To all Christian people to whom this present writing shall come. I, Dame Dorothy Packington, widow, late wife of Sir Thomas[2] Packington knight, lord and owner of the town of Aylesbury, sendeth greeting. Know ye, me, the said Dame Dorothy Packington, to have chosen, named, and appointed my trusty and well-beloved Thomas Lichfeld and George Burden esquires to be my burgesses of my said town of Aylesbury. And whatsoever the said Thomas and George, burgesses, shall do in the service of the Queen's Highness in that present parliament to be holden at Westminster the eighth day of May next ensuing the date hereof, I, the same Dame Dorothy Packington, do ratify and approve to be my own act, as fully and wholly as if I were or might be present there. In witness whereof, to these presents I have set my seal, the fourth day of May in the 14th year of the reign of our Sovereign Lady Elizabeth, by the grace of God of England, France, and Ireland Queen, Defender of the Faith, &c.'

Aylesbury had been granted a charter of incorporation, including a parliamentary clause, in January 1554, in consideration of its faithful adherence to Mary Tudor during the Duke of Northumberland's rebellion. Ostensibly, the charter was granted on the petition of 'the Queen's subjects of the town of Aylesbury', but who can doubt that its real deviser was Sir Thomas Packington? The borough sent its first representatives to parliament in April 1554. We know the names of its first Bailiff, aldermen, and capital burgesses – the leading townsmen – not one of whom ever sat in parliament. Indeed, it is obvious that from 1554 till the end of Elizabeth's reign Aylesbury always elected two outsiders.[3]

We need not hesitate to assume that the Packingtons invariably nominated both representatives. One of the borough's first two members was Thomas Smith, famous in his day as 'Customer Smith', being Customer of the port of London. He was a yeoman's son and London business man who in that expansive age attained to great

1. R. BRADY, *Historical Treatise of Cities & Boroughs* (1777), app. p. 50. The first edition of this work was in 1690.
2. Brady reads 'John' in error (cf. *Return of M.P.s*, i, 407 n.).
3. *Cal. Pat. Rolls, Ph. & Mary*, i, 45–7.

wealth and a fine estate in Kent. His younger son, continuing in the business, made a second fortune and became the first Governor of the East India Company, while in the elder line the grandson – 'young Tom Smith . . . a man of very near £5000 land' – married an Earl's daughter, a Sidney to boot, and was created a peer.[1] Customer Smith's two sons [2] and a relative by marriage [3] represented Aylesbury in 1584, 1586, and 1597 – all no doubt Packington nominees, as was the Thomas Lichfeld of Dame Dorothy's return, her son-in-law, who was member in 1571 as well as 1572, and Thomas Tasburgh, member in 1584, 1586, and 1597, who was her second husband.

Dame Dorothy died in 1577, but her son John – 'Lusty Packington', as he was called by Queen Elizabeth, who made a courtier of him and admired his athletic prowess [4] – carried on the family tradition. In 1586 and again in 1597 the Sheriff actually addressed his election precept to him and not to the Bailiff as the law enjoined, which suggests that in 1572 the precept may have been addressed to Dame Dorothy, thus furnishing an explanation of her extraordinary return. John Packington's returns were in his name 'and the community of the borough', the latter an empty form.[5] Altogether, Aylesbury is the perfect Elizabethan example of a pocket borough. Nor is its interest diminished by the fact that the Packingtons' chief estates were in another county, Worcestershire, where the family fulfilled their social role as Sheriff and Deputy-Lieutenant.

Our modern minds are prone to give a false notoriety to Dame Dorothy Packington. To contemporaries it was not the sex but the lordship of the borough that mattered. In fact, she was not the first woman to elect members of parliament, but had been anticipated by

1. *D.N.B.*; McClure, *Letters of John Chamberlain*, ii, 228.

2. John in 1584. Thomas in 1597. The *D.N.B.* identifies the 1597 member with Sir Thomas Smith, Master of Requests; but he was appointed Clerk of the Parliaments before the election, and could hardly have been a candidate. The association of Customer Smith's family with the seat virtually settles the question.

3. Thomas Scott of Scot's Hall, Kent, whose younger brother married Customer Smith's daughter. The Scotts were connected by marriage with the Sackvilles, from whom Customer Smith purchased Westenhanger, his Kent estate. Thomas Sackville was M.P. for Aylesbury in 1563. The Packingtons must have been connected in some way with this group.

4. *D.N.B.*

5. Brady, op. cit., app., p. 50; Browne Willis, op. cit., i, 128–30.

Dame Elizabeth Copley, widow of Sir Roger Copley, lord of the manor of Gatton.

Gatton, close to Reigate, Surrey, was to become one of the most scandalous rotten boroughs in our parliamentary history, whose fate in the Great Reform Bill of 1832 was certain. It was just as rotten, though not scandalous, in the sixteenth century; a mere village, or rather hamlet, which in 1621 was described as consisting of seven houses, all but one occupied by Copley tenants, none of whom was a freeholder.[1] Roger Copley became lord of the manor in Henry VIII's reign, and in 1539 it was noted that whoever had the parliamentary seats must take no wages, 'because there is but one house in the town to be any help to the same'. The election return for 1547, in which the word 'inhabitant' was used in a technical sense, declared that the members were elected by 'Sir Roger Copley knight, burgess and only inhabitant of the borough and town of Gatton'. A similar return had evidently been made in December 1541.[2]

Sir Roger died in 1549, and in February 1553, the son being a minor, the return was made in the name of Mrs Copley and all the inhabitants. Perhaps the same formula was used in September–October 1553 and March 1554, but all pretence was discarded in November 1554 and October 1555. On these two occasions the Sheriff addressed his precept to this lady, and she made the return in her own name. '... According to the tenor and effect of a warrant by the said Sheriff to her in that behalf addressed', runs the return of 1554, 'the said Dame Elizabeth Copley, after proclamation there duly made – an ironic formality! – hath chosen and elected William Wootton of Lincoln's Inn, gentleman, and Thomas Copley – her eldest son – of the Inner Temple, gentleman, to be burgesses for the said borough of Gatton.' The return was signed, 'By me, Elyzabeth Coppley'.[3]

In the following parliaments Thomas Copley, the new lord of Gatton, presumably made the elections and returned himself as one of the members in 1558, 1559,[4] and 1563. This young man was dis-

1. *Commons Journals*, i, 511–12; NOTESTEIN, *1621 Debates*, iv, 24.

2. *L. & P. Hen. VIII*, XIV, i, 645; *Return of M.P.s*, i, 376 n.; *Commons Journals*, i, 875.

3. *Cal. Pat. Rolls, Ed. VI*, v, 340; *V.C.H. Surrey*, iii, 198; *Commons Journals*, i, 875; *Return of M.P.s*, i, 391 n., 394 n.

4. No return survives for 1559. Browne Willis gives Thomas Copley; probably a guess, but probably right.

tantly related to Queen Elizabeth. In Mary Tudor's last parliament he shocked the Commons with 'unreverent words of the Queen's Majesty', saying that if a certain bill passed he feared the Queen might 'give away the Crown from the right inheritors'. It is difficult to see the ground for his fear, but the spell of imprisonment that followed his disloyal speech brought acknowledgement from Elizabeth on her accession, and in 1560 she stood godmother to his eldest son.[1] Unfortunately for Copley, he reverted to Catholicism in the new reign, and at the end of 1570, after the Rebellion of the North had tightened up the treatment of Catholics, he fled abroad. There he remained, a pensioner of Spain, pathetically anxious, as the years passed, to be regarded in his own country as a loyal Englishman, not a renegade, and in constant touch with Burghley and then with Walsingham, to both of whom he was related through their wives. He was one of the most eminent of the non-political exiles, a victim of conscience and of his times, and – if Charity interpret his story – a good Englishman at heart to the last. He died in exile in 1584.[2]

Who elected the members for Gatton in 1571 and 1572, we do not know. Since Copley had left the country and was staying abroad without licence, the revenues of his estates, according to an act of 1571, were sequestered by the Crown; but his wife, Catherine, remained in England until the Queen in 1574 generously licensed her to join her husband.[3] Perhaps it was she who chose the members; perhaps there was a farcical pretence of election by the inhabitants, directed by local magnates.[4]

When the next general election arrived, in November 1584, Copley was dead, but his widow and her eldest surviving son can hardly have got back to England. The heir was under age and therefore a royal ward. As Master of the Court of Wards, Lord Burghley wrote an extraordinary letter to the Sheriff, explained only, though fully,

1. *Commons Journals*, i, 50–1; *Cal. S.P. Dom. Add. 1580–1625*, p. 65; *D.N.B.*; *Surrey Arch. Coll.* xi, 157 ff.
2. KEMPE, *Loseley MSS.*, pp. 243–6; POLLEN, *English Catholics in the Reign of Queen Elizabeth*, p. 148; *Cal. S.P. Dom., 1547–80, 1581–90, Add. 1566–79, Add. 1580–1625*, passim; *Hatfield MSS.* ii, passim.
3. *Cal. S.P. Dom., Add. 1566–79*, p. 473.
4. Roland Maylard, M.P. in 1572, was Lord Howard of Effingham's servant and Clerk of the Peace for Surrey, which suggests the latter alternative (*H.M.C. Rep.* vii, 641, 652b).

by the unique circumstances of the case. The Sheriff, he wrote, had to return two representatives for Gatton, who heretofore, as 'there are no burgesses in the borough there to nominate them', had been nominated by Mr Copley. Since the heir and his lands were now under the jurisdiction of the Court of Wards, the Sheriff was to forbear making a return without direction from Burghley. In other words, Gatton was temporarily a pocket borough of the Court of Wards. The direction or nomination evidently followed within a few days, and included the name of Francis Bacon, though as he secured a more reputable seat at Melcombe Regis through the nomination of the Earl of Bedford – an early sign, maybe, of his readiness to sample the favours of rival patrons – Burghley afterwards wrote instructing the Sheriff to amend the return and appoint another person in his place.[1]

Catherine Copley and her son, William, returned to England, but were soon in trouble over their religion. In the aftermath of the Babington Plot a Catholic priest, a kinsman of the family, was captured at Gatton where the mother resided. In October 1586 William Copley was under restraint in a London alderman's house; and in the following summer the mother was in prison. Then, sometime during the next year or two William fled abroad, where, though he had 'more need of wit than a wife', he married. In January 1590 he was in Madrid, vowing that he would not return 'till England be converted, which I hope will be in three or four years'. He had become an avowed traitor, which his father never was. He returned to England on James I's accession, a chastened man.[2]

In the autumn of 1586, when a new parliament was summoned as a result of the Babington Plot, Catherine Copley, under the settlement of her husband's estates, had, as Sir Francis Walsingham wrote, 'the nomination of the two burgesses for the town of Gatton, being a parcel of her jointure'. And at this very time she had been caught harbouring a Catholic priest. It was a situation that justified government action. As Secretary, Walsingham wrote to the two Deputy-

---

1. Add. MS. 5702, fols. 86–7 (printed in MEREWEATHER and STEPHEN, op. cit., iii, 1648).

2. STRYPE, *Annals*, iv, 13; *Cal. S.P. Dom.*, *1581–90*, pp. 352, 365; *A.P.C.* xv, 179; *Cal. S.P. Dom.*, *Add. 1580–1625*, pp. 265, 298; *Surrey Arch. Coll.* xi, 174 ff.

Lieutenants and the Sheriff of Surrey. The Lords of the Privy Council, he announced, seeing that Mrs Copley was 'known to be evil affected', did not think it convenient that she should 'bear any sway in the choice' of Gatton's representatives. Consequently, their Lordships had thought good that the three recipients of the letter should recommend to the burghers William Waad, a Clerk of the Privy Council, and Nicholas Fuller, a counsel at law. Should the electors be unwilling to choose these two, care must be taken that discreet and well-affected persons be elected.[1]

It was a moderate letter in the circumstances. The final concession to the electors was a sop to local magnates. Nominally the election seems to have been made by 'the inhabitants' – presumably the tenants of six or seven cottages. In reality, Sir William More of Loseley and Sir Thomas Browne of Betchworth Castle, neighbouring squires and the two Deputy-Lieutenants, probably directed the election. They observed the general sense of their instructions, but ignored both recommendations. One of the new members was Burghley's nominee of 1584, no doubt chosen then, as he was re-elected now, because he was Sir Thomas Browne's relative. The other was Serjeant Puckering, the eminent lawyer, who had been Speaker in 1584 and was booked for re-election to this high office. Whether his villa at Kew in Surrey, or friendship with the Deputy-Lieutenants, or direct suggestion from Court, led to his choice, we know not.

For the rest of Elizabeth's reign, and afterwards until 1621, it seems fairly clear that the humble inhabitants of Gatton, on the Sheriff's precept directed to the equally humble constable – Shakespeare's 'Hugh Oatcake, sir, or George Seacoal; for they can write and read' – continued to elect the members.[2] They can only have been ciphers – a sort of Dogberry and Verges farce – doing as they were told by the Sheriff or, more probably, by neighbouring magnates. The members chosen include two members of the Browne family, John Herbert, Master of Requests and later Secretary, George Buck, an Esquire of the Body in the latter years of the reign and afterwards Master of the Revels, and Michael Hicks, the merry, influential secretary of Lord Burghley and bosom friend of Sir Robert Cecil. The Court flavour had no particular significance. Buck may have owed election and re-election to his patron, Lord Howard of

1. Kempe, *Loseley MSS.*, p. 242 n.   2. Cf. *Commons Journals*, i, 875.

Effingham, Lord Lieutenant of Surrey and its most eminent magnate.[1] The Cecils may have intervened for Michael Hicks, though, indeed, most people would have been glad to do him a favour, for his own favours, as witness his mounting wealth, had a high monetary value.[2]

We may conclude our story of Gatton with two reflections. If the recusancy and exile of its owners had not deflected its electoral history along very odd paths, this constituency would have continued a secure and peaceable pocket-borough like Aylesbury. But its singularity has some bearing on another point. Had the parliamentary system of the time really been corrupt in a monetary way, then those six or seven cottagers with their humble constable would have been in clover. Silence, of course, is no proof; but no one, looking at the list of Gatton's members and familiar with the Elizabethan social and electoral pattern, would believe that Gatton was 'corrupt'. Boroughs might be decayed, but seats were not bought in those days.

Another borough of some notoriety in our parliamentary history was Newton in Lancashire, described in its first return as 'the borough of Sir Thomas Langton, knight, baron of Newton within his fee of Makerfield'. It was one of three boroughs – Clitheroe, Newton, and Sudbury – all part of the Duchy of Lancaster, which first returned members to parliament in 1559. While Sudbury was a town of importance, Newton was an insignificant little place, hardly more than a village, and Clitheroe, according to a modern estimate, had a population of about six hundred and thirty. The conclusion seems irresistible that these boroughs were enfranchised through the mediation or action of the Chancellor of the Duchy, Sir Ambrose Cave, influential Privy Councillor and friend of Sir William Cecil. But that can only be half the story. The question, equally applicable to Clitheroe, still remains: why Newton? The initiative must surely have come from no one but the lord of the borough, Sir Thomas Langton. Unfortunately, evidence of this, or of friendship with Cave or Cecil, or of any other connexion with the Court completely eludes us. Oblivion has descended on the life of this knight.[3]

1. CHAMBERS, *Elizabethan Stage*, i, 98.
2. Cf. my Raleigh Lecture, *The Elizabethan Political Scene*.
3. *Return of M.P.s*, i, 400 n.; *Eng. Hist. Rev.* xxiii, 679; WEEKS, *Clitheroe in the 17th Century*, p. 6.

In 1594 a new Thomas Langton sold to his relatives, the Fleet-woods, 'the barony of Newton . . . and the nomination, election, and appointment of two burgesses of the parliament, which hath been used by the baron, lord, or owner of the said barony . . . with all other appurtenances belonging thereto'.[1] This description may have been true in all its implications in 1594, but from 1559 to 1572 it seems as if the members were suggested from the Court by the Chancellor of the Duchy. Probably, however, the baron of Newton made the appointments and the borough functioned as a proprietary borough.

Quite a number of boroughs were similar to Aylesbury, Gatton, and Newton – too small to do otherwise than return two gentlemen. But though some local family or families might have the disposal of a seat at any time, they were not pocket-boroughs in the thorough, blatant fashion of these three. They were evidently at liberty to grant their favours to other influential friends.

Heydon or Hedon in Yorkshire, 'restored' in 1547 in the first batch of Edward VI's new parliamentary boroughs, was such a place. There were two neighbouring families, the Constables and the Hild-yards, which obtained a privileged voice in the elections. Each ranked among the eminent families of the county, and filled the offices of Justice of the Peace, Sheriff, and member of the Council in the North.

Sir John Constable of Burton Constable and Halsham, the one a few miles to the north and the other a similar distance to the east of Heydon, was the most powerful man in Holderness; son of a Neville, married to a Neville, and brother-in-law of the sixth Earl of Westmorland. He sat for Heydon in the second parliament to which it sent representatives as a restored borough, and subsequently sat again on three or four, or possibly on five occasions,[2] in addition

1. *Eng. Hist. Rev.* xxiii, 680.
2. No returns survive for April 1554 and 1559. For the former parliament Browne Willis gives Constable's name with a query: that is, he guesses. In 1559 the Sheriff reported that there were no returns from Heydon, Thirsk, Ripon, Boroughbridge, Knaresborough, and Aldborough (BROWNE WILLIS, iii, 64); but since a return exists for Ripon (list of supplementary returns at P.R.O.), the others may be presumed to have made returns, either by-passing the Sheriff or being late. In that case, Constable may well have sat for Heydon.

to representing the county in 1555. His parliamentary service ended in 1566, perhaps as an indirect consequence of his removal from the Council in the North.[1] The cause of this disgrace was a feud with a rival faction on the Council; and it says much for his loyalty or his caution that in spite of such an inducement to discontent and in spite of his doubtfulness in religion, he kept clear of the Northern Rebellion, which left his noble brother-in-law a condemned traitor and exile. In due course his son and heir, Sir Henry Constable, was able to take up the parliamentary heritage. In 1584 Henry was elected for Heydon along with his Warwickshire relative, the famous Fulke Greville, whose mother was a Neville, aunt to Sir John Constable's wife. There can be little doubt that on this occasion both Heydon seats had been placed at his disposal. Sir Henry sat again for the borough in 1586, then for the county in 1588; after which, what with the stigma of a recusant wife and a recusant brother, and being under suspicion himself in the tense atmosphere of war, he did not re-enter parliament until 1604, when again he sat for Haydon.[2]

The second family, the Hildyards or Hilliards of Winestead, an estate little further away from Heydon than Halsham, did not rise to the honour of a county seat.[3] This was a measure of their inferiority to the Constables, just as their undisturbed membership of the Council in the North was a symptom of the stability which the lesser man could more easily attain. They did not enter parliament until 1563,[4] in which year and in the two subsequent parliaments of 1571 and 1572 Christopher Hildyard – who, incidentally, was Sir John Constable's brother-in-law – was one of Heydon's members. Although he continued active in local administration, remaining a member of the Council in the North from 1582 till his death in 1602,[5] his parliamentary ambitions seem to have been sated by three parliaments, covering six sessions. However, after an intermission of two parliaments, he brought the Heydon seat back into the family by securing the election of his nephew and heir, another Christopher Hildyard. Appropriately, this man's career was similar to his uncle's, except

1. *H.M.C. Longleat MSS.* ii, 19.

2. A. GOODER, *Parliamentary Representation of Yorkshire* (Yorks. Arch. Soc.), ii, 16, 33.

3. Cf. G. POULSON, *Hist. of Holderness*, ii, 467.

4. Of course, it is conceivable that Christopher sat for Heydon in 1559.

5. REID, *Council in the North*, p. 495.

that he developed a passion for parliament, and sat in every one save the Addled Parliament of 1614, from 1588 till his death in 1634. He moved only once from Heydon, when in 1621 he represented Beverley, close to the paternal estate of Routh.

CHAPTER 9

Borough Patrons

In the early seventeenth century Thomas Howard, Earl of Arundel, wrote to the Constable and inhabitants of Steyning, a small Sussex borough, informing them that a parliament was to be called: 'It were well if the old custom were duly observed, that every borough should elect members of their own body to undergo that service. But it hath been a usage of long continuance for most towns to make choice of such foreigners as were fit and worthy ... and herein to have recourse and respect unto the tender made to them of able men by their chief lords. And so my ancestors have done unto your predecessors.'[1]

His ancestors – the Dukes of Norfolk – had been longer at the game than he may have realized, for there is a list, compiled in 1464–5, of the towns 'in Sussex' – extending to Surrey – for which 'my Lord of Norfolk maketh burgesses of the parliament'. The towns mentioned were Lewes, Shoreham, Bramber, Reigate, Gatton, and Horsham. A later Duke of Norfolk, who in 1536 or 1539 was using his influence in many parts of the country on the King's behalf, gave 'the names of such towns as in times past I could have made burgesses of parliament of in the shire of Sussex', naming Horsham, Shoreham, Steyning, Lewes, and Gatton, 'where Sir Roger Copley dwelleth'. He was doubtful whether Reigate sent representatives – an odd, and maybe significant, display of ignorance: of course, it did.[2]

Still later, the ducal name crops up in connexion with Queen Elizabeth's first parliament – the parliament which finally severed the English Church from Rome. Writing in the early seventeenth century, William Camden in his *Annals* quotes catholic critics of this parliament as saying that the Duke of Norfolk and the Earl of Arundel 'had for their own turn or hope begged voices, as also

1. W. Albery, *Parliamentary History of Horsham*, p. 16.
2. Ryan and Redstone, *Timperley of Hintlesham*, p. 12; *L. & P. Hen. VIII*, x, no. 816.

Cecil had done by his cunning'. It is one of several statements which have been used to bolster up the contention that the Elizabethan Church settlement was enacted by a packed parliament. We need not tarry over this particular illusion: it has been subjected to detailed examination by a modern scholar and shown to be false.[1] All the same, there was a great deal of interference in borough elections in 1559, and still more in subsequent parliaments. The motive was not packing; it was patronage.

In the early part of Elizabeth's reign, nothing can have seemed more natural in Norfolk and Sussex than the pervasive influence of the Duke of Norfolk. He was England's sole duke, her greatest territorial magnate. 'I count myself', he said to the Queen, 'as good a prince at home in my bowling-alley at Norwich as she [Mary Queen of Scots] is, though she were in the midst of Scotland.'[2]

The Duke's home county of Norfolk possessed five parliamentary boroughs: Castle Rising, King's Lynn, Norwich, Thetford, and Great Yarmouth. He was High Steward both of King's Lynn and Great Yarmouth. At the former, as we know, he asked for and was given one of the two seats in 1559, nominating a dependant[3] who in 1555 had sat for Shoreham in Sussex and who in 1571 was to represent Thetford, always, we may assume, as his nominee. Again in 1563 there was an obvious nominee at King's Lynn. He was brother to the Duke's Chamberlain, and had sat for Shoreham in 1559.[4] At Great Yarmouth, the second Norfolk borough of which the Duke was High Steward, one of his servants, a man implicated later in the Ridolfi Plot, was a member in 1559, as he had been in Mary Tudor's last parliament.[5] In 1563 this man was transferred to the Sussex borough of Bramber, leaving the Yarmouth seat free for the Comptroller of the ducal household;[6] but in the following parliament he was back again at Yarmouth.

1. CAMDEN'S *Elizabeth* (1688), pp. 19–20; C. G. BAYNE, 'The First House of Commons of Q. Eliz.', *Eng. Hist. Rev.* xxiii, 455, 643.

2. MURDIN, *Burghley Papers*, p. 180.

3. Thomas Hogan esq. Cf. *Eng. Hist. Rev.* xxiii, 470; *Hatfield MSS.* i., 440.

4. Richard L'Estrange esq.

5. William Barker, gent. Cf. *Hatfield MSS.* i, 521 and passim.

6. Thomas Timperley esq., who also sat for Bramber in October 1553. Cf. RYAN and REDSTONE, op. cit., p. 32.

The tale continues with the other Norfolk boroughs. At Castle Rising one of the members from 1558 to 1571, the year of the Ridolfi Plot and the Duke's final downfall, was Sir Nicholas L'Estrange, Chamberlain of his household. Sir Nicholas had sat for King's Lynn in 1555; then, in 1558, his master, as High Steward of Cambridge, had tried to nominate him there, but, meeting with a refusal, recourse was had to the Castle Rising seat. At Thetford there may have been a nomination in 1559: certainly, one of the members in 1563[1] and both in 1571 were followers of the Duke. Finally, one of the members for Norwich, chosen at a by-election – probably in 1566 – and subsequently at the general election in 1571, was a dependant.[2] Thus, all the parliamentary boroughs of Norfolk were at least partially under the sway of their great lord. It may be that an actual nomination was not needed in every single instance, but who can doubt that the talisman of these servants and followers was their livery?

The Duke's influence is similarly evident in Sussex. Unfortunately we are handicapped by the loss of some returns for the parliament of 1559, but there was a fairly obvious nominee both at Bramber[3] and Shoreham.[4] In 1563 at least four of his servants were placed in this county – at Bramber, East Grinstead, Horsham, and Steyning,[5] while one of the members for Midhurst may have been a brother or relative of the member for East Grinstead.[6] In 1571 a member for Bramber, both members for Shoreham, and one for Steyning were connected with the Duke.[7]

The survey is necessarily incomplete, but none the less gives an excellent idea of the extension of territorial authority to borough elections. There is nothing sinister about it. So far as we can tell,

1. Edward Clere esq., who had sat for Thetford in 1558. Cf. *Hatfield MSS.* i, 439.

2. John Blennerhasset esq., also M.P. for Horsham, 1558. Cf. ibid., p. 527.

3. Robert Buxton, also M.P. for Horsham, 1563. Cf. *Commons Journals,* i, 58.

4. Richard L'Estrange.

5. William Barker, Laurence Banister (cf. *Hatfield MSS.* i, passim), Robert Buxton (cf. *Commons Journals,* i, 69), Robert Harris (cf. *Hatfield MSS.* i, 527, 549).

6. Edward Banister.

7. Robert Wiseman, William Dix, John Bowles, John Farnham. Cf. ibid., pp. 433, 435, 527; S.P. Dom. Eliz. 59, no. 5.

none of these boroughs was completely and persistently subject to the Duke's dictatorship; and, most interesting point of all, his nominees were not government men, but gentleman-servants and dependants. They did not even constitute a political party. If we had the evidence, we should almost certainly discover that they themselves asked for seats, and that in satisfying their wishes the Duke was merely carrying out the social obligations of his class. Other eminent Elizabethans did the same. The Archbishop of York, the Bishops of Winchester and Peterborough, a score and more of noblemen, statesmen such as Walsingham, Heneage, and Robert Cecil, and many minor gentlemen played this role of borough patron, some at a number of places, some at only one.

In the west country, where the Russell family had its origins, the second Earl of Bedford, a peer who for his charity and his puritan sympathies may be likened to the Earl of Huntingdon, exercised a territorial authority not dissimilar to that of the Duke of Norfolk. He was Lord Lieutenant of Devon, Cornwall, and the city of Exeter, and, at the end of his life, of Dorset.[1] In Devon he was lord of the manor of Tavistock, where the Portreeve, the returning officer, was his official. Both this borough's members were consistently 'foreigners' – his nominees. In making his nominations, the Earl, like many other magnates, employed the device known as a 'blank', by which the return was sent to the patron, complete except for the name of one or both members, which he then proceeded to insert, leaving clues for the historian both in the difference of handwriting and ink and in the inappropriate space usually left for the name.

The return for Tavistock in 1559 is lost, but in 1563, 1571, 1572, in a subsequent by-election, and finally in 1584 – the Earl died in 1585 – one of the members was a relative or connexion by marriage.[2] The second member in 1563 was Sir Nicholas Throckmorton, the prominent courtier and diplomat, who in 1559 had sat for Lyme Regis, another of the Earl's boroughs. Patron and nominee – for there can be little doubt of the relationship – were probably intimate friends. Both were of the 'hot-gospeller' type in religion. The same

1. G. SCOTT THOMSON, *Two Centuries of Family Hist.*; *Lords Lieutenants in 16th Century*, p. 48; *Foljambe MSS.*, p. 14.
2. J. J. ALEXANDER, 'Tavistock as a Parliamentary Borough', *Trans. Devon Assoc.* xlii, 258 ff.

religious affinity may explain the election of the second member in 1584, who was Valentine Knightley, son and heir of Sir Richard, whose Northamptonshire house, a little later in the reign, gave shelter to Puritans and their notorious Marprelate printing press. The Earl's hand may also be detected, again employing a 'blank', at Dartmouth, where his steward of the west, Hugh Vaughan – who entered parliament through a by-election at Bridport in 1581, replacing the Earl's eldest surviving son – became a member in 1584. Vaughan's subsequent election at Plymouth in 1586 and Tavistock in 1593, during the minority of the third Earl, was perhaps his own doing, though the Bedford prestige must have been decisive.

Among the Dorset boroughs, it is obvious that Bridport granted the Earl one nomination. The member in 1559 was his 'very faithful servant' William Page, whom he nominated as member for Oxford in 1563. In the second parliament of the reign, we need entertain no doubt about the diplomat John Hastings.[1] This gentleman in 1572 represented Poole, where the Earl also made nominations. He had been a Marian exile; another instance of a puritan link between patron and nominee. In 1571 Thomas Parry, son of the Queen's childhood servant and Comptroller of her Household, Sir Thomas Parry, was evidently the Earl's nominee; and once more we have the Court connexion, once more religious affinity. In the next parliament, that of 1572, the Earl's son was elected, to be replaced in 1581 by his steward. Then in 1584, the last election of the series, we find the active puritan physician, Dr Peter Turner,[2] returned for Bridport by means of a 'blank'.

At Lyme Regis, another Dorset borough, there can be little doubt that the Earl's influence was behind a succession of nominees with Court connexions: in 1559 Sir Nicholas Throckmorton, in 1563 Francis Walsingham, and in 1571 and 1572 John Ashley, Master of the Jewel House and another of the Queen's childhood servants. The Earl also nominated a member at Poole, and as his nominee in 1571 – a Puritan once more[3] – was elected for Dorchester in the

1. M.P. for Leicester 1559, Bridport 1563, Reading 1571, Poole 1572. Cf. *Foreign Cal. 1563*, p. 395; ibid., *1575–7*, passim; *Hatfield MSS.* ii, 126; *Cal. Pat. Rolls, Ph. & Mary*, iv, 299; *V.C.H. Dorset*, ii, 145.

2. Cf. KNAPPEN, *Tudor Puritanism*, p. 277.

3. George Carleton. Cf. HUTCHINS, *Dorset* (1861), i, 25; KNAPPEN, p. 264.

following year, we may assume that he also exercised some sway in the elections at this latter borough. The assumption gains weight from the appearance, as one of Dorchester's members in 1584, of Robert Beale, Walsingham's brother-in-law, a royal servant and a fervent Puritan. This clustering of courtiers, officials, and others with left-wing religious sympathies under the Earl's parliamentary patronage is a feature of very considerable interest. The Bedford influence made no small contribution to the strong puritan complexion of Elizabethan parliaments.

When we turn to Melcombe Regis, a borough which with the twin constituency of Weymouth provided seats for the merchant forbears of the Russells in the fifteenth century, we are blessed with direct evidence of the Earl's influence.[1] In 1559 he wrote to his 'loving friends', the Mayor and his brethren, thanking them for giving him the nomination of one of their members, at the same time naming a gentleman of Bridport for the place and releasing them from the payment of any wages.[2] In all likelihood he continued to extract one nomination at each election. In January 1576, on the death of a member – presumably his nominee – he asked to be allowed to name the substitute, suggesting that 'upon the return of your indenture, you will send the same ... with a blank for the name'.[3] The Earl's nominee on this occasion was one of Sir Francis Walsingham's secretaries, a keen Puritan.[4] Apparently this gentleman – as well he might, being so important a channel to Court favours – secured his own re-election in 1584 and 1586, thus leaving the Earl free in 1584 to nominate another person. He chose the incomparable Francis Bacon, who thus made his first entry into parliament, at the age of twenty-three. In the same year another noble patron appeared on the scene. This was the Earl of Pembroke, a dabbler in borough seats elsewhere, who had become Steward of Weymouth, and, from 1584 on, nominated one of its members, choosing in 1588 and 1593 his steward, Arthur Massinger, father of the dramatist.[5]

1. Cf. SCOTT THOMSON, *Two Centuries of Family History*.
2. *H.M.C. Rep.* v, 582a; H. J. MOULE, *Weymouth & Melcombe Regis Documents*, p. 128.
3. ibid., p. 97; *H.M.C. Rep.* v, 579b.
4. Lawrence Tomson. Cf. CONYERS READ's *Walsingham*, ii, 261.
5. MOULE, op. cit., pp. 22 n.3, 35, 39, 40, 48, 49.

The Earl of Bedford was not only a great territorial magnate. He was one of the outstanding personalities in the State and a very active man. Many aspirants for parliamentary seats must have sought his patronage, and there can be little doubt that his influence was even more extensive than our evidence reveals. During his brief period as High Steward of Oxford, as we have seen, he persuaded the city to depart from established practice and elect his servant, William Page, in 1563.[1] In 1571 and 1572 this gentleman sat for the Cornish borough of Saltash; and so we may surmise that the Earl's patronage extended also into Cornwall, as did his estates and his lord-lieutenancy.

Like the Duke of Norfolk, he suffered at least one rebuff. Though he was Lieutenant of the city of Exeter and maintained there a fine house, at which one of his daughters was born, the city authorities refused him a nomination in 1563. 'I thought,' he wrote bitterly, 'I had for my goodwill towards you somewhat better deserved than in so trifling a matter to have such a repulse.' 'If Mr Mallett do desire and obtain the place', he added, 'I shall be the better willing.' But even Mr Mallett was not elected. The city in 1554 had passed an act restricting election to resident citizens, but had not been averse to making Sir John Pollard a freeman in the following year, preparatory to electing him; nor did it show any repugnance to similar action in 1566. Yet on this occasion, in 1563, it refused to comply with its great Earl's wishes.[2]

This influential, kindly, and devout peer and statesman, one of the ornaments – in character but not in physical appearance – of Elizabeth's Court, died in July 1585: 'gone to his great master, the Devil', a Catholic was prompted to write.[3] Two or three hours before his death, his elder son and heir was slain in a foray on the Scottish border, and the earldom therefore descended to his grandson, a minor. The reign of the Russells in the west country was at an end. But before the memory of the great Earl dimmed, his son-in-law, the Earl of Warwick, Leicester's elder and more lovable brother, to whom the wardship of the new Earl of Bedford was granted, inter-

1. See above, p. 159.
2. *H.M.C. Exeter MSS.*, p. 43; J. J. ALEXANDER, 'Exeter M.P.s', *Trans. Devon Assoc.* lxi, 194 ff.
3. *Cal. S.P. Dom.*, *1581–90*, p. 261.

vened to prolong the family's parliamentary tradition. In September 1586, two Dorset gentlemen, acting as his intermediaries, forwarded a letter of his to the authorities of Poole, asking for the nomination of one of their members. The Earl of Warwick, they announced, 'hath written his like letters unto sundry other ports and privileged places of this county'. They hoped that out of respect for the young Earl of Bedford and the love borne them by his late grandfather, they would have 'no less consideration and due regard of my Lord of Warwick's request herein, who hath the wardship of the young Earl, than always heretofore you have had of your honourable good friend, the old Earl'.[1]

It is a curious happening, reminiscent of Burghley's intervention at Gatton in 1584.[2] Evidently, the Earl of Warwick made a similar request at Melcombe Regis,[3] which resulted in the re-election of Francis Bacon, and later in the substitution of his half-brother, Edward, when Francis preferred to sit for Taunton. Both these men had been Bedford nominees in 1584 — no doubt as a result of the close friendship, sealed by religious sympathy, between their father and the Earl. Pursuing this line of interpretation, we may guess that the Earl of Warwick solicited and obtained seats at Bridport, Dorchester, Poole, and Melcombe Regis simply to secure the re-election of his father-in-law's old nominees. It was an act of pious memory. The initiative may have come from the beneficiaries themselves; but we may surely regard the episode as a gesture of filial devotion by the Countess of Warwick, and as a demonstration of that sense of puritan brotherhood which was shared by her husband and which emerges so strikingly as a feature of the old Earl of Bedford's parliamentary patronage.

Though the Russell influence waned, west-country boroughs continued to elect outsiders. Who the patrons were, it is difficult to say. The lieutenancy held by the second Earl of Bedford was divided. In Devon and Exeter, his son-in-law, the Earl of Bath, was granted the office, but there is little evidence to indicate the extent of his interference in elections. At Barnstaple, where he had a special tie with

1. HUTCHINS, *Dorset*, i, 26. 2. See above, p. 179.
3. MOULE, pp. 35, 39, 40. I think the editor has misdated and obviously misread the 'draft letter to Mr Tomson' on p. 35. I assume the year to be 1586, not 1585.

the borough – it was only two miles from his house at Tawstock, and he became its Recorder in 1596 – he appointed one member at each election from 1586 on. His nominee in 1586 was his Devon agent and former tutor, who with two intermissions – in 1593 and 1601 – represented the borough from 1586 till 1611. In 1593 the agent's place was taken by 'a gentleman of my Lord of Bath', and in 1601 by a Devon lawyer. In this latter year, the lord of the borough, Robert Chichester, made a brief emergence from obscurity as the patron of the second member – also a Devon lawyer.

An incident in 1597, when the borough chose as its second member a man to whom the Earl took objection, showed how complete was this peer's dominance. It may well be that their unacceptable townsman belonged to a faction that was not sufficiently obsequious. Whatever the explanation, the borough dutifully held another election and chose a new member. As they told the Earl of Salisbury on the occasion of a collision in 1606, 'being poor men', they dared 'not withstand his lordship's command'. But their 'poverty', which induced dependence, was not in money or men. At the end of Mary Tudor's reign the borough had been electing two local burgesses – its Mayor and an ex-Mayor; and during most of Elizabeth's reign, it elected at least one townsman. What is more, it certainly paid wages to its local member in 1563–6, 1585, and 1589, and as late as 1640 paid the considerable sum of thirty-seven pounds to each of its two members.[1]

There were two other noble families with territorial interests in the west, the Paulets and the Blounts. At the beginning of her reign, Elizabeth entrusted the lord-lieutenancy of Dorset to James Blount, Lord Mountjoy, and by 1569 had associated with him Sir William Paulet, grandson of the Lord Treasurer, the Marquis of Winchester, that aged statesman born it appears in the year of Bosworth, who had served four sovereigns in office and survived all revolutions, being sprung, as he said, from the willow, not the oak. As for the old Marquis, he held the lieutenancy of Hampshire, of which county he had been Sheriff as long ago as 1512. James Blount died in 1581; and it was perhaps after this that the lord-lieutenancy of Dorset was

1. SCOTT THOMSON, *Lords Lieutenants*, p. 50; CHANTER and WAINWRIGHT, *Barnstaple Records*, ii, 103, 165–6; J. B. GRIBBLE, *Memorials of Barnstaple*, pp. 9, 14–16, 228; *Hatfield MSS.* xviii, 222.

added to the Earl of Bedford's other charges. On Bedford's death the office reverted to Sir William Paulet, now Marquis of Winchester.[1]

This nobleman, and the new Lord Mountjoy, were joint lords of a Cornish and a Devon borough, St Ives and Berealston, by descent through coheiresses.[2] At St Ives one of the seats was at their disposal, at any rate from 1584 on. Starting from this date there was a separate election return for each of the two members; and in 1584, 1588, and 1597 – the returns being missing for 1586 and 1593 – one member was specifically said to be returned 'with the consent' of the two lords.[3] By 1601 they had divided their inheritance, St Ives going to the Marquis of Winchester. At Berealston, which was only enfranchised in 1584, both members were included in a single return – the normal procedure; but the 1584 return stated quite plainly that they were elected 'at the request' of the two lords. The members were both 'foreigners', obviously their nominees;[4] and in 1586, 1593, and 1597 one member belonged to Lord Mountjoy's family.

Lord Mountjoy may or may not have enjoyed other parliamentary patronage. The Marquis of Winchester certainly did. This was in Dorset, though, significantly enough, it was only after the Earl of Bedford's death, when he reassumed the lieutenancy, that the opportunity for intervention seems to have come. In 1588 a Paulet was elected at Lyme Regis, while in 1593 one of the members was again his nominee.[5] Similarly at Bridport: in 1588 one member was a Paulet, and in 1593 one was a gentleman-servant of the Marquis.

Another noble family, comparable with the Russells for territorial greatness though not so happily situated for the number of parliamentary boroughs within their domain, was the Manners family, Earls of Rutland. Both the second Earl, who died in 1563, and the third, who died in 1587, were men of ability, as well as right mag-

---

1. Scott Thomson, pp. 48–50; *Foljambe MSS.*, p. 14.

2. J. J. Alexander, 'Bere Alston as a Parliamentary Borough', *Trans. Devon Assoc.* xli, 153 ff.

3. *Return of M.P.s*, i, 413, 422, 432. Note the different dates to the two returns. The *Return* omits a note about the consent of the Marquis of Winchester in 1601, which is in the original document.

4. ibid., i, 413 n.

5. G. Wanklyn, 'Lyme Regis Archives', in *Pulman's Weekly News*, 10 November 1931.

nificoes. Their influence extended into two counties, Nottingham-shire and Lincolnshire.

In the county of Nottingham there were two parliamentary boroughs, Nottingham and East Retford, the latter of which must have owed its enfranchisement in 1571 to the third Earl, who was its High Steward. His attempt to extend his patronage by securing the enfranchisement of Newark in 1579 failed.[1] The Rutland influence in the borough of Nottingham has already been described. With the exception of the parliament of 1571, it was exercised in every Eliza-bethan election until a minority in the earldom permitted the borough, from 1593 on, to enjoy the costly and, in the long run, undelectable privilege of freedom.[2] At East Retford, both members seem customarily to have been Rutland nominees. Certainly one, and sometimes both, are known to have had direct or indirect links with the Earl, and in 1586 the borough was ready enough to agree to his nomination of the two members.[3] Even after this powerful lord's death and during the minority that followed, the Rutland influence continued in the borough, for his devoted follower and relative, Sir George Chaworth, was made High Steward; and when his own health broke in 1590, this loyal knight wrote to the Bailiff and Steward advising them to choose the young Earl of Rutland as High Steward, should he die.[4]

In contrast, a Lincolnshire monopoly was out of the question, for two other powerful noblemen, both Privy Councillors, had territorial and electioneering interests in that county – the Lord High Admiral, Lord Clinton, who in 1572 was created Earl of Lincoln, and William Cecil, the great Lord Burghley. In 1569 Clinton was Lord Lieutenant of the county, and on his death in 1585 the Earl of Rutland, whose father had been Lieutenant in Edward VI's reign, was granted the office. In 1587, when Rutland died, the second Earl of Lincoln made suit for the lieutenancy; but Burghley objected strongly to the leader-ship of his 'native county' going to anyone other than himself, and such was his authority that he was given the office.[5] Thus each of these three families held the primacy of the county in turn.

1. See above, p. 139.   2. Above, p. 163.   3. Above, p. 145.
4. *Rutland MSS.* i, 280, 303.
5. *Cal. S.P. Dom., 1581-90*, p. 412; WRIGHT, *Queen Elizabeth & her Times*, ii, 338.

The Earls of Rutland possessed electoral influence in two of the county's five parliamentary boroughs – Lincoln and Grantham. At the former, there was no competition from Clinton or Cecil. The second Earl of Rutland was lord of the city, the fee-farm of which he sold to the citizens in 1559.[1] He began his intervention in the elections in 1553, prior to which the city seems customarily to have chosen two citizens: one of many indications that the surge of the gentry into the boroughs is largely a story of the second half of the century. Thereafter, he appears to have nominated one of the members more or less regularly. In 1555, 1559, and 1563 the nominee was his secretary.[2] When the next election came along in 1571, there was a new Earl, only just of age, and it is possible that the outside member in that parliament, Dr Thomas Wilson, Master of Requests, a Lincolnshire man, secured his own election and his re-election in 1572. However, in 1584 and 1586 the Rutland nominee was there again, without the shadow of a doubt. Then in 1587 came the third Earl's death, and a year later a long minority. The Rutland influence was in abeyance, leaving a vacuum that drew in the local gentry. In 1593 Sir Edward Dymock, a prominent Lincolnshire gentleman, whose mother was a Clinton and who at James I's coronation played the hereditary part of King's Champion, persuaded the city to elect his uncle, Charles Dymock, 'he having always showed himself very courteous to the citizens, and promising to attempt in parliament anything that may be beneficial to this corporation; and further, that he will not put the city to any charge for burgess-money.'[3]

At Grantham, both William Cecil and the Earl of Rutland were interested in the elections in Edward VI's reign. In February 1553 Cecil wrote to the borough authorities telling them of some service he had done them – the patron's side of the bargain – preparatory to asking for the nomination of their members at the forthcoming election. The authorities were grateful; 'As in all other your worthiness ye have won unto yourself an immortal fame, so in this ye have deserved a perpetual memory'. More to the point, they 'most gladly' granted him one nomination, adding that they had asked the Sheriff to repair to him for the name – that is, they had left a blank in their return. As for the second seat, they explained that before his letter reached them, they had already agreed, 'at the special suit of the

1. *H.M.C. Rep.* XIV, viii, 51.   2. ibid., pp. 47 ff.   3. ibid., p. 74.

Earl of Rutland', to re-elect their former member, Sir Edward Warner; 'from which agreement, made at the instance of so noble a man, we cannot with our honesties digress'.[1]

To what extent these two patrons of the borough nominated its Elizabethan members, it is not easy to say. The able, witty, and lovable diplomat, Thomas Randolph, was probably Cecil's nominee in 1559. In 1563 the two members, one of whom was Cecil's brother-in-law[2] and the other a Manners, proclaim their patrons. In 1571, here as elsewhere, the Rutland influence was in abeyance; but Cecil in this year placed another connexion by marriage[3] and may even have supported the second member, the egregious Arthur Hall who had been his ward; though as a Grantham man, stubborn, assertive, and neurotic, Hall probably steered his own fortunes.

For some unknown reason, Cecil seems to have refrained from intervention in 1584, and a new aspirant to patronage, the Earl of Lincoln, appeared. He and the Earl of Rutland both asked for seats. The Alderman and his brethren wrote to the latter, explaining that they had moved the electors to allow each Earl one nomination: 'The greater number of our commons, however, have given their voices to Mr Arthur Hall and Mr William Thorold, saying that they had promised them before the receipt of your letter. These two gentlemen', they added, 'are such as you may command in any lawful matter' – a comment certainly true about Thorold, for his family belonged to the Rutland *entourage*. The Earl of Rutland's request had arrived too late; and the writers assured him that 'hereafter you may command us all, if we hear from you before our voices be passed to others'.[4] They were as good as their word. At the next election in 1586, in compliance with his wish, they chose Sir Henry Bagenall.[5] What is more, the other member, a Nottinghamshire gentleman, belonged to the Rutland circle.[6] Lord Burghley's influence can be seen re-emerging in 1593, when one of his servants, who was also in

---

1. Lansdowne MS. 3. fol. 75: printed in MEREWEATHER and STEPHEN, *Boroughs*, ii, 1172–3.

2. William Cooke, gent. M.P. Stamford 1559, Grantham 1563.

3. William Killigrew, M.P. Grantham 1571, Helston 1572, Penryn 1584, Fowey 1593, Cornwall 1597, Liskeard 1604, Penryn 1614.

4. *Rutland MSS.* i, 170.   5. Above, pp. 143–4.

6. Robert Markham esq. M.P. Grantham 1586, Notts county 1588. Cf. *Rutland MSS.* i, passim.

the Queen's service, was elected.[1] The Rutland tradition was renewed in 1601 with the election of a Manners.

In the other Lincolnshire boroughs the Earls of Rutland had no electoral control. Cecil was, or rather became, the sole patron at Stamford; Grimsby was in Lord Clinton's sphere; at Boston both seem to have been active. Stamford was Cecil's paternal estate. He became lord of the borough, and he may have begun his parliamentary career – in which, as in all else he touched, his exceptional ability was manifest – as its member in 1543:[2] certainly this was his seat in 1547. At the next general election, in 1553, not needing the seat himself, he asked the borough to elect his father-in-law, Sir Anthony Cooke, Edward VI's scholarly tutor.[3] On this occasion, Lord Clinton, the Lord Admiral, also wrote for a nomination, apparently with Cecil's approval. There was no opposition to Cecil's nominee: 'all our company with a whole assent agreed ... without contradiction'. But for their other seat the burgesses had chosen the lawyer-son of one of themselves, a man, as it happened, attached to Lord Clinton's service, and they hoped that his Lordship would not take offence.[4] During Elizabeth's rein, the Cecils, with their authority so vastly enhanced, monopolized such patronage as there was at Stamford, frequently nominating both members, though occasionally only one.

At Grimsby, the Earls of Westmorland, as lords of the borough, had at one time nominated members of parliament; but on the eve of Elizabeth's reign we find prominent Lincolnshire gentlemen assuming this role. Then in 1559 Sir Robert Tyrwhit, who was one of the three men among whom the lieutenancy of the county was shared, and whose brother had sat for the borough in Mary's last parliament, passed on an earnest request for a seat from Lord Clinton, at the same time staying his brother's candidature in order to open the way for his Lordship's nominee. It was perhaps a sign of the new authority to which the Lord Admiral was attaining. Presumably he got his way. At any rate, when the next election came Clinton

1. Thomas Horseman esq. M.P. Grantham 1593, 1597, 1601, 1604 till death.

2. Our knowledge that he sat in 1543, aged twenty-two, comes from his diary (*Hatfield MSS.* v, 69).

3. For some unknown reason Sir Anthony withdrew, and his son was elected to the seat.

4. HAYNES, *Burghley Papers*, pp. 201–2.

wrote direct to the borough and was granted a nomination. He fared better than an obscure London lawyer who wrote offering himself and his services *gratis*, except – as he added in a greedy afterthought, sufficient in itself, apart from his obscurity, to damn him at this borough – 'you see cause freely to consider me with some small pleasure'. The Lord Admiral may or may not occasionally have nominated later members. At the end of Elizabeth's reign the family influence was certainly still there, for the heir to the then Earl of Lincoln, Lord Clinton and Saye, was member for Grimsby in 1601, and like the borough's other members signed a bond to save the community from all expenses.[1]

The story of the last Lincolnshire borough, Boston, is obscure. One of the members in 1559, 1563, and 1571 was Lord Clinton's surveyor of his estates in that county.[2] He had sat for the borough since April 1554, and, before that, for Stamford in 1545. He may have owed his elections to his master, or may have secured the seats for himself. Perhaps Cecil's hand may be seen in the election of the well-known courtier and statesman, Thomas Heneage, in 1563, and with far more assurance in the choice of Vincent Skinner, a servant of his and an Exchequer official, in 1584, 1586, and 1588. But Boston's electoral secrets elude us.

Burghley, of course, possessed influence in boroughs outside his native Lincolnshire. He succeeded Sir Nicholas Bacon as High Steward of St Albans in 1579, and the result can be seen in the election of his secretary, Henry Maynard, as one of the members in 1584 and in succeeding parliaments. He was also Steward of Westminster, where his son Robert, and his grandson Richard made their entries into parliament, and where the names of officials of his Court of Wards bear the Cecilian stamp. In 1563 he intervened at Peterborough to secure the re-election of his brother-in-law Robert Wingfield;[3] and doubtless he was active elsewhere. But, true to his characteristic qualities of restraint and decorum, he does not seem to have exploited his opportunities so thoroughly and shamelessly as some other borough-patrons.

As we have noticed, certain noblemen were High Stewards at one

1. *H.M.C. Rep.* XIV, viii, 250 ff., 279.   2. Leonard Irby esq.
3. S.P. Dom. Eliz. 26, no. 1. The borough concerned is Peterborough, not Stamford as the *Calendar* surmises.

borough or another; and it was by virtue of this position that they exercised a widespread influence in parliamentary elections, un-associated with their territorial power. Most boroughs, parliamentary and otherwise, had such an officer. It was the way to provide the community with a patron and protector, whose counsel and aid they could invoke whenever needed. The more influential their patron, the safer they felt. There were few boroughs which did not, from time to time, have interests to promote at Court, and if they were able to secure a courtier for Steward, who was in a position to under-take the promotion of their suits, so much the better. The point is aptly illustrated by the service that Sir Francis Walsingham rendered Colchester in 1584. True, he was Recorder, not High Steward; but, as the Bailiff later described the post to Sir Robert Cecil, it was that of 'patron or rather parent of this society'.[1] Walsingham took in hand their petition for a new grant of lands, held from the Crown. He spoke to the Queen and to Burghley about it, obtained the goodwill of the Chancellor of the Exchequer, and wrote to the Solicitor General instructing him to draw up the document ready for the Queen's signature. No wonder that in the same year the corporation, in their gratitude, resolved 'that Sir Francis Walsingham shall have the nomination of both the burgesses of the town for the parliament for time to come, according to his Honour's letters'.[2]

It seems that there was a growing though mild type of competition among magnates for High Stewardships. We should be guilty of a bad anachronism if we imagined that this had any connexion with electioneering: parliaments were not yet frequent enough, nor was the political atmosphere sufficiently modern for the prospect of parliamentary patronage to be a conscious inducement to seek the honour. More to the point, the office carried a fee: for example, £4 per annum at Nottingham, £5 at the much smaller borough of Dunwich, £6 13s. 4d. – ten marks – at Salisbury, £10 at wealthier boroughs such as Ipswich and Plymouth.[3] In the budgets of such

1. *Hatfield MSS.* ix, 163, 395.
2. *Egerton Papers*, ed. Payne Collier (Camden Soc.), p. 102; MERE-WEATHER and STEPHEN, ii, 1346.
3. STEVENSON, *Records of Nottingham*, iv, 200; *H.M.C. Var. Coll.* vii, 82; HOARE's *Wiltshire*, iv, 305; BACON, *Annals of Ipswich*, p. 384; *H.M.C. Rep.* X, iv, 540.

sumptuous livers as the Earl of Leicester and the Earl of Essex, or even of less dazzling courtiers, they were petty items; but these men, like lawyers, were inured to the art of picking up trifles, and were neither the first nor the last to know that a pound is made up of pence. The Earl of Leicester's fees from stewardships, and still more the fees of the Earl of Essex, must have totalled a respectable sum in a year, and it is unlikely that these grandees scorned them: certainly, they accepted them.

Yet it was not even the fee; it was the prestige and sense of power that rendered the office attractive. The same social urge that prompted a lord to scatter his livery abroad and extend his personality in a host of followers, and the same quality of convention that made a peer's funeral procession approximate to a king's – a fantastic spectacle, occasionally as ruinous as modern death duties – caused magnates to be as ready to accept as boroughs were to offer the office; and the same rivalry in the outward show of power, which was apparent in the competition for followers, keeping Elizabethan society ever tense, manifested itself over this particular honour. In January 1572, when the Duke of Norfolk was condemned as a traitor and in consequence King's Lynn lost its High Steward, two of its leading townsmen were sent to London to consult their Recorder, the eminent lawyer Robert Bell, as to whether they should choose a new High Steward, and whom he would recommend, Leicester or Burghley. Bell must have preferred the Earl of Leicester: at least, it was he whom King's Lynn chose.[1] It was a significant decision. Though Burghley was not a promoter of faction, and though faction had been momentarily stilled in the presence of treason, these two were the great rival party-leaders in the State; and one can well believe that if Burghley knew of the deliberate preference of King's Lynn for Leicester, he was conscious of defeat.

A list of High Stewards would not be easy to compile: available information is scant. But there can be little doubt that the Earl of Leicester far excelled anyone else in such honours during his lifetime, as did Robert, Earl of Essex, afterwards. Boroughs were prone to judge by external show. They hitched their fortunes to the leading favourite rather than the leading statesmen. And how natural! On Norfolk's fall, the Earl of Leicester succeeded to his High Steward-

1. *Archaeologia*, xxiv, 325; *H.M.C. Rep.* XI, iii, 175.

ship at Great Yarmouth as well as King's Lynn. He was also High Steward at Andover, Bristol, Reading, and Wallingford, and Steward at Abingdon and New Windsor. At Maldon in Essex he was Recorder.[1]

Curiously enough, Leicester did not have much success as a patron of elections in these particular boroughs. In 1572, after the Duke of Norfolk's fall and perhaps while the Stewardship was vacant, Great Yarmouth went local in its choice of members; but when one of these representatives died, his place was taken at a by-election in 1576 by Edward Bacon, son of the late Lord Keeper. If, as is not unlikely, he owed his seat to the Earl of Leicester, then we must attach a good deal of significance to the borough's resolution in 1583 that no one should be elected to represent Great Yarmouth who was not an alderman.[2] Certainly, the borough thereafter maintained its independence. At King's Lynn, John Peyton esquire, who was chosen to represent the borough at a by-election in 1580, was connected with the Sidneys and Leicester; but as he was also the son-in-law of the Recorder, Robert Bell, whose place he was taking in parliament, and as the Earl clearly obtained no other nominees in later parliaments, the odds are that the High Stewardship of this borough brought no parliamentary patronage. The same is possibly true of Reading, where members of his wife's family, the Knollys family, which was very influential in the vicinity, persistently sat for the borough. There was also a rival patron at Maldon – a political opponent, the Earl of Sussex. In 1584 the Earl of Leicester asked the borough authorities for a nomination, perhaps hoping to take advantage of the recent death of the powerful third Earl of Sussex. Without waiting for a reply, but understanding – so, at least, he said – that they were willing to grant him one seat, he wrote again, nominating his servant, Richard Brown, an Essex man. But he counted his chickens before they were hatched, for Maldon elected as its one outsider a puritan gentleman who was probably the nominee of the new Earl of Sussex, thus forcing Leicester to find an alternative seat for his servant Brown at Lichfield.[3] Windsor was perhaps an

1. *Biographia Britannica* (1750), iii, 1787–8 n.; A. B. BEAVEN, *Bristol Lists*, p. 231.
2. C. J. PALMER, *Contin., Manship's History of Great Yarmouth*, p. 200.
3. *Essex Review*, vol. xv, 1906.

equally fruitless borough, for though it mostly returned outsiders, they appear to have had no association with Leicester.

In contrast, Abingdon, a single-member constituency, was probably at his beck and call. In 1571 and 1572 the member was Anthony Forster, owner of Cumnor Place, where Amy Robsart met her mysterious death, and unfortunate victim of the legend that grew round that tragedy. Cumnor Place was only three miles from Abingdon, and Forster, as a neighbouring squire, may well have secured his own election; but even if there was no formal nomination, the name of his patron must have been a guarantee of success. Leicester appears to have resigned this High Stewardship to Lord Norris about 1580, and so lost the nomination. As for Andover, it sent representatives to parliament only once in Leicester's lifetime – in 1586; and as he was abroad in the Netherlands at the time, he missed placing anyone here.

If this were the whole story of Leicester's parliamentary patronage, it would accord ill with the nature of the man and with his heavy-handed intervention at his borough of Denbigh in 1572.[1] Fortunately there are sufficient rifts in the clouds to obtain a better impression of what this supreme patron of high Elizabethan days was doing. In 1584 he asked for and was granted a seat at Poole, Dorset. The man he nominated, who was secretary to Sir Francis Walsingham, a close friend of Leicester's at this time, was elected as the Earl of Bedford's nominee at Melcombe Regis, but another of Walsingham's secretaries was chosen as a substitute.[2] He also nominated one of the members at Southampton.[3] In his own territorial area, he nominated one of the members at Tamworth,[4] and was in all likelihood responsible for the election of two servants of his, one at Coventry and the other at Lichfield.[5] The member at Denbigh may also be placed to his credit. This gives him a total of seven nominations in the parliament of 1584. There must have been more; many more, one imagines. He asked for a seat at Gloucester, but was refused it.[6] Doubtless he asked elsewhere with better success. Unlike the great territorial magnates, he was promiscuous.

1. See above, p. 146.   2. HUTCHINS, *Dorset*, i, 25.
3. Thomas Digges, M.P. Wallingford 1572, Southampton 1584. Cf. DAVIES, *Hist. of Southampton*, p. 203 n. 9.
4. Add. MS. 28175, fol. 51.   5. Edward Boughton, Richard Brown.
6. Below, p. 263.

CHAPTER 10

Borough Patrons:
The Cinque Ports and the Duchy of Lancaster

As the practice of parliamentary patronage developed, it was only natural that certain royal officials, who exercised a peculiar authority in a number of boroughs, should exploit their opportunities. Two of these officials were the Lord Warden of the Cinque Ports and the Chancellor of the Duchy of Lancaster. There must have also been some degree of influence wielded in the Duchy of Cornwall, where an extraordinary cluster of parliamentary boroughs, most of them enfranchised in the sixteenth century, returned nominees as a matter of course, many being too small to do otherwise. An appreciable number of their representatives were obviously nominated, directly or indirectly, from London. It is equally obvious that others obtained their seats through the local gentry. Unfortunately, Cornwall's story remains obscure. All we can say is that it was no more sinister – if this word has any place at all in Elizabethan electoral history – than the corresponding stories of the Cinque Ports and the Duchy of Lancaster.

The Cinque Ports, seven in number though five in name, 'do lie towards France', as Sir Edward Coke wrote, 'and therefore prudent antiquity provided that they should be vigilantly and securely kept'.[1] They enjoyed extensive franchises, with courts and an organization of their own, and were under the jurisdiction of a special governor, the Lord Warden or Keeper of the Cinque Ports, whose administration was centred at Dover Castle, of which he was the Constable. The Warden, says Coke, 'in former times was ever a man of great fidelity, wisdom, courage, and experience, for that he had the charge of the principal gates of the Realm'. Among his powers were those of a Sheriff. All royal writs were delivered, executed, and returned through him, the Ports being exempt from county jurisdiction. Con-

1. *Fourth Institute* (1669), pp. 222–4.

sequently, it was to the Warden that the writs for parliamentary elections were directed, and *via* him that the returns were made – a strategic position that invited intervention, when this practice crept into elections. The seven Ports, citing them from east to west, were Sandwich, Dover, Hythe, New Romney, Rye, Winchelsea, and Hastings. Each sent two members, known as barons, to parliament.

At Elizabeth's accession, the Lord Warden was Sir Thomas Cheyne who was also Treasurer of the Household, in which capacities he had served Henry VIII, Edward VI, and Mary Tudor. He was retained in his offices, but died within two months, when the wardenship was granted to William Brooke, tenth Lord Cobham, who with his two brothers had taken part in Wyatt's Rebellion in February 1554.[1] The family had demonstrated both its protestantism and its partiality to Elizabeth in this rash venture; and the Queen was not one to forget past services. Cobham was also made Lord Lieutenant of Kent, which with his wardenship made him the unrivalled head of that county. Apart from a momentary cloud during the intrigues of the Duke of Norfolk with Mary Queen of Scots, he grew in favour at Court. Early in 1586 he was made a Privy Councillor, and finally in 1596 succeeded the Queen's cousin in the great Court office of Lord Chamberlain – a magnificent climax to his career, which, however, he was left little time to enjoy, for he died in March 1597.

His death came at the high season of faction at Elizabeth's Court. The young Earl of Essex was at the summit of his glory after the astounding victory at Cadiz, and in his intemperate way was prepared to brook no opposition to his will. The vacant wardenship of the Cinque Ports at once became the object of a bitter struggle between him and the Cecils. There were two aspirants to the office. The one was Henry Brooke, the new Lord Cobham, bound to the Cecils by the great friendship of his father with Lord Burghley and the marriage of his sister to Sir Robert Cecil. The other was Sir Robert Sidney of Penshurst, the famous Philip's younger brother, now head of the family, and a friend and follower of the Earl of Essex, to whom he was attached by intimate ties. Essex had tried to obtain for him the lord chamberlainship against Cobham's father in 1596 – an in-

---

1. *A.P.C.* vii, 37; *Chronicle of Queen Jane & Queen Mary* (Camden Soc.), p. 62; *G.E.C.* iii, 348.

sensate proposal. He now set heart, mind, and temper on procuring for his protégé the minor post of Lord Warden. Thus the honour of the nation's two outstanding party-leaders was engaged. Equally engaged was the honour of their clients, for there was far more at stake than an office. The wardenship virtually carried with it the lord-lieutenancy and the primacy of their native county, Kent.

After twice urging Sidney's suit on the Queen and being told flatly that she would not give way nor so wrong the new Lord Cobham as to confer the office on his social inferior, Essex, in his matchless folly, persisted with his advocacy, vowing to stand for the wardenship himself and later resign it to Sir Robert. At a meeting with his fellow-Councillors in Lord Burghley's chamber, he declared that he hated Cobham for his 'villainous dealing and abusing' of him, and that he would have right cause to think himself little regarded by the Queen if she conferred the office on this man. How monstrous of him to make so public and embittered a faction-issue of his sovereign's action; to face her with the alternative of humiliation or of seeming to give a partisan decision! But his 'violent courses' merely had the effect of causing the Queen's intellect to confirm her instincts of loyalty to the memory of a faithful old servant. She appointed the new Lord Cobham as Lord Warden, and later made him Lord Lieutenant of Kent.[1] Alas! He did not possess his father's qualities, and when Elizabeth died he became involved in the so-called Main Plot, was convicted of treason, and dragged out a miserable, pitiful life in the Tower.

Thus, for most of Elizabeth's reign the Cinque Ports were under the authority of the powerful tenth Lord Cobham. Already, before 1559, Sir Thomas Cheyne had exercised a degree of parliamentary patronage in some of the Ports. For example, members of his family were elected at Winchelsea in November 1554 and at Dover and Rye in January 1558, while his son-in-law, the notorious Sir John Perrot of Pembrokeshire, sat for Sandwich in October 1555. No doubt he nominated others during his period of rule, though his activities were probably on a modest scale, spasmodic and casual, indistinguishable from those of other magnates and lords of boroughs.

The first election of Elizabeth's reign took place a week or two

---

1. *H.M.C. De L'Isle & Dudley MSS.* ii, passim; COLLINS, *Sidney Papers*, ii, 26, 75.

after Sir Thomas Cheyne's death, and, with no lord to dictate their choice, at least five of the Ports elected local men. Winchelsea, already half a mile from the sea, hopelessly decayed, and perhaps intent on saving wages, chose a Kent genteman along with one of its jurats or aldermen, though as this person appears to have possessed property in the town, Winchelsea may perhaps be grouped with the five other Ports. We are left with Hastings, which may or may not have chosen one outsider. Lord Cobham's first election came in 1563. He was clearly feeling his way. He probably nominated one member at Hastings, Hythe, and New Romney,[1] and may or may not have nominated one at Rye and Winchelsea.

It was at the next election, in 1571, that trouble started. Since 1555 Sandwich had been regularly electing its Recorder, Roger Manwood, a distinguished townsman of outstanding ability and charm, who later rose to high legal rank as Chief Baron of the Exchequer and was a munificent benefactor of his native town and county, though his good name was to be besmirched at Court by corrupt practices, shocking both to the Queen and to Burghley. This lawyer, who also held the office of Solicitor to the Cinque Ports, wrote to the borough before the 1571 election, urging them to choose his brother, John Manwood. He understood that the Lord Warden would also nominate him; but, discovering afterwards that the Warden preferred someone else, he dutifully withdrew the proposal. Manwood might cringe; the portmen of Sandwich would not. They refused Lord Cobham's nominee. In 'all Sir Thomas Cheyne's time and in all your Lordship's time also', they wrote, 'we have had both or one at the least of our own inhabitants, according to the Queen's writ and our liberties; and by our customs and liberties, always used, one at the least must be such as was sworn to our liberties'. Since Roger Manwood, who was accustomed to be one of their representatives, was not a resident, the other, they added, must be one of their freemen. They elected Manwood along with his brother John.[2]

Hythe, too, was subjected to a good deal of pressure at this election; and very embarrassing it proved. At the forthcoming parliament they were in need of all the goodwill they could muster, since, as they

1. Sir William Daunsell, Receiver General of the Court of Wards; Edward Pelham; Sir Christopher Alleyn of Ightham.
2. MURRAY, *Constitutional History of the Cinque Ports*, pp. 95 ff.

said, 'we mean to be suitors in the behalf of the poor estate of this town, our poor Port'; and bitter experience had shown that in such circumstances it was dangerous to have strangers as members. 'We have great cause by a foreign burgess to be careful what burgesses we take for our Ports, for at the last parliament we had not a worse enemy than one of our own burgesses, being no portman.' The offender must have been Edward Popham, who in all probability had been the Lord Warden's nominee.

Someone unnamed – 'a good portman', a friend, a lawyer, and a prospective M.P., qualifications that would suit Roger Manwood – whose aid they required to support their bill in parliament, sent a message asking them to elect Mr John Hales,[1] a Kent gentleman, or Mr Robert Honywood. On top of this came a letter from the Lord Warden earnestly pressing them to choose Mr William Cromer, also of Kent. And as if these were not enough, another gentleman of Kent made suit for himself – Mr Keys, the giant Serjeant-Porter at Court, who as a middle-aged widower with children had infuriated the Queen and convulsed the Court in 1565 by marrying the diminutive, 'crookbacked and very ugly' young maid of honour,[2] Lady Mary Grey, with her perilous dowry of Tudor blood, a potential claim to the royal succession, and very little sense.

What were the perplexed townsmen to do? Make enemies they dared not, and yet they had to have one local M.P. They wrote to their Lord Warden granting him one nomination from among their four gentlemen-suppliants – a friendly gesture to everyone, as they fondly hoped. Back came a sharp letter from the Warden's Lieutenant of Dover Castle, conveying his master's strong disapproval. As a way of diminishing his Lordship's annoyance, he urged them not only to elect his nominee Mr Cromer, but to choose as their second member a Mr John Rede, thus adding a fifth name and claiming both seats for the Warden! This, however, was going altogether too far. They did elect Mr Cromer, but along with him one of their townsmen; and in a humble apology, they wrote to their Lord Warden: 'We may not deny your Lordship any reasonable request, and our

1. The name has been read as 'Jeames Hales' and 'John Heles'. I assume that he was John Hales, nephew and heir of the author of the *Common Weal of England* (cf. C. H. GARRETT, *Marian Exiles*, p. 174).
2. *Spanish Cal. Eliz.* i, 468.

full meaning was at the beginning that your Lordship should have the nominating of one of them.' Their late member, they told him, had been a 'great enemy to the Port'; Mr Cromer they hoped would be their friend. Whether he was or not, they failed to get their bill through the parliament, owing, no doubt, to the congestion of business.[1]

Lord Cobham was presumably active in other Ports during this general election. Dover chose an official of Dover Castle, New Romney a Kentish gentleman, and Rye an Exchequer official, a 'carpet-bagger' from Derbyshire, probably all of them his nominees.[2] Hastings chose two local men, as perhaps did Winchelsea, though we may be pretty sure that this poverty-stricken town paid no wages.

In 1572, the Warden's influence was, if anything, less. Winchelsea chose a Dover Castle official,[3] along with its Mayor, but Rye, New Romney, and possibly Hythe went entirely local.

As yet there had been no claim to a prescriptive right to one nomination at each Port. But it was near, and the Ports were evidently conscious of the danger. Strength lay in unity. At a Brodhull or Brotherhood assembly of all the Ports in the summer of 1572, after the end of the parliamentary session, it was decreed that none but resident freemen, or those of counsel with the Ports and receiving a fee from them – Roger Manwood, for instance – should be elected as their representatives. The practice of choosing 'persons ignorant of the privileges of the Ports', it was declared, had led to their liberties being weakened by acts of parliaments which did not contain a proviso protecting those liberties. Two years later there was a riposte from the Lord Warden, when in a draft agreement between himself and the Ports he inserted a clause recognizing the right of the Warden to nominate one parliamentary burgess in each Port. It was a significant, one might say a threatening, move. But the clause was omitted from the final agreement. The Ports had evidently stood upon the law – 'the only fortress of the inferior sort of people', as our 1571 member of parliament so truly said.[4]

1. G. WILKS, *Parliamentary Repres. of Hythe*, pp. 52–4; *H.M.C. Rep.* ii, 91–2.

2. John Pinchneyl (cf. J. B. JONES, *Annals of Dover*, pp. 378–9); Edmund Morrante; Thomas Fanshaw.

3. Richard Barry.

4. MURRAY, op. cit., p. 97; WILKS, op. cit., pp. 58, 61.

The Lord Warden had failed to gain his principle, but he retained his persuasive authority. In the next election of 1584 – a time of national alarm, of the Throckmorton Plot, of William the Silent's assassination, and of the Bond of Association – his authority received a casual fillip from a Privy Council letter instructing him to deal with all the Cinque Ports and exhort them to choose loyal and responsible representatives. If they would permit him to nominate their members, well and good; but he was to choose his own course – whether nomination or advice – as should seem best to him 'and shall stand with the liking of the said boroughs'.[1]

So far as Hythe was concerned, Lord Cobham fulfilled his instructions by talking to the Mayor and a jurat. They probably arranged for one nomination to be left to him, and subsequently he sent on the name of Thomas Bodley, the scholar-diplomat, as recommended from the Court.[2] Taken out of its historical setting, the entry of Bodley's election in the town's Assembly Book, with its use of the word 'elected' in a non-technical sense, might be most misleading. Bodley, it declared, 'is elected to be one of the said burgesses by the Lords of her Majesty's Privy Council, and also preferred unto us by the Lord Warden as a man very meet for the same'. Hythe's other member was the Mayor, a gentleman of note, whom they paid at the generous rate of four shillings a day, plus travelling expenses.[3] In this election, Dover elected the Lieutenant of Dover Castle, the Warden's right-hand man, New Romney chose one of his estate-agents, Winchelsea a gentleman of Kent who was Chancellor of Chichester diocese and an obvious nominee. Hastings perhaps accepted a nominee, Rye probably did not, and Sandwich certainly did not.

Thus, even with the unexpected help of the Privy Council, the Lord Warden did not attain his goal in 1584. On the other hand, the Ports definitely receded from their principle of complete independence, enunciated in 1572. Dover continued in subjection. For the rest of the reign it elected an official from the Castle, or, in 1601, his nephew. Perhaps it disliked paying wages: certainly, a member

1. *Hatfield MSS.* iii, 71.
2. Bodley was also elected, and chose to sit, for Portsmouth (D'EWES, *Journals*, p. 334b).
3. WILKS, pp. 62–4.

who sat four times between 1555 and 1572 noted in his will that his wages had not been paid, and another, the local man in 1593, complained that his were two years in arrears.[1] Hastings retained one local member, though the other was generally, perhaps always, a nominee. Hythe continued with unbroken regularity to elect a Kentish gentleman, probably the nominee of Lord Cobham, along with one of its jurats. Winchelsea more or less went to pieces: or so the names suggest.

The other Ports, however, still managed to demonstrate their independence. New Romney chose as its representatives in 1586 two jurats, members of a group or faction which lorded it in the town in the late eighties; and in 1588 this party seems to have defied the Lord Warden, refused him a nomination, and re-elected their ringleader, William Southland, along with a Kentish gentleman, one of the Scotts of Scot's Hall. Their behaviour provoked the Warden into ordering them to dismiss Southland from his seat; an overbearing and unwarrantable *démarche*, to which they replied that he was already elected and returned and it was contrary to their customs to make a second election. In 1590 the Privy Council had to be invoked to suppress this faction; and thereafter Romney, it seems, came to heel. Certainly it accepted a nominee in 1597 and 1601.[2] Rye may have admitted a stranger in 1588: otherwise it clung to its freedom during these years, until in 1597, with a new Lord Warden, it let in first one outsider, and then in 1601 two. As for Sandwich, unless Roger Manwood's son and heir was a nominee of Dover Castle, which hardly seems likely, the Warden appointed no member from 1588 to 1601, and apparently none throughout the reign.

Thus, by the close of Elizabeth's reign practice had drawn very close indeed to the theory propounded in 1574 by Lord Cobham. In the first year of James I the Ports gave a flutter of independence. They reiterated their old decree about choosing resident townsmen, this time under penalties of a twenty pounds fine on any offending town, afterwards increased to forty pounds and a ten pounds fine on any person voting for a stranger. Alas! It was little more than a gesture. New Romney tried to resist the Warden in 1604, but gave way after receiving an extremely vigorous, threatening letter. By 1614 the right

1. JONES, *Annals of Dover* (Dover, 1916), pp. 378–9.
2. *A.P.C.* xix, 5, 9, 64, 207, 232; MURRAY, op. cit., p. 97.

which Lord Cobham had boldly but vainly attempted to extort from the Ports in 1574, had, through a process of gradual usurpation, become a prescriptive, immemorial privilege. Or, at least, so the Lord Warden liked to think: 'the ancient usage and privilege that myself and my predecessors have ever had in the nomination of one of the barons to be elected in the several Ports'. By 1624 the usurper had become even more blatant: 'The Lord Warden', it was said, 'doth commonly recommend fourteen burgesses to parliament, seldom or never denied him, unless it be upon some great distaste betwixt him and the Ports.' Despite this extravagant claim, the spirit of independence did not die. Yet, such was the denigrating effect of persistent practice that it needed an act of parliament in 1689 'to declare the right and freedom of election of members to serve in parliament for the Cinque Ports'.[1]

In its modern form, the anomalous structure known as the Duchy of Lancaster originated with the decision of Henry IV to keep his ducal patrimony separate from the royal estates when he became King. Its core was the County Palatine of Lancaster, but ducal rights and estates, like those of other great lords, or, for that matter, of the King, were scattered. There were few counties in England and Wales which did not in some degree acknowledge the jurisdiction of the Duchy and swell its territories; and even in London it had its 'liberties'.[2] The central administration, housed at Savoy House in the Strand, was under the Chancellor of the Duchy, among whose chief officials were the Attorney of the Duchy, the Receiver General, Auditors for both the north and south parts, separate Surveyors for both lands and woods, divided also between north and south, and the Clerk of the Court of the Duchy. There were other central officials on the pay-roll, and doubtless many clerks whose pay came from fees. In addition there were the officials of the County Palatine, and a host of local officers: for example, in Edward VI's reign there were twenty-three 'particular' or local Receivers.[3] The head of this impressive administrative machine was a Privy Councillor, and though not a nobleman, and lacking both the aristocratic prestige and intimacy of the

1. WILKS, pp. 58, 66, 89; MURRAY, pp. 98–9.
2. HOLDSWORTH, *Hist. of Eng. Law*, i, 115; STOW, *Survey of London*, ed Kingsford, ii, 91 ff.
3. S.P. Dom. Eliz. Addenda, vol. 16; S.P. Dom. Ed. VI, 18, no. 40.

territorial magnate, he wielded a power over borough communities, which in extent far outran that of any magnate, and in degree often equalled or even surpassed that of a Norfolk, a Bedford, or a Leicester.

Elizabeth's first Chancellor of the Duchy was Sir Ambrose Cave, friend of Sir William Cecil, a staunch Protestant and one of the initial group of Councillors appointed before the new Queen left Hatfield for London. He is scarcely more than a name in history, but he was influential at Court.[1] On his death in 1568 he was succeeded by the elderly, cultured diplomat and statesman, Sir Ralph Sadler, who had begun his career in the household of Thomas Cromwell, served Henry VIII as diplomat, Councillor, and Secretary, and Edward VI as Councillor and Master of the Wardrobe. Like his friend, William Cecil, he went into retirement under Mary, but re-emerged as one of the earliest Councillors of Elizabeth, served her on missions that linked his story with Mary Queen of Scots, and finally was made Chancellor of the Duchy; an honourable, if unspectacular career, during which he amassed great wealth – 'got honestly', if we can believe the tradition which Fuller echoed.[2] He died in 1587, and his successor was Sir Francis Walsingham, the eminent Secretary, whose period of office covered only one general election – that of 1588. On Walsingham's death in 1590 the highly-favoured courtier, Sir Thomas Heneage, already a Privy Councillor and Vice-Chamberlain of the Royal Household, was made Chancellor. The status of the office was rising as the competition for place and power intensified. Heneage, too, served through only one general election – that of 1593.

Heneage's death in 1595 came at a time when the Earl of Essex, in his urge to monopolize all appointments, was sharpening the division of the State between his own followers and those of the Cecils. Burghley obviously wanted the chancellorship, with its extensive patronage and influence, for his son, Robert, who was already a Privy Councillor, but not yet Secretary. Probably the Queen sympathized: at any rate, she was not prepared to let it go to the Essex faction. Her tactics were amusingly subtle. She left the chancellorship vacant, appointed eight commissioners to carry on the work, and for a time took the

---

1. *Cal. S.P. Dom.*, *1547–80*, p. 117; *Cal. Pat. Rolls, Eliz.* i, 66; *A.P.C.* vii, passim.

2. Cf. Sir Walter Scott's memoir in *Sadler State Papers*, ed. Clifford, vol. i; *D.N.B.*

seal of office into her own keeping, employing Burghley – who thus kept a lien on the post – to seal and dispatch business as occasion arose. Then, two years later, on Saturday, 8 October at 11 p.m. – an interesting sidelight on the working habits of this extraordinary woman – she handed the seal to Sir Robert Cecil and made him Chancellor, at a time when Essex was out of the way, on the Islands Voyage.[1]

The appointment came barely in time to suit Cecil's parliamentary plans, since the writs for a new election had gone out about a month before. At least one of his letters to Duchy boroughs, asking for nominations, arrived too late. In 1599, when he became Master of the Court of Wards, Cecil had to resign the Duchy; and, plagued by the factions, the Queen once more had recourse to commissioners. Gossip was busy in 1600. Now the rumour went that Sir John Stanhope, a thoroughgoing Cecilian, 'shall be Chancellor'; now that it was to be Sir John Fortescue, Chancellor of the Exchequer, who temporarily held the seal of the Duchy, and was less obnoxious to opposite interests. In September 1601, with parliament and the legal term pending, and with Stanhope now provided for as Vice-Chamberlain, Fortescue was appointed Chancellor of the Duchy for ten days; and, after a new relapse to commissioners, the office was again granted to him in November. He certainly interfered in the elections to some Duchy boroughs in 1601; but so also did Cecil, who had retained his residence at the Savoy and perhaps took advantage of an anomalous situation.[2]

All the six parliamentary boroughs of Lancashire – Clitheroe, Lancaster, Liverpool, Newton, Preston, and Wigan – were within the Duchy. The Chancellor enjoyed a strategic position not unlike that of the Lord Warden of the Cinque Ports, for as this was a County Palatine its election writ issued from the Duchy office and was delivered to the Sheriff by the Duchy's pursuivant. He was therefore able to send his letters to the boroughs by the pursuivant, or merely give verbal orders through the Sheriff. At Liverpool, for example, Sir Ambrose Cave sent a letter to the Mayor and aldermen in 1563,

1. COLLINS, *Sidney Papers*, i, 357, ii, 64.

2. WINWOOD, *Memorials of State*, i, 41; COLLINS, op. cit., ii, 158, 165, 188; *De L'Isle & Dudley MSS.* ii, 465, 486; *Hatfield MSS.* ix, 246; P.R.O. Duchy of Lancaster, 12/16/74, 75; 41/82 (references I owe to Mr H. V. Jones Jr of Harvard); *Cecil's Letters to Carew* (Camden Soc.), p. 99.

while Sir Ralph Sadler in 1572 employed the other, less courteous and more peremptory method.[1] The Chancellor was tantamount to a viceroy in Lancashire, and numerous officials, great and small, were his subordinates. Little wonder that his will prevailed.

The result can be seen at Lancaster, Preston, and Wigan, where the list of Elizabethan members suggests that few sat without either the Duchy's nomination or at least its goodwill and support. Take Lancaster: Sir Thomas Benger, a Wiltshire gentleman who became Master of the Revels in January 1560, and William Fleetwood, a London lawyer of Lancashire descent, who was counsel to the Duchy, were the members in 1559; in 1563, John Hales, a Chancery official, author of *The Common Weal of England*, and along with him, Fleetwood again; in 1571, Henry Sadler, son of the Chancellor, and Miles Sandys, an official of the Queen's Bench and a 'carpet-bagger'; in 1572, two of the Chancellor's sons. Or take Preston: the two members in 1559 were Roger Alford, an Exchequer official, one-time servant of William Cecil, and Richard Cooke, Cecil's brother-in-law – obviously the nominees of Cecil's great friend, Sir Ambrose Cave. In 1597, when Sir Robert Cecil was Chancellor, the members were John Brograve, Attorney of the Duchy, and John Stanhope, Treasurer of the Chamber and Cecil's staunch friend. In 1601 the Mayor wrote to say that they had given Cecil the election of one member and that the Under-Sheriff of the county would attend upon him with the indenture, 'wherein we have left a space'.[2] John Brograve, the Attorney, was re-elected to the other seat, thus once more subjecting the borough wholly to London. At Wigan in 1572 one member was Edward Fitton, whom we shall meet again in the Duchy borough of Boroughbridge – a Cheshire gentleman, and therefore of the locality, though also *persona grata* at Court; the other was Edward Elrington, the Chancellor's son-in-law. In 1593 we have William Gerrard, member for Wigan previously in 1584 and 1586, nephew of the Duchy's Vice-Chancellor, and probably already connected with the Duchy himself, certainly its Clerk in 1600. The second member was Michael Heneage the antiquary, younger brother of the Chancellor.

However, conditions were not uniform throughout Lancashire. At Liverpool another patron confronted the Chancellor – his social

1. *Liverpool Town Books*, ed. Twemlow, i, 216–17, ii, 41.
2. *Hatfield MSS.* xi, 443–4.

superior, the Earl of Derby, Lord Lieutenant of Lancashire and Cheshire; and therefore the Chancellor's effective, though not always his actual claims were limited to one nomination. Little chance, one might have thought, for the borough to tread freedom's path. Yet, at the beginning of Elizabeth's reign, it happened that in Ralph Sekerston, whose story has already been partly told,[1] they possessed a supremely capable and ambitious alderman to lead them along that path. In 1559 they elected him as one of their members, ignoring – one must suppose – the wish of the Chancellor. As their Town Books show, they still thought Sekerston was their member a week after the date of the return; but when that return reached the Chancery, Sekerston's name had been erased and that of a second Duchy nominee, Richard Browne, inserted;[2] a lesson in dutifulness, which surely ought to have sufficed. Nevertheless, when in 1563 the Chancellor asked for only one seat, they flouted him completely, and, what is more, successfully. Only the mediation of the Earl of Derby stayed Sir Ambrose Cave from retaliating 'in his fumes' with the dreaded penalty of a *quo warranto*.[3] This time the town authorities did learn their lesson, and thereafter Liverpool reserved one seat for the Chancellor and one for the Earl of Derby, though the easy-going nature of the latter, who was not an aggressive seat-hunter, permitted them to retain their idol, Ralph Sekerston, in his seat till he died.

Newton, 'the borough of Sir Thomas Langton', assumed the pattern of Liverpool, whereas Clitheroe, the other Lancashire borough enfranchised in 1559, may have gone the way of Lancaster, Preston, and Wigan. 'In the first forty years after Clitheroe was made a parliamentary borough', says a modern writer who seems to be broadly right, 'not more than three gentlemen out of the eighteen elected had any local family connexion with the district . . ., and one of these was a barrister of Gray's Inn, and was therefore domiciled in London. A fourth may have been of a Lancashire family. All the others were "foreigners". Several were lawyers . . .; others were officers of the Crown, or in the service of the government.' Sir Thomas Heneage, Chancellor in 1593, obviously planted his granddaughter's husband, William Twysden, on the borough in that year. In 1601 'the Chancellor of the Duchy'—presumably Fortescue—wrote

---

1. Above, pp. 146–7.   2. *Town Books*, i, 108; *Return of M.P.s*, i, 400.
3. Above, p. 147.

asking for one nomination. The second member on this occasion was a neighbouring gentleman.[1]

The number of parliamentary boroughs outside the County Palatine, yet within the Duchy, was quite appreciable: East Grinstead (Sussex), Higham Ferrers (Northants), Huntingdon, Leicester, Monmouth, Newcastle-under-Lyme (Staffordshire), Stockbridge (Hampshire), Sudbury (Suffolk), Thetford (Norfolk), and a group in Yorkshire — Aldborough, Boroughbridge. Knaresborough, and Ripon.[2] Here the Duchy's authority was not exceptional, as it was within the County Palatine. It varied with the degree of direct control, and could be met and countered by the influence of local magnates or even of the local gentry. As we have seen, the borough of Leicester was protected by the Earl of Huntingdon. Sir Ralp Sadler may have placed a friend there in 1571,[3] and certainly did in 1584. But when Heneage overplayed his hand in 1593 a stop was put to this intrusion, and even Robert Cecil did not dare to renew the attack.[4]

The Hampshire borough of Stockbridge was only enfranchised in 1563, and for this reason one might have expected it to be susceptible to Duchy influence. Nevertheless, whether Cave or Sadler placed a nominee there seems very doubtful. Hampshire was the home county of the Paulets and Lord Sandys, and had a vigorous lot of gentry. The members seem too consistently local to fit the Duchy pattern, until in 1588, the year of Walsingham's chancellorship, an Exchequer official, sprung from a Wiltshire family, betrays the familiar hand. Then, in 1593, the aggressive Sir Thomas Heneage — who, incidentally must have placed a Duchy nominee at Monmouth, hitherto seemingly free from this interference — probably placed at Stockbridge a 'carpetbagger', whom he also nominated at Lancaster, perhaps as a form of insurance against the uncertainties of the other borough.[5] In 1597 Sir Robert Cecil got his request in too late. The borough had already

1. WEEKS, *Clitheroe in the 17th Century*, pp. 220 ff.; J. R. TWISDEN, *Family of Twysden*, p. 106.

2. *H.M.C. Kenyon MSS.*, p. 407.

3. Stephen Hales, citizen and merchant-tailor of London, *alias* of Coventry, brother of John Hales, Clerk of the Hanaper and M.P. for Lancaster in 1563 (cf. *Cal. Pat. Rolls, Eliz.* i, 197, 380).

4. Above, pp. 165–6.

5. John Awdeley, gent. of London (cf. *Foljambe MSS.*, p. 39), M.P. West Looe 1572, Bodmin 1584, Lancaster and Stockbridge 1593.

elected a nominee of Lord Sandys along with a local Justice of the Peace. By way of placating him, they explained that they had 'made stay' for a Duchy nominee until October 1st. 'Hereafter', they added, 'you shall not only request, but shall command anything which we may do.'[1] Whether the two obvious intruders who sat in 1601 were nominated by Cecil, or by the new Chancellor, Fortescue, we do not know. But, whatever happened then, Stockbridge, as we shall see, had by no means lost its aversion to London-placed 'foreigners', or its tradition of loyalty to Hampshire squires.

Even at Newcastle-under-Lyme, where – it is said[2] – Duchy influence in elections was an old tradition, and very few of its members in the Tudor period were local-born burgesses, an official nominee does not seem to have been invariable. There was probably none in 1559, 1586, 1593, and 1601.

Huntingdon, in contrast, appears to have succumbed to the Duchy regularly, though apparently not in 1559. On occasions – in 1563 and 1571 – it may have surrendered both seats. We know that Sir Thomas Heneage – how characteristic of him! – asked for both in 1593. He was given one.[3] We also know that Sir Robert Cecil wrote for a nomination. As for the Duchy borough of Sudbury, it was at least as subject as Huntingdon. It probably returned a Duchy nominee at every election, and perhaps two in 1559 and 1593.

Higham Ferrers, a single-member constituency, is a puzzle. It started the reign only too clearly at the Duchy's call, electing in 1559 and 1563 'The Right Worshipful John Purvey, Auditor of the south parts of the Duchy of Lancaster'[4] – a Hertfordshire gentleman, who had sat for the Duchy borough of Huntingdon in 1553, and for his own county in 1558. As likely as not, Christopher Hatton, the rising star among favourites at Court, though himself a Northamptonshire man, owed his seat in 1571 to Chancellor Sadler; and so presumably did the member in 1572. But thereafter, the influence of Mildmay,

1. *Hatfield MSS.* vii, 432.

2. T. PAPE, *Newcastle-under-Lyme in Tudor & Stuart Times*, pp. 35–6. This author is too reliant on the guesses of Wedgwood, *Parliamentary Repres. of Staffs.*

3. R. CARRUTHERS, *History of Huntingdon* (1824), p. 164. The quotation from the lost corporation ledger of the answer to Heneage, permitting him only to nominate 'them', should obviously read 'one'.

4. *Return of M.P.s*, i, 401.

Hatton, and Montagu of Boughton, great names in the county, would explain the elections; though it is just conceivable that these magnates operated through the Chancellor of the Duchy.

In the north, outside the County Palatine, the Chancellor was a remote figure. There were nearer powers to sway the boroughs – powers with whom he might not wish to compete. For example, many of the representatives of Aldborough, Yorkshire, were either members of the Council in the North or northern gentry.[1] The borough was perhaps regarded as primarily under the influence of the Lord President of that Council. Nevertheless, it seems likely that William Lambarde, the loyal and lovable Kent antiquary, was a Duchy nominee in 1563; and so, with more assurance, we may say of William Waad, member in 1584, servant of Burghley, diplomat, and Clerk of the Privy Council, who also sat for Thetford in 1588 and Preston in 1601, both Duchy boroughs. Finally, all doubt vanishes about George Horsey, Sir Ralph Sadler's son-in-law, who was a member in 1586. Sir Edward Cecil, who sat for Aldborough in 1601, was probably the nominee of his father, the Lord President of the Council in the North.

The position of the adjacent town of Boroughbridge was not dissimilar, though the Duchy seems here to have had better fortune. True, it got no member in 1571, 1572, and 1586: on the other hand, it may have named both in 1588, 1593, and 1597. John Ashley, Master of the Jewel House, member in 1563; Nicholas Faunt, Clerk of the Signet and secretary to Walsingham, member in 1584; Sir Edward Fitton – father of the fascinating, but alas! too amorous maid of honour, Mary Fitton, of mistaken Shakespearian fame[2] – member in 1588, a gentleman we have already met as member for Wigan in 1572; John Brograve, Attorney of the Duchy, member in 1593, and member for Preston in 1586, 1597, and 1601; and Henry Fanshawe, Auditor of the north parts of the Duchy, member in 1597: all these are people about whom it would be absurd to entertain any doubt. And others also look as if they had come out of the Duchy office.

At Knaresborough, the Slingsbys, chief landowners there,[3] and other northern gentry of note, occasionally monopolized the repre-

1. Cf. LAWSON-TANCRED, 'Parliamentary History of Aldborough and Boroughbridge', *Yorks. Arch. Journal*, xxvii, 325 ff.
2. Cf. NEWDIGATE-NEWDEGATE, *Gossip from a Muniment Room*.
3. Cf. G. R. PARK, *Parliamentary Repres. of Yorks.*, pp. 112–14.

sentation. Nevertheless, the Duchy probably placed at least one nominee there in each parliament from 1584 to 1597.

Ripon was in a class apart. It was described by the Archbishop of York as the 'only ... town in this bishopric having burgesses'; by which he presumably meant the only town where he could nominate a member. The Archbishop was its Steward, and apparently he and the Lord President of the Council in the North shared the two nominations. There is no sign of Duchy interference until in 1597 – some days before he was made Chancellor – and again in 1601, Sir Robert Cecil asked for a Ripon seat; but he secured the seat through the Archbishop and does not seem to have asserted Duchy authority.[1]

Broadly speaking, the members chosen by Elizabethan Chancellors fall into two classes. First, like dozens of other patrons, and for the same very human reasons, they appointed friends, dependants, and followers. The most conspicuous illustration is Sir Ralph Sadler's placing of his family. He had three sons and four married daughters.[2] The middle son had no taste for parliament; the eldest exhausted his appetite in a single parliament – that of 1572, with its three sessions – when he represented Lancaster; but the youngest sat for Lancaster consistently from 1571 to 1587 – that is, until his father's death withdrew the easy way to nomination, when his parliamentary service terminated. Of his sons-in-law, Sir Ralph placed three in parliament – George Horsey, Edward Baeshe, and Edward Elrington. Horsey was a Hertfordshire gentleman like his father-in-law, and was Deputy-Lieutenant and Sheriff of the county. He was brought by Sadler into the important office of Receiver General of the Duchy in 1576, and was member for Clitheroe in 1571, Preston in 1572, and Aldborough in 1586. He died in 1588. Baeshe, another Hertfordshire gentleman, was Surveyor of Victuals for the Navy, with which service he had been connected since Henry VIII's reign; and a very profitable business he made of it! In the parliaments of 1555, 1559, and 1563, his official interests provided him with a seat at the naval port of Rochester, but in 1571 he turned to his father-in-law and sat for Preston. The third son-in-law, Edward Elrington of Berkshire, sat for Wigan in 1572.

Duchy officials and officials in many branches of the royal service

1. *Hatfield MSS.* vii, 404, xi. 390, 409, 442.
2. *Sadler State Papers,* ii, 603 ff.

constituted the second class of nominees. It is here, if anywhere, that we should look for signs of packing parliament, for if a conscious government policy of this nature existed, it could scarcely fail to leave traces in so exceptionally large a group of boroughs under a single minister's control. But policy, unless framed and administered by lunatics, must surely possess some perceptible pattern or reveal some degree of planning and consistency. A desire to economize effort, if nothing else, would secure this. Yet, anything more haphazard and chaotic than the distribution of names in Duchy boroughs, it would be hard to conceive. The total lack of scheme can only be explained as the consequence of a system by which a large number of individuals – gentlemen, lawyers, and officials – seeking parliamentary seats, approached this or that patron, as opportunity and expectation prompted, whenever elections came along.

There is cause neither for surprise nor suspicion in the number of officials sitting for Duchy boroughs. The Chancellor himself was an official, he was advised by officials, he lived among officials. It was natural for them to seek his favours. Moreover, the relationship was not necessarily simple and one-sided. In the world of Essex and Robert Cecil, and, in a less acute form, in that of Leicester and Burghley, the faction-leaders carried their rivalry into the administrative service. Was it not said, though with gross exaggeration, that Leicester had placed so many of his supporters about the Queen that she found it hard to withstand him?[1] This was indeed the danger that Elizabeth perceived in Essex's passionate pursuit of appointments to office. And just as a statesman could bind a follower to his service by obtaining a post for him, so the gift of a seat in parliament was one of many ways by which he could attract an official into his constellation or retain him there.

As an epilogue to our story we cannot do better than recall a notorious scandal of 1614, when the electors of Stockbridge, who numbered but twenty-eight, paying no attention to a threatening letter from the Chancellor of the Duchy of Lancaster, dared to reject his two nominees. The Bailiff of the borough, perhaps an appointee of the Duchy and certainly more amenable to authority, ignored the election and returned the two nominees, while the Chancellor ful-

1. Cf. *Spanish Cal. Eliz.* iii, 267; *Secret Memoirs of Robert Dudley*, ed. Drake (1706), pp. 52 ff.

filled his threats by sending a pursuivant for two or three of the poor, intrepid townsmen, one of whom was cast into prison. It was a situation not unlike that at Liverpool in 1563. On this occasion, however, instead of an Earl of Derby, the House of Commons came to the rescue with its recently usurped jurisdiction over elections. The Chancellor, Sir Thomas Parry, was expelled from the House, and the weak-kneed James I suspended him from his office and the Privy Council. In the course of the debate, the Attorney General, hoping to deflate passion with a little realism, reminded members that 'we live not in Plato his Commonwealth'. He went on to say that it was 'the prescription of the Chancellor to have the nomination of one of the burgesses in every of the Duchy boroughs'.[1]

Thus, in the Duchy of Lancaster, as in the Cinque Ports, a process of repeated but piecemeal encroachment during Elizabethan times culminated under the early Stuarts in the formulation of a principle and a right.

1. *Commons Journals*, i, 477 ff.; *H.M.C. Portland MSS.* ix, 132; NOTESTEIN, *Debates 1621*, vii, 635; *J. Chamberlain's Letters*, i, 528; HOBART'S *Reports* (1724), p. 78.

CHAPTER II

Borough Patrons: Essex and Cecil

FROM time to time our narrative has caught echoes of the supreme faction-struggle of the Elizabethan period, the vital conflict between Robert, Earl of Essex, and the Cecils, which had its tragic end on the scaffold. As Essex himself said, when in the last hours of life the shafts of his chaplain's piety shattered all pride and revealed to his naked soul the true nature of his offence, it was 'a leprosy that had infected far and near'. A leprosy it was indeed. Lord Grey wrote in July 1598: 'My lord of Essex ... has forced me to declare myself either his only, or friend to Mr Secretary [Cecil] and his enemy; protesting that there could be no neutrality.'[1]

Faction was inseparable from personal monarchy. But hitherto, in the magical hands of Elizabeth, it had been used to guarantee her independence, while contributing to that intensity of spirit in both Court and country which made her reign splendid. Of her own generation she had gathered about her sufficient remarkable men to keep the balance of parties. The balance might sway, even on occasions look dangerous, but it had retained equilibrium.

It is the tragedy of old age to lose one's contemporaries and be ill at ease with youth. The Earl of Leicester died in 1588, Sir Christopher Hatton in 1591, another of the Queen's favourites, Sir Thomas Heneage, in 1595, and Sir Francis Knollys, highly privileged and influential among courtiers, in 1596. The flower of the nobility, the great Earls of Bedford, Huntingdon, and Shrewsbury, and the Queen's cousin Lord Hunsdon, were all dead by 1596; and so was Sir Francis Walsingham. While these men lived, the follies of an Essex could not have grown to such proportions nor become dangerous. But now, one only of the leading statesmen of the past remained – the ablest of them all, Lord Burghley. Intent on passing his power to his gifted son, Robert Cecil, he inevitably attracted the bitter opposition of Essex. In 1598 Burghley died.

1. SPEDDING, *Letters & Life of Francis Bacon*, ii, 285; *Hatfield MSS*. viii, 269.

Nature and accident conspired to enact the poignant tragedy that followed. Essex was endowed very far beyond common measure in spirit and personality; judgement alone was missing from his alluring compound of qualities. The passing of the Queen's generation left him supreme among courtiers; and war, personifying in his intrepid, careless leadership all the chivalrous instincts of a buoyant nation, made him the darling of the people and a magnet to adventure.

Times happen when history records circumstances in fateful concatenation. At this juncture there was an opportunity for monopoly of power such as had not existed before in the reign; and a young man – destined to play out his tragedy by the time he was thirty-four, before experience tempers hot folly – who was distantly related to the Queen, nobly-born, stepson of Leicester and son-in-law of Walsingham; a young man cursed with an urge towards monopoly that became a craze. His principal, his only real rival was Robert Cecil; and he was a mere knight, younger son of a newly-minted baron who had had to create a past as well as a future for his family. Moreover, he was puny and hunchbacked. In later years, the astutest man of that generation, Francis Bacon, looking back on his own mistaken certitude about the issue in the early years of the contest, was prompted to write his very curious essay 'On Deformity'.

We have previously noticed how certain boroughs, acting as barometers of the time, conferred High Stewardships on the Earl of Leicester.[1] When this prince of favourites died, Essex was but twenty-two; his fame and popularity lay a few years ahead. At Bristol and Great Yarmouth the people turned to Lord Burghley as Leicester's successor, while two years later, Ipswich, seeking a High Steward in place of Walsingham, chose the Queen's cousin, Lord Hunsdon.[2] Eight years passed, then ten. Essex's day had come, although the far-seeing Bacon, already sensitive to the signs of a storm, was trimming his sails. The less clairvoyant boroughs basked in the sun. Ipswich, Bristol, and Great Yarmouth elected Essex as their new High Steward; even St Alban's, on Burghley's death, overlooked Robert Cecil and chose Essex – a grievous slight, for Burghley had been

1. Above, p. 201.
2. BACON, *Annals of Ipswich*, p. 384; BEAVEN, *Bristol Lists*, p. 231; PALMER, *Contin.*, *Manship's History of Great Yarmouth*, pp. 321–3.

I. QUEEN ELIZABETH

Within the image (labels):
Procerum ... *Clerus* ... *Prolocutorem*

Cancellarii sedes

Prolocutor

Milites Provinciarum & Burgenses (quos vocant) utrinq, qui Cameram Parlamenti inferiorem constituunt, Prolocutorem conducentes.

2. THE PRESENTATION OF THE SPEAKER
NOVEMBER 1584

QUEEN ELIZABETH IN PARLIAMENT

A. Lᵈ Chancellor. B. Marquises, Earls &c. C. Barons. D. Bishops. E. Iudges. F. Masters of Chancerie. G. Clerks. H. Speaker of ȳ Comon. I. Black Rod. K. Seriant at Armes. L. Members of the Commons house. M. Sʳ Francis Walsingham Secretary of State.

3. QUEEN ELIZABETH IN PARLIAMENT

4. THE HOUSE OF COMMONS, 1624

Lord Lieutenant of the county, while Robert Cecil was a landowner, a Justice, and, since 1588, senior knight of the shire. True, Westminster, where Burghley had been High Steward, remained loyal to the Cecils: here the Dean and not the people chose the High Steward, and Robert Cecil had been his father's Bailiff. But at Cambridge University, where a somewhat similar situation had prevailed, Cecil being High Steward to his father's chancellorship, it was not he but Essex who succeeded Burghley.[1] Essex was also High Steward at the boroughs of Andover, Dunwich, Hereford – where he succeeded Sir James Croft – Leominster, Oxford, Reading, and Tamworth. The list undoubtedly would be longer if the information were complete.[2]

Sir Robert Cecil, for his part, was High Steward at Doncaster, where he succeeded Lord Hunsdon in 1596 and evidently secured the office through his follower, the Recorder; at Hull, where at his own solicitation he followed Sir Thomas Heneage in 1595; and at Plymouth and Westminster. He was also Recorder of Colchester, where again he asked for the post on the death of Heneage.[3] No doubt he held office in other boroughs; but in this competition, where as a rule popular favour adjudicated, we may conclude that he was a poor second to his noble and scintillating, though younger, rival. It is not without significance that at Doncaster, Hull, and Colchester the honour did not come spontaneously.

In February 1601, after his desperate and fatuous rebellion, Essex was executed. Cecil was then supreme, but he was odious:

> Little Cecil trips up and down,
> He rules both Court and Crown,
> With his brother Burghley clown. . . .[4]

Cambridge University made him its Chancellor.[5] But the less sophis-

1. *Cal. S.P. Dom.*, *1581–90*, p. 543; A. S. GIBBS, *Records of St Albans*, p. 296; *Vestry of St Margaret, Westminster, Annual Rep. June 1889*, pp. 22, 111; *Hatfield MSS.* xii, 459; COOPER, *Athenae Cant.* ii, 298.

2. *H.M.C. Var. Coll.* vii, 82; *Cal. S.P. Dom.*, *1595–7*, p. 476; *H.M.C. Rep.* XIII, iv, 331; *Hatfield MSS.* xvii, 360; ibid., xi, 114; COATES, *Antiquities of Reading*, app. no. xiv; PAPE, *Newcastle-under-Lyme*, pp. 46–7.

3. *Hatfield MSS.* vi, 317, v. 439–40; *H.M.C. Rep.* X, iv, 540; *Hatfield MSS.* ix, 163, 395.

4. C. C. STOPES, *Henry, Third Earl of Southampton*, p. 236.

5. *Cal. S.P. Dom.*, *1598–1601*, p. 576.

ticated boroughs, where popular opinion found expression, were not fickle. The ballads expressed their lament for Essex:

> He always helped the poor,
> Which makes them sigh full sore;
> His death they do deplore
> In every place.[1]

Cecil does not seem to have succeeded to any of Essex's High Stewardships. Great Yarmouth, despite its recent tie with Burghley, chose the Lord Admiral, Bristol and Ipswich the Lord Treasurer, and Oxford the Lord Keeper.[2] The emotional implication of these facts may perhaps be inferred from what happened at Reading. Here, according to the account sent to Cecil by a neighbouring supporter of his, the chief and secondary burgesses – the oligarchs – wished to make him High Steward in succession to Essex, and actually carried the nomination. But there was a rival party in the borough, led by the Mayor, the Steward or Recorder, and others, which was bent on choosing Essex's uncle, Sir William Knollys, Comptroller of the Royal Household. The issue may not have been simple. The Knollys family were local landowners, and the borough doubtless had its own reasons for faction. All the same, the Essex-Cecil cleavage had a tendency to merge itself into many local faction disputes, and there can be little doubt that on this occasion popular hatred of Cecil for the death of Essex was exploited. As Cecil's correspondent wrote: there was 'a kind of sub-threatening and secret depraving of your Honour'. 'Many flying speeches go about, and the bells ring evening, night, and morrow.' The Mayor refused to certify Cecil's election; the voters were canvassed and browbeaten; finally, Knollys was chosen as High Steward.[3]

It is not surprising that a man of Essex's temperament became engrossed in parliamentary elections during his meteoric career. Patronage was personified in him; it was the breath of his life. This spoilt child of fortune showed exceptional precocity. He was a few

---

1. C. H. FIRTH, 'Ballad History of the Later Tudors', *Trans. Roy. Hist. Soc.* 3rd ser. iii, 117.

2. PALMER, op. cit., p. 324; *H.M.C. Rep.* IX, i, 256a; BEAVEN, op. cit., p. 231; *Wood's City of Oxford*, ed. Clark (Oxf. Hist. Soc.) iii, 57.

3. *Hatfield MSS.* xi, 372; cf. *V.C.H. Berks.* iii, 297.

days short of eighteen when in 1584 he asked the borough of Tamworth to elect a nominee, John Bretton esquire; and although the
authorities found themselves embarrassed – having to grant the
other seat to the Earl of Leicester, and so to their sorrow exclude
from parliament their Recorder, who had omitted to insure against
such a calamity by making suit for a seat elsewhere – nevertheless,
as they reminded Essex in 1593, they were 'willing to gratify your
Lordship's first commendation'.[1] The Earl may have nominated one
of Tamworth's members in the next parliament. In 1588, as High
Steward and just after obtaining a new charter for the borough, he
was apparently granted both seats, for the members were his uncle
Edward Devereux, and his tutor and steward Robert Wright;[2] and
on this occasion he seems to have provided for the Recorder, Richard
Broughton – who was also his legal man-of-affairs – by securing him
a seat at Lichfield. He was probably also responsible for the election
of his kinsman, Henry Bourchier, at Stafford.

Staffordshire was the main, though far from the only, sphere of
Essex's influence. It was here that his principal estate was situated –
Chartley, where Mary Queen of Scots had been incarcerated. Also,
his mother, the Countess of Leicester, now married to Sir Christopher
Blount, lived at Drayton Basset. In 1593, by which time his mind
had turned to 'domestical greatness', the young Earl revealed his
nature by attempting to secure a virtual monopoly of the seats in this
county. He wrote to his friend Richard Bagot, a neighbouring squire
who looked after his interests there, sending him several letters which
he had written 'to Lichfield, Stafford, Tamworth, and Newcastle,
for the nomination and election of certain burgesses ..., having
named unto them: for Lichfield, Sir John Wingfield and Mr
Broughton; for Stafford, my kinsman Henry Bourchier and my
servant Edward Reynolds; for Tamworth, my servant Thomas
Smith; for Newcastle, Dr James'. After asking Bagot to have the
letters delivered, he added, 'I do earnestly pray your furtherance by
the credit which you have in those towns; assuring them of my
thankfulness if they shall, for my sake, gratify those whom I have
commended'. He also backed two candidates for the county election,
thus aiming at filling eight out of the ten Staffordshire seats. He was

1. Add. MS. 28175, fol. 51.
2. PAPE, *Newcastle-under-Lyme*, pp. 46–7.

successful with six, failing to get one county seat and to have Reynolds elected at Stafford.[1]

Essex's hunt for seats in this parliament ranged far afield. With little or no hesitation we can assign to him the nomination at Dunwich of his scholar-friend Henry Savile, Warden of Merton College, Oxford, and later Latin Secretary to the Queen and Provost of Eton; of an Exchequer official at Reading; of Arthur Atye – formerly Leicester's and soon to be his own secretary – at Shaftesbury; and of his steward Robert Wright at Shrewsbury. In the area of Wales where the name of Devereux, coupled with his own youthful sojourn in those parts, commanded a wide loyalty, sustained by the restless activities of his Welsh steward, Sir Gelly Meyrick – in this area another of his stewards, Thomas Crompton, sat for the borough of Radnor, while at Cardigan one of his most intimate followers, Ferdinando Gorges, was the member, and at Carmarthen the burgesses, rejecting a conflicting request from the Lord Keeper, gave him the nomination to their single seat.[2]

Appropriately enough, the supreme parliamentary effort of Essex's brief career was made in 1597, his last parliament, after the dazzling victory of Cadiz had carried him to the pinnacle of fame and popularity. Already his behaviour was becoming intolerable, and both Elizabeth and Burghley, whose ward he had once been, were by their astute moves blocking his way to inordinate political power. It was the year of the Islands Voyage, and in August Essex wrote to Robert Cecil from aboard ship at Plymouth, urging that parliament should not meet until the expedition was over.[3] At the same time he wrote to various boroughs: 'Being here at Plymouth expecting a good wind, I am advertised that her Majesty is resolved presently to call a parliament, which giveth me occasion before my departure to intreat this courtesy of you, that you will be contented to grant me the nominating of your burgesses, nothing doubting but I shall be returned from the present expedition ... in time convenient for this nomination, which if you do leave unto me, assure yourselves I will be careful to prefer unto this, very worthy and sufficient men. I pray

1. DEVEREUX, *Earls of Essex*, i, 280–2.
2. GUILDING, *Records of Reading*, i, 416; OWEN and BLAKENEY'S *Shrewsbury*, i, 550 n. 16; DEVEREUX, i, 279 n. 1.
3. *Hatfield MSS*. vii, 352.

you send your answer of this my letter to the Court, to my secretary Edward Reynolds.' We know that he sent the letter to Hereford and Shrewsbury, can infer that it went to Dunwich and Ipswich, and guess that other boroughs received it. The appeal, be it noted, was for both seats in a borough. Coming from victorious England's renowned hero, the darling of the people, as he set out on a naval campaign, how seductive the plea![1]

By the time the fleet returned – with childish rancour and little honour aboard – the elections had taken place and parliament had just met. Perhaps Elizabeth and Burghley had been far from averse to holding the elections in Essex's absence. At any rate, the Queen had seized on his absence and the meeting of parliament to promote his enemy, the Lord Admiral, to a well-deserved earldom – a move which gave the Admiral precedence of Essex and threw the returned and rather bedraggled hero into such a huff that he stayed away from both Court and parliament.

Essex's election campaign of 1597 must have been conducted by Reynolds and other servants. Their success did not correspond with the extravagant requests in their master's letters. Neither Hereford nor Shrewsbury conceded a single nomination;[2] Dunwich and Ipswich each gave one.[3] Yet the Earl's followers did well. Eight of his servants were elected, all obvious nominees: at Andover, Dunwich, Leominster, Lichfield, Oxford, Penryn, Tamworth,[4] and some unknown constituency for which Sir Gelly Meyrick sat, probably Carmarthen, which he had represented in 1588.[5] About a dozen or more of his friends and relatives, some intimately, some loosely attached to him, were also members, as were eighteen of that peculiar clientele of Essex knights, not all of whom, however, belonged to his

1. *H.M.C. Rep.* XIII, iv, 338; *Rep.* v, 342b; *Var. Coll.* vii, 85–6; BACON's *Ipswich*, p. 389.

2. For Hereford, cf. *Hatfield MSS.* xvii, 360. The M.P.s were: Gregory Price esq., member in every parliament from 1572 to 1597, and Mayor in 1573 and 1576 (cf. DUNCUMB, *History of Hereford*, i, 367); Anthony Pembridge esq., presumably a resident (cf. *H.M.C. Rep.* XIII, iv, 339). For Shrewsbury, see above, p. 162.

3. *H.M.C. Var. Coll.* vii, 85–6; BACON, op. cit., p. 389.

4. Edward Reynolds, Arthur Atye, Thomas Crompton, Joseph Oldsworth, Anthony Bacon, Edward Jones, William Temple.

5. Cf. D'EWES, op. cit., p. 575.

faction, nor had all, as yet, received from him their dubious honour. They constituted a substantial group; and our numbers are perhaps an under-estimate. Twelve of these M.P.s took part in the Essex Rebellion.[1]

Though many in the non-servant class secured their own seats, some were his nominees. Francis Bacon, elected at Ipswich, certainly was. Then, Edmund Baynham, a Kent man, involved later in the Essex rebellion, was a likely nominee, as was Herbert Croft, who found a seat at Launceston when Essex failed to place him at Hereford. In Staffordshire, Henry Bourchier sat again at Stafford, at Lichfield there were two nominees, and Sir Christopher Blount was re-elected for the county. But — and how revealing is the bare fact! — at the Duchy borough of Newcastle-under-Lyme, where Essex placed a nominee in 1593, now that Robert Cecil was Chancellor of the Duchy there was no Essex member.

How are we to interpret all this? In a notorious catholic tract, known as 'Leicester's Commonwealth' and described by Sir Philip Sidney as 'full of the most vile reproaches which a wit used to wicked and filthy thoughts can imagine', the author commented on the Earl of Leicester's 'most absolute and peremptory dealing in all things whereof it pleaseth him to dispose ... As in the universities, in election of scholars and heads of houses, in ecclesiastical persons for dignities of church, in offices, magistrates, stewards of lands, sheriffs, and knights of the shire, in burgesses of parliament ... and all other the like, where this man's will must stand for law and reason, and his letters for absolute laws.' It was gross caricature of course; but in some respects it was better caricature of Essex than of Leicester.[2]

The spread of the Essex 'leprosy' through all classes and many localities of the country would in any event have brought an appreciable number of the Earl's friends into parliament; but it may well be that in these elections of 1597, in addition to the ordinary motive of patronage, there was a conscious effort to secure what we may loosely call a party in the House of Commons. Those remarkable pioneers in political tactics, the Puritans, whose precocious modernity came from the organizing genius of Calvinism, had already in the

1. Cf. Miss C. M. Davey's thesis.
2. SIDNEY'S *Works*, ed. Feuillerat, ii, 61; *Secret Memoirs*, ed. Drake, pp. 55–6.

eighties done something of the sort. However, the Puritans had a parliamentary programme; and their electioneering – whatever it amounted to – was truly modern in its purpose. We need not, and should not, attribute the same precocity to the Essex group. It would be safer to liken their motive to that of many boroughs which wanted local representatives to safeguard their interests should anything arise in parliament affecting them. Between the two factions or parties in the country there was a fundamental difference of mentality and policy – a difference which once flared out in a dramatic scene between Essex and Burghley in the Council Chamber. The one loved war, the other peace. The presence of a well knit group of the Earl's adherents in the parliament of 1597 was a guarantee that – to quote once more a catholic stricture on Leicester – 'nothing passes in parliament ... that he dislikes'[1] Essex's secretaries and his infatuated followers, many of them able but irresponsible men who constantly played on the ruinous instincts of their impetuous young master, may have been conscious of this. If they deliberately imported such a motive into Elizbethan elections, it was a striking departure from current practice. Patronage, a natural and more or less harmless feature of aristocratic society, was being turned into a political weapon.

This, if true – and we are unfortunately reduced to speculation – would explain the counter-activities of Sir Robert Cecil. He, for his part, certainly employed new election tactics; or perhaps it would be more accurate to say, he revived the tactics of Henry VIII's minister, Thomas Cromwell. As Chancellor of the Duchy of Lancaster he had unique facilities for placing his clientele in parliament. But this patronage, extensive as it was, did not satisfy him. Perhaps he realized rather late that the Essex faction was making unusual efforts, and was provoked into doing the same himself. Both at Stockbridge and East Grinstead his letters asking for nominations arrived too late. His tardy appointment as Chancellor might explain these instances. But he was also too late at Colchester, where he was Recorder; which suggests some newly-realized need for more seats.[2]

The novel device to which Cecil had recourse was the transfer of nominations from other borough patrons to himself. His brother-in-law Lord Cobham, a principal enemy of Essex, gave him a nomina-

1. *Cal. S.P. Dom.*, *Add. 1580–1625*, p. 137.
2. Above, pp. 217–18; *Hatfield MSS.* vii, 385, 415.

tion at New Romney, received as Lord Warden of the Cinque Ports. Then, a distant relative by marriage, one Jonathan Trelawny of Poole, Cornwall, housed, as his Cornish contemporary Carew wrote,[1] 'far beneath his worth and calling', presented him with either one or two seats in that county – certainly one at Liskeard. In addition, Cecil asked the Archbishop of York for two seats, and was given one, at Ripon. Moreover, displaying a curious ignorance for a principal minister of State and an M.P. of long standing, he asked the Bishop of Durham for two borough seats, assuming that the County Palatine of Durham was represented in parliament. Surely the merest tyro ought to have recognized the absurdity of this! And not only Durham: there was also some misapprehension which led to an inquiry about non-existent seats at Doncaster.[2] These are merely instances of which evidence happens to have survived.

In the same indirect manner, or else by direct approach to the borough, Cecil presumably obtained the seat at Christchurch, Hampshire, to which his clerk, Simon Willis, was elected, and the seat at Queenborough, Kent, for his intimate friend, Sir George Carew. Also his relative, William Cooke, whom he placed at Westminster in 1601, sat for Helston in this parliament. It looks like another of his nominations; and either he himself or his father must have been responsible for the election of Vincent Skinner, Burghley's servant and later his own, at St Ives.[3] To appreciate the strength of the Cecilian group in the House of Commons in 1597, we must bear in mind that Lord Burghley also had his own far-from-negligible borough patronage.

In 1601, though Essex was dead and his faction discredited and impotent, Cecil continued the same policy. He probably received a Winchelsea seat from Lord Cobham: at any rate, a servant of his sat for this port.[4] Jonathan Trelawny, to quote his own words, was 'bold now again to present' him 'with two burgess-ships for this parliament'. Viscount Howard of Bindon, whose sphere of influence was

1. *Survey of Cornwall* (1723), p. 117a.

2. *Hatfield MSS*. vii, 429, xi, 405, vii, 404, 405, 442.

3. For Simon Willis, M.P. Knaresborough 1593, Christchurch 1597 and 1601, cf. *Cal. S.P. Dom., 1598–1601*, passim. For Vincent Skinner, M.P. Truro 1571, Barnstaple 1572, Boston 1584, 1586 and 1588, Boroughbridge 1593, St Ives 1597, Preston 1604, cf. *Cal. S.P. Dom., 1591–1603*, passim.

4. Hugh Beeston, esq. Cf. *Hatfield MSS.*, vols. v ff. passim.

Dorset, where he was Lord Lieutenant of the county and the town of Poole, wrote to say that some of the towns, trusting in his concern for their welfare, had given him the nomination of their burgesses, and if Cecil cared to appoint one or two, he would adopt his nominations. The Archbishop of York was induced to renew his gift of a seat at Ripon; and Cecil's clerk got in again at Christchurch.[1]

With Preston and maybe other Duchy boroughs, the borough of Westminster, and places that have left no trace in our evidence, Cecil must have nominated quite an appreciable number of the burgesses in this parliament. Shortly before the elections, he wrote to his friend Sir George Carew, President of Munster, promising to reserve a seat for him. 'I had kept a room for you in the parliament', he wrote later, when the Queen had refused to grant Carew leave of absence; 'though now I despair of it, I will hold a room for you in my heart.'[2] The comments of foreign ambassadors, none of whom spoke English or really understood the country, need to be treated with extreme caution.[3] However, in November 1601 the French ambassador wrote to his King: 'Today, according to what I hear, the greater number of the counties and towns send their returns in blank to the Secretary of State, and he names whom he pleases.'[4] A grotesque statement! but not without a substratum of fact.

There is a *fin-de-siècle* quality about the closing years of Elizabeth's reign. The Elizabethan system was in decline. Restraints, on which a wholesome life so largely depends, were being loosened, weaknesses magnified. The attempt of Essex to construct a single, dominant faction and thus establish a monopoly of patronage, was one sign of the change. It was later to find a less estimable but more successful exponent in the Duke of Buckingham, and so contribute to that revolt against a decadent political structure which merged into the Civil War. Political jobbery and corruption were another sign of morbidity. They were inherent in the Elizabethan system. Indeed, Court society was dependent on what seems to us, and often was, bribery. In an age when government finance, no less than conven-

1. *Hatfield MSS.* xi, 405, 401, 409.

2. *Letters from Cecil to Carew*, ed. Maclean (Camden Soc.), pp. 96, 100.

3. On this point, cf. my article, 'The Diplomatic Envoy', *History*, xiii, 204 ff.

4. P.R.O. Baschet Transcripts, bundle 32.

tion, made the payment to officials of adequate salaries quite out of the question, a system of gratuities was natural and, if kept within bounds, not unhealthy. The Queen set her face against abuse; and so did Burghley, though even he, a model of probity in his time, was not wholly free from taint and appears to have faltered in his last years.

In human affairs there seems to be a tendency for pressure to be maintained on the weak places of the social system. A new generation does not feel the old restraints. *Autres temps, autres mœurs.* Queen Elizabeth told Burghley that although he had brought up his son, Robert, as near as might be like unto himself, yet Burghley was to her in all things, and would be, *Alpha* and *Omega*.[1] 'As near as might be'! Father and son were not the same. The indications of jobbery and corruption in these last years when Robert Cecil was in power, and the instances with which his own name is associated, are too many to leave much doubt in one's mind. They tell of a deterioration in the moral climate. And when the last restraint was removed with the accession of a new monarch, as prone by nature to magnify this weakness of society as Essex had been to magnify faction, corruption and the sale of office and honours reached scandalous proportions.[2]

The argument holds good with parliamentary elections. While the Elizabethan electoral system may startle us, it was natural, it was free from corruption, and broadly speaking it was healthy. Before Essex and Robert Cecil appeared, it served social, not political purposes. But it too had inherent weaknesses. Essex, with his lack of all moderation, exploited one. Yet it was Robert Cecil whose activities were most noxious. His policy of organizing and canalizing nominations, inducing borough patrons to transfer their powers to him, was the antithesis of high Elizabethan practice. To a cynic, concerned with practical results, there may seem no essential difference between two strikingly comparable acts: between the Earl of Shrewsbury asking the Archbishop of York in 1593 to find a seat for his protégé, Anthony Wingfield, whereupon the Archbishop nominated him at Ripon; and Sir Robert Cecil asking his successor to transfer to him

1. ELLIS, *Original Letters*, 3rd ser. iv, 148.
2. Cf. my Raleigh Lecture, *The Elizabethan Political Scene*, where the theme is developed.

a nomination at the same borough in 1597 and 1601.[1] In fact, there was a profound distinction, both in method and morality. It was an abuse of the old system, and was to lead early Stuart sovereigns to those efforts at manipulating elections which brought their government into such disrepute.

Though, so far as we know, vulgar corruption did not foul elections before Elizabeth's death, it was not far off in the new atmosphere. We are passing into the Jacobean period, and only the still imperious though weakening hand of the aged Queen held the new forces in check. She herself felt the change. As she remarked to her faithful old antiquary, William Lambarde: 'Now the wit of the fox is everywhere on foot, so as hardly a faithful or virtuous man may be found.'[2]

1. Heralds' Coll. Talbot MSS. I, fol. 158; above, p. 157.
2. NICHOLS, *Progresses of Queen Elizabeth* (1788), vol. ii.

CHAPTER 12

Borough Elections

'Whoso desireth to discourse in a proper manner concerning corporated towns and communities', wrote a seventeenth-century antiquary, 'must take in a great variety of matter and should be allowed a great deal of time and preparation.' [1] In their electoral history they displayed all the individuality of persons – which, indeed, by a legal fiction, they were. Until the seventeenth century, when the interference of the House of Commons tended to modify and restrain the prevailing variety, each borough was left to evolve its own method of choosing representatives, so producing a confusion of practice far more perplexing than the notorious state of affairs on the eve of the Great Reform Bill of 1832.

In the boroughs there was no statutory franchise as in the counties. Indeed, the less we think in terms of a right to vote, the better we shall understand the complexity of the subject. It was the community, not the individual, that was represented. Even in the counties, with their forty-shilling freeholder franchise, this conception was still alive. On the theoretical side it explains the common practice by which the leading gentlemen of the county decided among themselves beforehand whom they should elect. We should regard these individuals, not as undermining the voting rights of the freeholders, but as facilitating a corporate act. The same practice prevailed in some boroughs. For example, at Exeter, where the parallel with the counties is more obvious because it was one of those parliamentary boroughs that were counties in themselves and held their elections at county courts, where the freeholders were the voters: here in 1588 and 1593, and no doubt on other occasions, the Common Council or governing body of the city discussed in advance who were the two 'most fit' persons to be proposed to the freeholders at the next

1. Madox, *Firma Burgi*, preface.

county day, adding in 1593 that if the freeholders preferred any other person, they were free to choose accordingly.[1]

It was only natural for the corporate acts of the borough to be performed by the governing body on behalf of the community; and therefore the election of members of parliament by what we term today 'the corporation' need not be considered a restrictive practice, denying the ordinary burgess or inhabitant the right to vote. The port of Rye, for example, when defining its procedure for the election both of its town officers and its parliamentary representatives, in 1580, vested the choice, as a matter of course, in the Mayor, jurats, and Common Council.[2] Our information is far from complete, but it seems fairly clear that in a substantial majority of Elizabethan boroughs the electorate was the corporation. At King's Lynn, the Mayor, twelve aldermen, and eighteen common councillors are regularly recorded as electing the Elizabethan members; at Leicester, it was the Mayor, twenty-four aldermen, and forty-eight assistants, meeting in Common Hall; and at Northampton, the Mayor, the twenty-four comburgesses – his 'cobrethren' – and the forty-eight commons. The procedure was the same at Reading and Salisbury.[3]

However, borough history conforms to no single pattern. Apparently by long-standing custom, some boroughs admitted a wider body to the franchise. Elsewhere, popular agitation broadened the franchise – agitation akin to the demand for a voice in the affairs of the town which led to the creation of a second chamber of 'commoners' in the governing body. The modern conception of a right to vote, implicit in any such movement, drew strength from the competition for parliamentary seats which developed in the second half of the sixteenth century. Rival candidates began seeking support from different elements in the community, thus provoking disputes about the franchise. Then, in the early seventeenth century, the House of Commons itself helped to break down the medieval preference of the community to the individual, when its standing committee,

1. WINIFRED TAFFS, 'Borough Franchise in the 17th Century' (London M.A. thesis), p. 107.

2. *H.M.C. Rep.* XIII, iv, 74.

3. ibid. XI, iii, 148, 175 ff.; BATESON, *Leicester Records*, iii, 136; MARKHAM and COX, *Northampton Records*, ii, 494; GUILDING, *Reading Records*, i, passim; *H.M.C. Var. Coll.* iv, 226 ff.

which dealt with election controversies, applied what we should describe as liberal principles. In 1624, in an election case concerning Cirencester, in which the issue was whether freeholders alone had the right to vote, the committee declared 'that there being no certain custom nor prescription' – and, as we know, for proof of prescription they demanded evidence which it might be impossible to furnish – 'we must have recourse to common right'. 'Common right' they held to be 'that ... all men, inhabitants, householders, resiants within the borough' 'ought to have voices in the election'.[1] Such decisions made good liberty; generally they were bad history.

Any classification of Elizabethan parliamentary boroughs according to the nature of the franchise must be both deceptive and inadequate. If, however, we indicate certain broad divisions, it may help to simplify the subject. In addition to the 'corporation boroughs', which have already been mentioned, there were some constituencies where the vote was confined to freemen of the borough; some where a particular tenure – for example, burgage tenure, or freehold – entitled the holder to vote; and still others with the widest franchise, extending to the inhabitants, the resident burgesses contributing to the town's charges, or to householders – descriptions which were not necessarily so broad as they seem.

Shrewsbury was a borough where resident burgesses, contributing to the town's charges, had the vote; but those 'living outside the town' were excluded. In 1584 there was a contested election, involving a poll, in which the three candidates secured 366, 299, and 176 votes respectively, indicating an electorate of about 420 – a large number for an Elizabethan borough. There was evidently another contested election in 1601, though all we know about it is a local chronicler's comment that there was 'great ado' in the choice of members.[2] Coventry, a 'freeman' borough privileged with county status, had an even larger electorate; or so it seems from a disputed election case in 1628, when it was said that about 600 electors were present – a number which few boroughs could have equalled in Tudor times.[3]

The small Surrey borough of Bletchingley furnishes an example

1. GLANVILLE, *Reports*, p. 107.
2. *H.M.C. Rep.* XV, x, 13; 'Early Chronicles of Shrewsbury', *Trans. Shrops. Arch Soc.* 1st ser. iii, 300, 347.
3. *Commons Journals*, i, 880.

of tenure determining the electorate. It was a manorial borough, presided over by the lord's Bailiff, an ancient borough by prescription, but without a charter of incorporation. It had belonged to Henry VIII's rejected Queen, Anne of Cleves, from whom it passed to Sir Thomas Cawarden, Master of the Revels, and from his heir to Lord Howard of Effingham, in whose family it remained from 1560 throughout the rest of Elizabeth's reign. During this period it is unlikely that the voters did anything more than follow the instructions of their lord's Bailiff. But in 1624 a majority of the electors ventured to revolt against a candidate recommended by the lady of the borough, and two rival elections were held, the Bailiff calling in ordinary inhabitants to offset the recalcitrant burgage-holders. Ultimately, the dispute came before the House of Commons, whose committee – again supporting freedom against patronage, even though it led them this time to favour the narrower franchise – reported that there were 'divers burgages or borough-tenements', the freeholders or tenants whereof, resident at the time of the election, had time out of mind chosen the members of parliament.[1]

Occasionally a borough adopted a form of indirect election. For example, throughout the sixteenth century Cambridge selected two men – one being chosen by 'the Mayor and his assistants for the bench', the other by 'the commonalty', in Henry VIII's reign – who then proceeded to choose eight men, who in turn made the final choice of the members of parliament. It was presumably a device to secure speed and orderliness in a borough with a wide franchise. But it did not always work smoothly. In 1556, to test 'what quietnesss may ensue thereof', they agreed that the second of the two men should be chosen by the twenty-four common councillors and the minor officials instead of by the body of commoners. The experiment was for that occasion only, and was probably abandoned afterwards. Difficulties continued. In 1571 an ordinance had to be passed declaring that a majority of five should prevail in the final selection of the members; and in 1600 both the 'two' and the 'eight' were each allotted one hour for making their selections, in default of which new groups of electors were to be chosen.[2] Great Yarmouth, a 'corporation borough' with as many as seventy-two members on its governing body, also

1. *V.C.H. Surrey*, iv, 257; GLANVILLE, *Reports*, pp. 29 ff.
2. COOPER, *Annals of Cambridge*, i, 272, 422, ii, 108, 227, 269, 600.

resorted to indirect election. In 1552 they nominated one of the Bailiffs, six aldermen, and six common councillors to choose their two members of parliament. This may or may not have been the invariable procedure at general elections. It was certainly not adopted at a by-election in 1575 when 'the whole house' or corporation chose the new member.[1]

A closer view of borough elections is happily supplied at Warwick. Just as Exeter in Elizabethan days had its notable antiquary, John Hooker, and Liverpool its redoubtable alderman, Ralph Sekerston, so Warwick produced an eminent worthy, a cross between these two. His name was John Fisher. He was a principal burgess, sometime Bailiff, and for a number of years Steward or Town Clerk; an able, rather smug authoritarian, who to his own greater glory and our delectation kept a remarkable descriptive record of municipal affairs, known to posterity as the Black Book of Warwick.

Under its charter of 1554, the government of this borough had been committed to a Bailiff and twelve assistants, 'to be called the principal burgesses'. The charter contained a clause which might have led to the creation of a second, or Common Council, as in other boroughs, if the oligarchs had not construed it in their own way. In 1570 they chose twenty-four townsmen to be their 'assistants'; 'to be called, used, continued and dismissed' as the principal burgesses willed, and to be 'as it were the mouth of the commoners'. Difficulties soon arose between the two bodies, as the result of which the Bailiff and his twelve colleagues decided that twenty-four commoners were too many, and after disbanding their assistants, later replaced them by a group of twelve. They were chiefly required to represent the whole body of commoners in the annual election of the Bailiff and the election of parliamentary representatives. As John Fisher wrote, this 'might better be done and with greater quietness' by the twelve assistants 'than if every rude fellow should have his speech'.[2]

For most of Elizabeth's reign, the lord of the borough was Leices-

1. PALMER, *Contin., Manship's Hist. of Gt Yarmouth*, pp. 197, 199. In the 15th century King's Lynn had used a method of indirect election (cf. HARROD, *Records of King's Lynn*, pp. 95–6).

2. *Cal. Pat. Rolls, Ph. & Mary*, ii, 19; TAIT, 'The Common Council of the Borough', *Eng. Hist. Rev.* xlvi, 22; *Black Book of Warwick*, ed. T. Kemp, pp. 16, 56 ff., 104 ff.

ter's elder brother, the Earl of Warwick, who was also Lord Lieutenant of the county. Under 'good Lord Warwick's' benign and generous patronage, parliamentary elections proceeded peacefully. There was no problem. The Earl asked for and was granted one nomination each time, and named his kinsman, Thomas Dudley, consistently from 1572 till 1588. The other member in 1571, 1572, and 1584 was the efficient and officious John Fisher – clearly, the nominee of the principal burgesses, and a choice always dutifully accepted by the body of assistants.[1]

Then in 1586 came trouble. It was caused by a neighbouring gentleman, Job Throckmorton of Haseley Manor, thrusting himself forward as a candidate. This Warwickshire squire belonged to a distinguished family. His father, Clement, was brother of the eminent Sir Nicholas Throckmorton and cousin to Queen Catherine Parr. In an active parliamentary career he had sat four times for the borough of Warwick and twice for the county. Job was his heir and succeeded to his father's estates in 1573. He carried the Protestantism of his father and uncle into the extremist ranks of the Puritans, of whose movement he was one of the most active lay supporters. Later, in 1588, his house at Haseley for a time harboured the secret Marprelate printing press, while he himself was suspected of being the author of these scurrilous, disturbing tracts.

Puritanism probably furnishes the clue to the borough of Warwick's troubles in 1586. After an initial experiment in 1584, these religious zealots were putting forth their maximum efforts in a political campaign, the scope and organization of which seem astonishingly out of place in the sixteenth century. As we know, they were at pains to secure the election to parliament of a number of their supporters, and as likely as not Job Throckmorton was one. Warwick was a centre of the movement. Within the last year the great puritan leader, Thomas Cartwright, had been appointed by the Earl of Leicester as Master of his Hospital or almshouse in the borough; and this eminent divine was a friend of Throckmorton's. He preached for him at Haseley.[2]

What is more, while the governing clique at Warwick were clearly

1. Cf. KEMP, op. cit., pp. 26–7, 409–10.
2. BANCROFT, *Survey of the Pretended Holy Discipline* (1593), p. 369; SCOTT PEARSON, *Cartwright*, pp. 290 ff., 303.

not Puritans – in 1564 John Fisher and two of his colleagues had been described by their Bishop as 'adversaries of religion', which must mean that they were sympathetic to the old faith [1] – there was a faction among the townsmen, led by a certain Richard Brook, which may well have belonged to this party. Brook in 1582 had been expelled by Fisher and his colleagues from the oligarchy of principal burgesses for 'his self-liking and resolute opinion, ruled by the loose lines of liberty, without respect or regard of the law of God or man'; and in the following year he had led 'the multitude' in their demand for a share in the choice of principal burgesses.[2] He was Fisher's *bête noire*: repeatedly the Black Book of Warwick reflects the antipathy of an oligarch for a demagogue. If also he was the leader of the local Puritans, then Fisher's venom would be doubly explained, for, as conservatives in religion, the borough 'bosses' must have detested such restless extremists.

Throckmorton had the support of a number of prominent gentlemen of the county, including the puritan-minded Sir John Harington and Sir Fulke Greville (the father), along with some of the principal burgesses and their assistants at Warwick. Further, he 'made very great labour to many of the inhabitants of this borough for their voices . . ., being much assisted by the busy Richard Brook and his complices'. With that touch of modernity which so startles us in the puritan movement, he visited Warwick, and, in order to rally his supporters and win voices for 'good cheer's sake', gave a 'solemn dinner' to sixty or eighty of them at the Swan Inn. Fisher, as well he might be, was shocked. These people, he scornfully wrote, were 'the meanest inhabitants of the borough'.

He was alarmed by the threat to the exclusive monopoly hitherto exercised by the principal burgesses and their submissive twelve assistants. If the election went to a contest, obviously the inhabitants at large, on whom Throckmorton was relying, would demand a part in it; a prospect as fearful to the oligarchs as it must have been pleasing to Brook and his faction. There was no escape by trickery. The authorities could not, as they might have wished, hold the election in secret, for the Bailiff had been compelled to promise Throck-

1. 'Letters from the Bishops to the Privy Council, 1564', *Camden Misc.* ix, 8.
2. KEMP, *Black Book*, pp. 367, 369, 344.

morton's supporters among the gentry – too influential a group to be flouted – that he would give two days' public notice of the election by proclamation. Nor could they look for countenance to their two great lords, the Earls of Warwick and Leicester. Warwick was a friend of Puritans, and Leicester the indulgent patron of Cartwright.

A week before the election, the Bailiff summoned the twelve assistants to meet him and his colleagues, the principal burgesses. After reproaching those who had promised to support Throckmorton, he expressed the hope 'that they would not be hasty with their voices until they somewhat understood the mind of their Bailiff and principal burgesses in the matter'. To prove that their representative should be a burgess, free and resident – which Throckmorton was not – and that none but free burgesses possessed a vote, he had the relevant statutes read to them. His speech seems to have had some effect on the hearers. But the canvassing for Throckmorton proceeded with such success, especially 'with the husbandmen in the Bridge end and West Street', that the authorities were left no alternative but to open direct negotiations with him.

At the interview, they began with the legal argument that as 'a gentleman and no burgess, nor having any interest' in the town's causes, 'nor any colour of freehold in the town', he was ineligible. To this he answered by citing the present example of Thomas Dudley and the precedents set by his father, Clement Throckmorton. His critics retorted that they had kept the law by swearing Dudley as a burgess, while his own father had not only been a good freeholder in the town and dwelt there, but had been made a burgess. In contrast, he himself had no habitation there, nor indeed did he wish to be a burgess 'but for the parliament, where peradventure some friends ... may have some causes in handling' – a sly dig, one imagines, at the impending puritan campaign in parliament.

Throckmorton would not budge. He intended, he declared, 'to put it to the jury by election'. He had no intention of creating 'a broil', and if the Bailiff gave two days' notice of the election, he would abide by the result. 'But he would not have this matter huddled up in a corner, as the most of your matters be', and rather than betray his supporters, he would challenge his opponents in the House of Commons. 'And if I fail them of it', he declared, 'yet, Mr

Rigeley, I mean to meet you at the parliament door to try the title between you and me.'

One of the gentlemen friends whom Thockmorton had brought to the interview suggested a way out of the difficulty. 'Well, brother Throckmorton', he said, 'I perceive that Mr Bailiff and his company are in doubt lest they may have something for the town to be done in the parliament, and therefore they would look to have such as they send thither sworn and assured to them. And they have reason so to do.' The solution was for Throckmorton to become a burgess. This he agreed to do and to swear an oath devised by John Fisher; though when it came to the oath, with puritan meticulousness he added a saving clause for his service to God and the Queen. The company then adopted him as their candidate, and the meeting ended with an officious homily by Fisher, reproaching Throckmorton for his familiarity with Richard Brook and for the 'diligent labouring of those that be ready to run headlong into any looseness', coupled with a burst of spleen at being ousted from the seat himself – though previously he had professed unwillingness to accept it![1]

The authorities had stooped to conquer. They were saddled with Throckmorton, but had kept the multitude out of the election. Their monopoly did not last. In 1620 divers freeholders and inhabitants assembled in the yard of the Shire Hall intent on electing two Warwickshire gentlemen, while the principal burgesses and their assistants in a room above were electing another pair. On this occasion the oligarchs managed to argue and sustain their case; but in 1628, when a similar challenge occurred, the issue was brought before the House of Commons, and though a petition was produced from about two hundred commoners disclaiming any right of election, the House, on its committee's report, decided that 'the right of election for the town of Warwick belongeth to the commonalty'. 'If but one commoner appear to sue for his right,' they declared with misplaced unction, 'they will hear him.' Their historical sense was wretched: the 'corporation' had in fact been ousted from an age-long monopoly by the competition and election tactics of intruding gentry.[2]

There were probably few contested elections in Elizabethan boroughs; certainly few compared with the total of members. This

1. *Black Book*, pp. 385 ff.
2. ibid., pp. 409–10; *Commons Journals*, i, 907.

is not surprising. In most boroughs the number of voters was small, and unless the monopoly of the town council or other select body was challenged, disagreement over nominations was not likely to occur. Also patronage reduced the opportunities for dispute. Yet there were some contests. Shrewsbury, as we have seen, had two successive lively elections at the end of the reign and maybe others of which there is no record. It was a borough with enough voters to encourage rival candidates.

The Court of Star Chamber offered little solace to the vanquished in these contests. It could not act quickly enough to unseat a member –a defect which, as we have noted, was remedied by the House of Commons in James I's reign, thus incidentally leading to an increase in the number of contests in borough elections. Again, Star Chamber suits were tedious and expensive. As a rule, the issue was not worth all the bother, for in boroughs a gentleman's social prestige was not at stake in the way it was in the counties. However, most rules have exceptions. Fortunately, there were a few people, vindictive, litigious, or touchy enough to take their grievances to this court. Such cases are pools of water in a thirsty land.

One case arose out of the 1571 election at Haverfordwest in Pembrokeshire, a single-member constituency where the population was between two and three thousand, though the franchise was confined to the burgesses or freemen, a body of about one hundred.[1] The story centres on Sir John Perrot, a characteristic figure of his age; 'a goodly gentleman, and of the sword'. He was of great physical strength, superb courage and spirit, but of a violent and arbitrary disposition, much addicted to brawling, possessing 'a native freedom and boldness of speech' which 'drew him on to a clouded setting and laid him open to the spleen and advantage of his enemies': an Earl of Essex, one might almost say, cast in a coarser mould. He was reputed to be a son of Henry VIII, 'a subreptitious child of the blood royal'.[2] Perrot was the oustanding personality in Elizabethan Pembrokeshire. His boyhood home and estate of Haroldstone adjoined Haverfordwest, of which borough he was Mayor in 1570, 1575, and 1576.

Such a man was fated to conjure up antagonisms. Early in Elizabeth's reign we perceive an anti-Perrot party among the Pembroke-

1. For references see my account of the election, *Eng. Hist. Rev.* lxi, 18–27.
2. *D.N.B.*; NAUNTON, *Fragmenta Regalia*.

shire gentry. Perrot himself was supported by the Wogans of Wiston and Boulston. Opposed to him were William Phillips of Picton, an estate close to Haverfordwest, John Barlow of Slebech, Perrot's neighbour in this part of the county who came into conflict with him over concealed lands, and two gentlemen who became Phillips's sons-in-law, George Owen of Henllys, lord of Kemys, the Pembroke-shire historian, and Alban Stepneth of Prendergast, the principal figure in our election story. Stepneth came of a Hertfordshire family. He settled in Pembrokeshire probably in 1561, and four years later married his first wife, whose father had been an enemy of Perrot's in Mary Tudor's reign. Through her he inherited the estate of Prender-gast, adjoining Haverfordwest.

So great was Perrot's power in this borough that no opponent would have stood a chance of election while he remained at home. But in November 1570 he was offered the post of President of Mun-ster, and in February 1571, a month before the parliamentary election, set sail for Ireland. It was Stepneth's opportunity. The Wogans, who might have led the Perrot party in their leader's absence, had no rights in the borough, whereas Stepneth himself was a burgess, as was William Phillips of Picton, and there were five other Justices of the Peace, one of them an esquire, and three ex-Sheriffs of the town on Stepneth's side. His party included most of the burgesses of gentle rank, and in the absence of Sir John Perrot was strong enough to control the affairs of the borough.

All should have gone well for him. But, alas! the borough offices for that year had been filled before Perrot left for Ireland, and both the Mayor, John Voyle, and the Sheriff, Edmund Harries, who was Voyle's son-in-law, were Perrot's adherents. The Sheriff was a key-man, because Haverfordwest enjoyed the status of a county. Conse-quently, it was his duty to preside over parliamentary elections, and, like his betters in the counties, if he had the effrontery he could do pretty well as he liked.

The candidate whom the Sheriff and his party put forward was John Garnons, a Herefordshire gentleman by origin, married to a Pembrokeshire woman. He was, or soon became, Clerk of the Peace for the county, an office which he probably owed to Perrot who was *Custos Rotulorum*. His age was thirty-six or -seven, and he had probably sat in parliament, as a lawyer of the Middle Temple, for

Pembroke borough in November 1554, at the early age of twenty. He stood excommunicate at the time of the 1571 election, having been openly denounced in the parish church of St Mary's; but as this solemn censure of the Church was notoriously abused, being inflicted for light offences, it may imply little, though it did give his opponents the opportunity of trying to have him expelled from the House of Commons.

There was a good deal of preparation for the election. William Morgan, a tailor, aged twenty-six or -seven, who became Sheriff of the borough in 1585–6, but in 1571 was not yet a burgess and had no right to a voice in the election – though he did, in fact, vote! – was the Sheriff's most active supporter. The two of them, with 'certain other unruly persons', 'did ... most earnestly travail and practise'; and some of the more timorous of Stepneth's supporters were in consequence induced to play safe, to stay at home on election day or go out of town. The Mayor was said to have made 'sundry new burgesses', conditional on voting for Garnons – a very early precedent of a notorious eighteenth-century practice.

The election took place in the Shire Hall of the town on 20 March 1571. The leading townsmen sat on the bench, and after the nominations the voters ranged themselves on opposite sides of the Hall. William Morgan moved among them, urging them to vote for Garnons. So did the Sheriff, who, if Stepneth can be believed, 'with strong hand and violence ... haled and pulled' some from one side to the other, drove some out of the Hall, and set porters at the door to keep out others. There happened to be one burgess in prison for debt, enjoying a burgess's right of incarceration in the 'free gaol of the town' – presumably with that liberty of movement which often made imprisonment in those days surprisingly less irksome than we might imagine. The Sheriff asked for whom he intended to vote, and when he replied 'Stepneth', rejoined, 'And thou shalt therefor into the lower gaol'. The same afternoon the unfortunate man was transferred to this straiter confinement.

A poll was taken. Each voter was called by name, his vote being entered in paper 'books' or lists compiled by the two parties; and if challenged by the opposing side he had to declare on oath that he was a burgess and was thus qualified to vote. The two original lists drawn up for Stepneth were put in as evidence in his Star Chamber suit and survive among the documents. The list of his own supporters has fifty names, authenticated by the signature or mark of each voter; and it is of incidental interest, as a measure of literacy, that twenty-eight signed their names, the others using marks. Only one of Stepneth's supporters was challenged: he took the oath.

The list of Garnons's voters – authenticated by five of Stepneth's side, signing as witnesses – contains forty-four names. Thirteen are noted as 'no burgess' and one as 'disgraded'; and these were all challenged and put to the oath, one apparently refusing to take it. We must presume that the other thirteen took the oath, and, according to Stepneth, perjured themselves. Actually, three of them, including William Morgan, confessed in their evidence that they were not burgesses. Thus, giving Garnons's side the benefit of all doubt, his list should be reduced to forty more or less legitimate votes.

Fifty against forty seems plain arithmetic. But the Sheriff could still juggle with names in his return. He calmly transferred to Garnons the names of two men who voted for Stepneth. A townsman who though present gave no vote because he was not a burgess, was afterwards called into Garnons's house by Morgan and the Sheriff, and asked 'to take up a seal fixed on wax on a parchment writing'. Not knowing what the document was, he refused; but Morgan told him that he would simply be doing what the Mayor had done, and so he took hold of the seal. It was the election return, and in this way one more vote was scored for Garnons. Another townsman, also unqualified, did the same in the house of one Elizabeth Nashe, widow. But the most casual and amusing of these incidents happened during the election. A simple townsman, Evan ap Powell, was standing in the street outside the Shire Hall. Morgan called to him from a window, 'With whom wilt thou give thy voice?' 'Where my master, Thomas Tanke, giveth his voice', answered Powell. Tanke, a former Mayor, was one of Garnons's supporters.

During the election there were angry scenes, with insults and opprobrious names like 'Jackanapes'; and Morgan told one of Stepneth's supporters that 'if he had had right, he should have been hanged twenty years ago'. The Sheriff was heard to say that if Garnons had only ten votes and Stepneth ever so many, nevertheless he would return Garnons. When reminded of the legal penalties for a false return, William Morgan retorted 'that the Sheriff should be saved harmless' – in other words, his fine be paid for him – 'whatever it should cost'. The Sheriff tried to brazen out his conduct by saying that Stepneth was disqualified as non-resident and not a burgess. The latter was a lie, and the former had little or no substance.

Though Garnons was clearly outvoted, he was returned as the town's representative, while Stepneth proceeded against the Sheriff in the Star Chamber and won his case. By good fortune the judgement has been preserved: Harries was sentenced to imprisonment and to a fine of two hundred pounds.

In 1572, the year following this election, Sir John Perrot was still away in Ireland, the new town officials, both Mayor and Sheriff, were now from the anti-Perrot faction, and, though William Morgan attempted to upset things by seizing and detaining the election writ, Stepneth won the Haverfordwest seat. It is a further sign of the collapse of Perrot's power during his absence that William Phillips of Picton, Stepneth's father-in-law and a leader of his party, captured the county seat. By a stroke of luck, the 1572 parliament with its several prorogations outlasted the period, from 1573 to June 1584, during which Sir John Perrot was resident again in Pembrokeshire. The next election came in November 1584, when he was back in Ireland, this time as Lord Deputy, the highest office in the land. Stepneth was thus enabled to win the Haverfordwest seat again, and to retain it at the next election in 1586. But with that, his run of luck ended. Perrot returned to Wales in July 1588, and marked his resumption of control over the town by standing for election there in November of that year. Needless to add, he obtained the seat.

CHAPTER 13

Borough Elections: Chichester and Gloucester

IN the sixteenth century the government of the Sussex city of Chichester was still centred on the medieval gild merchant – a curious but not unique survival.[1] The gild consisted of the Mayor, aldermen, and free citizens, who met for business in their common Council House and alone could make anyone a 'free citizen, enfranchised of the city' – a member of the gild. Outside this close and apparently small body of citizens were the commoners, who had certain rights and met in the common Gildhall or Townhall of the city.

Both sections of the community took part in the election of the Mayor and the members of parliament. In the mayoral election, the retiring Mayor put to the commoners the names of two or perhaps three chosen by the members of the gild from among themselves: that is, the gild had the right of nomination and the commoners of election. It was a situation likely to provoke occasional trouble, and in 1540 certain 'ringleaders of all the commoners' decided to defy the custom and elect their own nominee, a 'brother of the city'. They 'stood stoutly' against the Mayor and his brethren; but the chief conspirators were clapt in ward, and the Mayor, with the rump of the commoners, proceeded with the usual form of election.[2] There was another revolt in 1580. On this occasion the commoners ignored the two official nominees and elected another free citizen, one Robert Adams, who in fact became Mayor two years later, was re-elected after an interval of ten years,[3] and was Town Clerk and alderman at

1. My colleague, Professor C. J. Sisson, called my attention to the Chichester election case in the Star Chamber, on which this narrative is mainly based. The documents are: Star Chamber 5, C 41/1, bill, answers of Ralphe Chauntler, George Chatfield, Robert Addams, replication; c 26/36, interrogatories and defendants' depositions; c 23/37, plaintiff's and defendants' interrogatories for witnesses, with depositions; C 47/10, plaintiff's interrogatories.

2. This incident, mentioned in the 1586 election case, is clearly the one summarized in *Star Chamber Proceedings, Sussex Rec. Soc.* xvi, 17–18.

3. Cf. the list of Mayors in A. HAY, *Chichester*, p. 569.

the time of the 1586 parliamentary election. On this occasion the commoners were probably not guilty of a serious defiance of authority, but were simply choosing a man out of his turn. The Mayor and his fellow-gildsmen, however, would not tolerate the innovation. They chose one of their two nominees themselves.

In the election of members of parliament, the custom was for the gild to elect one member and the commoners the other, each body being responsible for the wages of its member. Normally, when relations between the oligarchy and the people were peaceful, it seems likely that the Mayor and his fellow-gildsmen not only elected their own man but also nominated the commoners' representative; though this was certainly not the theory of the constitution and there were conflicting views about the practice. It was generally agreed, however, that if the commoners chose anyone who was not a free citizen, the election was only valid if the gild of merchants agreed to confer the freedom of the gild and city on that person.

In the election for Mary Tudor's last parliament, 'the commoners and the baser sort did of a will make choice' of one, Roger Drue, then a commoner; this in preference to Peter Tolpett, a free citizen, who became Mayor in 1559 and who – though we cannot be sure of this – may have been nominated by the Mayor and his party. The gild refused to make Drue a free citizen, and the Mayor returned Tolpett as the alternative candidate. The principle was reaffirmed in 1563 when the commoners' member, John Sherwyn esquire, a free citizen and later an alderman, agreed, 'upon the tedious suit' of a mutual friend, to yield his seat to a local gentleman who was not a free citizen. The Mayor vetoed the proposal, as 'against our liberties'.

Up to this point, the city had perhaps kept its elections more or less free from outside interference. But in 1571 the name of Thomas West, probably brother of Lord De La Warr, a Sussex magnate, appeared as that of the commoners' member. He was made a free citizen to comply with the custom of the borough; from which we may infer that he was acceptable to the oligarchy. He was probably nominated by the Mayor and his brethren in response to a lord's letter, perhaps from the Earl of Arundel, whose castle dominated and still dominates the neighbouring country.

If, as seems likely, this was the first lapse from independence, it proved to be the beginning of a long story. In the following year,

1572, Dr Valentine Dale, a Master of Requests, used by the Queen on many diplomatic missions, came forward as a candidate. He probably needed a patron's aid for his first election and the Earl of Arundel again seems the most likely intermediary. Once elected, and made a free citizen as Thomas West had been, Dr Dale clung to the seat like a limpet. The city was in bondage. But such a bondage, which not only secured the community a friend at Court with ready access to the sovereign, but also served individual citizens who had suits in his Court of Requests, was very acceptable. A member of the gild – John Sherwyn – who tried to replace him with a friend, criticizing his complete ignorance of Chichester's affairs, presently added that he himself had no business in the Court of Requests: unlike others, he could afford to show independence.

Owing to his eminence, Dr Dale had to be the senior of the two parliamentary burgesses, and therefore the merchant gild's choice. In normal circumstances this made little odds. The junior seat was virtually at the gild's disposal; and no doubt it was on their recommendation that the commoners in 1572 chose as their member Richard Lewknor esquire, of the Middle Temple, a local Sussex gentleman who was probably already Recorder of Chichester. He was an able lawyer, who later became a Serjeant-at-Law and Chief Justice of Chester, and died owning several manors in Sussex as well as land in Shropshire.[1] In or before 1586 he possessed a house in Chichester.

When the next parliamentary elections came in 1584, the authorities found themselves tied to both these members; to Dr Dale on account of his Court influence, and to Lewknor because he was Recorder. All might have been well and the commoners might as before have followed the lead of their betters without demur, had it not been for an irascible citizen, a newcomer to Chichester since the last election. His name was James Colbrand.[2] He had been a member for Ludgershall in Wiltshire in the parliaments of 1571 and 1572, perhaps through the influence of his wife, who was the eldest daughter of Lord St John of Bletsoe; and maybe it was the death of his father-in-law in 1582 which made him turn to Chichester in 1584. He was a local gentleman, an esquire by status, who owned land in the neigh-

1. *Post Mortem Inquisitions, 1485–1649, Sussex Rec. Soc.* xiv, 143.
2. Cf. ibid., p. 54.

bourhood as well as a house in Chichester, where he had been living since 1580, or perhaps a year or two longer. He was a cousin of Lewknor's, or called him cousin, which implies some degree of relationship; but he was on bad terms both with him and his elder brother, Thomas Lewknor, as also with others. His contentious nature ultimately caused the 'better sort' in this part of Sussex to refuse to associate with him. At the time of the 1584 election, or certainly two years later, he was captain of the city's trained bands, which gave him a following among the humbler inhabitants and the equipment of a faction-leader. He was not a 'free citizen'.

After electing Dr Dale and agreeing to nominate the Recorder, Richard Lewknor, as the commoners' member, the Mayor and his colleagues fixed Friday, 6 November 1584, for this second election. No opposition was expected; and Lewknor was away in London for the legal term. When, however, it was realized that Colbrand was organizing a party for his own election, the Mayor postponed the day from Friday to Monday, thus giving Lewknor's friends among the aldermen time to take counter measures. The delay was prudent, for Colbrand, who had not yet exhausted his credit among the 'better sort', had managed to obtain, in writing, the support of alderman John Sherwyn, who had been busy canvassing on his behalf. But the majority of the people rallied to the voice of authority. The ex-Mayor, Ralph Chauntler, and others who clearly detested the intruder, were very active. If Colbrand can be believed, some of the voters, no doubt irretrievably pledged to him, were coerced into staying away, while, the night before the election, Chauntler sent for 'a great multitude of people' – a resounding phrase, signifying little in Star Chamber cases – gathered them in and behind his house, and the next morning issued forth with them. In Lewknor's absence, Chauntler personated him at the election and had 'great words' with Colbrand. Evidently it was a noisy scene. Colbrand was beaten, and was 'in a great rage', calling some who voted against him 'turncoats', and threatening to convene his leading opponents before the Lords of her Majesty's most honourable Privy Council – to 'make a Star Chamber matter of it', as Justice Shallow would have said.

Such was the background to the election which took place two years later, and which did lead Colbrand to make a Star Chamber matter of it. In the intervening years he strengthened his position as a demagogue and lost caste among gentlemen. Only two of the better citizens were supporting him in 1586.

Already, when the Sheriff's precept for the 1586 election arrived, the city was committed to Dr Dale, for on 20 September, in reply to an offer of his services, the Mayor, who was then John Farrington, had written in the name of the aldermen and citizens promising him the seat. The precept reached the new Mayor, George Chatfield, on 3 October. After consulting some senior colleagues, he summoned the aldermen and free citizens to a meeting at the Council House, where those present, numbering about thirty – a clue to the size of the ruling body – re-elected Dr Dale, 'had speech to nominate' Richard Lewknor for the other seat, and appointed the following Friday, 7 October, as the day for the commoners' election. The city Serjeant was sent through the town to give general warning of the assembly.

Everyone must have known that Colbrand would again stand for election; and therefore, in spite of the calls of the legal term, Lewknor on this occasion prudently remained in Chichester to fight for his seat. Though we hear little about it, we may be sure that there was a good deal of preliminary canvassing. Lewknor's side had a windfall in the shape of a circular letter from the Privy Council to all Sheriffs, urging the re-election of the old members. The Mayor had already told his fellow-gildsmen of this.

On the Friday morning, the Mayor, Recorder, and divers aldermen and free citizens assembled at the High Cross, 'a place of usual meeting', and when the hour of eight approached, went in procession to the Town Hall or Gildhall. The Mayor waited awhile for the electors to assemble before going to his seat at a table on the dais; and during this time, Colbrand 'came very hastily, furiously, and in quarrelling manner unto them'. Fixing in particular on Edward More esquire, a gentleman who – so the evidence suggests – had stood unsuccessfully for the county at the election held the day before at Chichester, he said: 'Master More, you are come now to be quittance with me for that I was against you yesterday.' To which More answered: 'No. I will keep that in store until another time, for I take it you did me little harm, because you were able to bring very few or none that are freeholders or copyholders of your own.' The gibe went home. In great heat Colbrand retorted: 'I can bring as many or more than you can. And my father might dispend three hundred pounds in Sussex when your father was chipping of bread in the pantry' – an allusion to the office in the Royal Household which More's father had held. More gave him the lie: if his father had no land in Sussex, he had land elsewhere. 'If thou canst dispend two hundred pounds', he continued, 'I can dispend four hundred pounds; and if thou canst dispend four hundred pounds, I can dispend eight hundred pounds.' 'Thou liest in thy throat', replied Colbrand. 'I have as much land as thou, and am as good a gentleman as thou art.' After which typical Elizabethan exchange, the Mayor and others with much ado quieted Colbrand and saved a tumult.

The Mayor and his brethren then went to their places on the dais, where a number of gentlemen, including some of the Cathedral Close, who had no vote but came to lend countenance to the Recorder, stood upon the Mayor's table. The Mayor explained the cause of the meeting, told the electors of the Privy Council's letter advocating the re-election of the former members, and 'commended unto them Master Richard Lewknor'. Thereupon the Town Clerk, Robert Adams, read both the Sheriff's precept and the Council letter, and urged them to have special care of the Council's injunction. This sore stroke at his candidature roused Colbrand to cry out angrily, 'What an impudent fellow is this! He hath read the Council's letters without a warrant, and hath abused the Council's letters, which he shall answer unto.' He claimed that they had no such force as Adams pretended.

After this 'the people fell presently into calling and crying out, some of one side and some of the other'. We might term it the election by voices. In the midst of the hubbub, the Mayor came down from the dais, and through the Town Crier commanded all serving men and all others who 'had no voice' to leave. He himself put them out and locked the hall door. Giving the rest charge to keep the peace, he ordered those supporting Lewknor to stand on one side of the hall, and those for Colbrand on the other. Perhaps it was now that the most active of Lewknor's backers did their utmost to dissuade many of their opponent's followers from voting for him. Colbrand 'was no gentleman', argued one. Another went up to a certain William Reigatt, a sadler and tenant of his, and said, 'Reigatt, get thee away!' But Reigatt stayed, knowing no reason why he should leave.

'Reigatt,' said the man to him later, 'thy coat shall be pulled from thy back.' And, sure enough, the following day he was told to clear his hay and goods out of a stable and garden, his landlord refusing to grant him grace even over the week-end.

The next stage in the election was a poll, two men from each side being assigned to compile the lists of names. They began with Colbrand's voters – described in the Star Chamber documents as 'most of them' Colbrand's soldiers, 'and the residue, of the meanest and basest sort of the people'. Lewknor's scrutineers were quickly challenging some on the ground that they were under-tenants, whereupon the Mayor ordered them to complete the lists for both sides, setting a mark against any name they wished to challenge. Apparently forty-five or -six, fairly evenly divided between the two sides, were challenged for this reason. These men were sent into an adjoining jury chamber and called for scrutiny one at a time. After long debate, it was agreed 'that he that did watch and ward for the house of himself, and paid lot and scot and had no allowance of any of the rest that dwelt in the house with him, was accounted to be the upper-tenant, and the other that did not watch or ward of himself was accounted to be the under-tenant' and therefore voteless.

Seemingly, some of the inhabitants of the Cathedral Close voted for Lewknor. The Close was outside the city's jurisdiction and its inhabitants were not contributories to the town; nor – it was said – had they voted in previous elections. Colbrand's scrutineers objected to them, and probably the objection was sustained. But a fierce controversy arose over the right of the free citizens, or gildsmen, to vote. In the last election of 1584, Colbrand had had some support among those privileged few, and the question had not then arisen. On the present occasion, there was only one on his side. He naturally objected to such votes; and he might think with reason, for this was the election of the commoners' member. The free citizens had already held their own election, from which the commoners were excluded. But, clear though the logic seems to us, it was evidently a moot point; and well it might be in a constituency that had had few contested elections. Certain free citizens refrained from voting because they did not think they possessed a vote; others voted with the words, 'if he may', added to each name; and perhaps, as Colbrand complained, some of these names were added quite late in the proceedings.

It was obviously touch and go for Lewknor. At eleven or twelve o'clock that morning he was heard to say – or so one of Colbrand's witnesses testified – that he would lose the election and had rather lose three or five hundred pounds. As the proceedings dragged on, a sadler, voting for him, wanted to get back to his work: Lewknor promised to pay his day's wages rather than lose his vote. On the legal aspect of the free citizens' vote, as might be expected, he was quite emphatic. In his opinion, they alone ought to be the voters: at least, they should participate in the election.

Tempers and speeches were inflamed. It may have been at this time, when the outcry was great, that Edward More, sitting near Colbrand, said to him: 'Master Colbrand, I pray you, speak you to them to be quiet; they will peradventure hear you.' 'What will you have me to do?' answered Colbrand. 'If you will have them quiet, you must please them.' To this More replied: 'Must we please the people ? No, no; the people must be governed, not pleased.' Some of the boasting words used by Colbrand's soldiers have been preserved. 'If they could not have him by their choice there, they would choose him at the High Cross or in the fields.' 'They cared not for the laws: law, or law not, they would have him.' 'They would go up with him to the parliament-house door.' Colbrand – so it was said – stimulated their enthusiasm by promising them corn 'all the year after' for 2s. 6d. a bushel, if he became a member of parliament; and they should have their woading or dyeing again.

The Mayor, who, while committed to the Recorder's side, behaved with admirable judgement throughout, refused to accept his interpretation of election law, since he was a party to the issue. Once more going down from the dais to pacify the rowdy voters, he decided to have the voting lists wrapped in a paper and sealed in two places with hard wax by each of the candidates, pending conference with the aldermen in the Council House and the taking of outside legal advice. Also, there was a further question to be settled, which Lewknor had naturally raised. This was, whether Colbrand was eligible for election, since he was not a free citizen.

The Mayor then asked Lewknor and Colbrand to announce that an agreed procedure had been reached, and request the electors to depart peacefully. Lewknor spoke first. He was sorry, he said, that the election had been so troublesome and that anyone should think ill of him. He did not believe that he deserved to lose any of their voices, for he had served as a citizen in parliament these fourteen years, and never yet charged the city one penny towards his expenses. Moreover, he was careful of their interests and had brought some things to good pass for them. Colbrand then stepped upon the table to speak. 'The gentleman', he irritably declared, 'was driven to preach of himself and of his doings.' Though unable to imitate Lewknor and preach of his own doings, yet he thought that he had done, or was willing to do, as much as his opponent. The assembly dispersed about five o'clock. They had been at it since 8 a.m., apparently without a break.

The next day, Saturday, the Mayor called together his brother-aldermen, who resolved to summon a meeting of aldermen and free citizens for the Monday at 8 a.m. The Mayor also brought a lawyer, Thomas Bowyer, to the city to give legal advice. On the Monday, after much discussion, it was decided – with Colbrand's one supporter as the sole dissentient – first that the free citizens were legally entitled to vote, and secondly that Colbrand, not being a free citizen, was disqualified from election. Thereupon, the Mayor sent for Colbrand, announced their decision, showing him its statutory basis, and – superfluous though this had become – broke open the sealed voting lists before him and the whole company. According to the Mayor, the lists revealed four more names for Lewknor than for his opponent. A number – 'a great many more', says the Mayor, with questionable exactitude – of the free citizens present at the meeting would have liked that morning to add their names for Lewknor, but the Mayor would not permit it. In his Star Chamber bill Colbrand claimed that he was elected 'by a far greater number of voices of electors'. No doubt he had a majority of commoners' votes; it may also be that some free citizens, imagining in the first stage of the election that they had no voice, added their votes as the poll proceeded – technically a questionable act; but, when all has been said for Colbrand, the Mayor's sober account of the election seems far preferable to his outpourings.

The same day, in the afternoon, Colbrand came to the Mayor's house with a strange request. Would he ask Lewknor to surrender his seat? Lewknor, he naïvely argued, would retain the credit of winning the election, he would be freer to attend to his legal business, and he, Colbrand, would be greatly beholden to him. The next morning the Mayor and seven or eight aldermen went to the Recorder with this curious plea. Understandably, he would not be persuaded. If, said he, Colbrand had written to him before the election, he could have had the seat with his goodwill. But after what had happened, it stood not with his credit to yield.

Balked this way, Colbrand, supported by many friends, next asked the Mayor to make him a free citizen and return him to parliament in place of Dr Dale, who was not a resident and was therefore not qualified; moreover, they argued, he could have his choice of other seats. The Mayor must have been a singularly peace-loving man, for, following this request, he actually wrote to Dr Dale, asking if he would surrender his seat. The messenger took the letter to the Court at Windsor, and not finding him there, proceeded to London. But Dr Dale was at Fotheringay at the trial of Mary Queen of Scots, and the Mayor was therefore kept waiting for an answer, with his election return held in suspense. During this delay, the selfish Colbrand badgered the Mayor to return him, offering bonds of eight score pounds or thereabouts should he get into trouble.

At last the answer came; but not from Dr Dale, from the Privy Council. It was a sharp reprimand, dated 22 October, which sent the Mayor scurrying with his return to the Sheriff. The Councillors reminded him of the promise of re-election made to Dale in September, and of their own circular letter to Sheriffs. They now understood that there were some practices to oust Master Dale and defraud him of the seat to which he had been nominated by general consent and which he had held so long. They advised the city authorities, as well in respect of the Queen's general advice to constituencies, as also for the credit of Dr Dale, which was 'greatly touched', to continue him as their member, reminding them that he 'both hath, and is likely further to stand you in very good stead for the causes of the city'.

Thus Colbrand's pertinacity came to nought. However, he seems to have drawn up a rival indenture and to have gone to Westminster, pretending that he expected the Mayor to return him as one of Chichester's members, though one suspects that legal or other business took him to town. If he attempted to get the Clerk of the Crown to accept his own rival indenture and return, he certainly failed. Presumably, he also lost his Star Chamber case, for the Privy Council judges in that court were not likely to approve of his attempt to discredit Dr Dale's election, nor sympathize with his demagogic role.

It is interesting to reflect that if this election had taken place in the 1620s, the result in all likelihood would have been different. Privy Councillors would not then have dared to write directive letters to an independent borough; Colbrand's challenge to the validity of the election would have gone to the House of Commons, not the Star Chamber; and the House would almost certainly have construed the law in favour of the commoners – as, in fact, they did later, in 1660.[1]

Subsequent Chichester elections also indicate that Colbrand lost his Star Chamber case. He lived till October 1600, but though he was prominent enough to become Sheriff of the county in 1598–9, when next he secured a seat in parliament – in 1597 – it was at Appleby, not Chichester. In 1588 Dr Dale and Richard Lewknor were once more returned. Dr Dale died in November 1589, and in the parliament of 1593 Richard Lewknor became the merchant gild's representative, while the commoners meekly acquiesced in Lord Lumley's nominee, William Ashbie, 'a mere stranger unto this place', as the Mayor wrote, 'and unknown to us all, and only liked and allowed of by your Lordship's commendations'.[2] Lord Lumley may be presumed to have represented the Arundel interest in Chichester while his nephew, the Earl, was prisoner in the Tower. Perhaps he was the city's High Steward. His nominee was clearly sponsored by the Mayor and his fellows, and so, in effect, after the disturbing interlude of Colbrand, the commonalty of Chichester had returned to the old custom of accepting the merchant gild's nominee as their member. It would have been decribed as a 'free election': indeed, the Mayor and others had not hesitated to affirm this in 1586. To the sixteenth-century mind, it was not incompatible with freedom for humbler people to acquiesce in the proposals, even insistent proposals, of their betters.

The city of Gloucester had a far more troubled and varied history than Chichester. It was a county in itself, and therefore election writs went direct to the two Sheriffs, while elections were held, as in the counties, on the county day in the county court, which, on these occasions, because of the number present, met in the Gildhall instead of the Tolsey. There was a relatively large electorate, perhaps – as

1. T. CAREW, *Elections*, p. 144.   2. Egerton MS. 2598, fol. 277.

was suggested in the Star Chamber – some four to five hundred;[1] but it was as free citizens or burgesses, not as suitors to the county court, that electors were entitled to vote.

The first dispute of which we hear was in October 1555. The evidence is vague, but apparently many of the electors, including a minority of the Common Council of the city, supported a rival candidate against one of the two whom the Mayor and 'the worthier' aldermen and councillors wished to be elected. There was – to quote the city's records – 'great busyness', 'long debating', 'discord, contentions, and strife'; and some of the burgesses who obstructed the poll were fined by the city authorities sums varying from 3s. 4d. to 1s. od. Perhaps the official candidate was John Pollard esquire, the city's Recorder, 'profoundly learned in the laws of this realm', as the Clerk of the House of Commons noted in his Journal. He had been Speaker in 1553, and was again to be Speaker in this parliament, but had evidently been forced to seek a borough seat in lieu of his recent Oxfordshire county seat.[2] A most attractive candidate he must have seemed to responsible city governors. But he was an alien, and the ordinary Gloucester crowd, with its dislike of 'foreigners', could easily be persuaded to prefer a good Gloucestershire squire. If this guess be right, the rebels won. John Pollard, Speaker-designate, had to find a Wiltshire borough seat a week later, while Gloucester elected Arthur Porter esquire, who had been Sheriff of the county in 1548–9 and senior knight of the shire in November 1554. Following their reverse, the city authorities passed an ordinance forbidding any burgess, on pain of disfranchisement, to give his vote or canvass for anyone who was not a burgess and freeman, or else Recorder of the city.[3]

The ordinance was observed in the following election of 1558, when the new Recorder, Richard Pates, a worthy lawyer and speculator in chantry lands,[4] was chosen along with an ex-Mayor of the city. Pates was re-elected in 1559 and 1563, but the authorities violated their ordinance on both occasions by choosing as their senior member an eminent Gloucestershire squire, Sir Nicholas Arnold, who had

1. Star Chamber 5, A 1/5, interrogatory no. 9.
2. The *D.N.B.* is inaccurate in its life of this man.
3. *H.M.C. Rep.* XII, ix, 452–3.
4. *Trans. Bristol & Glos. Arch. Soc.* lvi, 201 ff.; *Cal. Pat. Rolls, Ed. VI*, ii, 260.

been in royal service under Henry VIII and Edward VI, was in
trouble and for a time imprisoned in the Tower under Mary, and for
a year acted as Lord Justice of Ireland under Elizabeth.[1] The place of
such a man was clearly in the county seat: indeed, he had sat for
Gloucestershire in 1545, 1553, and 1555, and was to sit again in 1572.
But, being a keen parliament man, when a county seat was not available he turned to the boroughs, sitting for Gloucester in 1559 and
1563 and Cricklade in Wiltshire in 1571. He was brother-in-law to
Arthur Porter;[2] and perhaps the same local faction which seems to
have secured Porter's election in 1555, was responsible for this palpable breach of the city's ordinance.

We do not know whether there was any trouble over the election
of 1563. In 1571 there certainly was. By this time, Mr Pates, who had
sat in every parliament since he was made Recorder, had come to
regard his Gloucester seat as an incident, nay a right of office. He
reckoned without the factions. Though not an alien like his prede-
cessor, he was probably not a sworn burgess – or so it was suggested
many years later.[3] In any case, he had enemies. 'By the sinister practice of some evil men of this city', he was ousted from his seat in 1571
– ousted by the Town Clerk, an Oxford graduate and lawyer named
Thomas Atkins, who was a 'young' man of about thirty-three compared with Pates's staid fifty-four years,[4] and, more humiliating still,
as Town Clerk was technically his deputy. Atkins seems – at any rate,
later in his life – to have counted on the backing of the commoners,
and perhaps the old tradition of resistance to authority was a factor
in the election.

Pates, however, had friends in high places. He took his grievance
to the Master of the Rolls, Sir William Cordell, a contemporary of
his at Lincoln's Inn, evidently wanting the election quashed on the
ground that the Recorder ought to be one of the members. Cordell
spoke to Lord Burghley, and on his instructions had search made for
precedents. He found a writ of Henry VIII's reign ordering the city
of London to proceed to a new election because they had failed to

1. No return survives for 1559. The names of the members are given in
the city's Minute Book, 1486–1600, fol. 133.
2. *Trans. Bristol & Glos. Arch. Soc.* xxviii, 153.
3. Star Chamber 5, A 20/11, interr. no. 8 for Hutchins.
4. For Atkins's age, cf. ibid., L 5/22; for Pates's age, *Trans. Bristol & Glos.
Arch. Soc.* lvi, 201 ff.

elect their Recorder; and in reporting this to Burghley, he wrote of Pates: 'He hath been of long time a good parliament man and very diligent and painful there.'

Whether Burghley would have been so injudicious as to sanction the extension of a unique precedent from a unique constituency to the entirely different conditions and tradition of Gloucester, may be doubted; but as Pates then wrote to him, there was scarcely time before parliament met to execute such a writ, and he 'feared lest the doing thereof might breed more unquietness' in the city than his 'needless service in that parliament could recompense'. He let Atkins enjoy his triumph.

But when in the following year this man again defeated him – 'the like wrong being now again offered to me and to mine office here, by gathering together of a multitude by great labour, and by some threatening words, contrary to the law' – he appealed direct to Burghley, urged on, he said, by 'a great number of good citizens', who considered the election 'a wrong done to the state of this city'. No doubt Burghley would have been glad to help one who could describe himself as no 'shrinker from any her Majesty's service or your Lordship's commandments'; but it seems clear that he prudently refrained. Atkins continued to hold his seat in parliament.[1]

Twelve years elapsed before the next election. Against the historical background just described, we can appreciate how inapt, if not inept, was a letter that arrived from the Earl of Leicester in October 1584, asking for the nomination of one of Gloucester's members. 'I will thank you for it', he wrote, 'and will appoint a sufficient man and see you discharged of all charges in that behalf.' 'If you will send me the election with a blank, I will put in the name', he added in a complacent postscript.

Perhaps the Earl was Gloucester's High Steward: if so, it would explain his request. But the city authorities, meeting in Common Council, were clear that they dared not even mention the letter to the electors. 'Experience hath taught us', they answered, 'what a difficult thing it hath always been to deal in any matter where the multitude of burgesses have voice.' At the last election, they continued, 'there grew so great variance and offence amongst our burgesses upon like occasions ... that ... we are persuaded that it will

1. S.P. Dom. Eliz. 77, no. 32; 86, no. 23.

not be convenient to publish that motion unto them, perceiving already how a great number of those burgesses are affected.' They were fully convinced that the electors could not be persuaded to choose anyone 'not sworn to the franchises of this city'. Moreover, the Sheriffs, conscious of their oath of office, scrupled 'to deliver any return not warranted by the writ of summons and the statute'. One can only marvel at mere citizens being willing to take such explicit responsibility for crossing so great a man. The city's members in 1584 were a wealthy draper and prominent alderman, Luke Garnons, and our Town Clerk, Thomas Atkins.[1]

Silence descends on the elections for a time. In 1586 Richard Pates, now seventy and 'aged and weak in body' – he died in October 1588 and was buried in the south transept of the cathedral – re-emerged for a final session in parliament, as senior colleague of the persistent Thomas Atkins. There must surely be a story to that ill-yoked team, though, alas! we do not know it. But there happens to be another, a remarkable story, illuminating the pattern of affairs in Gloucester at the time; and this is worth telling.

In November 1586, while in London at the parliament, Pates took steps, on account of age, to resign the recordership. He wished to hand over to 'his friend', William Oldsworth; which probably indicates – though of course it may not – that he aimed at selling the succession to his office. Now the choice of a Recorder rested with the Mayor and aldermen; and the new Mayor was Luke Garnons. Pates must have anticipated opposition; and no doubt it was this anticipation that led him, despite his official oath by which he was bound to preserve the liberties of the city, to imitate his action in 1571 and 1572 and exploit his credit with Privy Councillors. He prevailed on the Council to write a letter to the Mayor and aldermen desiring them to elect Oldsworth. Apparently, the Council also invoked the aid of the Lord Lieutenant of Gloucestershire, Lord Chandos, who replied that while all the aldermen, having special good liking of Oldsworth, were willing enough, the Mayor was not. Consequently, in January 1587 the Council wrote again to the Mayor and aldermen, in terms calculated to bring any normal city official to heel.

Garnons, however, was no ordinary Mayor. He continued wilful. On 5 April, 'moved to find this his obstinacy so strange', the Council

1. *H.M.C. Rep.* XII, ix, 457.

wrote to Lord Chandos ordering him to give the Mayor the alternative of compliance or of appearing before them in London. The threat had some effect. Along with the aldermen, Garnons carried out the formal election of Oldsworth, and wrote reporting this to the Council. But then, on the ground that the Common Council of the city, and not the aldermen alone, had the right of election, he refused to admit him to the office. The Justices of Assize and the Queen's Serjeants-at-Law were called in to construe the city's charter, and the Privy Council wrote yet again. But still he was obdurate. In June the issue was referred to the two Chief Justices, who summoned the Mayor and Mr Oldsworth before them to state their case; but the Mayor 'failed in his proof of the matter' in Trinity term, and, given time till Michaelmas term, simply did not appear. In November, by which time Garnons had finished his year of office, the Council itself again took up the question. They wrote to the new Mayor and the aldermen, and also to Lord Chandos, peremptorily ordering the admission of Oldsworth as Recorder; and at last, with the principal obstacle removed, they got their way. So far as we know, Garnons suffered no punishment for his defiance of all England's might.[1]

It is an extraordinary tale – tribute to the astounding courage of a relatively humble, if wealthy, citizen, and also to the respect of powerful Councillors for a legal argument. The Council believed that Garnons's wilfulness sprang from support of a rival candidate. Doubtless they were well informed. He obviously counted on backing from the commoners in the corporation; equally, he had little or none among the aldermen. One is inclined to see in this the same division of opinion – a cleavage between the few and the many, with some of the few in the role of demagogues – which runs through the electoral history of the city.

It can surely be no accident that the new Recorder was not chosen as one of Gloucester's representatives in the next election of 1588. The senior seat went to Thomas Atkins, with his former superior, Luke Garnons, in the junior place – a double triumph for the popular party. During the last ten years Atkins's fortunes had been in the ascendant. He had become Queen's Attorney and member of the Council in the Marches of Wales, and perhaps in consequence had

1. *A.P.C.* xiv, 321, xv, 17, 136, 291, xvi, 75.

resigned the office of Town Clerk in 1578.[1] In 1593 his influence in the city was still irresistible, for in that year he was re-elected to parliament as senior member to a Gloucestershire man, Richard Birde, his successor as Town Clerk.

Then fortune changed: indeed, it may already have been on the wane, for in 1590 he was selling his office of Queen's Attorney.[2] In or about 1596 he was apparently in prison for debt; and at the time of the next parliamentary election, in 1597, according to his enemies he was not only deep in debt but had no lands or possessions, save some household goods, books, and apparel, and an annuity of forty shillings from the city. Said these same enemies, he was 'a man noted to be very dangerous for any trust to be committed unto him, and such a one whose courses were greatly disliked'; a judgement not without support from more trustworthy sources.

Nevertheless, he hoped to retain his seat in parliament. The very day before the election he wrote to the Mayor, aldermen, Common Council, and citizens offering his services, 'with many protestations of sincerity and great performance . . ., and desiring . . . to be elected for wiping away of such blemishes which he had before received'. A few weeks later, in early October, he was apparently outlawed for a debt of three pounds and thirty-three shillings and fourpence costs, and remained an outlaw for at least two years.[3] As likely as not, one motive for seeking membership of parliament was to visit London and move about there with impunity, under the protection of a member's privilege of freedom from arrest.

Unfortunately for Atkins, the Mayor, Grombalde Hutchins, was no friend of his. He had been imprisoned by the Council in the Marches of Wales, so Atkins said, and blamed him for it. Nor was the Town Clerk at this time, Richard Baker, a friend; which is not surprising, for Atkins was a busybody, who kept inflicting his advice as a lawyer and quondam Town Clerk on the magistrates. He had been very critical of Baker, who dubbed him an ass for his pains. Nor again did the two Sheriffs, John Baughe and Nicholas Langford, like him. He cited all four of these men as defendants in his Star Chamber suit after the election, directing particular venom against Baker.

1. RUDDER, *Hist. of Gloucestershire*, p. 119.
2. COLLINS, *Sidney Papers*, i, 314–15.
3. Star Chamber 5, A 49/5, demurrer.

Perhaps the common people, and they alone, remained true to him: he claimed to have been 'trusted and beloved' 'of the greatest multitude' of citizens. If so, the election was a last, but distorted, episode in our long electoral story.

We might have expected to find Luke Garnons and one or two other aldermen in the role of demagogues, on the side of Atkins. But the man's decrepitude was probably too much for them. Among the respectable, only one or at most two not very insistent voices – those of close friends – were raised for him. Atkins, with an optimism worthy of Mr Micawber, seems to have expected more favour from the new magistrates who were due to take up office shortly after the receipt of the writ, and accused the retiring Mayor and Sheriffs of undue haste in holding the election. The charge was absurd, for the officials were, of course, bound by law to execute the writ at the first county court after receipt of it. But apart from this solid defence, there is no evidence that the new Mayor would have supported his candidature. Atkins seems to have been too pitiable a figure for that.

The writ, dated 23 August, 1597, arrived in time for the county court due to meet on 6 September. The Sheriffs showed it to the Mayor and some of the aldermen; and thereupon the Mayor caused public proclamation to be made summoning the citizens to meet at the Gildhall at 8 a.m. on that morning. The day before the election, the Mayor, aldermen, and others of the Common Council – whether meeting formally or informally, as a whole or a select number, the evidence does not state – met to confer about candidates. They decided that Atkins was not fit to be elected, and presumably agreed to nominate the Recorder, William Oldsworth, and along with him alderman Luke Garnons – perhaps a balancing of the parties.

When the county court met on 6 September in the upper chamber of the Gildhall, under the presidency of the Sheriffs, there was a great assembly of citizens. All who were not burgesses were ordered to depart, and then the writ was read, the necessary proclamations made, and the Town Clerk proceeded to declare the business, showing 'what kind of persons were fit to be chosen' – not Atkins, of that we may be sure. Next, the Mayor addressed the electors: 'My masters, we have considered for the election of the burgesses of the parliament for the city, and have thought Mr Oldsworth and Mr Garnons to be fit men for the place. Notwithstanding, we leave the same to you.' After this, the Town Clerk, 'as prolocutor for the said Mayor, aldermen, and Sheriffs', recommended Mr Oldsworth. Whether he also recommended Mr Garnons, he does not say.

Disliking the order of the names, the electors shouted, 'First Mr Garnons, Mr Garnons!' The crying of names probably went on for some time. According to the defendants in our Star Chamber case, only one or at most two persons were heard to name Atkins. When 'the cry' ceased, the Town Clerk stood up and said twice: 'This is your election. You do elect, according to the tenor of the writ, Mr Luke Garnons and Mr William Oldsworth to be citizens for the commonalty of the city ...; and this is the election of you all.'[1] To which the electors answered, 'Yea, yea!' As there was no dispute, there was no need for a poll, and the county court was immediately adjourned, to meet an hour later at the Tolsey for normal business, thus freeing the Gildhall for a session of gaol delivery.

Such was the simple story – too simple, perhaps – as told by the defendants. According to Atkins the whole business was rushed. There were many electors, he declared, outside the upper chamber of the Gildhall, below the stairs, at the gates, and at the windows, who called out that they would not have Mr Oldsworth, and 'with exceeding great noise and loud voices, to be heard very far off, did name' Atkins 'and made choice of him'. What is more, one of his two friends in the upper chamber told the magistrates that 'the commons and all those which were below the stairs in the said hall' would have Atkins. To this the Mayor answered that 'they were but Jacks and lewd fellows'. When the court was adjourned to the Tolsey, says Atkins, these voters went there, expecting the election to be continued.[2]

The two versions of the story are irreconcilable, and not having the evidence of witnesses in this Star Chamber case, we cannot really judge their veracity. It may well be that the magistrates started the proceedings promptly on time, before many of the humbler electors had arrived, and carried them through with unwonted speed, being determined to avoid a poll. Again, they may have paid little attention to anyone outside the upper chamber where the election took place.

1. Oddly enough, Oldsworth's name was apparently placed first in the return. Cf. *Return of M.P.s*, i, 433.

2. The documents in the case are Star Chamber 5, A 10/6, 20/11, 1/5.

But what are we to make of the statement, in which Mayor, Sheriffs, and Town Clerk all concur, that one or perhaps two persons at most made election of Atkins, and that they did not hear any of the burgesses who were outside so much as name him? Either they lied or Atkins did. It would be unwise to place great faith in the latter's word; and some of his charges are palpably baseless. At best, his supporters were burgesses of little substance. The reponsible and respectable — those in the upper chamber — fought shy of him.

Thomas Atkins was re-elected as Town Clerk in October 1598 on the death of Richard Baker. It was probably an act of charity rather than a triumph for his old party in the city. He had resigned the office in the day of his prosperity, and presumably now needed the emoluments in impoverished age. In 1601 he was unable to prevent the re-election to parliament of William Oldsworth, who again sat with Luke Garnons. Times had changed; and Richard Pates had at last, though posthumously, been revenged. Atkins resigned the clerkship finally in January 1603, when he was said 'to be then very old and weak'; in fact, he was sixty-five.[1] Judging from the Star Chamber and other evidence we have, he was not an attractive nor a truthful man, nor particularly upright.[2]

1. RUDDER, op. cit., p. 119.
2. Cf. *A.P.C.* xi, 72, 272, xix, 439–40; Star Chamber 5, A 49/5, 56/27; C. SKEEL, *Council in the Marches of Wales*, p. 117.

CHAPTER 14

The Government and Elections

WE are now sufficiently familiar with the pattern of our subject to return to the question of government influence in elections. The conventional generalizations of the past need not trouble us. While contemporary writers, both from the catholic side and the protestant, accused the Tudors of packing their parliaments, the extravagance and *ex parte* character of these charges rob them of authority; and, as we have seen, the wholesale creation of new parliamentary boroughs, stressed by modern writers, has really little or no connexion with the problem. The Tudors did, however, influence elections. There is no doubt about that. In what way, to what extent, and for what purpose, it is our business to discover.

Some degree of interference was inevitable, at least in the first half of the century. It was required as the government took to framing a programme of official legislation – a recent innovation in parliamentary procedure, and a sign of modernity. The planned society of the sixteenth century, with its great measures of religious, economic, and social regulation, could not have sprung spontaneously from a haphazard assembly of country gentlemen and townsmen. Preparation and organization were needed; and no statesman capable of carrying through the programme of the Reformation Parliament of 1529–36 – the first demonstration on a grand scale of parliament's coming of age – could have failed to perceive that he must have a core of leaders in the House of Commons.

The northern rebels in the Pilgrimage of Grace saw what was happening. 'The old custom', they protested, 'was that none of the King's servants should be of the Common House; yet most of that House were the King's servants.' Similarly, Sir Thomas More's nephew, William Rastell, complained that the King in 1529 engineered the election of 'divers of his own Councillors and Household servants and their servants'. We are not concerned with the degree of accuracy in these statements. Their interest is that of an old-world protest against a new order of things; a protest that may be likened to the famous clause in the Act of Settlement of 1701 excluding all persons holding office or place of profit under the Crown from the House of Commons, which, if not speedily modified, would have prevented the evolution of our Cabinet system of government.[1]

For the efficient working of a post-Reformation parliament, it was essential that the House of Commons should contain what Rastell so much deplored, a group of King's 'Councillors and Household servants and their servants'. A numerical majority was not needed; leadership was. An early Elizabethan lampoonist illuminated this truth in a piece of bombast, entitled 'a lewd pasquil'. After brief characterizations of forty-three members of the 1566 parliament — for the most part jejune witticisms, such as 'Goodier the glorious', 'Strickland the stinger', and 'Wentworth the wrangler' — he ended with the reflection,

> As for the rest, they be at devotion;
> And when they be pressed, they cry 'A good motion!'[2]

In due course the electoral system, in its own peculiar way, came automatically to assure the government of its nucleus of 'King's friends'; but until that happened, some thought had to be given to securing the same result deliberately.

Our story can only find its proper perspective by harking back to the Reformation Parliament; but as very little is yet known about this, one of the most crucial of all English parliaments, we must begin with a sketchy and uncertain introduction. That Henry VIII took a personal interest in the elections of 1529 seems quite clear, and doubtless he was assisted by the Duke of Norfolk and others at Court who had electoral influence and were ready to place seats at his disposal. It may be that the King intervened directly in elections as his opponents accused him of doing. But the first assured evidence of organized and systematic interference comes, appropriately enough, with the rise to power of that astute and able politician, Thomas Cromwell. Even before the two general elections of his

1. *Harpsfield's Life of More*, ed. Hitchcock and Chambers (E.E.T.S.) pp. 350–2; K. M. PICKTHORN, *Early Tudor Govt. Hen. VIII*, pp. 129–32.
2. Camb. Univ. Lib. MS. Ff. v, 14, fol. 82b. Another copy in Stowe MS. 354, fol. 18.

career, those of 1536 and 1539, gave full scope to his manipulative talents, he was active filling vacancies in parliament at by-elections, and conning lists of members.[1]

Several documents have survived from Cromwell's first general election. They include a list of some suggested candidates, compiled by him, and a letter – if it belongs to this year – showing that the Duke of Norfolk exercised widespread influence, both in counties and boroughs, to secure, as he wrote, that 'such shall be chosen as I doubt not shall serve his Highness according to his pleasure'. The choice piece is the correspondence concerning the election at Canterbury, where Cromwell's recommendation of two candidates only reached the city after the election was over. The magistrates wrote him a humble letter of explanation; but it was swept aside. 'At your own wills and minds', answered Cromwell, 'contrary to the King's pleasure and commandment', you have chosen others; 'whereat the King's Highness doth not a little marvel'. Ordering them to proceed to a new election and choose the royal nominees, he continued: 'And if any person will obstinately gainsay the same, I require you to advertise me thereof that I may order him as the King's pleasure shall be in that case to command.' Needless to say, the city did as it was told. Ninety-seven citizens, 'freely with one voice and without any contradiction', as the Mayor with unconscious irony wrote, elected Cromwell's nominees.

In the next general election of 1539 the Earl of Southampton was very active on this minister's behalf. He went so far as to defer the elections in Surrey and Sussex in order to ascertain whom the King and Cromwell wished to be elected, asking for a new writ to the Sheriff to regularize his arbitrary action. Cromwell himself, with blunt assertiveness, used the King's name to secure the two Norfolk seats for particular candidates.[2]

Episodes of this nature naturally impress us, but it would be wrong

1. MERRIMAN, *Life & Letters of Thomas Cromwell*, i, 67 (Taunton, Cromwell's constituency in 1529, belonged to the Bishop of Winchester); A.F. POLLARD, 'Thomas Cromwell's Parliamentary Lists', *I.H.R. Bulletin*, ix, 31 ff., and 'The Reformation Parliament as a Matrimonial Agency', *History*, xxi, 219 ff.

2. *I.H.R. Bulletin*, ix, 43; *L. & P. Hen. VIII*, x, no. 816, XIV, i, nos. 520, 564, 573, 598, 645, 672, 706, 800, 808; MERRIMAN, i, 126–8, ii, 13–14, 209–10.

to exaggerate either their scale or effect. Cromwell was not creating a pliant majority in the House of Commons. He was providing a group of 'King's friends' to lead the House; and in the counties it was not so much a case of planting nominees, as of selecting the most acceptable among the leading local gentry and throwing official weight on their side. We might have likened his activities to those of Sir Robert Cecil at the end of Elizabeth's reign, if it had not been for two highly significant differences: Cromwell operated in the counties as well as the boroughs, and acted in the name of the sovereign.

Other men, other ways. In the first election of Edward VI's reign, Protector Somerset's liberal-minded government, so far as is known, did not indulge in widespread electioneering. True, the Privy Council, by letters to the Lord Warden of the Cinque Ports and the Sheriff of Kent, did attempt to secure the election for that county of Sir John Baker, who as Privy Councillor and prospective Speaker was doubly needed in the House of Commons. Evidently, the proposal cut across the plans of the local gentry, and when construed by their two officials into a 'commandment' and a 'menace', aroused protests. Hearing of this, the Council wrote a further letter enjoining respect for the county's 'liberty of election'. How different from Cromwell's pitiless, heavy-handed authority! In the end, Sir John Baker failed to obtain the Kent seat: he sat for the county of Huntingdon.[1]

But this remarkable restraint did not outlast the Protector. His successor, the unscrupulous Duke of Northumberland, had to take thought for the success of his policy, as Henry VIII and Cromwell had done. In two by-elections at the beginning of 1552, one for Hertfordshire and the other for Surrey, the Council instructed the Sheriffs to secure the election of particular persons, though with what result, we do not know: it is unlikely that tender scruples mitigated the pressure.[2]

Then came the general election of 1553. On this occasion, a circular letter was sent out in the King's name, instructing the Sheriffs to impress both on freeholders and burgesses 'that they should choose and appoint ... men of knowledge and experience'. If this had been all, the letters would have been innocuous; just a little paternalism, characteristic of the age, and unobjectionable on constitutional

1. *A.P.C.* ii, 70, 516, 518–19.   2. ibid. iii, 459, 470.

grounds, for were not the efficiency and discipline of parliament the Crown's concern? But the letters went on to enjoin that if the Council, or any Councillors 'within their jurisdiction', recommended in the King's name men of learning and wisdom, their directions were to be followed.[1]

What is more, we know that eight counties received special letters, containing fifteen nominations. Twelve of the nominees were elected, and if, as seems likely, last minute changes were made in the lists, fourteen, or possibly all fifteen seats went as the Council wished.[2] The facts are arresting; but once more they are not so dark as they seem. Most of the nominees were appropriate persons for their seats, who may or may not have needed the Council's backing to turn the scales in their favour.[3] In addition to the corporate action of the Council, individual Councillors presumably operated in both counties and boroughs. But, whatever the extent of their activities, and striking as official intervention undoubtedly was on this occasion, it would be absurd to speak of the government as either achieving or aiming at what has been called a 'nomination parliament'.[4]

There appears to be no evidence that for her first two parliaments Mary Tudor made any official attempt to influence the elections. However, by the autumn of 1554, when the writs went out for her third parliament, the warm surge of loyalty inspired by Northumberland's conspiracy was gone and the spectre of a divided nation had appeared. Wyatt had risen in rebellion, the hated Spaniards had arrived, and Mary was set on her final and supreme purpose, the reconciliation with Rome, 'the restitution of God's honour and glory'. In letters to the Sheriffs and others she called on them to admonish electors both in counties and boroughs to choose representatives 'of the wise, grave, and catholic sort'. It was one of the safety measures promised by her Councillors in the previous March to induce Philip of Spain to come and marry the Queen.

1. Lansdowne MSS. 3, fols. 36a, 37b; 94, fol. 19. Printed in Strype, *Memorials*, II, ii, 64.

2. Brit. Mus. Royal MS. 18C, 24 (Docquet book of the Council). Original minutes of two letters are in Lansdowne MS. 3, fol. 36. Also cf. STRYPE, *Memorials*, II, ii, 65–6.

3. Cf. the Council letter to Hoby, quoted FROUDE'S *History*, v, 126 n.; *A.P.C.* iv, 200.

4. Cf. FROUDE, v, 125; POLLARD, *Pol. Hist. 1547–1603*, p. 74.

Already there had been trouble-makers in parliament; and in all likelihood they had been mostly among the gentry representing the boroughs. In the circular letter there was a clause urging constituencies to choose members from 'their inhabitants, as the old laws require'. Of its significance there can be no doubt whatever, more especially if the Venetian ambassador – who alone supplies the information – was right in reporting that in the next parliament the government attempted to pass a bill enforcing the law against non-resident members; timorous townsmen being preferable to independent gentry. The bill failed, says the ambassador, because the opposition, giving tit for tat, ingeniously tacked a place bill to it, prohibiting the election of any official or paid dependant of the government. It is difficult to know what to make of the story. The tactics described are so precocious as to be hardly credible. However, even if a bill against non-residence had passed, it would surely have failed to stem the tidal advance of the gentry into the boroughs. Nor were circular letters assured of much cogency. They could have only a limited effect on an electoral system that was rapidly developing a pattern of its own and becoming less and less responsive to alien manipulation.[1]

A modern scholar has described the circular letter of 1554 as 'a mere platitude'.[2] It was more than that. The Sheriff of Lincolnshire, for instance, wrote to Grimsby enjoining them to choose an inhabitant of their own town, one of the catholic sort; and there is an admonitory letter to the city of Hereford – one of a number sent out by Nicholas Heath, Bishop of Worcester and Privy Councillor – which contains a postscript commending for re-election the two citizens who had represented the city in April 1554. In fact, neither of Heath's nominees was chosen, one being passed over because he was elected for the county.[3]

At the next election in 1555 the government took similar precautions. Before he left England in August of that year, Philip had discussed the autumn elections with Privy Councillors, who were

1. STRYPE, *Memorials*, III, i, 245; BURNET, *Hist. of the Reformation*, ed., Pocock, vi, 313; E. H. HARBISON, *Rival Ambassadors at the Court of Queen Mary*, p, 142; POLLARD, *Pol. Hist.*, p. 148.
2. *Eng. Hist. Rev.* xxiii, 647 n.
3. *H.M.C. Rep.* XIV, viii, 255; *Rep.* XIII, iv, 319–20.

instructed to see that 'none but Catholics and none who are suspect' were elected. Once more Nicholas Heath sent out circular letters to secure the choice of 'grave men and of good and honest behaviour and conversation, and specially of catholic religion'. This time his Hereford letter contained no nominations, but one sent in his capacity of President of the Welsh Council to the Sheriff and others of Carnarvonshire, included a postscript recommending a Welsh knight, who was duly elected for the county. Whatever the government's efforts, they fell palpably short of success, for this parliament proved the most obstreperous of the reign, with 'many violent opposition members'.[1]

Mary Tudor's last general election was again preceded by circular letters to Sheriffs and Mayors, urging the choice of 'men given to good order, catholic and discreet, and so qualified as the ancient laws of the realm requireth'. This final qualification was more clearly defined in one of the two versions of the letter – probably an early draft. The Sheriff was told to secure, 'by all the ways and means you can', that members 'be taken as near as may be of the inhabitants of the city or town' – a further sign that the intrusion of the gentry into the boroughs had been producing intractable parliaments.[2]

When Queen Elizabeth came to the throne, her ministers must have been well aware of this historical background; aware of circular letters and of the more blatant electoral devices of Thomas Cromwell and the Duke of Northumberland. Not oppressed, as Mary's government was, by gloomy thoughts of opposition, and inspired by the new Queen's buoyant faith in popular support, their minds were probably receptive to the simple but profound truth that already the development of the electoral system had rendered the methods of the recent past crude, out of date, and ineffective; receptive also to the fact that Councillors and prominent courtiers, by the ordinary process of election, could count on securing seats for themselves, and, through their prestige and territorial power, possessed sufficient influence in boroughs to bring their friends and followers into parliament. Granted harmony between government and people, no official action was required to obtain that essential core of 'King's friends',

1. HARBISON, op. cit., p. 257; H.M.C. Rep. XIII, iv, 320; Cal. Wynn Papers (N.L.W.), no. 19; POLLARD, op. cit., 143 ff.
2. Eng. Hist. Rev. xxiii, 647 n.; BURNET, vi, 313 n.

of 'Councillors and Household servants and their servants', whose presence in the House of Commons thirty years previously had offended the conservative William Rastell.

Whatever the reason, the old policy was dropped. We can be fairly confident that there were no circular letters and no royal or official nominations of the Cromwell and Northumberland type in 1558–9. Nor is there the slightest trace of official intervention in the general election of 1563.

Then in 1571 came the revival of the circular letter – a revival, but also a transformation. The letter was not at all concerned with the religious or political opinions of candidates; and it went to Lord Lieutenants and other influential persons throughout the realm, not to Sheriffs. We possess the text in the copy sent to Archbishop Parker and Lord Cobham for Kent.

Though most representatives, states the letters, are properly chosen, yet in many places care is not taken to choose persons able to speak for their constituencies and treat discreetly on the business before parliament. 'Many in late parliaments (as her Majesty thinketh) have been named, some for private respects and favour upon their own suits, some to enjoy some immunities from arrests upon actions during the time of the parliaments, and some other to set forth private causes by sinister labour and frivolous talks and arguments, to the prolongation of time without just cause, and without regard to the public benefit and weal of the Realm.' Parker and Cobham were instructed to confer with the Sheriff of Kent and others of repute in the county, and with the head officers of cities and boroughs, to remedy this state of affairs.[1]

The sentiments are admirable; the diagnosis of parliamentary ills sound. As some of our election stories have shown, there were gentlemen, in danger of arrest for debt, who sought election mainly to be covered by parliamentary privilege. There were others anxious to be in London for private business, not public. Moreover, private bills were pursued in the Commons with a zeal and expenditure of time that endangered public business and the accepted ideal of short parliaments. It may even be that in the wording of these letters the

---

1. *A.P.C.* viii, 15; *Correspondence of Abp. Parker* (Parker Soc.), pp. 379–80. For action at Wells on this letter, cf. MEREWEATHER and STEPHEN, op. cit., ii, 1252.

Queen was not unmindful of the rash young men in her last parliament, with their 'lip-laboured orations', who, though intensely loyal, nearly caused the assembly to founder over the agitation for naming a successor to the throne.[1] In any case, it all mattered little. So far as we can tell, the Council's amiable exhortations had no effect on the composition of the new parliament. Nor could much have been expected from the vague, brief echo of this letter circulated in 1572.

When the next parliament was summoned, in 1584, it was a time of crisis. William the Silent had been assassinated that year, the Throckmorton Plot had been discovered, and throughout the country people had been appending their seals to the Oath of Association, a declaration of lynch law aimed at Mary Queen of Scots. In this atmosphere of alarm, the Council seems to have revived the precedents of Mary's reign. At any rate, the letter to Lord Cobham as Warden of the Cinque Ports, to which allusion has previously been made, can hardly have been unique. Perhaps the Sheriffs received similar letters, though none are known. Cobham was instructed to see that the members for the Ports 'be not only discreet and sufficient persons, but known to be well affected in religion and towards the present state of this government'; and it was suggested that the Ports might be willing to grant him the nominations. This particular letter certainly had some effect, but it did not amount to much.[2] Possibly here and there, at other elections, a little more thought may have been given to the occasion; though no traces are perceptible in the composition of the parliament, and frank scepticism would not be out of place. Truth to tell, such letters were more or less impotent. They were also needless: however troublesome Elizabethan parliaments might be, their loyalty never wavered.

The Queen was well satisfied with this parliament, and intended to keep it in being. Its life was continued by several prorogations until at last it stood prorogued till 14 November 1586. But late that summer the Babington Plot was discovered, and the Council, with the trial of Mary Queen of Scots in prospect, was insistent upon the immediate calling of parliament. 'We stick upon parliament', wrote Burghley on 8 September, 'which her Majesty mislikes to have, but

1. Cf. my article, 'Parliament and the Succession Question', *Eng. Hist. Rev.* xxxvi, 497 ff.
2. *Hatfield MSS.* iii, 71; above, p. 210.

we all persist, to make the burden better borne and the world abroad better satisfied.'[1] From the government's point of view, the old parliament was eminently suited to deal with the crisis. It had discussed the Oath of Association and passed the Act for the Queen's Safety under which Mary was to be tried. But it could not be legally assembled before the date to which it stood prorogued, 14 November; and delay until then was intolerable. There was therefore no option but to dissolve it by commission, which was done on 14 September, and to send out writs for a new parliament. Along with the writs went letters to the Sheriffs, telling them that the Queen had thought good to hasten the parliament with a new summons. As the elections for the last parliament, both in counties and boroughs, had resulted in 'a very good and discreet choice ... of ... wise and well-affected gentlemen and others', they were instructed to assemble three or four of the 'well-affected gentlemen' of the locality, as also the principal persons of the cities and boroughs, and let them know that in the Council's opinion they would do very well to re-elect their former representatives.[2]

The letter was as extraordinary as the situation that evoked it. It certainly influenced the elections, as can be seen by comparing the number of members re-elected for the same constituencies in 1586 with the number in other parliaments. There were 186 on this occasion, compared with 131 in 1588 and 106 in 1593. The increase was more striking in the counties than in the boroughs: 43 in 1586, 25 in 1588, 24 in 1593. Moreover, 14 counties re-elected both their members, as compared with 3 in 1588 and 4 in 1593. Sheriffs and responsible county magnates, as one might have expected, were more susceptible to official advice in the nation's crisis than borough patrons.

But let us not be unduly impressed. Sixty per cent of the seats – 274 against 186 – were occupied by different persons; and the Council's letter must often have operated merely as a stimulus to old members to seek re-election, where otherwise they might have had the grace – or been compelled – to yield place to others. In Leicestershire, it seems that the letter was a godsend to the Earl of Huntingdon, enabling him to prolong a family monopoly and have two brothers re-elected for the county; in consequence of which he had to support the application of the same principle to Leicester borough.

1. *Scottish Cal.* viii, 701.   2. *A.P.C.* xiv, 227; *H.M.C. Rep.* vii, 642b.

In Chichester, as we have seen, the letter was used as a trump card in a contest quite detached from government policy. And at Warwick – though the result would in any event have been the same – the Earl of Warwick cited it to support the re-election of his nominee.[1]

On the other hand, the borough authorities at Warwick, under electoral pressure, ignored the letter in their choice for the second seat. More impressive still, Sir Henry Bagenall, a courtier, wrote from the Court itself asking the Earl of Rutland for a borough seat as an insurance lest his election as knight for Anglesey were 'hindered by the direction sent to all Sheriffs'.[2] He secured both seats, county and borough, thus making a double breach in government policy. In certain counties, prolific in borough patrons and 'foreign' burgesses – some of them officials – the Council's letter had no effect at all. Cornwall, with its two county members and forty-two burgesses, only re-elected five burgesses for the same constituencies; Devon, with sixteen burgesses, re-elected one county member and two burgesses to their old seats.

So far as we know, a circular letter was issued only once more during the reign. This was in 1597. The purpose was entirely innocent and commendable. The Queen wished to have members fit for their task and familiar with their constituencies. She was concerned, as she had been in 1571, and as Mary Tudor had been before her, with the effects of the gentry's intrusion into the boroughs. But whereas Mary Tudor's government had been fundamentally opposed to this development because it strengthened the opposition in her parliaments, Elizabeth's only worry was efficiency. She was perturbed about the worst type of 'carpet-bagger' and her idea might perhaps be described as that of the anonymous member who spoke in the debate on the subject in 1571, wishing to see 'home-dwellers', men 'either of the town or towards the town, borderers and near neighbours at the least'. As the Council's letter put it: They did not doubt that in the counties the principal gentlemen would have good regard to the choice of meet men, 'without partiality or affection, as sometimes hath been used'; but in the boroughs, 'except better regard be had therein than commonly hath been, there will be many unmeet men and unacquainted with the state of the boroughs'. The Sheriffs

1. Above, pp. 38, 165, 254–259; *Black Book of Warwick*, p. 387.
2. *Rutland MSS.* i, 207.

were instructed to inform the boroughs; and if, contrary to these orders, the parliament proved to be 'evil supplied', the Council threatened to inquire and find out who was responsible.[1]

In all likelihood, the Council's letters were written on the direct orders of the Queen herself; but an examination of the composition of this parliament suggests that it was all a waste of breath. No one was ruffled. There is not even a sign of the sting in the tail of the letter being applied. Indeed, could anything else be expected? The two most egregious borough manipulators of the reign – the Earl of Essex and Sir Robert Cecil – whose personal activities, as this very election proved, were really malignant, were both members of the Council. It was a case of Satan rebuking sin.

In addition to general directives to Sheriffs, Tudor governments, as we have seen, had had recourse to the nomination of particular candidates. The practice ceased abruptly with the accession of Elizabeth. True, in the latter part of her reign the Council did on a few occasions intervene in defence of men who might be described as Court candidates. The case of Dr Dale at Chichester in 1586 has already been told. The other incidents are well worth scrutiny, if only to demonstrate the limits within which the Elizabethan government felt that it could act.

The first concerned the Essex election of 1588, for which Sir Thomas Heneage, Privy Councillor and Vice-Chamberlain, and Sir Henry Gray, Lieutenant of the Queen's Pensioners, were candidates. Both were Deputy-Lieutenants of the county and therefore eminently suitable. According to the Privy Council, 'most part of the gentlemen and freeholders' were disposed to choose these two; but Lord Rich, the unfortunate husband of Penelope Devereux, Sidney's 'Stella', had come forward to impugn the choice 'by preferring of some other'. It was obviously Sir Henry Gray's candidature which was to be contested. Heneage, who, after his move from Lincolnshire to his fine new house at Copthall, Essex, consistently represented the shire as first knight from 1584 to 1593, was much too important a person to suffer challenge, whereas Gray had not previously sat in parliament. Lord Rich's intervention was dangerous. He was a very wealthy landowner, with a large tenantry, and, as the 1604 election later proved, was a keen and most active election agent. Moreover,

1. *A.P.C.* xxvii, 361–2.

the Sheriff, Robert Wroth, was his cousin; and since both were Puritans, in a county where this movement, with its precocious sense of politics, was notoriously strong, it is not unlikely that the two were intent on putting in a puritan member.

Heneage was probably behind Gray's candidature, and doubtless it was he who persuaded his colleagues on the Council to intervene. Their first official letter was one to the Sheriff forbidding him to hold the election elsewhere than at the customary place, Chelmsford, thus suggesting that they feared the employment of Sheriff's tricks. The opposition was not abashed. They went on with their electioneering; and a fortnight later the Council wrote to Lord Rich himself, 'advising and requiring' him to desist from his purpose. The reasons given were two: the undesirability of bringing together so large an assembly at that time, and 'the worthiness of both the parties nominated for that place'. Rich was told to return his answer by the messenger.[1]

We must conclude that Lord Rich yielded to the heavy hand of authority, for both Heneage and Gray were elected. The Council for its part had the excuse of wartime. It was but two months since the defeat of the Armada, certainly not a 'fit time' for setting the county by the ears with a resounding election fight, bringing its evil aftermath of faction. Perhaps in itself this is adequate explanation of their action; but there is a flavour of Stuart rather than Elizabethan times about it, and Heneage, who must have been responsible, showed himself, as a parliamentary leader, officially-minded and tactless, not in the high tradition of the age.

In 1601 the Council – as we have already noticed – reprimanded the Sheriff of Warwickshire for irregular conduct, suspected to be directed against Fulke Greville, the distinguished courtier. Their intervention achieved its purpose, and though too partisan for modern approval, it was provoked by the misbehaviour of the Sheriff, and was justified as an act of discipline.[2]

On the same day that the Council wrote to Warwickshire, a letter was directed to the Sheriff of Worcestershire.[3] Here one of the candidates was Sir Thomas Leighton, a Worcestershire gentleman, who could have spent but little time in his home county, for he was

1. *A.P.C.* xvi, 298, 318; *Eng. Hist. Rev.* xlviii, 395 ff.
2. Above, p. 49; *A.P.C.* xxxii, 247.　　　　　3. ibid., p. 251.

Governor of Guernsey. He was a man of consequence who had been in the Queen's service for over thirty years and had been brought into greater prominence at Court by his marriage with Elizabeth, daughter of Sir Francis Knollys, a relative of the Queen and in her service till she married. She and her husband continued in highest favour at Court, exchanging New Year's gifts with the Queen. On one occasion, Lady Leighton, then in Guernsey, acknowledged a letter from Sir Robert Cecil containing greetings from her Majesty: 'such affectionate words', she declared, 'as, were not the writer [Cecil] of very sufficient credit, her faith would fail her therein'. No doubt religion, as well as the usual mercenary motives of the Elizabethan marriage market, had brought husband and wife together, for like his father-in-law and his wife, Leighton was puritan in outlook. As the Privy Council hinted in their letter, this trait in his character can hardly have endeared him to the conservative gentry of Worcestershire; nor was his residence in distant Guernsey a commendation.[1]

The Council told the Sheriff that they understood there was likely to be division over the election, and 'some opposition, made out of faction'. They thought that Leighton's special services to Queen and State, and the good account in which he deservedly stood with her Majesty, should 'sufficiently recommend him'. 'It is not our meaning', they continued, 'in any sort to restrain or hinder the liberty of a free election, which ought to be amongst you'; but since there was suspicion that some undue proceeding might be used against him, 'especially out of animosity of religion', which would greatly displease the Queen should she learn of it, they admonished the Sheriff, as a man of judgement, not to be 'transported with any such passion'. The Queen would be very pleased with any favour shown to one whom she so well esteemed, and equally she would be sensible of any evil done him by irregular practices.

The Council's action was cautious and tactful, ostensibly prompted by anticipation of trickery at the election. The broad hint was taken: Leighton was returned as the senior knight of the shire.

Though it is abundantly clear that the Elizabethan government did

1. NICHOLS, *Progresses* (1788), vol. ii; *Hatfield MSS.* xiv, 111; B. BROOK, *Memoir of Thomas Cartwright*, p. 434; SCOTT PEARSON, *Cartwright*, p. 160; *Seconde Parte of a Register*, ed. Peel, ii, 49, 64; KNAPPEN, *Tudor Puritanism*, pp. 283-4.

not employ the crude electoral methods of its predecessors, never-theless we are confronted by what may seem a paradox, namely that Elizabethan parliaments probably contained a larger Court element than any in earlier times. An analysis of the parliament of 1559, made some years ago, put the number of such members at fifty-four. It is probably too low an estimate, though we may assume that there were fewer at the beginning of the reign than at the end. In 1584 the number of members who were attached to the Royal Household or held such civil and legal offices as would justify inclusion in the Court group was approximately seventy-five. In addition there were fourteen gentlemen-servants of noblemen and statesmen, who may be regarded as indirectly associated with the government. If we put the Court element in the last parliament of the reign as not much short of one hundred, or between twenty and twenty-five per cent of the total membership, we shall be near the mark.[1]

It is an impressive, indeed a surprising proportion of the whole House. The question arises, did this happen naturally, or was it in some subtle way achieved officially and deliberately? Let us first, by way of a cautionary tale, look at a document among the Wynn of Gwydir papers – a copy of a letter to the Sheriff of Carnarvonshire, written in 1597 and couched in the form of a Council letter, the original having evidently been signed by the Lord Keeper of the Great Seal, Sir Thomas Egerton, and the Secretary, Sir Robert Cecil. Its purpose was 'to recommend unto you a gentleman of that country, her Majesty's servant, Mr Ellis Wynn', as knight of the shire. 'We have known him long and thereby have had that experience and trial of him that we think there cannot be made a better choice, especially at this time, when it greatly concerneth her Majesty's service to have the House furnished of persons discreet, sufficient, and well-affected. We have no doubt but by your good means, your neighbours will in their choice so respect this gentleman as both his own merits and our good opinion of him do require.'

The official language of the letter might easily deceive us: it de-ceived its modern editor. But two notes appended to the copy reveal its real nature and origin. Ellis Wynn – a Welshman whose 'good fortune' his more famous brother, John Wynn of Gwydir, ascribed to the English veneer received at Westminster School, citing this as

1. *Eng. Hist. Rev.* xxiii, 681; Miss Matthews's thesis.

an example for his son to follow with his own children – had risen through service in the household of Sir Robert Cecil to the position of Gentleman Harbinger at Court, an office with excellent scope for bribes on top of the annual fee of ten pounds. Like other ambitious officials, he wished to sit in parliament, and it was obviously his own idea to stand for Carnarvonshire. The two Privy Councillors came into the story simply because he needed influential backers. Normally, he would have turned to his patron, Sir Robert Cecil; but, as this was a county seat, and Sir Thomas Egerton had much influence in North Wales, he evidently picked on him as his first line of support. Though well enough known to Egerton, he seems to have approached him through a cousin in this official's service. Probably it was Wynn himself who suggested that Egerton should ask Cecil to add his signature to the letter. When subscribing his name, Cecil was conscious that his and Egerton's roles had been reversed. He remarked that he, as Wynn's patron, 'should have rather moved my Lord' on his behalf.

In the event, Ellis Wynn did not get the seat. It went to the eminent family of Griffith of Carnarvon. The natural order of things prevailed against the Court intrusion; and even the great John Wynn of Gwydir apparently resisted his brother's objectionable method of electioneering. The defeated man had to be content with a seat at Saltash in Cornwall, where Cecil, or Egerton, or some other courtier presumably placed him.[1]

It is an appropriate story: a case of a minor Court official and what might be mistaken for a Council letter. Egerton and Cecil, in this period of declining scrupulousness, may have been abusing their authority. Whether they were or were not, every incident in the tale was unofficial and personal.

There were many officials like Ellis Wynn, who by the very nature of their life were unusually eager to enter parliament; and at Court there was available a large number of seats, dependent on the territorial and other influences of leading statesmen and courtiers. The Court was a large family. Many, perhaps most, owed their offices there to the patronage of the great; and close bonds of friend-

1. N.L.W. Wynn of Gwydir Papers, Panton group, MS. 9052 E, nos. 197, 195; *Cal. Wynn Papers*, nos. 195, 197 (wrongly dated), 429; *Hatfield MSS.* vi, 454–5.

ship and clientage bound them together. Demand and supply were in contact; and the factional and party structure of the society made it incumbent on the leaders to please their followers.

There can be no reasonable doubt that in the great majority of instances men about Court secured their seats in this natural way and not through any deliberate government policy. But on occasions a little thought with an official tinge to it may have been given to ensuring that certain individuals found seats. William Cecil once jotted at the foot of a memorandum of business for the forthcoming parliament, 'Mr Walsingham to be of the House'; which suggests concern of more than a personal nature to see this future statesman in parliament.[1] If the note was made in 1563, then precautions were taken against failure, for Walsingham was elected both at Lyme Regis and Banbury. Cecil presumably sought and found borough patrons, willing to adopt his protégé, the patron at Lyme Regis being almost certainly the Earl of Bedford. It is also true that all Privy Councillors who were commoners were expected to find seats in parliament. But in Elizabeth's reign there is neither indication nor likelihood that official backing was required to achieve this, as it had been in the case of Sir John Baker in Edward VI's reign.

Possibly the Queen herself took some interest in the competition for seats. She had an insatiable curiosity and was notoriously alive to even trifling happenings about her. When parliamentary elections were in the offing, her Court must have been a miniature market; and, if in no other way, she no doubt heard, through the gossip of her ladies, of this, that, and the other person seeking a seat. A word from her in the right quarter would help a lot; and no doubt, directly or indirectly, by plain request or innuendo, her help was sometimes sought, though it was not in her nature to be indiscriminate in granting it.

By happy fortune an illustration of this survives – a unique item, so far as we know. In 1586 Sir Francis Walsingham, as Recorder of Colchester, wrote to the magistrates of that borough: 'I have received your letter and understand by the same that before mine came unto you the election for the burgesses of your town was already passed

1. S.P. Dom. Eliz. 40, no. 68. The document is difficult to date. It cannot be 1566, as given in the *Calendar*. Perhaps the 'act for apparel' mentioned may date it 1563.

with Mr James Morice and Mr Francis Harvey; which choice I do very well like and allow of, both for that it was so ordered by her Majesty, if those gentlemen were extant' – that is, if they were without seats – 'as also in respect of their sufficiency for that place. I heartily thank you that at my commendation you would so gladly have chosen Mr Gorges; which I would not have desired, if I had known of your good choice already made.' Mr Gorges, it may be added, was another Court official, who was found an alternative seat at Downton, the Bishop of Winchester's borough.

The implications of the letter are of great interest. In the previous parliament of 1584 Walsingham had been given both the Colchester nominations, and the two members – Morice, who was Attorney of the Court of Wards, and Harvey, a Gentleman Pensioner – must have been his nominees. In 1586 these two gentlemen may have placed such reliance on the Council's circular letter advocating the re-election of former members, that they did not bother to approach their patron, Walsingham. At any rate, the borough obeyed the Council's directive, while Secretary Walsingham, the embodiment of conciliar authority, ignored it! Nor is that all. Clearly, Elizabeth had told Walsingham or someone else to see that these two officials were found seats. Yet such was the informality of the whole business, and so complete the lack of organization, that Walsingham quite involuntarily came near to frustrating the Queen's wishes.[1]

Walsingham's action at Colchester in the following parliament of 1588–9 again emphasized the casual nature of patronage. He put in his friend Sir Nicholas Throckmorton's eldest son, Arthur, thus ousting Harvey from the seat he had held in 1571, 1584, and 1586.[2] But he gave the latter a Duchy of Lancaster seat at Knaresborough, Yorkshire, instead. In the next parliament, with Walsingham, his patron, dead, Harvey had to move once more – this time to the Wiltshire seat of Chippenham, where, in all likelihood, another patron at Court placed him.

The Colchester episode simply confirms the conclusion arrived at by a different line of approach, namely, that the election of royal

1. *Biographia Britannica* (1766), article on Walsingham, VI, ii, 4141–2 n.; MEREWEATHER and STEPHEN, ii, 1346.
2. *Biographia Britannica*, VI, ii, 4141–2 n.

officials and courtiers was a haphazard business, achieved without government planning, and with no official policy behind it, except the knowledge that normal processes would by themselves bring ample representation of the Court into any Elizabethan parliament.

CHAPTER 15

The Quality of the House

MOST of the famous men in Elizabethan history sat in parliament: statesmen, as a matter of course – the Cecils, Sir Thomas Smith, Sir Francis Walsingham, Sir Christopher Hatton, Sir Thomas Heneage, and many less well-known; courtiers such as Sir Thomas Sackville, created Lord Buckhurst and later Earl of Dorset, Sir Philip Sidney, Sir Walter Raleigh, Fulke Greville, and Francis Bacon; eminent lawyers, among whom were William Fleetwood, Thomas Egerton, and Edward Coke; men famous in voyage and adventure, Sir Humphrey Gilbert, Sir Francis Drake, Sir Richard Grenville, Thomas Cavendish; and men known in the realm of scholarship and letters, such as Thomas Norton, John Lyly, Sir Henry Spelman, Sir Edward Dyer, and Sir Robert Cotton. Social eminence also had its place. In the parliament of 1584, twenty-four of the members were sons of peers, and another thirteen intimately related to the peerage.[1]

Increasing competition for seats operated as a sieve, excluding the indifferent or colourless. Even in the counties it was not necessarily sufficient for candidates to belong to the more substantial families, with their powerful following of friends and tenants. They had usually to show some initiative and will. In the boroughs, whether patrons nominated the members or candidates made their own approaches to the constituency, competition tended to eliminate the less vigorous, less intelligent, and unambitious, while the minority of townsmen who secured seats were generally the more prominent and assertive in the community – Mayors, ex-Mayors, Bailiffs, Town

1. The information and figures in this chapter are largely derived from four M.A. theses on the personnel of parliament, written under my supervision: by Helen Brady and Constance M. Davey on the parliaments of 1571 and 1597 (Manchester, 1927); and Hazel Matthews and Evelyn E. Trafford on the parliaments of 1584 and 1593 (London, 1948). Miss Fuidge has supplied me with tentative figures for 1563. Occasionally I have seen reason to amend the calculations.

Clerks, and aldermen, or, as they were called in the Cinque Ports, jurats.

Occupationally, the largest class was that of the country gentleman, whose chief concern was running his estates. Such men numbered approximately 240 in the parliament of 1584, more than half the total membership of the House, which was then 460. Royal officials – men in the political or legal service of the Crown or attached to the Royal Household – constituted the next largest class: there were approximately 75 of them in this parliament. As an appendix to these two principal classes, we might place a miscellaneous group of 14 gentlemen-servants of noblemen and statesmen, 8 ecclesiastical officials, about half a dozen gentlemen who made the sea or the army their career, and 2 medical doctors. The third significant class was that of practising lawyers. Their number in this parliament has been calculated as 53, tallying exactly with the estimated number of townsmen. For many reasons, not excluding the difficulty of classification, exactitude is elusive, but the figures give a fairly reliable impression of the composition of the House of Commons in the latter half of Elizabeth's reign. In parliaments subsequent to 1584, the number of gentlemen-servants and probably the Court group tended to increase; the lawyers also may have added slightly to their number; but there were no violent fluctuations.

While native talent will display itself whatever a man's education and stupidity be tempered but unchanged after even the best training, it still remains true that the effectiveness of an assembly is inevitably and profoundly affected by the quality of education its members have received. Fortunately, it is possible for us to discover, with some accuracy, which of our members of parliament received what we may describe as higher education – that is, went either to the university or the Inns of Court, or to both. The figures are remarkable, and the trend they reveal very significant. Of the 420 members in the 1563 parliament, it has been calculated that about 67 went to Oxford or Cambridge, and 108 to the Inns of Court. Since 36 of the latter prefaced their legal with a university education, the figures give us a total of 139 members with a higher education. By 1584 the numbers had grown strikingly. The university figure is 145, and the Inns of Court 164, of whom 90 also went to the university – a total of 219 members out of a House now numbering 460. In the 1593 parliament 161 of the members had been to the university and 197 to the Inns of Court, with an overlap of 106 who attended both, giving us a total of 252, or appreciably more than half the House.

Though the figures for the 1563 parliament are less reliable than the others, the upward trend is stark and staring. No doubt the growing attraction of a seat in parliament was in part responsible, but the underlying cause of the increase was the invasion of the universities and the Inns of Court by the gentry. An anonymous planner, who in the flush of enthusiasm at the opening of a new era drew up a programme of social and economic reform for the first parliament of the reign, wanted to speed on this cultural revolution by act of parliament. 'That an ordinance be made – he wrote – to bind the nobility to bring up their children in learning at some university . . . and that one-third of all the free scholarships at the universities be filled by the poorer sort of gentlemen's sons.'[1] His secular and aristocratic purpose was achieved; but not by act of parliament. The simple march of time and fashion and spirit accomplished it. William Harrison, author of the 'Description of England' which prefaced Holinshed's *Chronicle* in 1577 and 1587, commented on the result. He was a clergyman, and conservative in temperament. Conceiving of the universities as vocational and ecclesiastical seminaries, he regarded the invasion of the gentry as an 'encroachment', an ousting of poor men's sons by men of birth and wealth.[2]

An incidental point of some interest is the predominance of Cambridge men in the earlier parliaments of the reign and the reversal of the position in later parliaments. In our 1563 figures, 49 belong to Cambridge and 18 to Oxford – a relationship confirmed by less complete figures for the parliament of 1571. In contrast, Cambridge men numbered 62 in 1584 and 72 in 1593, against Oxford's 83 and 89. On the whole, easterners went to Cambridge and westerners to Oxford, but presumably there was a neutral range of families ready to patronize either. One likely reason for the greater attraction which Elizabethan Oxford seems to have had for the politically alert gentry was the fame of the great puritan scholar, Laurence Humphrey, Regius Professor of Divinity and President of Magdalen College from 1561 to 1589, who had been abroad with the Marian exiles, im-

1. *Hatfield MSS.* i, 163.
2. HOLINSHED's *Chronicle* (1587), i, 149b.

bibed Calvinism, and returned to be a thorn in the side of authority over vestments. 'Mr Doctor', Elizabeth is said to have remarked to him when at Oxford on a Progress, 'that loose gown becomes you mighty well; I wonder your notions should be so narrow.' He had friends in high places – Burghley, for example, and Sir Francis Knollys who had been a fellow-exile in Mary's reign and afterwards sent his sons to Magdalen. Sir Thomas Bodley, who, as a child, accompanying his father, had also been a Marian exile, tells how he was sent to Oxford, 'recommended to the teaching and tuition of Doctor Humphrey'. Many Elizabethan members of parliament went to Magdalen College, where, according to a much later authority, Dr Humphrey 'did . . . stock his College with a generation of nonconformists, which could not be rooted out in many years after his decease'. His influence was reflected in the strong puritan tone of the Elizabethan House of Commons.[1]

Another change which our educational figures reveal is the notable increase of members with a legal education, and especially of members who went both to the university and the Inns of Court. One explanation is the expansion of the legal profession in Elizabeth's reign, but more significant is the spread of a fashion for finishing a gentleman's education with some study of the law. As Shakespeare's singularly stupid country gentleman, Justice Shallow, said: 'There was I, and little John Doit of Staffordshire, and black George Barnes, and Francis Pickbone, and Will Squele, a Cotswold man; you had not four such swinge-bucklers in all the Inns of Court again.'[2] The amateurs as a rule did not trouble to take a degree at the university, nor to be called to the bar after their law courses. Of the members in 1584, only 54 out of the 145 who went to the universities took a degree, and only 64 out of 164 were called to the bar. The figures for the 1593 parliament are similar, but slightly progressive: out of 161 only 62 took a degree, and out of 197 only about 60 were called to the bar.

We know Justice Shallow and his friends. Let us meet a few people from real life. Thomas Sackville, Lord Buckhurst, sent his son and heir, Robert, to Oxford, from which, after graduating, he proceeded

1. *D.N.B.*; BROOK, *Lives of the Puritans*, i, 363 ff.; NICHOLS, *Progresses* (1788), anno 1566, p, 3; *Trecentale Bodleianum, p. 5.*
2. *Henry IV,* pt 2, 3, ii.

to the Inner Temple, but was not called to the bar. At twenty-three he entered parliament, and, until his father's death raised him to the peerage, sat in each parliament, representing his county, Sussex, as befitted such an aristocrat, except in 1588 when he sat for Lewes. Fulke Greville, another gilded youth who set the pattern for his times, was at Cambridge and the Middle Temple, but neither graduated nor was called to the bar; and three of the parliamentary sons of Sir Francis Knollys, including his eldest surviving son and heir, William, went to Magdalen College, Oxford, and afterwards to an Inn of Court, again without any form of graduation.

This changing fashion, of incalculable benefit to our civilization, can be seen in the 'Memorials of the Holles Family'. Denzil Holles of Irby in Lincolnshire, a substantial gentleman linked with the peerage by marriage to Lord Sheffield's daughter, and member of parliament for East Retford in 1584 and 1586, was – according to Gervase Holles, the seventeenth-century memoralist of the family – educated at Cambridge. He sent his eldest son John, a precocious boy and the future Earl of Clare, to Cambridge in 1579 at the age of thirteen or fourteen. And then – marking an educational novelty in the family tradition – the youth, in November 1583, proceeded to Gray's Inn, in order, as Gervase Holles puts it, 'that by the study of the laws he might be the better fitted for the service of the Commonwealth'. On his father's death in 1590, followed by his grandfather's within nine months, John became the head of the family, responsible for two brothers who as younger sons had their own fortunes to make. He sent the elder of the two to his own College at Cambridge; but, as happened to others in those spacious and spirited days, the impulse of the adventurer and the fame of his kinsman, Sir Francis Vere, took him to the Netherlands, where he became a great soldier. The other brother was sent to the same College in 1597, and then, two years later, to Gray's Inn, 'being designed to the profession of the law'; but on a visit to his brother in the Netherlands he too felt the adventurer's call and forsook the law.[1]

This story of three brothers illustrates the place of university and Inns of Court in the life of the gentry in the latter part of Elizabeth's reign. Young Holles abandoned Gray's Inn, but others in his position

1. *Memorials of the Holles Family* (Camden Soc.), pp. 67, 88–9 (cf. p. 248 for the question of age), 73, 83.

stuck to the law and prospered. Thomas Wilson, who, between 1596 and 1600, wrote an acute and invaluable, if sometimes unreliable, description of 'the State of England', commented bitingly on the swollen 'estate of common lawyers', 'grown so great, so rich, and so proud that no other sort dare meddle with them. Their number', he went on, 'is so great now that, to say the truth, they can scarcely live one by another, the practice being drawn into a few hands of those which are most renowned, and all the rest live by pettifogging, seeking means to set their neighbours at variance, whereby they may gain on both sides. This is one of the great inconveniences in the land, that the number of the lawyers be so great, they undo the country people and buy up all the lands that are to be sold.' The wealth of some, he added, is incredible: 'Not to speak of the twelve chief judges and the multitude of serjeants, which are most of them counted men of £20,000 or £30,000 yearly, there is one at this day of a meaner degree, namely the Queen's Attorney – Edward Coke – who within these ten years, in my knowledge, was not able to dispend above £100 a year, and now ... may dispend betwixt £12,000 and £14,000.' [1]

There was a double reason for Wilson's jaundice. He was the younger son of a country gentleman, and he professed the Civil Law – the first ever a misfortune, and the second, since the fatal blow of the Reformation, little better. Some few Civilians, he tells us, lived in good credit; 'the rest, God wot ... take great pains for small gains'. [2] For him, fortune proved tardy and sparing, and he looked on the prosperous estate of Common Lawyers with resentment. He had been born too late. In the new society of his days, it was the Common Law which was the career open to talents, just as in pre-Reformation times it had been the Church, associated with the Canon and Civil Laws.

Wilson wrote contemptuously of 'my young masters', the sons of rich yeomen, who, not content with the state of their fathers – 'to be counted yeoman and called John or Robert (such an one)' – 'must skip into his velvet breeches and silken doublet, and, getting to be admitted into some Inn of Court or Chancery, must ever after think scorn to be called any other than gentleman.' [3] As Sir Thomas Smith

1. *Camden Soc. Misc.* xvi, 24–5. 2. ibid., p. 25.
3. ibid., pp. 18–19.

wrote in his *De Republica Anglorum*, 'Whosoever studieth the laws of the realm, who studieth in the universities, who professeth liberal sciences, and to be short, who can live idly and without manual labour, and will bear the port, charge, and countenance of a gentleman, he ... shall be taken for a gentleman; ... and if need be, a king of Heralds shall also give him for money, arms newly made and invented, the title whereof shall pretend to have been found by the said Herald in perusing and viewing of old registers'. 'Such men,' he added, 'are called sometimes in scorn, gentlemen of the first head.'[1]

Smith, who originally wrote his book in France and was conscious of the contrast with that country's more rigid conventions, thought this social flexibility 'not amiss'. And the history of many a Tudor family would justify him. But not everyone was so liberal-minded. Our anonymous planner at the opening of Elizabeth's reign would have excluded upstarts from the law. His outlook was aristocratic, his argument entrenched in *noblesse oblige*: 'That none study the laws, temporal or civil, except he be immediately descended from a nobleman or gentleman, for they are the entries to rule and government, and generation is the chiefest foundation of inclination.'[2] Let it be added, that few lawyers, being 'gentleman of the first head', appear to have found seats in Elizabethan parliaments.

Little wonder that the House of Commons showed initiative and ability, when – the stage reached by 1593 – forty-three per cent of the members possessed a legal education and fifty-four per cent had been to the university or the Inns of Court, or to both. Such men spent more and more time in debate. They set and maintained a high standard of parliamentary oratory.

But knowledge and ability are not the sole requisites for legislators. Practical experience is needed. It was present in good measure. As a matter of course, all Privy Councillors eligible for membership secured seats. Normally they represented the counties. Numbers fluctuated, varying from a maximum of nine in 1559 to a minimum of three in 1597.[3] They constituted a managerial core, anticipating in some respects, but in some respects only, cabinet ministers of

1. Ed. Alston, pp. 39–40. 2. *Hatfield MSS.* i, 163.
3. In 1559 nine; in 1563 eight, diminishing to seven in the second session; in 1571 and 1572 five, rising to eight in the session of 1581; in 1584 six; in 1586 and 1589 seven; in 1593 four; in 1597 three; in 1601 five.

modern times. In the last three parliaments of the reign their number was dangerously small; but in Elizabeth's days there never was that cleavage between Crown and Parliament which made a similar dearth of leadership in early Stuart parliaments so disastrous.[1] All her parliaments, even when critical, were loyal to her, and she never lost the art of playing upon their devotion. Moreover, there was plenty of experience, personality, and ability in the Court group of royal officials and others, which, as we have seen, numbered not far short of one hundred in the last parliaments of the reign. They did not act as a party in any modern sense of the word, nor even to the extent expected of them by the early Stuarts: that was part of the secret of successful parliaments in Elizabeth's reign. But they did contribute to the restraint and responsibility of the House of Commons.

Nor were the country gentlemen, in the narrower sense of the term, lacking in practical experience. The type which sought election was broadly that which ran the administration of the county as Justices of the Peace. Fully half the country gentlemen in the parliament of 1584 held county office, and another thirty odd, not yet qualified by age or succession to their fathers' estates, were later to hold office. In fact, the number who never attained to the dignity was less than eighty.

But parliamentary sessions in those days were very brief and the qualifications we have analysed, invaluable though they were, would have been sadly frustrated without the addition of parliamentary experience. The patient growth of tradition, the broadening of privilege from precedent to precedent, and the consolidation of victories in the long march towards political supremacy – all were dependent upon the presence in each parliament of a number of old hands ready to guide the new. As a rule, about half the members of an Elizabethan House of Commons had sat before. In 1571, with no general election since 1563 and moderate appetites satisfied by the two sessions of that parliament, the proportion of newcomers was higher than usual. They numbered 272 out of 437 – sixty-two per cent. The disparity was even more marked in 1584, when twelve years and three sessions intervened, and only exceptionally could a man under thirty have sat before. The newcomers then numbered 322 out of 460 –

1. Cf. NOTESTEIN, *The Winning of the Initiative by the House of Commons* (Raleigh Lecture, 1924); D. H. WILLSON, *Privy Councillors in the House of Commons, 1604-29.*

seventy per cent. They numbered 221 – forty-eight per cent – in the parliament of 1593, the normal type.

Of the newcomers, 135 in 1571, 109 in 1584, and 134 in 1593 never sat again, the number in 1584 being unduly small owing to government action. Reversing the line of thought, over two-thirds of the House normally sat more than once – a high proportion. Of the members who sat in the 1584 parliament, 241 sat again in 1586, and 153 in 1588. The corresponding figures for the 1593 parliament – the average type – are 157 re-elected in 1597 and 116 in 1601.

Some members, especially higher officials and the more important country gentlemen, were returned again and again, with impressive regularity. Some sat spasmodically. Some – usually lesser folk who, whatever their inclinations, had to yield to competition – sat in few parliaments. The appropriate figures decline sharply. Approximately forty-six per cent of the members in the 1584 parliament sat either once or twice, forty-five per cent sat between three and six times, seven per cent sat in seven or eight parliaments – a considerable achievement, remembering how infrequently parliaments then met – and two per cent sat more often still.

The 'Old Parliament Man', as he was called – the habitué of the House of Commons – was already a conspicuous figure. The example *par excellence* was Sir Francis Knollys, who, so he tells us, sat in the Reformation Parliament in 1534, when the act for the submission of the clergy was passed.[1] He was then about twenty years old. Though the evidence is defective, it is conceivable that he sat in all the remaining parliaments of Henry VIII's reign as well as in the first parliament of Edward VI. In Mary's reign he was in exile, but with the accession of Queen Elizabeth, his wife's cousin, and with the new dawn for his fortunes, he sat in every parliament until his death in 1596. In his last parliament in 1593 he could look back over sixty years' experience gained in perhaps fourteen parliaments; a member whose cousinly loyalty to Queen Elizabeth was ever tempered with puritan frankness and independence.

Probably no other Elizabethan equalled his achievement, but there were three who had twelve parliaments to their credit before they died. One was Sir William More of Loseley, Surrey, who had repre-

1. Cf. his speech printed in the pamphlet, *Information on a Protestation ...* (1608), pp. 94 ff., and (somewhat inaccurately) in STRYPE, *Whitgift*, ii, 124.

sented Reigate at the age of twenty-seven in 1547. When fifty years later he sat for the last time, he had as fellow-members three men who, forty-three years on, in the Long Parliament, were still members of the House of Commons. In his last four parliaments, Sir William was accompanied to Westminster by his son and heir, Sir George More, who, beginning in 1584 at the age of twenty-one, sat in twelve consecutive parliaments between that date and 1626, ringing the changes between the family borough of Guildford and the county, as his father had mostly done. Both were influential parliament men. Sir Walter Mildmay, Elizabeth's Chancellor of the Exchequer and Privy Councillor, scored the same record as the Mores. He entered parliament in 1545 at the age of twenty-five, and, in spite of a hiatus in Mary's reign, managed to sit in twelve parliaments before his death in 1589. In practically all the sessions of Elizabeth's reign, there were one or two or more men whose parliamentary memories carried them back over the Elizabethan religious settlement and the Catholic reaction of Mary Tudor to the Protestant Reformation under Edward VI, and even into the reign of Henry VIII. What a pageant of history, what a wealth of precedent, of the maxims born of long, rich experience, must have been in those wise old heads! And what continuity there was! In the parliament of 1593, along with Sir Francis Knollys whose membership went back to 1534, there was a young man, Sydney Montagu, whom he probably knew well, who was a member of the Long Parlimant in 1640 – a span of more than a century.

Though only four Elizabethans seem to have sat in twelve or more parliaments, there were a few who managed to get ten into their lives. One of the choicest of these was Sir Robert Wroth. He was the son and heir of an eminent and wealthy gentleman, one close to the King in Edward VI's reign, who acquired great estates in the home counties. During Mary's reign the son was abroad in exile with his father. Then, back in England under Elizabeth, he entered parliament in 1563, aged about twenty-three, and after sitting twice for boroughs, assumed his father's seat for the county of Middlesex and held it without a break till his death in 1606. 'I have been of this House these forty years,' he said when giving his views on a point of procedure in 1601.[1]

1. TOWNSHEND, *Historical Collections*, p. 279.

Many others were habitual parliament men: for example, Sir Thomas Cecil, Burghley's eldest son, member of every parliament from the age of twenty-one in 1563 until he succeeded to his father's peerage in 1598; Sir Anthony Cope – one of Oxfordshire's leading gentlemen, a hot Puritan who 'was collecting a fine assortment of puritan ministers' in the Banbury district [1] – who sat nine times, from 1571, when he was twenty-two years old, till his death in 1615; and William Howard, second son of William, Lord Howard of Effingham, who from the age of twenty or thereabout in 1559 till his death in 1600 sat for the family borough of Reigate in all but one parliament.

The peripatetic member, to whom the nineteenth century contributed the oppropbrious name of 'carpet-bagger' – though in Elizabethan days he very rarely needed to pack his bag and visit his constituency – was already a familiar figure. We have come across a number in the course of our narrative. They were usually but not invariably without strong territorial ties – royal officers, lawyers, gentlemen-servants, and the like, who did not care where they sat as long as it was somewhere. There was Arthur Atye, scholarly secretary to the Earl of Leicester and later to the Earl of Essex. He resided at Kilburn in Middlesex, but sat for Liverpool in 1584, Fowey (Cornwall) in 1589, Shaftesbury (Wiltshire) in 1593, Dunwich (Suffolk) in 1597, and Berealston (Devon) in 1604 until his death in that year. Miles Sandys, a royal official, sat in every parliament from 1563 to 1597, but never twice in the same seat. His constituencies, in chronological order, were Taunton, Lancaster, Bridport, Buckinghamshire (his second wife's county), Abingdon, Plymouth, Andover, and Stockbridge. Sampson Lennard, a prominent gentleman of Kent and Sussex, claimant to the barony of Dacres in right of his wife, and a person with friends at Court, sat for Newport (Cornwall) in 1571, Bramber (Sussex) in 1584, St Mawes (Cornwall) in 1586, Christchurch (Hampshire) in 1589, St Germains (Cornwall) in 1593, Rye (the Cinque Port) in 1597, Liskeard (Cornwall) in 1601, and Sussex in 1614. Henry Macwilliams of Essex, a Gentleman Pensioner, sat in only four parliaments, but made a remarkable jump from Dorchester and Liskeard in the south in 1571 and 1572, to Appleby and Carlisle in the far north in 1584 and 1586. How eloquent are these bare facts

1. KNAPPEN, *Tudor Puritanism*, p. 292.

of the haphazard way in which such gentlemen secured their seats! The instinct to be methodical, which ought to have prompted some degree of continuity in patron, client, and constituency was not easily evoked when parliaments met so occasionally and elections were few and far between.

Being dependent on their own communities, and these in turn subject to so much external pressure, townsmen furnish few examples of continuous parliamentary experience. Yet there were a few. Richard Lyffe, a jurat of Hastings, sat for his town eight times, from 1563 till his death in 1605, missing only two parliaments; and Edward Peake, a prominent jurat, five times Mayor of Sandwich, sat for his native town from a by-election in 1576 till his death in 1606.

Continuity; and now cohesion. The family ties of members almost defy description. As a *jeu d'esprit*, a student has compiled a series of genealogical tables, which link together like the tale of the House that Jack built and contain the names of ninety-three members of the 1563 parliament. Fathers and sons, brothers, sons-in-law, brothers-in-law, cousins, and more distant relatives all sat together. Among intimate groups, the most conspicuous was the Knollys family, a parliamentary family if ever there was one. In the sessions of 1576 and 1581 there were actually seven of them in the House of Commons: Sir Francis, the head of the family, his younger brother, Henry – a 'carpet-bagger' like many younger brothers – and five sons. Sir Francis had seven sons. The youngest took to soldiering and probably had neither inclination nor time for parliaments. The other six – most of whom were educated at Magdalen College, Oxford, and afterwards at the Inns of Court – entered parliament on the first possible occasion after they were twenty or twenty-one, and with one exception sat consistently throughout the reign or till death closed their careers. The eldest entered in 1563, the second and third sons in 1571, the fourth in 1572, the fifth in 1584, and the sixth at a by-election in 1575.

Apart from the Knollys family, there were nine instances of father and son sitting together in the 1571 parliament: the Crofts of Herefordshire, the Dormers of Buckinghamshire, the Gargraves of Yorkshire, the Gates of Yorkshire, the Hoptons of Suffolk, the Lanes of Northamptonshire, the Mildmays of the same county, the Musgraves of Cumberland, and the Russells of Worcestershire – a geographical distribution that reveals how nation-wide this custom was. All the fathers sat for their county and the sons for boroughs, mostly within the county. Among brothers in this parliament were three Killigrews and three Newdigates, and several pairs including the Bowes, the Careys, sons of Lord Hunsdon – four of whom sat in the parliaments of 1584 and 1589 – the Cordells, the Heneages, the Pophams, the Snagges, and the Stanhopes. In later parliaments instances of close relationship were still more numerous. In 1584 there were actually twenty-two families from which two or more brothers went to parliament.

A striking example of the family group in a broader sense is furnished by the Cecils. In the 1597 parliament Sir Robert Cecil had as fellow-members a half-brother, a nephew, and seven first cousins, not to mention more distant relatives. There was Thomas Cecil, Lord Burghley's heir, whom we have already mentioned, and with him his second son, Richard, whose first constituency, in 1593, at the age of twenty-three, had been the Cecil borough of Westminster. Robert Cecil's mother was one of the celebrated daughters of Sir Anthony Cooke, tutor to Edward VI and scholar-gentlemen, who in the enlightened tradition of the English Renaissance, of which the incomparable Sir Thomas More was the examplar, lavished the finest classical education on his daughters. Another was mother to the brilliant Anthony and Francis Bacon, both members of parliament in 1597, and a third was mother of Sir Edward and Sir Thomas Hoby, also in this parliament. A fourth daughter, equally renowned for her learning, married Sir Henry Killigrew, an Elizabethan diplomat, and though he had given up parliament long before 1597, a brother and a nephew were members in that year. There was also another cousin of Cecil's on his mother's side, William Cooke, who certainly owed his Westminster seat in 1601 to Sir Robert, and probably his Helston seat in 1597. On his father's side, Cecil had an aunt whose two sons, Robert and John Wingfield, were likewise members.

If we were to trace the relatives of all these men and their wives, the ramifications would spread hither and thither. The Bacons bring in their half-brother, Nathaniel, also a member of parliament; one of the Hobys married a Carey, sister to two sons of Lord Hunsdon sitting in this parliament, and they in turn were related to the Knollys family and to Charles Howard, afterwards second Earl of Nottingham; one of the Wingfields married a Croke, sister to two more members. And so we might go on. Sir Henry Sidney's family affiliations in the parliament of 1571 ramble in a similar way. There was a brother-in-law, Sir William Dormer, a nephew, Robert Dormer, another nephew, John Harington of Exton, and still another, William Fitzwilliam. Fitzwilliam was the son-in-law of Sir Walter Mildmay, the Mildmays were connected with the Walsinghams, the Walsinghams with the Wentworths, and the Wentworths with the Stricklands and the Lanes.

As a sample of a minor constellation we may take the family circle of Sir John Fortescue, Chancellor of the Exchequer and Privy Councillor. For fellow-members in the parliament of 1597 he had a brother, two sons – there had been three in 1593 – and a nephew, Sir Henry Bromley – son of Sir Thomas, Lord Chancellor from 1579 to 1587 – who brought into the group a cousin, Edward Bromley, and two brothers-in-law, Oliver Cromwell of Hinchingbrooke, and John Little of Worcestershire. Nor dare we omit from our tale the East-Anglian family of Gawdy, which contributed eight of its members to parliament between 1558 and 1621 and actually had five sitting in 1597. One of the Gawdys married a daughter of Sir Nicholas Bacon, and so this little group, with its own ramifications, could be attached by a tenuous thread to the Cecils. As for west-country members, they were notoriously clannish, and family relationship certainly had something to do with this. A Carew of Anthony, for example, married a daughter of the Edgcumbes of Mount Edgcumbe; and in the parliament of 1584 the combination occupied five borough seats in Cornwall and one in Somerset.

Our rather prolonged genealogical excursion will have shown that the English gentry, or the more substantial and ancient families among them, were a closely integrated class – a fact written deeply in our history and of untold importance in the history of parliament. Social customs and institutions secured this. Marriage was not normally a question of romance, dependent on acquaintance and so tending to inter-marriage within the county, the social unit. There was romance, of course, but not to the extent that the lyrical poetry of the age might suggest. Marriage was a matter for negotiation between parents. It was often very mercenary. An heir or heiress or a wealthy widow was a bargain piece in a national rather than a local market. Cornwall married into Norfolk, Warwickshire into Somerset.

The retinues of gentlemen-servants that great men maintained, and the custom of sending young ladies into some noble or distinguished household as a finishing school, also contributed to meandering relationships. So did wardship, a feudal prerogative which survived until 1645 and conferred upon the Crown the guardianship and marriage of all minors inheriting land held in knight-service. Few of the country gentry, indeed none of any standing, were immune from this archaic and now irrational and irritating burden. The Crown sold the wardship and marriage of a minor, sometimes to a relative, but often to strangers. It was a coveted investment or speculation, especially if the purchaser had a son or daughter of his own to marry.

No wonder that gentlemen knew one another's names, pedigrees, and heraldic showings, with their many quarterings of arms. Mutual acquaintance was widespread. Starting in the county, it broadened at the university and the Inns of Court and later in London and at the Court where so many gentlemen came on business and paid their respects to the Queen. Edward, Lord Herbert of Cherbury – who incidentally was a royal ward allotted to Sir George More of Loseley, with whom he afterwards remained on terms of affectionate friendship – tells how as a young Welsh squire of seventeen or eighteen, 'curiosity rather than ambition' brought him to Court. 'As it was the manner of those times for all men to kneel down before the great Queen Elizabeth', he tells us, 'I was likewise upon my knees in the Presence-Chamber when she passed by to the Chapel at Whitehall. As soon as she saw me, she stopped, and swearing her usual oath, demanded, "Who is this?" Everybody there present looked upon me, until Sir James Croft, a Pensioner, finding the Queen stayed, returned back and told who I was, and that I had married Sir William Herbert of St Julian's daughter.'[1]

One has only to turn over the pages of John Chamberlain's gossipy letters to his friend Dudley Carleton, with their scores of names of country gentlemen, to realize how intimate a society this was. The parliamentary diarists of the time, themselves gentlemen, jotting

1. *Autobiography*, ed. Lee, pp. 81–2.

down speeches in the House, seem rarely to have been at a loss for the name of a speaker.

To complete our picture we must obtain some idea of the age of members. As we have noticed, the eldest sons of prominent families – younger sons, too, on occasions – heirs by birth and custom to parliament, frequently made their entry into the House of Commons at the first possible election. Not many entered before they were twenty-one, and very, very rarely were they knights of the shire while under age. The vigour and bitterness with which Sir John Harington opposed the election of his own nephew in the Rutland election of 1601 illustrates conventional feeling,[1] as does Lord Burghley's restraint in waiting till his son, Robert Cecil, was twenty-five before seeking a county in place of a borough seat for him. Yet there were exceptions. The man who was possibly the babe of all Elizabethan members sat for a county, and sat, by virtue of his birth, as senior member. He was Edward Dudley *alias* Sutton, the profligate son and heir of the fourth – or, according to another reckoning, the eighth – Baron Dudley. He sat for Staffordshire in 1584 at the age of seventeen, a striking example of noble blood overcoming all obstacles. Not very different was the example of Charles Howard, second son but eventual heir of the Armada hero, who in 1597 at the age of eighteen, after election to the family borough of Bletchingley, Surrey, suddenly found the county seat vacant through a mistaken idea that his elder brother's new courtesy title prevented him from sitting. Gilbert Talbot, aged eighteen, and his stepbrother Henry Cavendish, aged twenty, jockeyed into the two Derbyshire seats by Bess of Hardwick and the Earl of Shrewsbury in 1572; Robert Sackville, heir of Lord Buckhurst, planted in the Sussex seat by his father and Viscount Montague in 1584 at the age of twenty-one; and Robert Sidney, elected for Glamorganshire at the age of twenty-one by the persuasive intervention both of his father, who was Lord President of the Council in the Marches of Wales, and of his brother-in-law, the Earl of Pembroke, and also by virtue of his own marriage to a rich heiress of that county:[2] all these bear the stamp of exceptional privilege.

For the sixteenth century dates of birth are much more elusive than those of death. We cannot give a complete age-picture of any

1. Above, p. 125.   2. *Stradling Correspondence*, ed. Traherne, pp. 21, 77.

Elizabethan House of Commons; but we can, with a fair measure of reliability, compare the ages of 40 per cent of the members in two parliaments, those of 1584 and 1593. The earlier of these was a notoriously young parliament, partly, no doubt, because there had not been a general election for twelve years: the interval had piled up candidates under the age of thirty, and the novelty of the occasion was in itself an attraction to youth. In our 1593 figures age may be unduly stressed, either because it was in fact a slightly older House than usual, or because the sample has distorted the truth. Of 183 members in the 1584 parliament, 44 were under thirty, 13 of these being twenty-one or less, and 15 aged twenty-two to twenty-five; 111 were aged thirty to forty-nine; and 28 were fifty or over, of whom 5 were sixty-five or more. In 1593 the total of our sample is 190. Of these, 34 were under thirty, one being nineteen, and 18 aged twenty-two to twenty-five; 109 were aged thirty to forty-nine; and 47 were fifty or over, 6 of them being over sixty-five.

Though 40 per cent is an unreliable sample for such a question as age, there is good reason to believe that the complete figures, if they were obtainable, would maintain much the same relation between the three broad divisions of youth, middle, and old age: certainly they would not be likely to favour youth at the expense of the older age-groups. Consequently we can assume that in an Elizabethan House of Commons appreciably more than half the members were middle-aged, and the rest divided, on the average not very unequally, between impetuous youth and staid old age – surely a judicious balance. 'The young heads', as Elizabeth bade them in 1563, could 'take example of the ancients'.[1]

In the 1586 parliament the oldest member of the House was Sir Ralph Sadler, Chancellor of the Duchy of Lancaster and Privy Councillor, who had been born in Henry VII's reign, had first entered parliament – so far as our defective records show – in 1541, and was now sitting for the last time at the age of seventy-nine. But he was not the Nestor of Elizabethan parliaments. This proud record must surely go to 'Old Grimston' – Edward Grimston esquire of Rishangles, Suffolk, born either in 1507, the same year as Sadler, or in the previous year. He had been Comptroller of Calais under Edward VI and Mary, and having been captured at the fall of the town and

1. *Eng. Hist. Rev.* xxxvi, 500.

unable to pay the heavy ransom demanded for his release, endured nineteen months' imprisonment in a high room of the Bastille before he made a daring escape. After filing through the great bars of his prison window and successfully concealing the work, one night, while his guard slept in his room, he descended by torn bed-sheets to freedom, where further adventures awaited him before he finally reached home. The tale was famous in its day, and for ingenuity, coolness, and courage is worthy of a place with the best of escape-stories. 'This good old man', his daughter tells us, was ninety-two when he died early in 1600. He was therefore eighty-five when in wintry February he took the toilsome journey from Suffolk to Westminster to sit in the parliament of 1593.[1] In age he eclipsed the 'father of the House', Sir Francis Knollys, who was probably seventy-nine when he sat for the last time in 1593; and Knollys in turn eclipsed that other grand old man, Sir William More of Loseley, who was seventy-seven when he sat in 1597.

Birth and education, expert knowledge, practical experience, and corporate solidarity – all were present in abundant measure in the Elizabethan House of Commons. And so was character. It was an assembly which never failed to display high and independent spirit, moral and religious fervour, and patriotism. By a paradox which must be accounted one of the supreme felicities in the history of the Mother of Parliaments, flagrant violation of the law and of medieval representative principles, indeed those very episodes in our story which most shock our modern democratic sense, resulted in assembling in parliament the élite of the country – 'the flower and choice of the Realm', 'many grave, many learned, many deep wise men, and those of ripe judgement'.[2] Already the House might have in-

1. *H.M.C. Earl of Verulam's MSS.* pp. 13 ff. I prefer his daughter's explicit statement of age to Cooper (*Athenae Cant.* ii, 280–1) who puts his birth as 'about 1528'. The inscription in Rishangles church need not be taken literally: indeed, it gives a wrong date for his death. The parish register at Rishangles (for the entry in which I am indebted to Miss Fuidge) confirms the daughter on this point. It reads: 'Edward Grymstone Esqr, that Ancyent Justyce & worthy magistrate of our Commonweal in these partes, Dyed at Ipswich upon Satterday the xiii of February and was buried, Tuesday 26 Feb. 1599.' Moreover, a parliamentary diarist of 1593 (Cotton MS. Titus F II, fol. 79a) described him as 'Old Grimston', which seems incompatible with Cooper's surmise of his age.

2. D'EWES, *Journals*, p. 98a; Cotton MS. Titus F II, fol. 22b.

scribed upon its portal the sentiment of one of its members, no other than the famous Sir Christopher Hatton, though the words, uttered in the parliament of 1586–7, seem to come strangely from a bachelor: *As I and my posterity trust to serve for ever in the same.*[1] The House of Commons reached maturity in Elizabeth's reign. The instrument was tempered with which the Crown was to be resisted and conquered. It was not from the Stygian darkness of Tudor despotism that early Stuart parliaments emerged. They succeded to a rich heritage, to great traditions.

1. Harleian MS. 7188, fols. 88 ff.

CHAPTER 16

Members' Wages and Election Costs

IN the Elizabethan period members of parliament were still entitled to wages: 4s. od. per day for knights of the shire, and 2s. od. for burgesses, including travelling time to and from Westminster. The legal position was as clear as it had been in the Middle Ages; and any member had only to pay a fee in Chancery to secure a writ *de expensis* ordering the payment of the sum legally due to him. To what extent these writs were used is, however, quite another question. The Chancery had ceased enrolling them – keeping an office copy on the Close Rolls – nearly a century and a half before; and we must therefore look at the receiving end, in borough accounts or other sources, for any traces. Nor is this the only intricacy. A writ *de expensis* was far from being the invariable way of obtaining payment: indeed, why should a member put himself to the trouble and cost of a writ, if he could secure his money without it?

In the boroughs, wages were usually a matter of mutual arrangement between the community and its members. The rate might or might not be the statutory one, or there might be no wages at all. Such local arrangements naturally excluded resort to the Chancery, unless, as sometimes happened, a member had difficulty in extracting his wages, or a borough omitted to obtain a formal renunciation of them and its curmudgeonly representative afterwards sued out a writ with the object of extorting payment, contrary to his verbal promise.[1] In the counties writs might be necessary to justify the Sheriff in levying a rate to provide the money; but in the boroughs the authorities could do this without a warrant from outside. Where borough members had faith in their constituencies, there was little or no point in buying a writ from Chancery; and in Elizabethan times the mere existence of one seems often to imply that the member despaired of a settlement by amicable means.

Normally, wages were not paid to outsiders. In the competition

1. See above, p. 149.

for seats, these people would have stood no chance of election on different terms. Consequently, many small boroughs paid no wages at all; and, taking borough members as a whole, only a minority were paid. There was every degree of variety. Some boroughs were consistent, always paying both members or one member; others were inconsistent; others paid intermittently. The statutory two shillings was the usual rate. Some, however, paid less, some more, while elsewhere the rate fluctuated.

The city of London, which had four members, two chosen by the aldermen and two by the commons, paid its senior pair, who ranked as knights, 4s. od. a day, and its juniors 2s. od. – 'such fees as are allowed by act of parliament', as an entry of 1587 put it. In 1450 the authorities had laid down that when parliaments were held at distant places their members should be allowed 40s. od. a day, presumably for the whole party of four – a generous allowance; but the occasion for such exceptional treatment did not arise in Elizabethan times. In addition the city provided a livery allowance, for cloth and fur. An ordinance of 1429 fixed the quantities and price, according to civic rank, and made provision for attendants, two being allowed each member when parliament met away from London, reduced to one each for the junior members when the meeting was at Westminster. Practically the same allowances and gradings were in force in 1571, when the total cost amounted to £38 14s. 2d. But in 1581 the luxury of the seniors was reduced, and all four members were to receive a scarlet gown for each session – subject to a maximum of one a year – or in lieu thereof, £6 13s. 4d. In 1571 the members were also allowed 1s. od. a day each for boat-hire. It was probably an ancient fee, but – reminiscent of the economy in liveries – it seems to have been deliberately stopped in 1587.[1]

London was not the only constituency where distinctions were accorded to civic rank. In 1584 Hythe undertook to pay its Mayor 4s. od. a day, as well as his 'charges and expenses' to and from Westminster, whereas in the following parliament, when the local member

1. Repert. xxi, 446; Jor. v. fol. 32; SHARPE, *London and the Kingdom*, i, 273–4; Chamber A/cs. i. 16th cent. fols. 48b ff.; Repert. xx, 183, xxi, 446, xxiv, 212. I owe these and the later extracts from the City records to a former student Miss Winifred Jay, who generously placed her transcripts at my service.

was merely a jurat, he received 2s. 0d. a day, with 9s. 0d. each way for the journey. In 1588 the Port again elected its Mayor, and, though less generous on this occasion, paid him 3s. 0d. a day. In each of these parliaments, the other member was a 'foreigner', serving *gratis*. Apparently, Hythe ceased to pay any wages at all after the end of Elizabeth's reign.[1]

Despite the intervening fall in the value of money, Cambridge, in the first of Elizabeth's parliaments, was still paying its members 1s. 0d. a day, in accordance with an ordinance of 1427; but in 1563 the ordinance was repealed and the rate doubled. Once begun, generosity, or the community's finances, continued to expand. In 1571 a member was allowed 'charges'; in 1585 the moderate sum of 15s. 4d. was paid for horse-hire. Then in 1589 each member was allowed 4s. 0d. a day, and after a lapse to 2s. 0d. in 1593, the new rate was paid again in 1598 and finally established by ordinance after the parliament of 1601.[2] Sandwich was another borough where payments fluctuated. The normal wage was the statutory 2s. 0d., but in 1544 only 1s. 6d. was paid; and then, from 1576 till the latter part of Elizabeth's reign, when, as at Dover, payments appear to have ceased, the rate jumped to 4s. 0d. a day.[3] In all probability Plymouth had few occasions to pay its Elizabethan members, though when, for the last parliament of the reign, it did pay one of them, a local merchant, he received the handsome reward of 10s. 0d. a day for himself and his man – a total outlay of £32.[4] The incident shows clearly enough that if poverty drove many small boroughs to welcome the free service of nominees, and if thoughts of economy led others to a mixture of free and paid service, for some boroughs economy was not necessarily a motive in accepting the intrusion of the gentry.

Salisbury clung with commendable tenacity to two citizens for its members, and faced the financial consequences, though from time to time it was helped by the civic patriotism of representatives. The two members in Elizabeth's first parliament, John and William Webbe – sons, perhaps, of the William Webbe who sat in the

1. WILKS, *Barons of the Cinque Ports*, pp. 63–5.

2. COOPER, *Annals of Cambridge*, i, 178, ii, 158, 177, 178, 278, 410, 476, 521, 593, 617.

3. WM. BOYS, *Sandwich*, i, 402.   4. *H.M.C. Rep.* X, iv, 540.

Reformation Parliament, remitted part of his wages in 1535, and on his death left a benefaction for 'the setting of spinners, weavers, and clothiers awork' – brought a writ against the city for £24 16s. od. in January 1560, eight months after the end of the parliament. Perhaps it was customary at Salisbury to obtain payment through a writ; perhaps the city was a bad payer. In any case, John Webbe then proceeded to remit his half of the bill, while William, who had been heavily hit by his journey to town, 'forasmuch as he hath been long sick at London', remitted £2 8s. od. 'for the good will he beareth to this chamber', and was promised payment of the remaining £10 the following March. Their example was later followed by Giles Estcourt, citizen and Recorder, who inserted a clause in his will in 1587: 'I do forgive the Mayor and commonalty of Sarum all such money as is due unto me for serving of them in divers parliaments as a citizen for this city.' Estcourt had sat in eight sessions, from 1563 to 1586, and if his wages were outstanding for all or most of these, then his generosity was great. We know that the city paid both its members for the parliaments of 1589, 1593, and 1601. In one instance, the cost was £22, in another £20.[1]

Wherever wages were paid, they were certainly the main expense connected with parliamentary elections. But there were many minor costs as well. In accordance with the conventions of the time, every official involved in the peregrination of writs and returns probably looked for his fee or reward. In 1584 the Clerk of the County received 3s. 4d. from Barnstaple for bringing the Sheriff's precept to the borough. Then there was the cost of drawing up the certificate of election – the indenture between the borough and the Sheriff. Barnstaple paid 2s. 6d. early in Elizabeth's reign for a pair of indentures, but in 1586 and 1593 managed to get them written and ingrossed for 1s. od., with an additional item of one penny for wax in 1586. Chippenham in 1587 paid but sixpence for 'parchment and the making of the indenture', while Bridgwater in 1571 merely noted the cost of the wax – again one penny, though at Plymouth it cost twopence. Some boroughs recorded a charge by the Sheriff for making the return to Chancery; and in all likelihood a fee was general. The joint borough of Weymouth and Melcombe Regis,

1. HOARE's *Wiltshire*, iv, 282, 708; *H.M.C. Var. Coll.* iv, 217–18, 222, 228; will in P.C.C. 1587 (47 Spencer).

with its four members, paid the Sheriff 8s. od. on one occasion. Bath and Maidstone each paid 4s. od., while Bath also paid 7s. 6d. for horse-hire and service in carrying the indenture to the Sheriff. Chippenham escaped with a modest fee of 2s. 6d.[1]

Next, the Clerk of the Crown in Chancery had to be paid for receiving and filing the writs and returns. In 1593 a parliamentary diarist noted that the fee was 2s. od., which may have been the rate for a burgess, and 2s. 6d. the rate for a knight of the shire.[2] London in 1571 paid 8s. od. to this official's deputy, on presentation of his bill.[3] In 1559 Cambridge recorded two payments: 6s. 8d. 'for certifying of the names of the burgesses of the parliament'; and 2s. od. to one of the members, 'for the entry of his name', probably a fee to the Serjeant of the House. In 1589 the borough noted a single payment of 8s. od. 'for the return of the indenture'.[4] Members themselves may, as a rule, have discharged these fees, and if serving *gratis* may not have sought repayment. All the same, we find Haverfordwest paying 7s. 6d. in 1593 'for entering Sir Nicholas Clifford's name when he went into the parliament house'.[5] In addition to paying £28 5s. od. to one of its four members for 113 days' wages at the substantial rate of 5s. od. per day,[6] Weymouth in 1597–8 paid £4 10s. 6d. 'for the establishing of the burgesses in the parliament house'. The item was unusually heavy, doubtless owing to a dispute over rival election returns to that parliament; but we may assume that it included some or all of those small charges that we have been examining. In the same parliament Portsmouth advanced £6 to one of its members to pay his 'fees and charges' and to serve as instalment for his wages

---

1. CHANTER and WAINWRIGHT, *Barnstaple Records*, ii, 103; GOLDNEY, *Records of Chippenham*, p. 339; Bridgwater Borough Archives (I am indebted to Mr T. Bruce Dilks, who kindly sent me various transcripts of these); WORTH, *Plymouth Records*, p. 121; MOULE, *Records of Weymouth & c.*, p. 131; *Somerset Rec. Soc.* xxxviii, 182; *Records of Maidstone*, pp. 189–90.

2. D'EWES, *Journals*, p. 468b.

3. Chamber A/cs. 1. 16th cent. fol. 48b. 'Paid to Master Dyster', who (*A.P.C.* vii, 291) was the Clerk of the Crown's deputy.

4. COOPER, *Annals*, ii, 158, 476. I think that this payment 'to the clerk of the parliament house' was really to the Clerk of the Crown.

5. J. PHILLIPS, 'Glimpses of Elizabethan Pembrokeshire', *Arch. Camb.* 6th ser. iv, 265.

6. MOULE, op. cit., p. 135, gives 5s. 8d. a day, but arithmetic and probability suggest 5s. od.

at 2s. od. a day. The other member, being a nominee, cost the town nothing.[1]

A few boroughs made festive at election time. Bridgwater – which followed the principle of one local member and one self-supporting outsider – paid 2s. 3d. in 1571 'for a pottle of sack and a pottle of white wine when the burgesses were chosen, and sugar'; and 4s. 6d. 'for fish the same time for their dinner'. In the same year Nottingham paid twelve pence to wife Bomford for ale and bread 'on the Monday when the burgesses of the parliament were chosen'. In 1588, on the order of the Mayor and borough council, Cambridge contributed £2 7s. 9d., half the cost, for the dinner given at the Falcon 'at the time of choosing knights of the shire'. As its own borough election took place the day before, perhaps there was something of a joint festivity about the occasion. Similarly, Ipswich at the previous general election disbursed a modest 3s. 8d. 'for wine given to them that chose the knights of the shire'. We are not told whether it celebrated its own elections.[2]

County wages are something of a mystery. There are no local records to solve the problem, and other contemporary documents do not give a clear lead. As late as 1523 knights of the shire were apparently purchasing their writs *de expensis* and looking for their wages, as a matter of course; at any rate, Sir Richard Cornwall, member for Herefordshire, was doing so.[3] That seems to be the last tangible clue. There are later items of evidence, but they are not so direct and they are compatible with a practice that was dying out. In 1543 there was an act of parliament – a delightful curiosity for the legal-minded – which incorporated the two knights for Cambridge-shire and the Sheriff as 'wardens of the fees and wages of the knights of the shire of Cambridge' to receive an annual rental of £10 devoted to freeing the inhabitants of the county in perpetuity from levies for their members' wages. Then in the following year, there was another act which, when dealing with the payment of Welsh county and borough members, referred to the same obligation in England as if it

1. MOULE, op. cit., p. 135; D'EWES, p. 554; EAST, *Portsmouth Records*, p. 212.

2. Bridgwater Archives, Water Bailiff's A/cs.; *Records of Nottingham*, iv, 142; COOPER, *Annals*, ii, 476; *H.M.C. Rep.* IX, i, 250b.

3. *L. & P. Hen. VIII*, IV, iii, no. 5962. The letter is misdated, as internal evidence shows.

were still a reality. In 1554, 1558, 1559, and 1566 we come across instances of tenants on ancient demesne in six different counties obtaining confirmation of their rights to exemption from contributing to the expenses of knights of the shire; not very impressive evidence, for this was only one of several rights that such tenants enjoyed, and its inclusion may have been purely formal.

Again, we need not take *au pied de la lettre* an order made by the House of Commons in 1581, when, worried by the unauthorized absence of many members, it resolved, as a mild course and by way of warning, that knights of the shire and burgesses who had departed without licence should lose their wages, and that the Clerk of the Crown, who issued the writs *de expensis*, should in future proceed only on warrant from the Clerk of the House. Supposing that county members were already accustomed to forgo their wages, nevertheless the House, on theoretical grounds, could not have excluded them from an order which did, in fact, have substance for many burgesses.[1]

We need better evidence than all this before assuming that wages were still being paid in many counties as late as Elizabeth's reign. True, they were not entirely extinct. In the Denbighshire election of 1588 a candidate was accused of seeking election 'only to the end to have the country's money to maintain his brabbling causes in London', and again in 1601 there was mention of wages.[2] Then, the Earl of Pembroke, when urging the election of his brother-in-law, Robert Sidney, for Glamorganshire in 1584, took care to add that he would 'demand no charges of the country at all'.[3] But these were Welsh counties. They may have lagged behind the times, and perhaps some of the poorer and more remote English counties lagged likewise. It is hard to believe that in counties rich in substantial gentlemen, where the honour of election was highly valued and eagerly sought, squires would show themselves less ready to forgo their wages than they were when forced to take second-best in borough seats. However, this is a mere guess, and in money matters sixteenth-century conventions were often odd.

As in the boroughs, some counties made merry on election-day.

1. 34 & 35 Hen. VIII, c. xxiv, 35 Hen. VIII, c. xi (*Statutes of the Realm*, iii, 924, 969); *Cal. Pat. Rolls, Ph. & Mary*, ii, 206–7, iv, 231; ibid., *Eliz.* i, 127; MEREWEATHER and STEPHEN, ii, 1436; *Commons Journals*, i, 136.
2. Above, pp. 108, 116.   3. *Stradling Correspondence*, p. 77.

Here it was the candidates who entertained the constituents. The custom was not new. Among the family papers of the Carews of Beddington, Surrey, there is an account, drawn up by a servant, John a Chamber, showing the 'costs of election to be knight of the shire'. It probably refers to the Surrey election of 1515.[1] There is no indication that the expenses were shared by a colleague, as later happened, and it may be that this candidate merely feasted his own supporters. The number must have been substantial. Items include sixteen dozen bread, nine dozen ale, nine and a half kilderkins – a kilderkin being eighteen gallons – of beer, and a considerable quantity of wine; two 'beefs', eight sheep, two carcasses of veal, four pigs, nine geese, four hens, sixteen capons, four dozen 'birds', pasties, fish, etc. Probably the food was consumed at dinner at some house and not at free buffets in various inns, for the bill mentions fire in the chamber and in the kitchen, candles, and wages of cooks and scullions. The total outlay, including the candidate's own costs staying at Leatherhead the night before, came to £10 1s. 8d. – a far from negligible sum in 1515.

Unfortunately, there seems to be no itemized Elizabethan account for comparison. As we have seen, Cambridge paid half the cost of a dinner in 1588. Since the total expenditure was only £4 15s. 6d., in money very much depreciated since 1515, the dinner was probably confined to gentlemen. For a closer parallel with the feast of 1515 we must take a much later bill – the 'charges at Chelmsford' incurred by Sir Thomas Barrington, elected first knight of the shire for Essex in March 1640. The two principal items of expenditure – 'diet and wine and beer' at the Lion inn, and 'a hogshead of wine and a butt of beer given at the Bell' – were shared, presumably with the second member, or, if there was a contest, with the candidate who paired with Barrington. Barrington's share of the first item was £20 2s. 6d., and of the second £4 8s. 0d. In all probability it was a case of free meat and drink – at one inn, drink only – available for the mass of voters. There are thirty-six items in the bill, which totalled £42 2s. 3d. A number of gentlemen and servants were paid their charges, amounting to a few shillings each: for example, the accountant

1. Add. MS. 29597, fol. 12. The B.M. catalogue assigns the document to Elizabeth's reign, but the handwriting and the dated account overleaf suggest 1515.

himself, 5s. 6d., 'for charges that I was at with two companies' – doubtless two bands of freeholders placed under his charge. A charge of £2 11s. 6d. for 'horsemeat etc.', must indicate free stabling for gentlemen supporters. The 'Colchester waits by appointment' received 6s. 0d., bell-ringers 5s. 6d., George Burke, who brought 'the good news' to my Lady 5s. 0d., 'for opening of gates through the fields as we went and came' 2s. 0d., and 'the poor' 1s. 9d. The Under-Sheriff received a gift or fee – the one was apt to develop into the other – of £3 0s. 0d., 'another man of the High Sheriff's 5s. 0d., and bailiff Benson £1 10s. 0d.[1]

The tradition of entertainment was perhaps an old one in Essex. As early as 1559 there had been a dispute, which led to the intervention of the Privy Council, about taking up an inn for the occasion. It may of course have been simply a question of housing some of the gentry; but a similar dispute in 1604 was certainly concerned with lodging and diet on a large scale. Lord Rich, who was supporting the Barrington of that time, urged that they must know both the number and quality of their voters, 'else provision cannot so fitly be made for them'; and he himself helped by sending supplies from his own private stores. One of the three candidates – who withdrew from the contest – wrote: 'I perceive it is expected that I should defray some good portion of the charges at the election, which I am loth [to do] because it is likely to be extraordinary.'[2]

Our 'bill of charges' for 1640 was probably more elaborate than any which Elizabethans had to meet: electioneering by this later date had become more intense, more sophisticated, more costly. Certainly, with its payments to officials and others, and its numerous petty items, especially the recouping of gentlemen and servants for small outlays, presumably in managing groups of freeholders, the 1640 bill is strikingly different from the simple bill of 1515; though, when allowance is made for the drastic fall in the value of money between the two dates, the main expenditure on food and drink was not so different as might have been expected.

In Hertfordshire they appear to have been well on the way to the

1. One of certain Barrington MSS. in the church at Hatfield Broad-Oak. I owe the opportunity to transcribe the document to the Vicar and to my friend Professor Wallace Notestein of Yale University.
2. *A.P.C.* vii, 38; *Eng. Hist. Rev.* xlviii, 400 ff.

1640 pattern by 1584. As we have seen, Sir John Brockett and Charles Moryson ran Edward Denny in that election, and were defeated. Afterwards, Brockett wrote to Moryson: 'Touching the charges, all things were done by Mr Denny's man, who yesterday with my man did seek to pay every man; but ... many would not receive one penny. I do hope we are nothing indebted at Hertford, for you had discharged where you did lie.' In the light of the later Barrington bill this may be taken to mean that anyone who had been put to expense in looking after freeholders was offered his costs. Many gentlemen refused payment: commercialization had not yet reached the 1640 standard. Though not a candidate, Moryson himself gave a dinner to the men of St Albans who voted for Denny. At least, that is how I construe a letter to him from the Mayor of the borough: 'Touching your benevolence to certain of this borough who attended with me at Hertford ... it is thought best by us, if it shall so please you, to appoint the day either the Monday, Tuesday, or Thursday next after Christmas Day.' The Mayor appended the names of those who 'very willingly did perform their promise in the journey'. Besides himself, there were three principal burgesses, and twenty-three others. At the foot of the list, he added: 'Andrew Coltman, James Lee, were there of their own good will, but wanted ability of freehold.' They too, let us hope, got their dinner.[1]

There is evidence from other counties of Elizabethan candidates playing host to the voters. In the Wiltshire election of 1559, one of the three candidates, George Penruddock, who was Steward to the Earl of Pembroke and was successful in the election, though the Sheriff afterwards fraudulently returned his opponent, stood up at the end of the election and 'gave thanks, as well to them that gave their voices to him as to Sir John Thynne – his opponent – and desired them all to come to dinner to Wilton House – the Earl of Pembroke's – and they should be welcome'. The Sheriff, the second successful candidate, 'and divers and many other gentlemen and others came thither and dined there, as well such as gave their voices with Sir John Thynne as with ... Mr Penruddock'. Again, in the first of the two Rutland elections in 1601, Sir John Harington and Sir Andrew Noel, the two elected representatives, joined together 'in the charges of the entertainment of the freeholders there assembled

1. Add. MS. 40630, fols. 6, 8.

... as the usual manner hath been there at the time of such elections'.[1]

Confessedly, our examples are few. The entertainment of voters was not a universal custom. An allusion to freeholders 'fasting and far from home' at a Hampshire by-election in 1566 would seem to indicate that even in this comparatively central and important county, no arrangements were made to feed the voters.[2] Such hospitality may still have been exceptional in Elizabeth's reign, but in these matters a precedent casually set by some wealthy, prodigal, or merely generous candidate could easily start a stubborn custom.

Apart altogether from election expenses, knights of the shire must have found their seats an expensive pleasure, what with the cost of lodgings in London at a congested season and the various fees and gifts that confronted them at Westminster. James Harington, who sat for Rutland county in 1597 and therefore knew from experience what outlay was involved, is alleged to have said in 1601 that membership would cost him £200; and both as a younger brother and by temperament – for in 1597 he departed from parliament without leaving the customary gift for the poor and the minister – we may assume that he was less lavish than some.[3]

1. *Eng. Hist. Rev.* xxiii, 472 n.; ibid. lxi, 36.
2. Star Chamber, Ph. & Mary, P 7/18, answer. The documents are wrongly placed in Mary's reign.
3. Above, p. 131; D'Ewes, p. 566a.

CHAPTER 17

The Officers of the House

THE House of Commons had only three officers in the pay of the Crown – the Speaker, the Clerk, and the Serjeant-at-Arms. By ancient usage that can be traced back to 1485, the Speaker received a fee of £100 for each session of parliament.[1] On occasions, royal generosity may have gone further, for in 1523 Cardinal Wolsey wrote a letter to the King on Sir Thomas More's behalf in which he declared that, for the better maintenance of their household and other charges imposed by the office, it was customary, 'though the parliament hath been right soon finished', to pay Speakers 'a reward of £100', over and above 'the £100 ordinary'.[2] Whether he was stating the truth or making a princely gesture at his sovereign's expense, we do not know. 'Rewards' were a device employed by sixteenth-century monarchs to supplement inadequate salaries; but unless the two payments were made separately and from different treasuries, Speaker Audley certainly received no more than a single payment of £200 for the first two sessions of the Reformation Parliament.[3] In Edward VI's reign only the ordinary fee seems to have been paid.[4]

Uncertainty also exists about Elizabeth's reign. When a session lasted over two legal terms, the Queen may have paid what she termed 'double hire';[5] a reasonable convention for Speakers who were practising lawyers. At any rate, John Puckering, who was Speaker in two parliaments of this nature, 1584–5 and 1586–7, asserted that the Speaker's allowance 'was never certain', but varied according to the length of the session.[6] Then, in a catalogue of

1. *I.H.R. Bulletin*, xii, 25 n. 102.
2. More received the extra £100. Cf. *Harpsfield's Life of More*, pp. 320–1.
3. P.R.O. Duchy of Lancaster, 28/7/1, p. 15. I owe this reference to Mr G. Elton.
4. *A.P.C.* ii, 163, 379, iv, 39.   5. *I.H.R. Bull.* xii, 25.
6. *Cal. S.P. Dom., 1601–3, & Add.*, pp. 534–5. This document is wrongly dated and ascribed. The reference to Fisher's debts, for which there was a private act in 1584–5, settles the date and the name of the Speaker.

lamentations, written, one surmises, in 1595 when he was successfully begging one hundred pounds land in fee farm from the Queen, and with naïve and typical effrontery, while about to entertain her with prodigal magnificence at his Kew house, claimed that he had served her as Lord Keeper at a net loss of £1000 a year – in this later writing he described the parliaments when he was Speaker as each containing two sessions. 'I never had recompense,' he wrote, 'albeit £400 was due fee for those four session, and recompense meant me by her Majesty.' This statement, too, was disingenuous, and lest another notch be cut in the mythical tally of Queen Elizabeth's meanness, let us add what he so conveniently forgot to say, that he had asked for his fee as Speaker to be set against a debt which he owed the Queen. Puckering was a man whom Elizabeth might have described as a 'greedy grasper'; a notoriously corrupt person, for whose death little grief was shown. His estimate of his fee may have been as fraudulent as the claim that it was still owing him.[1]

The Clerk of the House of Commons, known officially as the Under-Clerk of the Parliaments – the Clerk proper being in the Lords – was appointed by letters patent at a fee which had been £5 per annum under Henry VIII, jumped to £10 under Edward VI, reverted to £5 under Mary, and was again £10 under Elizabeth; this in contrast with the £40 paid to the Clerk of the Upper House.[2] During the whole of Elizabeth's long reign there were only two Clerks: John Seymour, who died in 1567 and deserves to be held in pious memory for inventing the Commons Journals – one of the salient landmarks in our constitutional development; and Fulk Onslow, who completed the evolution of the Journal and died at the ripe age of eighty-six in 1602. Seymour, who had been member for a Wiltshire borough in 1545, apparently officiated in the autumn session of 1547 but was not appointed to the clerkship until May 1548. He held office 'during pleasure', which compelled him to renew his patent under both Mary and Elizabeth, and exposed him to the temporary halving of his salary in Mary's reign. Onslow's patent was

1. Harleian MS. 7042, fol. 170b; COLLINS, *Sidney Papers*, i, 376; *Cal. S.P. Dom.*, *1601–3*, pp. 534–5.

2. *I.H.R. Bull.* xvi, 147; *Cal. Pat. Rolls*, *Ed. VI*, ii, 3; *Ph. & Mary*, i, 262; *Eliz.* i, 56; *L. & P. Hen. VIII*, xvi, 107 (22), 1056 (64).

for life. Illness and advancing age caused him to use a deputy in 1587 and 1589 and during the whole of his last parliament in 1601.[1]

In addition to his salary, paid half-yearly, the Clerk received a reward or gratuity from the Crown at the end of each session. In 1534 and 1536 the amount was £10, in 1549 forty marks (£26 13s. 4d.), in 1550 and 1552 fifty marks.[2]

The Serjeant-at-Arms, who in social status was an esquire or gentleman like the Clerk, held office for life by letters patent. Ordinarily, he was 'specially attendant' on the sovereign, presumably merging in that corps of twenty-five Serjeants-at-Arms provided for in Queen Elizabeth's Household establishment. In parliament time, however, he was 'to be attendant upon the Speaker' and 'carry the mace before him', a duty appropriate to the streets of Westminster and London no less than the precincts of parliament. In 1606, for example, 'Mr Speaker went to St Clement's church with the mace before him to the marriage of the Lady Verney's daughter'.[3] More domestically – as a contemporary, John Hooker, relates – he was charged with the cleaning of the Commons' House and keeping the doors. 'He ought to keep the inner door fast and to suffer none to come into the House during the time of sitting, unless he be one of the House, or come [with] message from the Higher House, or be willed by the House to come in.'[4] He also acted as tipstaff and jailer, to whose safe custody the House might commit anyone infringing its dignity or privileges.

His fee from the Crown was that of an ordinary Serjeant-at-Arms, twelve pence a day and a yearly livery of clothing at Christmas. Apparently, he received no additional 'reward' at the end of a

1. Cf. my article, 'The Commons Journals of the Tudor Period', *Trans. Roy. Hist. Soc.* 4th ser. iii, 136 ff., and A. F. POLLARD in *I.H.R. Bull.* xvi, 144 ff., xvii, 1 ff. Pollard's statement that Seymour functioned in the 1547–8 session is confirmed by a reference in the London records (Repert. xi, 415). His suggestion that Seymour delegated his work to a deputy, possibly Onslow, in 1566–7, is not borne out by the handwriting of the Journals.

2. *I.H.R. Bull.* xvi, 147–8; *A.P.C.* ii, 270, 389, iv, 48.

3. *L. & P. Hen. VIII*, II, ii, 3433; *Cal. Pat. Rolls Ph. & Mary*, ii, 224; PECK, *Desiderata Curiosa*, i, 62; *Bowyer's Diary, 1606–7*, ed. Willson, p. 199 n.

4. Hooker, 'The Order of Kepinge of a Parlament', Exeter City Records, Book 60h, fols. 12 ff. I am indebted to Professor W. J. Harte for a transcript of this MS.

session, as did the Commons' Clerk and many officials in the Upper House; which was a reasonable distinction, for he was not involved, as they were, in the laborious business of drafting and writing public bills. Nevertheless, though nominally no better paid than an ordinary Serjeant, his post brought perquisites that made it a coveted promotion.[1]

For all three officials, Speaker, Clerk, and Serjeant-at-Arms, salaries and gifts from the Crown were a minor part of the profits of office. This was characteristic of the whole royal service. One has only to scan the Queen's Household list, with its hundreds of officials at more or less static and therefore progressively inadequate salaries, and consider the modest limits of Crown revenue, to realize that the financial structure of official life just had to be of that nature. Those needing the services of officials partnered the Crown in supporting them. The same principle held in the private households of the great. Sir Christopher Hatton's secretary told his master in 1584, 'I never charged you with any kind of wages, nor other gift or bounty of your own whatsoever': in other words, he served for board and lodging plus tips. 'There liveth not so grave nor so severe a judge in England,' he declared, 'but he alloweth his poor clerk under him, even in the expedition of matters of greatest justice, to take any reasonable consideration that should be offered him by any man for his pains and travail. It is the poor man's whole maintenance, and without it he could not live.' The following items of expense incurred by the small Pembrokeshire borough of Haverfordwest in a suit before the Privy Council in 1597 will illustrate the process: Mr Waad, Clerk of the Privy Council, 'to solicit our cause' £2; Mr Waad's man, 'to remember his master' 2s. od.; the Earl of Essex's secretary, 'for his pains' 10s. od.; at 'two several times' to Mr Sandford, my Lord of Pembroke's secretary, £1.[2]

In parliament, an obvious source of supplementary income was the private bill – parliamentary measures drafted in the interests of one or more individuals or communities and promoted by them. Public bills – measures concerned with the common interest –

1. e.g. THOMAS HALE, in *Cal. Pat. Rolls, Ph. & Mary*, ii, 224 (cf. ibid., i, 280, 325).

2. NICOLAS, *Memoirs of Hatton*, pp. 389–93; *Arch Camb.* 6th ser. iv, 266–7. Cf. my *Elizabethan Political Scene*.

brought officials no fees; nor did public business of any kind. Theoretically, the salary of office was quittance for this work, though the appreciable gratutities paid by the sovereign at the end of a session to the judges and other legal assistants in the Upper House and to the Clerks in both Houses recognized the need for further payment.[1]

The borderline distinguishing public from private bills was obscure, and continued to be obscure even in the eighteenth century. But our parliamentary officials must have looked at the problem in a very simple way. Could they extract fees from someone? If so, it was a private bill. In 1607 when a member desired to hasten the ingrossing of a bill for amending highways in Sussex, Surrey, and Kent, the Speaker answered that the bill was long and of much labour to the Clerk; that it was followed and pressed as a public bill, but since it concerned only three shires it was by all former precedents a private bill; that no fees had been paid and no one was prepared to answer for them. The House sided with the Speaker. Pay up, it declared, or the bill lapses. What money could do on the fringe of private legislation was demonstrated by the city of London, always lavish in its parliamentary expenditure. In 1571 it sponsored a bill for bringing the river Lea to the north side of the city. Having paid all the fees as for a private bill, it then, by an additional fee of fifty shillings to the Clerk of the Upper House, had the act enrolled as well as exemplified, with the result that it has always appeared in the collections of printed statutes with chapter number as though it were a public bill.[2]

The Speaker was entitled to £5 for every private bill before the first reading – 'before he deliver it out of his hand'. If it concerned party and party the charge may have been '£5 the piece' – £5 from each person; a principle already existing in the Speaker's right to £5 for every name in a bill making denizens, unless 'he agree for less'.[3] The number of private bills was always large, always increasing, always too great for the time available. To compute their exact

---

1. *A.P.C.* ii, 37, 154, 265, 270, 389, iv, 21, 48, v, 22; *H.M.C. Rep.* VIII, ii, 22; *Hatfield MSS.* iii, 100.
2. *Commons Journals*, 1, 388; City of London, Chamber A/cs. 1, 16th century, fol. 78b; *Statutes of the Realm*, iv, 553.
3. Lambarde's tract, Add. MS. 5123, fol. 14, and version in Lord Braye's MSS.

number in any session is a hopeless task, for they cannot all be distinguished from public bills. The most cautious estimate of those read in the parliament of 1597 would be forty; and one can say with confidence that Speaker Yelverton on that occasion must have received between two and three hundred pounds from this source.[1]

Recognized fees were not all. By 1553, if not earlier,[2] the city of London, which had bills to prefer or interests to defend in every parliament, was giving the Speaker 'a free gift', 'for his lawful favour to be borne and showed in the Parliament House towards this city and their affairs there'. The customary sum seems to have been twenty nobles in gold – £6 13s. 4d. – presented in a purse. In 1576 he was given six yards of velvet – whether as a substitute for the money or in addition to it, we cannot tell.

It is in the nature of regular tips to be taken for granted and to lose their potency unless increased. In 1589 Serjeant Snagge received the conventional £6 13s. 4d. By 1597 the gratuity was £10. We do not know what Edward Coke was paid in 1593. At a guess, it was the higher figure, for in that parliament there was an innovation in the city's procedure. Instead of leaving the tip, like yeast, to its own beneficent operation, the Court of Aldermen sent a deputation, including three aldermen and the Warden of the Fishmongers' Company, to Mr Speaker 'for his favour in a cause concerning the said company of Fishmongers'.[3]

In the next parliament they went further. Serjeant Yelverton was given the Speaker's gift – this time £10 – in November 1597. On 24 January the city sent a deputation of four to seek 'his furtherance' in its bill 'for the reformation of the abuses in new devised stuff', and the City Chamberlain, one of the deputation, paid him £5. Though this was the amount of the Speaker's fee for a private bill, the use of the words 'for his furtherance' seems clearly to exclude any notion of a fee and dub the gift what we should call a direct bribe. The Speaker's goodwill could make all the difference to a bill's fate,

1. Cf. *I.H.R. Bull.* xii, 27–31.

2. For a century before this, occasional Speakers had received gifts: in 1454 one pipe of red wine and two barrels 'vini dulcis' (Jor. v, fol. 149); in 1472, £5 and 40s. each to 'other persons' (Jor. vii, fol. 33b); in 1512 £5 (Repert. ii, fol. 171b); in 1531 ten marks (Repert. viii, 183b).

3. Repert. XIII, i, fol. 92, XIII, ii, fol. 344, xix, fol. 39b, xx, fol. 163b, xxi, fols. 112b, 355, 396b, xxii, fol. 24, xxiii, fol. 31, xxiv, fol. 153b.

especially if it were facing heavy weather, for unless the House intervened – an exceptional occurrence – it was he who decided the order in which bills were read; and since many private measures expired for lack of time to read them, his power amounted to life or death. In this instance the bill was unpopular. If, as is probable, strong opposition had been manifest even at the first reading, it should have been allowed, as the phrase went, to sleep. Yelverton earned his five pounds by giving it a second reading. Then, although the House cried 'Away with the bill!' he put the question for committing it, and presumably in the face of a decisive negative, even ordered a division. Knowing that they were hopelessly outnumbered, the *Ayes* refused to divide; and as a last service he put the question for ingrossing. With a denial of this, the limits of his favour were reached. The city's money had been wasted.[1]

In the last parliament of the reign, London's 'free gift' to the Speaker was again increased. It was now forty nobles – £13 6s. 8d. – twice the amount paid from 1553 to 1589. The Speaker on this occasion was their own Recorder, which may have prompted the new generosity.[2]

The city of London was unique. It is unlikely that any other city or borough patronized the Speaker in each parliament, and yet likely enough that promoters of private bills, particularly corporate promoters, occasionally added a gift to the regular fee. There is indeed evidence to suggest that this happened.[3] On the other hand, the city of Westminster, whose statement of costs in connexion with the act for the good government of the city, passed in 1585, will subsequently illuminate our story, aspired no higher than the Clerk with its tips. In this instance, tips at a high level may have been unnecessary because the great Lord Burghley was Westminster's High Steward and the bill had his backing.

The Clerk of the House of Commons spread more tentacles than the Speaker. Naturally, he received a fee for private bills – £2. The

---

1. Repert. xxiv, fols. 153b, 180, 186b; *I.H.R. Bull.* xii, 18 (the conjectural date of 17 December for the second reading is proved wrong by the City records. The date was probably 25 or 26 January).

2. Repert. xxv, fol. 297b.

3. *H.M.C. Rep.* v, 579b. Also cf. payments in 1536 listed in FRANCES CONSITT, *The London Weaver's Company*, pp. 240, 241, 243.

figure was still maintained in the eighteenth century, though with certain elaborations. For example, even by 1649 the sixteenth-century principle that two or more parties to a bill were each liable for a full fee had been extended so that a bill for a corporation or society or shire counted as 'a double bill' – a refinement unknown to Elizabethan officials. The Clerk also received a fee – whether the Speaker did, we do not know, though he certainly did in the eighteenth century – for a proviso benefiting a private person, were the bill private or public. In 1571 London paid him ten shillings for such a proviso to the usury act. By 1649 the fee was the same as for a private bill – £2.[1]

Any writing that could be debited to someone other than the sovereign produced a demand for fees. Usually, the original paper text of a private bill was prepared by legal counsel, but in its passage through parliament it might have to be rewritten by the Clerk after amendment in committee, or, if it got as far as a third reading, there was the ingrossing on parchment, which was done by the Clerk of the House in which it originated. The Clerk was paid for this work. Then again, members or parties who were interested in a bill, whether public or private, and wanted to study the text, had to procure a copy from the Clerk. One imagines that he did a considerable business. Paper copies were charged by the line; and, as happened in the Star Chamber and elsewhere, the number of words to the line probably showed an understandable tendency to shrink. In 1571 the cost to members was one penny for ten lines, which may perhaps have been a preferential rate. In 1585 Westminster paid 'Mr Onslow's man' 5s. od. for 'a new paper book' after the committee's amendments, and there was a further charge of 7s. od. 'for new writing of the bill', apparently after the Lords' amendments had caused the Commons to introduce a new bill. The charge must have been fifty or one hundred per cent more than the penny rate. By 1649 the rate had risen to 1s. od. for a sheet of sixteen lines. For ingrossing on parchment the charge was by the skin or sheet, or, as it was later called, the press. The Westminster bill cost 8s. od., and Onslow was paid a further 5s. od. for embodying 'the last amendments which came from the Lords'. We happen to have a scale of fees operative

1. Above p. 323 and n. 3; *Commons Journals*, vi, 287; *Orders of the House of Commons* (1756), pp. 15 ff.; Chamber A/cs. 1, 16th cent. fol. 78b.

in the Upper House in 1623. The charge for ingrossing was then 3s. 4d. the skin. In the Lower House by 1649 it was 10s. the 'press': a very steep rise.[1]

When John Seymour invented the Commons Journals he provided future Clerks with a new source of income, though he could scarcely have been aware of the vision delectable and perhaps never profited from it himself. On the principle of doing nothing *gratis* in the private interest, it became the custom to charge for entries in the Journal or copies of orders and committee lists. We cannot say how soon these new fees were introduced. In 1585 the city of Westminster included two such items in its statement of costs: 10s. od. 'for the order set down for the committees meeting four times with the Clerk of the Lower House his book, at 2s. 6d. the time'; and 2s. 6d. 'for entering of the bill brought down from the Lords'. By 1649, though committee lists remained at 2s. 6d., the cost of orders had risen to 6s. 8d. In the eighteenth century they were at a level 6s. 8d.[2]

Other charges were evidently creeping in. From 1649 on, the officials of the House were restrained by a scale of fees established by authority, but there was no such precaution in the Elizabethan period. It was the Clerk's opportunity. By 1601 he appears to have attached a fee of his own to the older and more legitimate fees charged by the Serjeant-at-Arms when a culprit was brought before the House. Presumably it was the entries of commitment and discharge in the Journal which furnished the excuse for this innovation; and in 1649 the charge duly found a place in the official tables of fees.[3]

As with the Speaker, fees were not all. To secure the Clerk's 'favour' towards a bill was perhaps the commonest instinct of promoters: certainly, it was easier, as it was cheaper, to tip him than the Speaker. London was again conspicuous. Already in 1548 their

1. HOOKER, 'Order of Kepinge a Parlament'; *Local Government in Westminster* (Annual report of St Margaret's vestry, 1889), pp. 24–5; *Commons Journals*, vi, 287; Lord Braye's MSS. at Stanford Hall, vol. entitled 'Miscellaneous', which contains scales of fees for the House of Lords.

2. *Local Government in Westminster*, pp. 24–5; *Commons Journals* (hereafter referred to as *C.J.*), vi, 287; *Commons Orders* (1756), p. 17.

3. D'EWES, pp. 634a, 643a, 658a, 686a; NOTESTEIN, *1621 Debates*, ii, 487, v, 229, vi, 450; *C.J.* vi, 287. The fee was evidently unknown as late as 1589, when the Serjeant's fee only is mentioned (D'EWES, p. 435a, and cf. for 1576 *C.J.* i, 113, and for 1585 Trinity Coll. Dublin MS. N. 2, no. 12).

records mention 'such accustomed fee as the Clerks of the Parliament House have heretofore commonly used to have at every session of the parliament, of the free gift of the said city'. In 1549 the amount was five marks – £3 6s. 8d. – in 1550 and 1552 four marks, and then in 1553, for the last brief parliament of Edward VI and the first of Mary, five pounds. In 1554 there was a decline to forty shillings, paid 'albeit that nothing passed for the city'; and at forty shillings it appears to have remained until 1571, after which the records fail us. Repetition threatened to destroy its voluntary character. In 1567 the Clerk 'claimed' his gift 'as due' to him, and in 1571 Fulk Onslow, the new Clerk, in addition to his claim for certain regular fees, 'demanded' forty shillings 'for an ordinary reward'. The city of Westminster in its turn gratified the Clerk in 1585. In addition to the regular fee, it paid twenty shillings 'to Mr Onslow . . . to further the suit'. We may be sure that other promoters of bills acted similarly.[1]

Initially, the Serjeant-at-Arms, whose services in the labour of legislation were not obvious, as were those of Speaker and Clerk, may have had no share in the fees for private bills. By 1550 he was claiming a fee, but the variation in the amount paid suggests that the claim was not long established. In 1550 he demanded from the city of London 14s. 0d. for certain unnamed acts; in 1552 the fee was 6s. 8d. for one act, and in 1567 10s. 0d., again for one act. Westminster paid 11s. 6d. in 1585. By 1649 the fee was £1, and in the eighteenth century £1 5s. 0d.[2]

In the opinion of suitors the Serjeant, like Speaker and Clerk, was evidently one who could help or hinder the passage of a private bill. This was probably because he was responsible for their admission, along with legal counsel, to give evidence to the House. Certainly, they tipped him. 'Here be the shoe-makers, crying and following, ready to pull their bill out of my hand', said a member of 1585. 'I pray you, Mr Speaker, let the Serjeant call them in. He knows them: they be his clients.' Westminster tipped him 10s. 0d. for its bill. And he also appears in another item of the costs: 'To the Serjeant of the

1. Repert. xi, fol. 415, xii, fols. 69, 217b, XII, ii, fol. 488, XIII, i, fols. 103, 167, XIII, ii, fol. 353, xiv, fols. 13b, 161, xv, fol. 233, xvi, fol. 162b; Chamber A/cs. 1, fol. 78b; *Local Government in Westminster*, pp. 24–5.

2. Repert. xii, fol. 209, XII, ii, fol. 480, xvi, fol. 162b; *Local Government in Westminster*, pp. 24–5; *C.J.* vi, 287; *Commons Orders* (1756), p. 21.

Lower House and for musledyne [? muscadine] and cakes for the burgesses, 2s. 2d.'. In due course, though seemingly with some reluctance, London found itself adding him to the recipients of regular gratuities. In 1581 he was given twenty shillings as a free gift 'for his good will showed to this city in the parliament time'. Perhaps this was the initial precedent: at any rate, when twenty shillings was again paid in 1587, it was 'upon condition that he shall not at any time hereafter make suit . . . for the like'. What optimism![1]

Then there were his peculiar functions as tipstaff and jailer, the dim beginnings of which went back to the famous Ferrers case of 1543, when, after initial failure in which the Serjeant broke his mace during an undignified scuffle, the Commons first haled a delinquent before them. By 1585 these activities were bringing the Serjeant a fee of twenty shillings for the arrest of a culprit, and ten shillings a day – apparently only 6s. 8d. in 1571 – while in his custody. The culprit, of course, paid the fees.[2]

In the eighteenth century the Clerk's department was responsible for collecting all fees and distributing them to the Speaker and other officers of the House. As the London records show, this simplified but advanced procedure was not established in the sixteenth century. Each official collected his own fees. There was, however, one occasion, in 1581, when the city received a single bill from the Clerk for the formal fees due to the Speaker, the Clerk himself, and the Serjeant, for a private bill and a proviso. The total charge was £18 9s. 0d.; but, alas! we are not told how this sum was made up.[3]

Though neither the Crown nor the House had formal knowledge of any other officer than Speaker, Clerk, and Serjeant, each of these had one or more clerks or assistants. They were not on the Queen's pay-roll, but led a semi-private, semi-public existence, being appointed by their masters and paid by them out of fees, as professors' assistants were in the not remote past of some of our universities. It was the way the administrative services were expanding at this and in later times; and just as formal salaries furnish no clue to real earn-

1. Lansdowne MS. 43, fol. 171a; *Local Government in Westminster*, pp. 24–5; Repert. xx, fol. 183b, xxi, fol. 420.
2. Lansdowne MS. 43, fol. 164b; D'EWES, p. 367a; Hooker's tract. The first mention of these fees is in November 1555 (*C.J.* i, 44).
3. *Commons Orders* (1756), p. 20; Repert. xx, fol. 183.

ings, so the long tale of officials in royal Household lists is no guide to the actual number of people engaged in what we may broadly call the civil service. The tendency was for these subordinates or 'servants', as they were properly designated, to emerge from the obscurity of private employment into an official twilight by appearing as yet another item in the growing schedule of fees confronting suitors and litigants.

This stage had not been reached by the close of the Elizabethan period. The city of Westminster, for example, mentioned only one subordinate in the section of its 1585 account recording fees proper: 'the doorkeeper, 12d.' And this was probably by way of a gratuity for admitting the city's learned counsel or representatives to give evidence. Among tips, Westminster gave 12d. to 'the Porter', a second servant of the Serjeant, who by 1593 had at least three such men under him. The account also includes 5s. od. for the Clerk's 'man' for writing a new paper bill after the amendments in committee. The Speaker's clerk does not appear.[1]

The Clerk's servant or servants – Fulk Onslow certainly had more than one [2] – must have done much of the copying and ingrossing for their master, and no doubt received an agreed proportion of the fees. If a similar custom to that of the Star Chamber prevailed – where, for example, out of 2s. 4d. for examining each witness the Clerk received 1s. 6d., the Usher 4d., and the Examiner, who did the work, 6d. – the master received the lion's share. But fees, as we have constantly noticed, did not exhaust the possibilities. Those who sought the Clerk's favour must often have found themselves, according to the custom of the age, paying tribute also to his servants. When paying the Clerk's bill of £18 9s. od. for joint official fees in 1581, the city of London added the substantial gratuity of twenty shillings 'in reward to his clerks'.[3]

A fortuitous bounty came to Fulk Onslow's chief clerk in 1601

1. The version of Lambarde's tract in Lord Braye's MSS., gives fees for private bills to the Speaker's chief clerk, the Clerk's man, and the Serjeant's man. But they are probably later insertions and do not appear in the printed or earlier manuscript versions of the tract; *Local Government in Westminster*, pp. 24–5.

2. D'EWES, p. 431b.

3. SKELTON, 'Court of Star Chamber' (London thesis), i, 54; Repert. xx, fol. 183.

when he deputized for his master throughout the session, for the Commons, in recognition of his services, made a collection for him of one shilling from each member, amounting in all to about twenty-five pounds.[1] In the sixteenth century the servant did not sit with his master in the House; and in 1606 we find him referred to as 'the Clerk's man without'. But a print of 1624 shows two clerks sitting at the table, thus demonstrating that the Clerk's chief clerk was by then well on the way to an official existence. Twenty years later he was designated 'Clerk Assistant'; and in 1649 he and the other subordinates made a line in the official table of fees: 'the under-clerks, for every bill, beside the Clerk's fee', 10s. 0d. By the eighteenth century there were five subordinate clerks, with specified duties, titles, and fees. They had become 'officers and servants of the honourable House of Commons'. But the past still left its traces, for the Clerk retained the right of nominating his subordinates – echo of those sixteenth-century days when his assistants were in the full sense of the word his servants. Hatsell, author of the famous eighteenth-century collection of *Precedents*, who was appointed Clerk Assistant in 1760, tells us that 'appointment to these offices made a considerable part of the Clerk's income, as it was the usual practice to sell them'. He himself was the first of the under-clerks to be appointed on merit and without price – thanks to the magnanimity of the then Clerk, who, though he had bought his own office at the cost of six thousand pounds, wished to put a stop to the old, pernicious custom.[2]

Even members of parliament were gradually caught in this fee business. They were so many that it was only natural for officials to nurse any opportunity of turning their stray tips into a system of fees. As we have seen, there was a fee of 2s. 0d. – perhaps 2s. 6d. from knights of the shire – which members or their constituencies had to pay to the Clerk of the Crown in Chancery for the return of their election indentures.[3] From these returns it was his duty to compile a list of members – *Liber Parliamenti* was its official title – and certify a copy into the House of Commons, where it was known as the Clerk's Book and was used in calling the House. If only the Clerk of the

---

1. D'EWES, pp. 623a, 688b; TOWNSHEND, *Hist. Collections*, pp. 331, 332.

2. *Bowyer's Diary*, p. 96; HATSELL (1796), ii, 242, 249; *C.J.* vi, 287; *Commons Orders*, pp. 15 ff.   3. Above, p. 312.

House could have claimed it as his own private compilation! But he could not. It was official; it was mentioned in a statute of 1515.[1] He was debarred from making it an excuse for fees.

The Serjeant was more fortunate. He too possessed a 'book'; and it was not official. He either made a copy of the Clerk's Book himself, or had one made for him, to facilitate his work as the officer responsible for admittance to the House. By 1571 – perhaps earlier – burgesses were paying 2s. od. and knights 2s. 6d. 'for entering their names into the Serjeant's book'. By 1587, if Lambarde can be trusted, the knights' fee had risen to 4s. od.; and at the beginning of the 1597 parliament it was resolved 'that none do come into this House before they have paid the Serjeant's fees ... due unto him according to the accustomed usage of this House'.[2] Moreover, by 1593 his subordinates had managed to insinuate themselves into this lucrative game.[3] They received a 'reward', as distinct from a fee: 'The reward unto the doorkeepers, being three, is eighteen pence.'[4] In a full parliament at the end of Elizabeth's reign, the Serjeant must have received from this source alone about fifty-five pounds, and his subordinates about thirty-four pounds.

As for the Clerk, so far as we can tell,[5] during Elizabeth's reign he succeeded in tapping members' pockets only if they received licence to depart before the end of the session; and the justification for this charge, as the fee of 2s. 6d. suggests, was probably that he had to enter the licence in his Journal. Even as late as 1597 it may have been regarded as a novel imposition, lacking official sanction, for in that session the Clerk made the following entry: 'Mr Doctor Muffet ... being licensed to depart, left two shillings and six pence with Mr Fulk Onslow, Clerk of this House, for the poor and the minister, but nothing for the said Clerk himself.' By 1607, when on

1. Cf. my article, *Trans. Roy. Hist. Soc.* 4th ser. iii, 143–4.

2. Hooker's tract; Add. MS. 5123, fol. 14 (cf. *C.J.* vi, 287); D'Ewes, pp. 468b, 550a.

3. Plymouth's member or members paid 'the porter' 8d. in 1571 or 1572 (WORTH, *Plymouth Records*, p. 121).

4. Bodley, Tanner MS. 264 gives this reading of the obviously incorrect passage in D'Ewes, p. 468b.

5. Plymouth's records (WORTH, p. 121) show that 'the clerk of parliament had 4s.' in 1571–2. I am inclined to interpret this as the payment of 2s. per member for the Clerk of the Crown. But I may be wrong.

the Speaker's motion the House confirmed the fee, it had mysteriously become 6s. 8d. By 1649 the Clerk had reached his goal: he had the whole House paying him tribute. Either by analogy with the Clerk of the Upper House, who enjoyed substantial fees from the peers on their first admittance to parliament, or by mere imitation of the Serjeant's singular prerogative, he had established a right to a fee of 5s. od. from every knight and 2s. 6d. from every burgess.[1]

Elizabethan members were also mulcted – very willingly, for the most part – in the cause of charity. As Sir Edward Hoby said in 1601: 'It hath been a most laudable usage, that some contribution or collection should be made amongst us *in pios usus*. And I pray you, let us not forget our parliamentary charity.' The origins of the practice are a little obscure. Doubtless there had long been a poor-box in the House. Late-comers and early-goers were obliged to contribute their fourpence per misdemeanour. We first hear of a general collection for the relief of the poor at the end of the 1566 session, when £19 10s. od. was gathered in and two members appointed to distribute it; and again in 1576 and 1584, when, however, we are not told how much was collected. Presumably it had become a regular custom.[2]

In 1593 the convention took on a new and compulsive character. It was war-time, and Sir Robert Cecil rose to move 'for some course of necessary relief . . . for the great number of poor people pressing everywhere in the streets to beg', especially for maimed soldiers and mariners, the pathetic victims of war. From the large and influential committee appointed to consider the problem there emerged not only legislation but a proposal that some present relief for 'poor maimed and sick soldiers' might be provided by a collection from members of the House, every Privy Councillor paying thirty shillings, everyone returned as knight of the shire, or a knight by status, or a serjeant-at-law or doctor of law, ten shillings, every burgess five shillings, and all who had departed without licence double the appropriate rate. The levy was made at a roll-call of the House, and took so much time that only one bill was read that morning. James

---

1. D'EWES, p. 568b; *Bowyer's Diary*, p. 228; Cotton MS. Titus F. iv, fol. 97; *C.J.* i, 351, vi, 287.

2. TOWNSHEND, op. cit., p. 269; *C.J.* i, 76, 81, 82; T.C.D. MS. N. 2, no. 12; D'EWES, p. 365b.

Quirke, member for Minehead, 'a poor burgess', refused to pay his 5s. od.: he would only pay 2s. 6d. 'The Speaker', wrote a diarist, 'would have committed him to the Serjeant for disobeying the order of the House; but most of the House were against it.' Mr Quirke was lucky.[1]

Now it happened that the House had acquired a clock this session; and so, at the same time as the charitable levy, members were called on to pay 1s. od. each to the Serjeant-at-Arms 'for attendance and for a clock set up in the Parliament House'. The gratuity was a novelty; its occasion the clock; the association of the two levies quite fortuitous. But what a chance for the Serjeant to attach himself permanently to the collection *in pios usus*! When some four years later the next parliament came to distribute the 'fourscore pounds and more' collected from members at the rate of 10s. od. for knights and 5s. od. for burgesses, 'question was moved for the Serjeant's money, and agreed he should have £20 for himself and £10 for the men which were door-keepers'. On this occasion, thirty pounds was devoted to ransom the son of John Foxe, the martyrologist, ten pounds to the minister, and the rest to poor prisoners in seven of London's prisons.[2] The Clerk got nothing. Charity, unlike tips, passed him by; and as his men were merely private servants, serving outside the House, they too got nothing. By 1601 the 10s. od. and 5s. od. rates of the levy had become fixed, and so had the basis of distribution: 'part of the whole to the minister, part to the servants here – that is, the Serjeant and his men – and part to the poor; the rest at your disposements', as Hoby explained. The way the Serjeant had insinuated himself into this charity is worthy of an Elizabethan cautionary tale.[3]

As a final point of interest, the moral of which has wide application in Elizabethan times, it may be useful to compare the formal salary of one of these House of Commons' officials with an estimate of his receipts from fees and gratuities. Unfortunately, we can offer no calculation for the Clerk, where the divergence would be most startling: there are too many unknown and unknowable items. But

1. ibid., pp. 499, 503, 507; Cotton MS. Titus F. II, fol. 70b.
2. ibid., *I.H.R. Bull*. xii, 22–3; TOWNSHEND, p. 269; D'EWES, p. 566a.
3. TOWNSHEND, pp. 269, 333; D'EWES, pp. 687, 688b. Cf. *Bowyer's Diary*, p. 228.

the Serjeant's earnings are less elusive. His salary from the Queen was £18 5s. od. per annum and a livery. His receipts from fees and gratuities in the parliament of 1597–8 must have totalled about £130. The estimate is cautious, perhaps much too low; but at the end of the sixteenth century, in a year when parliament met, his official salary could have constituted no more than one-eighth or one-tenth of his total earnings.

CHAPTER 18

The Opening of Parliament

THE opening of an Elizabethan parliament was one of the great ceremonial occasions of the reign. Normally the Queen was in residence at the Palace of Whitehall, though in 1584 the routine was changed for St James's Palace. In attendance was an unusually full Court, reinforced by the peers who had come to London for the parliament. Before 1593 morning was the time for the state procession, but then, owing one imagines to the Queen's advancing age, a change was made to the afternoon.

If we may judge from the procedure in 1584, it was usual the day before to proclaim in the Presence Chamber at Court the hour at which everyone was to be ready. On that occasion it was 9 a.m., at which hour the nobles and bishops put on their parliament robes and the gorgeous pageant was marshalled. Beginning with the messengers of the Court, the procession ascended by order of precedence, emphasized by the intermittent placing of heralds, to the great noblemen who carried the Cap Royal and the Sword of State, the one accompanied by the Earl Marshal, the other by the Lord Steward, and all four preceded by Clarencieux King-of-Arms, two Serjeants-at-Arms with silver-gilt maces, Garter King-of-Arms, and the chief Gentleman Usher. Then came the Queen, with four Esquires of the Stable and her footmen in rich coats, and, as an outer escort, the Gentlemen Pensioners carrying their axes. After the Queen followed the Master of the Horse leading a spare horse of state, and accompanying him the Lord Chamberlain; then the Vice-Chamberlain, with many noblewomen, ladies, and other noble courtiers; and finally the Captain of the Guard followed by the Guard. Virtually the whole House of Lords was incorporated in the procession; not, however, the Commons, except individuals belonging to the Court, for this was the full Court in motion, and peers were by rank part of it.

The procession was a long time either marshalling or waiting, for though the hour of assembly in 1584 was 9 a.m., it was not until about 11 a.m. that the Queen joined it. In 1563 – when the opening ceremonies were postponed for a day because of 'the foul weather' – her Majesty rode on horseback: she 'took her horse at the Hall door'. At later parliaments she used an open chariot or horse-litter. In 1584 we are told that the chair, carried between two white horses, was like a throne, with two silver pillars at the back supporting a crown of gold, and with another two at the Queen's feet, on which were a lion and a dragon, 'made with wonderful cunning', 'glistering with gold', and supporting the royal arms. As she sat, 'in her imperial robes, with a wreath or coronet of gold set with rich pearls and stones on her head', the lofty, dazzling centrepiece of unsurpassed pomp and splendour and colour, many an English heart must have stirred at the spectacle.

The procession had but a few hundred yards to go – to Westminster Abbey, where the Dean and clergy in their copes received the Queen and delivered to her the sceptre of St Edward. Then, under a royal canopy and accompanied by her Court in ceremonial manner, she entered the Abbey and listened to a service and a sermon.

After restoring St Edward's sceptre to the Dean's keeping, the Queen left the Abbey and crossed on foot to Westminster Palace. She stayed awhile in her Privy Chamber till the Lords and others took their places in the Parliament Chamber. Then she came forth, the Sword, the Cap, and the Marshal's gilt rod borne before her, and seated herself on the throne or Chair of Estate. On her right was a nobleman holding the Cap. and with him Garter King-of-Arms; on her left, another with the Sword, and by him the Lord Chamberlain. Behind the cloth of state and the traverse or rail on either side of the throne, noblemen under age and noblemen's sons and heirs were permitted to stand, while three or four of the Queen's ladies sat at her feet on the steps of the throne.

The Parliament Chamber or Upper House contained four wool-sacks covered in red cloth, forming an inner square, on which sat the judges and royal counsellors, summoned to parliament by special writs of assistance. The upper sack, nearest the throne, was for the Lord Chancellor or Lord Keeper, but when the Queen was present he – as we might say – vacated the chair and took his place on the Queen's right hand behind the traverse. On the lower sack, opposite the Lord Chancellor, sat the Clerk of the Parliaments and the Clerk of the Crown, with a table before them, and behind knelt other royal clerks. Outside the inner square – the historical core of parliament – were benches, seating on the right the spiritual peers in order of precedence, and on the left the temporal peers, for whose overflow a transverse bench was provided behind the clerks' sack. At the back of this bench came a rail, 'and between that rail and the lower part of the house a void room for all suitors and such as shall have occasion to come before the King and the Lords'. Here, when they were summoned to these ceremonial sittings, stood the Commons, with the Speaker in their midst raised on a small stool or platform.[1]

Meanwhile, the Commons had met in their own Chamber; 'out of all order, in troops standing upon the floor, making strange noises', as the witty Recorder of London, William Fleetwood, described the scene in 1584.[2] They waited for the Lord Steward, who, with the Privy-Councillor members of the Lower House, quitted the royal procession at the Abbey, and during the service saw to the roll-call of members and to administering the Oath of Supremacy according to the act of 1563. This business was usually transacted in the room known as the White Hall or Court of Requests, the Lord Steward first administering the oath to Privy-Councillor members and then appointing them deputies to assist in the swearing.

As with other procedural activities in this formative period of parliament's history, the details seem to have varied on occasions. Sometimes an efficient mind took hold of the task; sometimes there was confusion. When the haughty Earl of Leicester was Lord Steward in 1584, characteristically he went off and left his deputies to do the job. They were unable to swear all the attendant members before the summons came to the Upper House, 'whereby', says Fleetwood, 'we lost the oration made by my Lord Chancellor'.[3] In 1593 all went smoothly. There was no state procession or Abbey service on that occasion, owing to the plague.[4] The Queen went privately to

1. Processional and ceremonial details varied. This description is based mainly on the account in THOMAS MILLES, *Catalogue of Honour* (1610), pp. 64 ff. Also cf. D'EWES, pp. 58 ff. 136–7; Cotton MS. Titus F. I, fols. 59, 129; *I.H.R. Bull.* xii, 4; TOWNSHEND, p. 173; DE MAISSE, *Journal*, ed. G. B. Harrison, p. 30; Hooker's tract.

2. Lansdowne MS. 41, fol. 45.

3. D'EWES, p. 332; Lansdowne MS. 41, fol. 45.

4. Add. MS. 5758, fols. 110 ff.

parliament by water, between 1 p.m. and 2 p.m., and the Lord Steward was therefore free in the morning. Moreover, the efficient Sir Thomas Heneage organized procedure. The Lord Steward was set at the door of the White Hall, where he called the knights and burgesses in regular order, each of whom then went to the door of the House of Commons, where the deputies administered the oath as he re-entered the House.[1] In 1597, when the royal procession did not start till about one o'clock, members were in attendance, with nothing to do, from 8 a.m.; and it was 2 p.m. before the Lord Steward arrived. Then, after a slow start, a method of mass swearing was quickly devised and the laborious business was got through in half an hour. Our diarist on this occasion estimates that 'above four hundred' members were present. If this estimate can be trusted, it was a large muster for the first day of parliament; for in the first parliament of James I, when 'three hundred at least' took the oath, the Clerk described them as 'a great multitude, more than was ever seen on the first day of a parliament in any man's memory'.[2] In the last parliament of Elizabeth's reign, the procedure was again awkward and confused. The Lord Steward and Secretary Cecil had to go to their places in the Upper House in the middle of their task, but others kept on and finished the business in time.[3]

After being sworn, members took their places in their own chamber to await notice that the Queen and Lords were set and expected them. Even this simple ceremony, so familiar in modern days as the summons of Black Rod, was not yet formalized or free from mishap. The space behind the bar in the Upper House, where the Commons stood, was quite inadequate. It was always a matter of 'as many as conveniently could' getting in, or, as a member more descriptively said, 'with great thrusting'. Those who knew the ropes infiltrated into the Upper House without waiting for the summons. At least, that is what they did in 1593, with the result that the Queen, thinking the Commons were present, began the proceedings before the rest arrived. The doors were closed, and the Lord Keeper was launched 'a good step into his oration' before the hubbub of the excluded and angry members reached her ears and she ordered the doors to be opened. Much the same happened in 1601, due, it was said, to the

1. Cotton MS. Titus F. II, fol. 20.
2. *I.H.R. Bull.* xii, 4–5; *C.J.* i, 140, 141.   3. TOWNSHEND, p. 173.

fault of the Gentleman Usher. On this occasion the door was not opened: indeed, to add insult to injury, the Usher, speaking through it, threatened the excluded members 'that if they were not quiet, they should be set in the stocks'. The majority of the Commons returned disgruntled to their own House – an unfortunate beginning to a stormy session.[1]

Bad management – the nemesis of too little formality – was not peculiar to Elizabeth's reign. At the opening of James I's first parliament, a number of strangers – royal servants and others – got into the Upper House behind the bar, and the Commons were forgotten. Reminiscent of the gaffe in 1601, a Yeoman of the Guard repulsed some members with the words, 'Goodman Burgess, you come not here', and shut the door on them. It was not until the King was drawing to the end of an inordinately long speech that the error was perceived and rectified. However, at the next sitting James obligingly repeated his speech – it occupies nine long columns of the printed Journals; which no doubt gave mutual satisfaction. In 1614 the Commons again found themselves excluded by interlopers; but in 1621 steps were taken to oust all strangers.[2]

When the Commons had arrived, the Queen opened the proceedings by bidding the Lord Keeper of the Great Seal 'show the causes of the parliament'. In 1571 she prefaced her command with a few words: 'My right loving Lords, and you all, our right faithful and obedient subjects, we, in the name of God, for His service and for the safety of this State, are here now assembled to His glory. I hope and pray that it may be to your comfort and the common quiet of us, you, and all ours for ever.' In 1601 the French ambassador noted that the Queen spoke a few words; and, though our diarists are silent on other occasions, it may well be that a brief royal preface of this nature was customary.[3]

At the Queen's bidding, the Lord Keeper, as the mouth of the sovereign, began a set oration – the prototype of our modern King's Speech – which varied in length from two thousand words or less to

1. *I.H.R. Bull.* xii, 5; Cotton MS. Titus F. II, fol. 20b; D'Ewes, p. 620; Townshend, p. 182.

2. *C.J.* i, 141 ff., 455; Notestein, *1621 Debates*, v, 424.

3. Cotton MS. Titus F. I, fol. 129b; P.R.O. Baschet Transcripts, bundle 32, Boissize to the King, 16 November 1601.

at least six thousand. It dealt only in the most general way with 'the causes of parliament'. There was no allusion to specific items of legislation, although the need for money was usually stressed. Rather it was a survey of the religious and political state of the country, sometimes including foreign affairs. In 1589, after the defeat of the Armada, Sir Christopher Hatton used the occasion for a spirited, eloquent, and patriotic oration, not unworthy of comparison with Winston Churchill's great war-speeches.[1] And at the next parliament of 1593, in Lord Keeper Puckering's hands, it again took the shape of a war-speech.[2] The oration ended with an injunction to the Commons to return to their House and choose a Speaker. Then the Clerk of the Parliaments read in French the names of the receivers and triers of petitions – an antiquarian survival; and so the sitting was brought to a close.

Thereupon, the Commons returned to their chamber, where, on the nomination of the senior Privy Councillor present, they elected their Speaker. 'Elected' was the formal description; but as a matter of fact the government had already decided who he was to be. In Edward VI's reign, for example, the Duke of Northumberland wrote to the Lord Chamberlain on 14 January 1553, seven weeks before the actual election, saying that it was time the King chose the Speaker of the House, so that 'he might have secret warning thereof, as always it hath been used', and be able to prepare his speeches to the satisfaction of his audience. In 1593 Edward Coke, the famous lawyer, was 'named to be Speaker ... at Hampton Court' by the Queen and Lords of the Council on 28 January; he was elected by the House of Commons on 19 February. Little wonder that in his *Institutes* he declared that 'the use is (as in the *congé d'élire* of a bishop) that the King doth name a discreet and learned man whom the Commons elect'.[3]

This apparently farcical procedure had a very simple and human explanation. When the Commons met at the opening of parliament, they had no chairman; and yet someone had to begin the proceedings. By a natural courtesy, enforced in those days by the all-pervading

1. Lambeth MS. 178 fols. 75 ff., quoted in my *Queen Elizabeth*, pp. 302–3.
2. Printed by me in *Eng. Hist. Rev.* xxxi, 129 ff.
3. TYTLER, *Reigns of Ed. VI & Mary*, ii, 163; *H.M.C. Rep.* IX, ii, 373a; COKE, *Fourth Institute* (1669), p. 8. Cf. NICOLAS, *Hatton*, p. 482.

sense of an ordered society, it was left to the senior member to speak first; and he was the chief Privy Councillor present – the Treasurer of the Household, or, failing him, the Comptroller. As Sir William Knollys, who was Comptroller of the Household, so aptly said in 1597: 'Necessity constraineth me to break off this silence.' In 1601 he was even more explicit: 'Some man should break silence; and I must confess at this time it belongs to my place.' Being able to count on this priority, what could be more natural than for Sovereign and Councillors to prepare the nomination? They had much to gain from the right choice.[1]

The situation was admirably diagnosed by an anonymous member of Elizabeth's fourth parliament, who, sometime before the 1581 session, wrote to a Councillor friend and patron offering excellent advice. 'The House hath used, and as I think will use, to like of such a person as the Councillors present; not arrogating to themselves the right of nomination, but leaving the House to their full liberty, who in their greatest liberty will be most frankly obsequious.' It was beneficial to them to have a Speaker who was 'most acceptable' to the Queen: that he acknowledged. And it might be thought that a Privy Councillor would therefore be best. For several reasons he was opposed to such a choice. First, it would lose the Queen a Councillor's voice in the House and exclude him from committee work; a comment which shows that already the strategy of parliamentary management was grasped. Again, if the Speaker was to handle his task efficiently, he must be skilled in the Common Law; and there was no great choice of such men among the Councillors. There was another reason; and here the writer used an argument the historical interest of which can scarcely be exaggerated. 'In some heads there may be a jealousy that a Councillor, being specially sworn to her Majesty's service, is not a person so congruent with the liberties of the House as another; and thereupon some men ... may move question, and of such question may rise a pike in the beginning of the session, which cannot be but perilous, *ominosum*, and to all discreet men very grievous.'[2]

The theory of a free choice, of a right to oppose the official nominee and propose another name, was carefully maintained and explicitly

1. *I.H.R. Bull.* xii, 6; TOWNSHEND, p. 174.
2. Harleian MS. 253, fols. 32 ff.

stated by Treasurer or Comptroller in Elizabeth's reign.[1] In James I's first parliament there was, in fact, a 'muttering' of alternative names, though 'the more general voice ran upon' the official nominee.[2] Only once was there opposition in Elizabeth's reign. This was in 1566 when the death of their Speaker between two sessions involved the election of another. The official candidate was Richard Onslow, member for Steyning, who had recently been made Solicitor General and was therefore serving in the House of Lords, whence he had to be brought down to the Commons. No doubt there was an element of independence in the resistance to his election, for this House was not a new one: it had sat in 1563, learnt the art of opposition, and was to display amazing skill in parliamentary tactics in the new session.[3] But it was Onslow's own argument in his disabling speech, urging that the office was incompatible with his Solicitor's oath to the Queen, which gave the critics their lead. There was a division. Eighty-two voted for him, seventy against; which incidentally reveals how small was the attendancce on this occasion.[4]

Though aware of his coming nomination, convention required a Speaker-elect to show becoming modesty and reluctance. When first named, Serjeant Yelverton, in 1597, 'blushed and put off his hat'. In 1601 Mr Coke went one better: he 'put off his hat, with a kind of strange admiration'. The House gave approval by calling the chosen member's name, or simply by 'Aye, Aye, Aye!' Then the Speaker-elect made the first of his 'disabling speeches', exposing his lack of the qualities needed for so responsible an office and praying the House to proceed to a new election.[5]

We are fortunate in possessing Serjeant Yelverton's own text of his speech in 1597.[6] 'The very name of the place', he declared, 'is so weighty, the ordinary travails of the service so difficult, and the

---

1. Cf. D'EWES, pp. 281, 333, 469; I.H.R. Bull. xii, 7; TOWNSHEND, p. 174.

2. C.J. i, 141. 3. Cf. my article in Eng. Hist. Rev. xxxvi, 497 ff.

4. C.J. i, 73. The Spanish ambassador reported (Span. Cal. Eliz. i, 583) that two other men were nominated; but he was a poor authority on such matters, and I am not inclined to believe him.

5. I.H.R. Bull. xii, 6; TOWNSHEND, p. 174. The Lord Mayor of London made a 'disabling speech' on his election (cf. Hatfield MSS. ii, 117; WRIGHT, Queen Elizabeth, ii, 240).

6. Yelverton MS. at Elvetham, 121, fols. 15b ff.

extraordinary charge that doth accompany it so excessive, as I must needs sink under the burthen of it ... Since this is no common nor mean place, it may not be supplied by a common and mean person, nor cannot be supported by a common and mean expense. And my estate of living, as many of you do know, is but small, my continual charge great ...; and to defray this I can in effect draw nothing to it but mine own industry, being a younger brother, little advanced by my father and left in some troubles of the law.' Also, he lacked countenance in the world, and that special favour with the Queen which the office required. 'The last, and yet I assure you not the least want', he continued, 'is my timorous and fearful nature, which at the very name and thought of her Majesty's presence so trembleth as I fear I shall fall down amazed and dumb when I shall be presented to speak unto her.'

Generally, a second Privy Councillor replied, commending the choice, and with the concurrence of the House the two Councillors escorted the Speaker-elect to the chair, where he briefly thanked them, though indicating his intention to seek release from the Queen. Details of the procedure sometimes changed a little. Our busybody, Recorder Fleetwood, thought that the performers mulled their parts in 1584: actually, there was precedent for their actions, as also for the critic.[1]

Convention exacted these disabling speeches. They were artificial; and self-depreciation in the mouth of an Edward Coke was humbug. Nevertheless, they were not necessarily lacking in sincerity or point. Elizabethan Speakers were all eminent lawyers, and as parliament met in term-time, the office temporarily withdrew them from practice – 'from the best time of my benefit', as Yelverton put it. The mercenary Serjeant Puckering – doubtless under temptation to fit his figures to the occasion, which was a begging suit to the Queen – calculated that the loss of legal fees and the expenses of office as Speaker in 1584–5 and 1586–7 amounted to two thousand pounds.[2] The office was not always coveted, nor even welcome. Our unknown member of Elizabeth's fourth parliament, when offering advice on the Speakership, suggested two names, John Popham and George Bromley. In loyalty to the established religion, 'in skill of the laws of England, in honesty and discretion, they be both equal', he wrote. 'In

1. Lansdowne MS. 41, fol. 45.   2. Harleian MS. 7042, fol. 170b.

all other learnings, Mr Bromley is far superior, and his deliverance in speech shall be found very good.' It would, he added, be difficult to persuade him to 'like of the place'. 'Commonly the fittest men do least seek for offices.' But as Attorney of the Duchy of Lancaster he held a good office of the Queen, and therefore she might better burden him with this service. Moreover, his private legal practice was now small, and the Speakership would not 'be hurtful to him as to Mr Popham for losing of clients, nor so hurtful to poor clients for losing their counsellor'. In the event, Popham was selected, doubtless to his immediate and grave financial loss.[1]

The next stage in the Speaker's election was his presentation to the Queen. It took place two or three days later and was the occasion for another ceremonial sitting in the Upper House. When in residence at Whitehall, the Queen came privately by water in the royal barge between 1 p.m. and 3 p.m., and, after robing, entered the Upper House and awaited the arrival of the Commons. Both in 1597 and 1601 the Commons grew impatient of the long, silent wait, and of their own accord went towards the Upper House to be close at hand when summoned. In 1601 they waited half an hour outside the Lord's door.[2] The Speaker was led to the rail between two Privy Councillors. As they entered the chamber they made an obeisance, and as they moved to their places, made three more.

Again bowing thrice, the Speaker embarked on his second disabling speech. He first announced his election, which required the Queen's approval. 'As in the heavens a star is but *opacum corpus* until it hath received light of the sun', said Coke, 'so stand I, *corpus opacum*, a mute body, until your high, bright, shining wisdom hath looked on me and allowed me.' Then came what Yelverton aptly described as 'an anatomy of ... my wants'. The modern debasement of a word has added a droll flavour to Speaker Williams's plea in 1563: 'I, therefore, knowing my own imbecility ..., as one amongst the Romans, chosen from the plough to a place of estimation, and after to the plough again; even so, I, a countryman, fit for the same and not for this place, most humbly desire your Majesty to discharge me hereof and to appoint some other, more able'.[3]

Calling the Lord Keeper to her, the Queen gave instructions for

1. ibid. 253, fol. 33.   2. D'EWES, pp. 550a, 621b.
3. Cotton MS. Titus F. II, fol. 22b; D'EWES, p. 63b.

the answer. Yelverton says that the Lord Keeper afterwards 'told me in private that the Queen gave him in commandment to say unto me ... that the eloquence which I had used was natural and not affected, which words in his speech unto me he did indeed use'.[1] It was the usual gambit to declare that the Speaker's very ability in decrying himself proved his fitness. His election was invariably confirmed: it would have been a rude shock had it not been.

Thereupon, the Speaker began his 'ornate oration', one of the great rhetorical feats of his career. Although Speaker Williams modestly protested that his was not an oration but 'an epistle with a request', it was an elaborate composition, divided into time past, time present, and time to come, and rich in classical and biblical allusions – to Androcles and the lion, Tantalus, Marcus Aurelius, Alexander the Great, Julius Caesar, Cato, Hannibal. The traditional theme was the orderly government of a Commonwealth; and the time-worn simile of the state and the human body was as ready an aid as the *cliché* today. Serjeant Wray in 1571 and Robert Bell in 1572 made excursions into English constitutional history, while Coke's speech in 1593, after a preliminary comment on the present, 'tended wholly – and how characteristically! – to come out of the history of England and the old statutes'. Yelverton's felicitous masterpiece was cast in more philosophical form, tracing the growth of society in Aristotelian fashion, analysing the advantages of monarchy – the best type of state – and commenting on the 'two only golden and glorious pillars that do uphold a throne', religion and justice, without which, as the mutability of fortune shows, no Commonwealth can long endure.[2]

Every speech contained its encomium upon the Queen's rule. 'Your country', declared Yelverton, 'now is religious in profession, peaceable in tranquillity, rich in treasure, strong in forces, wise in counsel, and populous in subjects. This happiness, this wonderful, rare, and most desired happiness hath begun, increased, and continued as well by your Majesty's most hearty embracing and constant professing of true religion, as by the admirable policies of your most wise, deep, forseeing circumspection.' When in 1601 in a parallel passage Speaker Croke spoke of 'the prosperous estate and peace of this land, which

1. Yelverton MS. 121, fol. 18b.
2. D'EWES, pp. 64–6, 141; Trinity Coll. Dublin MS. N. 2, no. 12; Cotton MS. Titus F. II, fol. 23b; Yelverton MS. 121, fols. 18b ff.

had been defended ... by the mighty arm of our dread and sacred Queen', Elizabeth interrupted with the exclamation – 'No! but by the mighty hand of God, Mr Speaker.'[1]

The Speaker ended his speech with the petition for privileges: two concerning himself, and two the general body of the Commons. His own were the right to amend any faulty reports he might make, and right of access to the Queen. The former, which had a very long history – with origins, perhaps, in the formal nature of legal procedure, being akin to a medieval litigant's right of amending his counsel's plea – was an antiquarian survival, the ancient purport of which evidently eluded Elizabethan Speakers, for they made varying attempts to rationalize it. The request for access, in the two first petitions of the reign, included access to the Lords as well as the Queen; but thereafter the Lords were omitted – deliberately omitted we may conjecture, for the Commons were rapidly emerging from subjection to the Upper House.

The two general privileges were freedom from arrest – a privilege increasingly invoked, and tending to abuse – and the fundamental privilege of all, freedom of speech.[2] The order in which the several Speakers placed the privileges varied. In 1559 and 1563 the personal took precedence of the general: a sound historical order. But in later parliaments the order was usually reversed: indeed, except in 1581 and 1601, when it was placed second, freedom of speech headed the list, as its importance, though not its pedigree, warranted. In 1572 the Speaker forgot to ask for freedom from arrest, and in consequence it was not formally granted that session. His blunder made no difference, for the privilege reposed on ancient custom, not on its inclusion – which was only recent – in the Speaker's repertoire.

When the Speaker had finished his oration, the Lord Keeper received instructions from the Queen for his reply. He usually recapitulated the points of the Speaker's speech, incorporating – often with a turn of phrase or sentiment that reveals its royal origin – some modest disclaimer of the encomiums bestowed on the Queen. 'Her Majesty', he said in 1593, 'hath no delight to hear her own praises blazed before her face.' She attributeth all the blessings, good fortunes, and victories of her reign 'to the omnipotent and miraculous goodness of

1. TOWNSHEND, p. 177.
2. On this privilege, cf. my article in *Tudor Studies*, ed. Seton-Watson.

our merciful God; and so much the more with humblest thanks to be acknowledged' because 'He enableth the weakest sex, and maketh them to admire it that ere now were wont to doubt their success ... For her part, she beseecheth the living God never to bless her longer than she study with all endeavour to do that may best please Him, and most prosper and preserve you. And though, she saith, you may have a wiser prince (for I must use her own words) she dare avow you shall never have one more careful of your safeties, nor to give more even stroke among her subjects, without regard of person more than matter. And of such mind, she beseecheth God ever send your prince.' The same dedicatory note had been struck in the first parliament of the reign: 'Her Highness wisheth ... that for England's sake there were as many virtues in her as would serve for the good government of this her Realm.'[1]

The principal purpose of the Lord Keeper's speech was to answer the petition for privileges. These were always granted, but with appropriate comments, warnings, and qualifications. Warning was given against the abuses to which the privilege of freedom from arrest was open; and as the lively problems of the period opened up the issue of free speech, so the granting of this privilege was accompanied with comments and qualifications that aimed at defining it. Sometimes the Lord Keeper closed his speech with an exhortation to make the new laws as few and as plain as may be, and to deal with weighty matters first – that is, to give public bills precedence over private. The object was short parliaments, assumed to be a boon to everyone.

Here the sitting should have ended; but occasionally – perhaps more often than our evidence tells – Elizabeth added a personal touch of her own. In 1571, as she rose to depart, mindful of the stormy and all-but-addled parliament of 1566, she spoke, 'wishing they would be more quiet than they were at the last time'. In 1572, as a diarist tells us, after the end of the Lord Keeper's speech, 'the Speaker was called for to the Queen's Majesty, and, kneeling, her Majesty had a quarter of an hour's conference with him under the cloth of state'. The story of a similar informality in 1597 comes from Speaker Yelverton himself: 'After her Majesty had confirmed me for Speaker, and after that I had then ended my oration, her Majesty passing by me, pulled

1. *Eng. Hist. Rev.* xxxi, 135; D'EWES, p. 16b.

off her glove and gave me her hand to kiss, and [using a figure of speech from archery] said, "You, sir, you are welcome to the butts, sir", and laid both her hands about my neck, and stayed a good space, and so most graciously departed; and in her Privy Chamber after, amongst her ladies, said she was sorry she knew me no sooner.'[1]

Very different is the tale from the last parliament of the reign. The magic touch, the mutual response of actress and audience, momentarily were missing. 'After some room made, the Queen came through the Commons to go into the Painted Chamber, who graciously offering her hand to the Speaker, he kissed it; but not one word she spake unto him. Neither, as she went through the Commons, few said. "God bless your Majesty", as they were wont in all great assemblies. And the throng being great, and little room to pass, she moved her hand to have more room; whereupon one of the Gentlemen Ushers said openly, "Back, masters, make room". And one answered stoutly behind, "If you will hang us, we can make no more room"; which the Queen seemed not to hear, though she heaved up her head and looked that way towards him that spake.' Perhaps she was unwell. A correspondent tells us, 'The Queen in all her robes had fallen the first day of the parliament, if some gentlemen had not suddenly cast themselves under that side that tottered, and supported her'.[2]

After retiring to her Chamber to put off her parliament robes, the Queen returned to the Palace of Whitehall by water, being escorted to her barge by the nobility. The Commons went back to their own chamber, where one bill was read to give the Speaker seisin of his chair before they too rose for the day. William Lambarde, presumably generalizing from his experience in the parliament of 1563-7, describes how after the Speaker's presentation, 'Then goeth he away with the Commons to their House, and is there set in his place by them, and thanketh them again for their good opinion of him, praying them to aid and inform him for the having the credit of their own election, without accusing or charging him abroad. And that for the better order of the House, they will frequent the common prayer,

1. *Trans. Devon Assoc.* xi, 475; T.C.D. MS. N. 2, no. 12; Yelverton MS. 121, fol. 30.

2. TOWNSHEND, pp. 178-9; *Secret Correspondence of Sir Robert Cecil with James VI* (1766), p. 26.

deal with the most weighty matters, use pithy and avoid tedious speeches, not abus[ing] the time but redeeming it. And not to speak to any bill upon the first reading, but rather to expect till they have advised upon it.'[1] But in 1581, and perhaps on other occasions, time or audience did not favour such an hortatory address: the Speaker postponed it to the next sitting.

1. Add. MS. 5123, fols. 6b-7.

CHAPTER 19

Procedure: 1

THE Commons met in St Stephen's Chapel, within the precincts of the Palace of Westminster, and here they continued to meet until the building was destroyed in the disastrous fire of 1834. It had come into the Crown's hands but recently, by the Chantries act of 1547, and the upper part of it, above the lower chapel or crypt, had been 'assigned for the house of parliament' possibly in time for the third session of Edward VI's first parliament in November 1549, certainly before July 1550.[1] Oddly enough, there seems to be no clue to the Commons' meeting place in Henry VIII's reign, but it was doubtless the Chapter House of Westminster Abbey, across the way, as it had been in the fifteenth century. Bringing the Commons under the same roof, figuratively speaking, as the Lords was symbolic, and in many subtle ways speeded on the new age of parity between the Houses.

Probably, the seating arrangements of the Chapter House, hallowed by long tradition, influenced the adaptation of St Stephen's Chapel to its new use, and, coupled with the arrangement in the House of Lords, determined our time-honoured place for the Speaker's chair, at the end of the chamber. The scene has been described for us by the member for Exeter in 1571, who was John Vowell, *alias* Hooker, Chamberlain of the city. He was uncle of the 'judicious' Hooker but is worthy of memory in his own right as a local patriot, no mean antiquary, and editor of Holinshed's *Chronicles*. 'This House', Hooker wrote, 'is framed and made like unto a theatre, being four rows of seats one above another, round about the House. At the higher end, in the middle of the lowest row, is a seat made for the Speaker, where he is appointed to sit; and before him sitteth the Clerk of the House, having a little board before him to write and lay his books upon. Upon the lower row, next to the Speaker, sit all such of the Queen's Privy Council and head officers as be knights or burgesses for that House; but after, everyone sitteth as he cometh,

1. *Cal. Pat. Rolls, Ed. VI.* iv, 13, 325.

no difference being there held of any degree, because each man in
that place is of like calling, saving that the knights and burgesses for
London and York do sit on the right side, next to the Councillors.'
At one period of the reign there was a 'scaffold' put up round the
walls, for those to sit on who wore great breeches stuffed with hair.
When the fashion went out, it was taken down, leaving marks that
prompted someone to hand on this titbit of information.[1]

This picture of the House, with its front government bench on the
Speaker's right, and on his left our front opposition bench, evidently
occupied by other 'head officers' of the Queen, is strikingly familiar.
The basic setting has remained unchanged through the centuries.
But there was no doorway in the east wall of the Chapel, behind the
Speaker, and the cross benches at that end of the chamber came
right up to the Speaker's chair, thus enabling Privy Councillors and
officials – 'the honourable persons which assist this chair' – to whisper
advice and instructions to him and so guide the course of business.
An incident from 1601 will illutrate what happened: 'Mr Secretary
Cecil ... spake something in Mr Speaker's ear'; whereupon the
Speaker shortly rose and closed the sitting without fulfilling his
promise to let a member move the reading of a bill against monopolies. Angry at the 'great disgrace', the member said to the Speaker
that 'he would complain of him the next sitting'. He 'answered not
one word, but looked earnestly on him; and so the press of people
parted them'.[2]

The upper part of St Stephen's Chapel, which was all that
Edward VI granted to the Commons, provided them with the barest
accommodation. They had a committee-chamber of their own. Possibly it was an upper room over the vestibule or lobby of the House,
referred to in 1593 as 'the Serjeant's room'.[3] But it was little used by
members except when a committee was required to give immediate
consideration to a bill during the sitting, or to meet in the early
morning before the House assembled. They obviously preferred not
to return to Westminster in the afternoon, when most committees

1. Hooker's tract (City of Exeter MSS.); Harleian MS. 980, art. 357, fol.
465.
2. D'EWES, p. 652b; TOWNSHEND, p. 224.
3. Nicholas Saunders's letter, printed by Miss de Haviland from the
Loseley MSS. in *The Times*, 12 December 1929.

met. Instead, they arranged the place of meeting to suit their convenience – at the Guildhall, the Temple Church, the halls of various Inns of Court, or, if Privy Councillors were on the committee, then in a room close at hand at Westminster, the Exchequer Chamber and the Star Chamber being most usual. On occasions, to give least trouble to their most eminent member, committees met at Court in Mr Treasurer's chamber or Mr Secretary's, at the Savoy for the Chancellor of the Duchy, at Sir Thomas Cecil's house, even 'at Mr Recorder's'. A member of James I's first parliament tells us that the Temple hall was not very good for this purpose, 'because the table there at which they sit is all in length, by reason whereof they are not so well heard as in other places where the table be square'.[1]

The only other room that the Commons possessed was the vestibule or lobby of St Stephen's – the 'outer room' as it was called – which was under the control of the Serjeant and his doorkeepers. 'Without this House [the main chamber]', wrote Hooker, 'is one other in which the under clerks do sit, as also such as be suitors and attendant to that House; and whensoever the House is divided upon any bill, then the room is voided.'[2]

There was not even a room in which to keep the Commons' records. In this respect the Lower House was worse off than the Upper. The Clerk in the House of Lords had an official repository for his papers – the Stone Tower in Old Palace Yard. Historically, his privilege was right and proper. Parliament was a unity and he was its Clerk, though he officiated only in the Lords. Its ingrossed acts, which were records in the technical sense of the word, were in his custody. On the other hand, the House of Commons, as the egregious Arthur Hall unwisely but with striking perspicacity said, was a new person in the Trinity. It possessed no 'records'. There were its journals, but they were of very recent origin, and in 1559 were still unofficial and jejune in scope and appearance. Also, there were the paper texts of bills, and other manuscripts. The Clerk had to keep these papers at his private lodgings, thus exposing them to grave risk of loss, especially at his death. The fair copy of all the

1. Cf. *C.J.* i, passim, especially pp. 83, 85, 124, 128; D'EWES, passim; Stowe MS. 354, fol. 35b.
2. HOOKER, *The Order and Usage of the Keeping of a Parliament* (?1575); *Bowyer's Diary*, p. 18.

353

Commons' Journals from 1584 to 1601 was lost in the early seventeenth century, and a volume of the rough drafts for the same parliaments, saved from this first catastrophe, disappeared later, probably just before the Restoration. In fact, it was not until the last quarter of the seventeenth century that the Commons secured a room in which to preserve their records. They were then safe from minor hazards, but alas! not from fire. Everything was lost in the destruction of the Palace of Westminster in 1834, except the Journals, already much impaired by the casual nature of their custody in the sixteenth and seventeenth centuries.[1]

From the lobby of the House, stairs led down to Westminster Hall. Members' servants were wont to stand on them, waiting for their masters, and, as idle youth will, made a considerable nuisance of themselves. There were constant efforts, continuing even in the eighteenth century, to keep the stairs clear and control disorder. In 1581 the House was driven to beg assistance from the Warden of the Fleet Prison, asking him to station two of his servants at the stairhead and lay hands on two or three of the miscreant serving-men and pages so that an example might be made of them for their 'lewd disorder and outrage'. We hear of no result; and the pages were at it again in the following and later parliaments.[2]

The House sat every day of the week except Sunday, nominally from 8 a.m. till 11 a.m. – the hours of the law courts. It filled slowly, and, evidently with a view to a better if later start, the Speaker in 1571 moved that prayers should be said at 8.30 a.m. every day and any member absent pay fourpence to the poor-box. The experiment was unsatisfactory, and six days later, when the House adjourned for five days over Easter – having sat on Good Friday – they made up for lost time by agreeing to meet in future at 7 a.m.[3] After that, they do not seem to have made any more experiments with the customary hour of beginning – 8 a.m. – though occasionally a committee might meet in the committee-chamber or in the House at 6 a.m. or 7 a.m.[4] As for the actual, as distinct from the nominal hour of rising, this was determined by the exigencies of business and debate, tempered by thoughts of dinner. It was evidently nearer noon than 11 o'clock.

1. Cf. my article, *Trans. Roy. Hist. Soc.* 4th ser. iii, 136 ff.
2. *C.J.* i, 121; D'EWES, pp. 334b, 629b; *Commons Orders* (1756), p. 6 ff.
3. *C.J.* i, 82, 84. 4. *C.J.* i, pp. 93, 96, 97.

In 1601 long arguments on a bill kept them till 12.45 p.m.; and even that was not a record.[1]

The day's proceedings began with the Litany, said by the Clerk, and was followed by prayers. This custom – symptom of the new protestant era with its puritan flavour – was initiated two or three weeks after the opening of Elizabeth's first parliament. When urging the Lord Mayor of London in 1574 to begin the City's meetings with prayer, Thomas Norton, the great parliament-man, wrote: 'It is so used in the parliament; and though such use be but of late, I trust it shall be continued and grow to be old.' Old it has indeed become. In 1571 the earnest, puritan-minded members gave greater solemnity to the occasion by asking the Speaker to provide and read a prayer; and the Speaker's prayer became a regular parliamentary feature. In 1597 the House for the first time imported a minister to read the prayers. For his pay he ranked with the poor as beneficiary of the end-of-session collection, and members who departed early were expected to leave something – as varying and personal in amount as modern tips – with Serjeant or Clerk towards his gratuity.[2] He did very well out of it. In 1597 he received £10 as his share of the collection.[3]

The primitive character of the early Commons Journals and the lack of any supplementary members' diaries before 1571 leave us very ignorant of detailed proceedings in pre-Elizabethan days. This, which might well seem a snare, tempting us to see novelty where none existed, is in fact one of many indications that the Elizabethan period was a great age in the formalizing of procedure, a process which denotes maturity in a legislative body. Without a Journal to record the orders, rulings, and proceedings of the House, building precedents upon a surer foundation than the corporate memory of an intermittent and changing assembly, refinement and rigidity could not reach very far. It was only in 1571 when the new Clerk, Fulk Onslow, introduced a new technique in compiling his Journal, writing a second or fair copy from the rough notes scribbled in the

1. D'Ewes, p. 667b; and see below, p. 388.

2. *C.J.* i, 54, 82, 118; *Archaeologia*, xxxvi, 103; D'Ewes, p. 566 and passim; Townshend, p. 179.

3. Townshend, p. 269. Townshend's 1597 diary (*I.H.R. Bull.* xii, 23) states that it was first agreed to give him £5, 'and after, the House gave him £10 more'. The final word, 'more', is perhaps an error.

House, and at the same time changing its format from a small dishevelled quarto, 6ins. × 8ins., to a neat and orderly folio, 8ins. × 13ins., that there was scope for the Clerk's private diary or notebook to become the official Journal of the House. Significantly enough, it is from a member of this parliament that we get the first hint of the House taking any cognizance of the Journal. Among the Clerk's duties described by this member, John Hooker, is the following: 'to enter and make true records and truly to write all such orders as be taken in that House'. And in 1572 comes the first recorded instance of the House ordering an entry to be made in the Journal. The Journal was no longer the private diary or *aide-memoire* of the Clerk. It had become the official record of the proceedings of the House.[1]

In itself this was a sign of maturity. But it does not stand alone. The Elizabethan period produced the first two[2] in that very copious succession of modern treatises on parliamentary practice, of which Erskine May's standard work – so modest in its beginning, so ponderous today – is the current exemplar. And along with this second novelty, the reign witnessed the appearance of members' own parliamentary diaries, synchronizing with the appearance of written texts of speeches and other unofficial parliamentary papers – documents to which an American scholar has applied the descriptive term 'separates'.

Though, as we shall see, there still remained a certain flexibility in the procedure of passing bills at the end of the sixteenth century, the modern practice of three readings, with no debate on the first reading, and the committee and report stages taking place after the second reading, was already evident at the beginning, and more or less established by the end, of Elizabeth's reign. In Henry VIII's reign it was not unknown for bills in the House of Lords to be read a fourth, a fifth, even an eighth time, and to be ingrossed not after the second but the fourth reading; and in the same House in Edward VI's reign a bill could be read a sixth time.[3] In the House of Commons between 1547 and 1558 there were many instances of a fourth, a fifth,

1. Cf. my article, *Trans. Roy. Hist. Soc.* 4th ser. iii, 136 ff.; T.C.D. MS. N. 2. no. 12.
2. By John Hooker and William Lambarde.
3. *Lords Journals*, i, 25–8, 35, 55–6, 169, 269–71, 361.

or even a sixth reading, and of committings on any reading.[1] But in spite of extravagances the main tendency was obvious.

Three readings became the settled rule in English parliamentary practice, not by chance, nor, as some have surmised, through any mystical quality about the number, but as a result of the exigencies of procedure. Bills were in manuscript. That was the determining factor. Save for acts of grace, coming from the Crown with the royal signature, the initial text of a bill was by Elizabeth's reign always on paper. The House was informed of its contents, not by printed copies, nor even by the distribution of manuscript copies, but by the Clerk reading the text. The reading of a bill was literally a reading: for example, reading the subsidy bill in 1585 occupied 'almost two hours'.[2] Very tedious these mornings would have seemed to us, especially when not enlivened by much debate, which was often the case in early days; and even hardy Elizabethans, for whom time flowed more serenely and prolonged listening was second nature, felt the tedium. They had no smoking room, no library, no room at all to which to retire and yet be on call. Inevitably, the man who bore the full drudgery of it all was the Speaker: he had no deputy, and sat in his chair six days in the week from eight o'clock till eleven, or even later. So no doubt did some stalwarts.

Usually, the first reading of a bill was the first disclosure of its contents to practically all members. The bill 'was disliked of many', notes a diarist of 1571, 'but not effectually argued unto of any man, for that it was the first reading'.[3] However, as yet there was no prohibition on debate at this stage, and perhaps in the earlier years of Elizabeth's reign not even any conscious prejudice against it. Nevertheless, convention inevitably crystallized round normal procedure; and the normal practice was to postpone debate. In 1581 in an hortatory talk at the beginning of the session, the Speaker asked members 'to forbear speaking to bills at the first reading', as time was short; while six years later, William Lambarde explained that after the first reading the Speaker should proceed to the reading of another bill, 'without suffering any man (if he may stay him) to speak unto it, but rather to advise thereof until the next reading, which is a mean, not only to have effectual speech, but also to save a

1. *C.J.* i, 2–49 passim.   2. Lansdowne MS. 43, fol. 167a.
3. Cotton MS. Titus F. I, fol. 157a.

great deal of time'.[1] By the 1620s, as a treatise interpreted procedure, it was 'not the use' to speak on the first reading, though not altogether without precedent 'in cases when the matter of the bill is apparently inconvenient and hurtful to the Commonwealth and so not fitting to trouble the House any longer'; which, he added, occurred 'very seldom'.[2] Here, obviously, is the explanation of our modern practice.

Between the first and second readings, members specially interested in a bill could either 'ask the sight' of it, reading it in the presence of the Clerk, or purchase copies from him – 'the writer-out of the copies of bills is set awork', as Arthur Hall put it – the recognized charge for which, when John Hooker wrote his treatise about 1571, was one penny for ten lines.[3] Others relied on hearing it read a second time. Thus after the second reading, informed debate could take place. If the House now approved of the body of the bill but thought that it required amending, this was the time to refer it to a committee – or, as they said, eschewing the collective noun, refer it to 'committees'. Commitment was not an essential stage in procedure. Indeed, at the beginning of the reign it was not employed unless amendment was expressly desired; and the bills committed were only a minority. Even at the end of the reign, when practice had quite changed, the principle remained. The Speaker on one occasion declared that he could not put the question for committing, if no one spoke to the bill; whereupon a member immediately rose to urge that it be committed. Much the same doctrine is found in an early-Stuart tract.[4]

After the committee came the report stage when a member of the committee explained any amendments that he and his colleagues had made. Already by 1581 – and maybe before – such formalism had entered procedure that each amendment, though a single, unimportant word, was solemnly read twice by the Clerk to bring it into line with the readings given to the rest of the bill. 'The Clerk', states our early-Stuart tract, 'ought to read every amendment and interlining two times, that so it may have as many readings as the rest of the bill hath had'; and though very many times the alterations will make no sense in isolation, 'yet notwithstanding, the Clerk ought only to

---

1. *C.J.* i, 118; Add. MS. 5123, fol. 7.   2. Add. MS. 36856, fol. 32b.
3. Hooker's tract; HALL, *Account of a Quarrel* (1815 reprint), p. 94.
4. Cf. D'EWES, p. 583a; TOWNSHEND, p. 187; Stowe MS. 354, fol. 32a.

read the new amendments, without meddling with any of the rest of the bill, for it is intended that the reporter hath declared ... the reason of the amendment and the connexion thereof to the rest of the bill'. Debate might ensue at the report stage, but unless the bill was re-committed, the question now put by the Speaker was for ingrossing – that is, for writing out the final text of the bill on parchment.[1]

At this point a new text – the official one on which the House was to pass judgement – had emerged. It was obviously essential to read this to the House. And so we arrive at our famous three readings, which was the minimum number of readings required to pass the normal bill in an age that did not use the aid of printing. It was left to time to eliminate the abnormal.

Between Edward VI's reign – when thanks to the Commons Journals there is some evidence on the subject – and the end of Elizabeth's reign, there was much tightening of procedure, due both to the growing congestion of business and the increasing independence and loquacity of the House. Under Edward VI and Mary procedure seems to have been flexible and natural, and the Commons were normally a rather easy-going assembly. The majority of bills were not committed in the Lower House. Apparently, in these early days it was the House of Lords, with its expert service of judges and other high legal officials, that was the more critical and responsible body. But by the latter part of Elizabeth's reign the roles of the two Houses had been reversed. Unless strategy so demanded – and it might prove a blunder for either the government or a private promoter to initiate a measure in the Upper instead of the Lower House – most bills by then were introduced first into the Commons; and what with having fewer bills to read and their quicker, less argumentative pace, time and again the Lords found themselves with little or nothing to do. They had to send to ask the Commons if they had any bills ready for them.

This new relationship of the Houses was clearly revealed by Lord Chancellor Hatton, who, two months before the meeting of the 1589 parliament, wrote to the Speaker of the previous parliament, wanting to consult him about bills, of which 'the Lords had good liking', left over from the last parliament for lack of time. 'The use of the Higher

1. *C.J.* i, 125; D'Ewes, p. 438a; Add. MS. 36856, fol. 35.

House', he wrote, 'is not to meddle with any bill until there be some presented from the Commons'; and so, to avoid having the Lords sit idle at the beginning of the parliament, he proposed to introduce these old bills.[1]

Again, in Edward VI and Mary's reigns bills were read as many times as the Commons wished, provided there was a minimum of three; though even this proviso may need qualification, for if the entry in the Journal can be trusted, which is doubtful, there was one instance of a bill passing after a second reading.[2] Committing or ingrossing a bill at this period could take place on any reading, from the first to the fourth or sixth. In Elizabeth's reign, by contrast, no bill was read more than four times, and a fourth reading was very exceptional. In 1581, after two sessions without abnormality, two bills were read a fourth time; but when a third seemed fated to similar treatment, the House decided that an actual second reading should 'stand for no reading'. The doctrine of three readings, neither more nor less, had finally triumphed.[3]

Similarly with commitments: a little flexibility still remained. There were instances of committing on the first, the second, and the third reading in Elizabeth's reign, though not of ingrossing after any other than the second. In 1571 when the main government bill stimulated a great debate on its first reading and there was inclination to commit it at once, Recorder Fleetwood opposed haste. 'The sudden commitment of bills', he declared, 'doth often occasion the lack of convenient qualifications, and very often is the cause that the bills be never heard of again': in other words, a first-reading debate could not reveal all the weaknesses of a bill. Nevertheless, two bills were committed in this way as late as 1584–5, but apparently none thereafter; and the tract written about 1587 by William Lambarde stated categorically that 'a bill may not be committed upon the first reading'. Occasionally bills were still debated, and might be rejected, on the first reading. For example, in 1601 Serjeant Harris, an influential common lawyer, 'stept up to' a bill, pointed out – a good hunting cry for this assembly – that it would enable ecclesiastical judges to determine laymen's inheritances and that it contained another 'gross fault'; whereupon 'all the House cried "Away with

1. D'Ewes, pp. 441a, 450b; Nicolas, *Hatton*, p. 482.
2. *C.J.* i, 15.　　　　3. ibid., pp. 127, 128, 131.

it"', and 'gave a very great No' to the question for reading it a second time.[1]

From time to time in the earlier part of the reign bills were committed on their third reading. Whether this was in order, was questioned in 1585. 'Before the law is passed', said Mr Lewknor, arguing for flexibility, 'we are judges of it; after it is passed, it is judge of us'. The House agreed that such bills might 'presently – that is, immediately – be amended, if need be, but not committed'. Procedure, however, still remained uncertain. The point was raised again in 1593 and once more in 1597 when 'it was agreed that if a bill be read three times, it cannot after be again committed, but with consent it may be amended at the table or presently in the committee-chamber'.[2] Perhaps one reason for this ruling was a new, a more formal attitude to the ingrossed text of a bill, as distinct from the paper draft, for commitment meant entrusting it during several days to some member for production at a meeting held at an Inn of Court or elsewhere. Certainly, the House was becoming much more particular. In 1601 when in the course of argument at the third reading the Solicitor General reached for the bill to look at a word in it, afterwards laying it on the Clerk's table, another royal official stood up and said, ' "Mr Speaker, you should, after a bill is ingrossed, hold it in your hand and let no man look into it"; which was confessed by all. And so the Speaker took it.'[3]

How casual, by contrast, earlier parliaments could be! In 1585, when urging the House to reverse a previous decision, William Fleetwood, Recorder of London, first expounded his argument – namely, that since parliament was one day in law it could do as the courts of justice, where, the term being theoretically one day, the same judges might reform any error, during the same term. Then he told a merry tale by way of precedent. 'I remember', he said, 'in a bill against vintners which was dashed, ... afterwards I and a company were had to a tavern by the Vintners and had good cheer, and came in the afternoon and reviewed it, and it passed. I remember

---

1. Cotton MS. Titus F. I, fol. 142b; T.C.D. MS. N. 2, no. 12; Add. MS. 5123, fol. 7b; TOWNSHEND, p. 222.

2. Lansdowne MS. 43, fol. 164b; D'EWES, p. 415b; Cotton MS. Titus F. II, fol. 48a; I.H.R. Bull. xii, 14.

3. TOWNSHEND, p. 209.

Mr Horsey said it was a good bill.' Much to his surprise, the tale misfired. 'We are not to follow precedents made in an afternoon, when commonly men are more merry than wise', said one. 'We are not to follow precedents made in taverns and tippling houses', echoed another. Apparently Fleetwood, who was an incorrigible raconteur, had told the same story to make the same point in 1576; but according to Arthur Hall it then had a different twist. The House, in this version of the story, first passed the bill on a Saturday afternoon after many had been feasted by the Vintners – Bacchus speaking for his ministers; but on the Monday morning, in restored sobriety, they made no bones about reversing the decision. Fleetwood's principle, though not his shameful illustration of it, was in fact applied on occasions. In 1581, finding that a bill, passed the day before, was 'mistaken in some words', the House amended it, read the amendments thrice, and then passed the bill a second time; but our diarist, an expert on procedure, placed the word '*nota*' against his entry, to denote its exceptional interest.[1]

In all likelihood, the march of formalism, at once subtle and obvious, was influenced by the differing personalities of the Speakers. Two stand out, the first especially. Edward Coke, prince of lawyers, a domineering man, with great legal learning, a love of precedent, and an inflexible, dogmatic mind, was not content to be a relatively passive chairman in 1593. Craving leave to speak 'for their better information' on a troublesome privilege question – 'which the House willingly granted', says our diarist, 'for they desired it, at least I did' – Coke explained that since the beginning of the parliament he had 'thought upon and searched ... this point of the privileges of the House, for I judged it would come in question upon many occasions'. In a sentence which biographers of Coke might note, he asked their pardon 'if I be round in that I say, for it is my fault, I cannot speak so mildly as some, but my manner is that that I speak is sharply' said.[2] It was not in the nature of such a chairman to tolerate loose procedure: the rule was bound to be enemy to the exception. In the following parliament, 1597, under the able chairmanship of Christopher Yelverton, a very different type of Speaker, but one whose

1. Lansdowne MS. 43, fol. 170a; HALL, *Account of a Quarrel*, p. 32; T.C.D. MS. N. 2, no. 12.

2. Cotton MS. Titus F. II, fol. 86b.

fine speeches are tribute to his capacity, procedure appears to have become quite settled, and, it would seem, consciously settled. Adolescence was over.

But far more dynamic than any Speaker was the House itself, developing in quality, experience, and independence. Between the days of Edward VI and Mary, when – a sure indication of immaturity – most bills were not committed, and the parliament of 1597, when practically every bill was committed, what a transformation! During Elizabeth's reign a critical, contentious tradition was forming, helped, as we shall see later, by the lobbying and organized intervention of outside private interests. 'I do much wonder to see the House so continually divided, and to agree upon nothing', said Francis Bacon in 1601; 'to see many laws here so well framed and offences provided against, and yet to have no better success and entertainment.'[1]

In the changed atmosphere time was more precious than ever; though in the nature of things members frittered much away, especially over privilege cases. The House could no longer afford to debate bills on the first reading, save indeed to kill a project out of hand and so save time. Committees came to be used, not as before solely for the purpose of amendment, but to transfer as much of the debate as possible from the floor of the House to the committee chamber. Hence the committing of virtually every bill, and the conversion of this into a normal stage in procedure.

Furthermore, there was a change in the type of committee. In the earlier part of Elizabeth's reign committees, generally speaking, were small: ten or so for normal, and twenty or so for special occasions, with rare exceptions. Members who had spoken in the debate and who perhaps had suggested amendments formed the core of these committees, and anyone opposed to the body of the bill was excluded. The tendency was for numbers to grow. In 1585 someone – the Speaker, if the form of address is a reliable sign – said, 'My Masters there, you call upon men to have them committees. You think to please them, but they con you no thanks for your labour, for they are unwilling.'[2]

In the last three parliaments of the reign, it is evident that the House was having increasing recourse to extraordinary committees.

1. TOWNSHEND, p. 194.   2. Lansdowne MS. 43, fol. 172a.

For example, we find all the Privy-Council members, all Serjeants-at-Law, and sixty others on one committee in 1593; then, all of the Privy Council, all knights of the shire, the members for all port towns and London, York, Derby, and Rochester, and thirty-seven others on a committee in 1597; and similar committees in 1601.[1] In 1597 two rival bills concerning the making of malt — not a major issue — were committed to the members for ten cities and boroughs, the knights for one shire, and thirty-eight other members by name; and still more striking, eleven bills about the relief of the poor and the punishment of idle and sturdy beggars were committed to all Readers at the Inns of Court, all Serjeants-at-Law (five in number), all knights of the shire, all citizens of cities, the burgesses for Hull, and forty-five other members by name.[2]

These were obviously very different committees from those that the House was wont to choose mainly from participants in the debate. The motive, in fact, was to avoid debate, to free the time of the House from long, contentious speeches. In 1621, by which date these large committees had become regular parliamentary practice, it was asked why they appointed so many members to committees, seeing that 'in Henry VIII's time there were not wont to be above six and in Edward VI's time not above ten'. The answer came pat: Nowadays, 'few matters are debated in the House, but are referred to a committee and there debated. So either we must order ourselves to the old course of debating matters before we correct them, or else there is reason for more committees' — that is, for larger committee-membership.[3]

It must also have been in these later years of Elizabeth that a custom emerged which is referred to in a letter written by a member in 1593: 'Our form in the Lower House is that if some members ... be chosen committees, to meet in the afternoon, ... yet any of the House may freely have access ... and there with them yield his objections and allegations ...; and these occasions of commitment give great, sudden occasions of attendance, so that none of the House can prescribe well any day to bestow his business elsewhere.' In 1601 the diarist, Hayward Townshend, gives us the debates of some im-

---

1. D'EWES, pp. 499a, 555, 561a, 624, 635a.   2. ibid. pp. 561a, 578a.
3. Add. MS. 26637, fol. 10b.

portant committees at which, though not a committee-member, he was present. He had a right to speak, but not to vote.[1]

In 1593 – when Coke was Speaker – the custom took root of holding some of these large committee-meetings in the House itself;[2] and on occasions the attendance must have resembled that of an ordinary sitting of the Commons. Sir Robert Cecil, reporting one of these meetings to the House in 1601, spoke of 'so good attendance, being little inferior to our assembly at this present'. In this unpremeditated way the Commons stumbled upon the substance of a new procedural device, the committee of the whole House, though realization of its possibilities and formulation of the procedure did not follow until the next reign. Townshend, the diarist, instinctively wrote of 'the House' on these occasions: 'And so the House, about six o'clock at night' – it was a November Saturday and dark, and they had sat from two p.m., in addition to a full morning session – 'rose confusedly'. Members tended to speak as in the House: 'Let us ... leave our orations and speeches, fitter for a parliament than a committee', said one impatient member, following a speech by Sir Walter Raleigh. True to type, he was unaware of the beam in his own eye.[3]

In early-Stuart parliaments one of the virtues of the committee of the whole House was that it got the officially-minded Speaker out of the chair. In February 1593, there was a meeting of the committee for supply, which was so contentious 'that all the afternoon until seven of the clock at night was spent and nothing concluded' and they agreed to meet again next morning in the Exchequer Chamber – probably before the House met, though renewed contention caused the meetings to overlap. According to our diarist, the Speaker was present and in the chair. The incident is puzzling. If accurately reported, it was perhaps a characteristic exhibition of Edward Coke's self-assertiveness. Mercifully, the precedent of having the Speaker in the chair at these embryonic committees of the whole House did not stick, and in 1601 Townshend, on the single occasion when he notes the point, tells us that a member, Mr Anthony Maynard, 'by the

1. *H.M.C. Rep.* iv, 335b; *I.H.R. Bull.* xii, 13; TOWNSHEND, pp. 192, 197; Stowe MS. 354, fol. 35a.
2. There was a precedent in 1589 (D'EWES, pp. 432–3).
3. TOWNSHEND, pp. 198, 200, 202.

consent of the whole House sat in the chair, as clerk, to register the order of this committee; and by consent also was licensed to put on his hat'.[1]

In the earlier part of Elizabeth's reign, when the Commons found themselves pressed for time towards the end of a session, they took to sitting in the afternoon as well as the morning. There had been a few precedents in Edward VI's reign, but only one such sitting between 1553 and 1563. Then in 1563 they met on twenty-one afternoons, and after a lapse to two in 1566, renewed the practice in 1571 with a vigour and deliberateness that promised to make it a regular feature of parliament. Parliament in that year met on 2 April and was dissolved on 29 May. On 9 May Thomas Norton, one of the natural leaders of the House, moved that they should sit from 3 p.m. till 5 p.m. every Monday, Wednesday, and Friday until the end of the session and employ the time solely in the first reading of private bills. On 21 May the order was extended to every afternoon, and the readings to the second as well as the first.[2] These sittings were the sixteenth-century equivalent of our all-night sittings; and it is not without interest that the reason for them, at this period of the reign, was the pressure of private, not government, business. They were confined to the initial reading of bills because of the smaller attendance in the afternoon, when members might be engaged on committees, or on their own business, or just soporific and lazy after the midday dinner.

When parliament met again in the following year, Norton's motion was not forgotten. It was an extraordinary session, called to deal with the Ridolfi Plot and Mary Queen of Scots, and held in May and June when Elizabeth preferred not to have London crowded, owing to the danger of plague in the hot weather. The Queen told the House not to deal with 'private matters', hoping to keep the parliament as short as possible; but the interests of both suitors and members overrode her injunction, and after using their spare time for such measures, they decided half way through the brief session of eight weeks to sit in the afternoons from 3 p.m. till 6 p.m., dealing

1. NOTESTEIN, *Winning of the Initiative*, pp. 36 ff.; WILLSON, *Privy Councillors in the H. of Commons*, p. 225; Cotton MS. Titus F. II, fols. 50b ff.; TOWNSHEND, p. 200.
2. *C.J.* i, 88, 91.

only with private bills but not passing any measure that concerned town or shire unless the members for the constituency were present.[1] In 1575–6 the House again held afternoon sittings. But then they almost disappeared, and in two parliaments vanished completely. Norton's conception had shrivelled and died, and there can be little doubt that this was due to the increasing demands made upon all competent and assiduous members by afternoon committee work. When the custom was revived, near the end of Elizabeth's last parliament, it was not on the initiative of any private member, but of Sir Robert Cecil, anxious to bring the session to a speedy end: 'We consume our time now in unnecessary disputation', he ill-temperedly remarked. And the next day the Queen herself added her own injunction, to support Cecil. Thus our story draws close to the present day, with these extended sittings imposed by the government.[2]

Time was an increasingly anxious problem. Elizabeth's parliaments were few, their sessions brief. One parliament, that of 1572, was quite fortuitous, and would not have been summoned but for the Ridolfi Plot. The Babington Plot probably caused another parliament to be held a year sooner. Even so, there were only ten parliaments, with thirteen sessions, in a reign of just over forty-four years – an average of more than three years between each session. Moreover, these sessions averaged less than ten weeks each in duration. The shortest – 1576 – lasted four weeks and two days, the longest – 1559 – fourteen weeks six days, including a recess of ten days at Easter.

The Queen claimed credit for her policy of few parliaments. 'Her Majesty', the Lord Keeper told parliament in 1593, 'hath evermore been most loth to call for the assembly of her people in parliament, and hath done the same but rarely.'[3] In so far as parliaments meant subsidies, there was justice in her claim; but her concern for the convenience and expense of members was becoming increasingly out of date as the lust of the gentry for parliamentary experience grew. Even the boroughs which still paid their members might have wished for increased facilities to promote their interests in parliament, while, in the latter part of the reign, private interests as a whole would probably have asked for more, not fewer parliaments. With numerous extra fees to officials, and the diversion of Councillors and royal

1. ibid. pp. 100, 101. 2. D'Ewes, p. 675b; Townshend, p. 309.
3. Eng. Hist. Rev. xxxi, 130.

servants from normal business, parliaments were of course a great expense and nuisance to the Crown. Supreme artist though she was in handling them, Elizabeth was personally antipathetic. She never liked their heady 'popularity'.

If Elizabeth had been a lax disciplinarian, sessions would have drifted on much beyond their actual duration: witness the petulant remark of Robert Cecil in 1601. Cecil's father, Lord Burghley, always had periodic lists prepared of the stages reached by bills in each House in order to fix the date for ending a session,[1] and also, through the Speaker's and other help in the Commons, to speed the bills which it was essential to have passed. After he moved from the Lower to the Higher House, he still remained the Queen's chief-of-staff in parliamentary affairs – tribute to the premier-like position of this supreme statesman, and incidentally to the new strategic importance of the Commons in parliament. Elizabeth never slackened the reins in driving her parliaments to a time-schedule. Even in her last parliament, when the Commons took the bit between their teeth over monopolies, she brought them to journey's end in very good time for Christmas, after just under eight weeks sitting.

But the pressure from promoters of private bills, the novel procedure of committing all bills, the great attendance, verging on the whole House, at important committees, the growing disputatiousness of the Commons; all were straining at the time-conserving discipline of a domineering Queen. When James came to the throne, with less nerve and authority, the result can be seen. His first parliament held five sessions in fewer than seven years, which was without precedent since Henry VIII's Reformation Parliament; and in each of the first four sessions the House sat on an average approximately nineteen weeks, twice sitting on into July. But then, unlike Elizabeth, the pleasure-loving James felt no obligation to be at hand in London while parliament sat. Not for him the irksome round

1. There are many such in the State Papers.

CHAPTER 20

Procedure: II

As today, parliamentary bills were divided into two classes, public and private, the one general in application, serving the commonwealth as a whole, the other particular, and concerned with personal or sectional interests. It was not a precise differentiation: we have already noticed that. In a debate on a bill in 1584–5 Recorder Fleetwood said, 'I did advise him to make [it] a private bill but he would not, and therefore he shall see what will come of it'.[1] The one infallible distinction was that of the officials: they levied fees on private, but not on public bills.

In terms of parliamentary time, private bills were much more important than they are today. Indeed, with that slight violence to truth which sustains an epigram, we might say that if for the Crown parliaments meant subsidies, for the Commons they meant private bills. 'If her Majesty's meaning be to have the session short', wrote a member, advising a Privy-Councillor friend in 1581, 'then it is good to abridge the things that lengthen the session'; and the first he mentioned were 'the number of private bills of singular persons', and 'the bills of occupation, mysteries, and companies, and specially the bills of London'. He suggested – and his advice was followed – that at the beginning of the session there should be a motion for a committee to consider bills offered to the House and prefer 'the most necessary'; 'but in no wise', he added, 'to make mention of rejecting any, although indeed it amounteth to a rejecting of those that be of small importance, for private bills ever be eagerly followed and make factions'. He proposed tackling the problem of London bills by calling the London members together before one was read and asking them whether it could not be dealt with among themselves; if this was possible, then to commend it to the Lord Mayor and Aldermen, thus ridding the House of it – a course which, as the London records

1. Lansdowne MS. 43, fol. 166b.

show, had been adopted in 1566. He thought it would 'do the City a marvellous benefit'.[1]

Present-day treatises draw a sharp distinction between the procedure in public and in private bills, the main feature of which is the quasi-judicial process of hearing counsel and witnesses both for and against private bills, at the committee stage. The distinction was unknown, or at any rate unacknowledged, in Elizabethan days: indeed, in the earlier part of the reign many private bills were not committed at all. However, since the contemporary mind still thought of parliament as a court – as witness the word *judicium* which the Clerk of the House of Commons employed to denote the passing of a bill – members were bound to react sympathetically when parties to bills which affected private rights asked to be heard in person or by counsel, either in the House itself or in committee. In bills of attainder the Commons had long considered that they should proceed judicially, hearing evidence; and in bills affecting property rights they were obviously inclined in Elizabeth's reign to demand evidence from the parties concerned, along with their learned counsel.[2] The development of a similar procedure with the normal private bill was probably the result of advances in the technique of lobbying.

The pioneer in this business of lobbying was London. It stood pre-eminent. As early as 1445 the Common Council of the City allotted a sum of five hundred marks for the defence and promotion of City affairs in the forthcoming parliament.[3] In the sixteenth century the whole procedure was organized and canalized. Citizens were not supposed to pursue any bill or suit without the knowledge and consent of the Lord Mayor and aldermen – a regulation which was reiterated in 1555.[4] As the regulation worked in the Elizabethan period, City companies and crafts with bills to promote submitted them to the Court of Aldermen, where they were read and possibly committed to the Recorder or someone else to amend. If finally approved, the promoters were authorized to proceed with the bill, and sometimes, when the Aldermen felt prompted to add their own weight to the cause, the City's four members were 'specially moved'

1. Harleian MS. 253, fol. 34; Repert. xvi, fol. 262 (The many excerpts from the City records in this chapter I also owe to Miss Jay).
2. Cf. *C.J.* i, 97, 133b.   3. Jor. iv, 62.   4. Repert. XIII, ii, fol. 323b.

to further it. At least once, a bill was disliked and its presentation in parliament forbidden; on another occasion, though disliked, the promoters were authorized to proceed if they wished.

Preparations were also made for concerted opposition to any bills injurious to City interests. In 1572 there was a bill 'against injuries offered by corporations in the City of London to divers foreign artificers'. On its first reading in the Commons, the Recorder of London declared it 'slanderous to the City', though admitting that if its allegations were true, the extortioners deserved to be punished. His speech secured its immediate commitment. Some weeks later, the wardens of various City companies affected by it came to the Court of Aldermen and were charged to prepare their defence, with the aid of learned counsel, and 'to deliver the same in fair writing' to Sir Rowland Hayward and Mr Recorder, the two senior City members, in order that 'they with others may the better answer the said bill in parliament', and overthrow it 'if they can'. In fact, the bill was crowded or manoeuvred out and did not reach a second reading.[1]

In 1584–5 there was a bill before the House of Commons to diminish the statutory width of cloth, on which London opinion was divided. Taking his cue as an official from the Lord Mayor and the main body of aldermen, William Fleetwood, the Recorder, spoke against it on the second reading. 'There was an alderman of London and a draper at the door the last day', he said, 'and spake to me to further the bill, for, quoth he, it is a good bill and you shall have cloth as good as ever it was and a yard as good cheap. And I do believe him; but you shall have a yard of cloth narrower by half a quarter. And you, my masters, that buy a hundred or two hundred yards for liveries, reckon what you lose by that half quarter only.' 'In the twenty-seventh of Henry VIII', he reminded them, 'there passed a bill for the clothiers that they might make them but seven quarters broad; and now in the twenty-seventh of Elizabeth they attempt to bring it to six and a half. I believe they be seen in astronomy and think to have good luck always in the twenty-seventh year.'

They did have good luck. The bill passed the Commons, whereupon the Lord Mayor and aldermen wrote to Lord Burghley sending him the arguments against it, and asking that if these did not satisfy

1. Repert. xvii, 337; C.J. i, 97b; T.C.D. MS. N. 2, no. 12.

the House of Lords, skilful witnesses might be called to testify against it. For all this weighty opposition, the bill also passed the Lords and became a statute.[1]

Londoners pulled all the strings they could in promoting and opposing bills. In 1544, for example, the Recorder was instructed to move the Lords of the Council for their favour in a bill, while the water bailiff was 'to resort to the parliament house and to solicit the same matter with all diligence'.[2] Asking for the good offices of the great – of the Privy Council, the Lord Chancellor, or the peers – which had been so notable a practice earlier, seems most significantly to have lapsed more or less in Elizabeth's reign; although in 1576 the aldermen took care to make Lord Burghley privy to a particular bill, and in 1593 sought his and two other eminent Councillors' favour in another bill, both of them measures that required official backing. They also advised the beer-brewers, whose bill had been rejected in the Lower House in 1563, to amend the bill and put it into the House of Lords, 'and try what they can do therein by the help of their friends'.[3] But in Elizabeth's reign London's legislative activities were concentrated on the House of Commons and its lobby – another of very many signs that in this period there was a new constitutional climate.

For the last three parliaments of the reign, the Court of Aldermen appointed a committee 'to consider what bills are fit to be preferred at the next parliament for the good and benefit of this city'; in short, to prepare a legislative programme. And both in 1593 and 1597, they adopted what apparently were new tactics by sending a deputation to the Speaker at his private residence to ask for his favour in a bill; a request the cogency of which may be measured by the gratuity they paid the Speaker.[4]

This promoting of private bills was, and still is, an elaborate business. It could be quite expensive, which also remains true today. There were lawyers to be paid for drafting the bills, and if need be for acting as counsel. London paid James Altham £6 13s. 4d. for drawing seven bills for the parliament of 1601, and his clerk 40s. for

1. Lansdowne MS. 43, fol. 174a; S.P. Dom. Eliz. 177, no. 12; *Statutes of the Realm*, IV. i, 724.
2. Repert. xi, fol. 44.   3. Repert. xix, fol. 38b, xxiii, fol. 31, xv, fol. 189.
4. Repert. xxiii, fols. 22b, 31, xxiv, fols. 153b, 180, xxv, fol. 275.

writing them.[1] Westminster had several items in its bill of costs for the act of 1585: 10s. 'to my Lord Treasurer's man for drawing the book at my Lord's commandment' – Burghley was High Steward of the city; 20s. to Mr Atkinson for counsel, and 3s. 4d. to his man 'for writing a paper book'; 6s. 8d. to Mr Grafton's man for another paper book after the second committee; and 20s. to Mr. Grafton for counsel.[2] Some – perhaps much – of this business went to lawyer-members; for by employing them, friendly, influential, and informed voices were secured in the House. Then there was the lobbying, briefing, even feeing of members to speak for the bill; activities in which opponents also indulged. 'He that spake first', said a member in 1585, 'his tale deserves the less credit, because I can show it him in writing, for he hath it from the searchers ... I prefer the clothier before the searcher, and the truth before them both.'[3] Our diarist, Hayward Townsend, tells us that in 1601, when a private bill was read, 'I stood up to speak against it, according to a note given me by Mr John Stephens, an honest young gentleman of Lincoln's Inn' – presumably counsel for the opposition.[4] Some of these 'notes' or briefs survive among the State Papers.[5]

In 1589 a gentleman named Thomas Drurie, who was party against a private bill, was brought to the bar and charged, among other offences, with offering 'great threats' to some members, 'and to some others ... great sums of money to speak ... for him and not against him; and likewise in using of hard speeches both to some of them and of some of them'. Mr Drurie was clumsy, hot-tempered, indiscreet. The trouble he got into is no proof that subtler methods were not prevalent. 'Mr Speaker', began a member in 1585, 'I am not feed; I speak my conscience.' And the Liverpool Town Books boast of their local Admirable Crichton, Ralph Sekerston, their member in 1563; 'Where other town burgesses had and did retain speakers for them in the parliament house, he retained none, but stood up after the manner there and was speaker himself.'[6]

1. Repert. xxv, fol. 323.
2. *Local Government in Westminster* (1889), pp. 24–5.
3. Lansdowne MS. 43, fol. 174b.   4. TOWNSHEND, p. 267.
5. E.g. S.P. Dom. Eliz. 148, no. 7; 177, no. 44; Addenda, 20, no. 19.
6. D'EWES, pp. 448–9; Lansdowne MS. 43, fol. 174b; *Liverpool Town Books*, i, 218.

A borough naturally expected its own members to promote its interests. The Recorder of Exeter, one of the city's members in 1563, was entrusted with two private bills. He wrote to the city's Chamberlain explaining that he had introduced one into the Lords and the other into the Commons: 'If we should have put both in at one place, then peradventure the House would not be best contented with two bills for our private city.' But it was probably seldom sufficient to rely merely on the skill and devotion of one's own members. 'Before a man mean to move a matter', says a tract written in or about 1610, ' 'tis a good course to acquaint some of his friends therewithall and to desire them to second him, especially such men as are gracious with the House.' Our Exeter member in 1563 asked for ten pounds to be sent him, 'as I have retained divers in these causes and must give money about the same'.[1]

Thomas Howard, who was in London during the parliament of 1581, looking after the interests of the joint borough of Weymouth and Melcombe Regis, was more explicit. He was evidently critical of the borough's four members and sore at not being given the seat which had gone to the Earl of Bedford's nominee at a recent by-election. 'Such hath been the slender dealings, or such hath been the indirect dealings, of some of Melcombe', he wrote in one letter, 'as the money already gathered, I doubt me will return small or no benefit unto the town at all; therefore provide no more money until the same may be better employed.' And in another letter to William Pitt of Weymouth, he declared that it was impossible to do anything in parliament; 'for when I should have bestowed chargeable sums of money in framing bills, in rewarding them that should speak favourably in them, in gratifying the Speaker and other men of authority, then should I look for a hard passage of the bill, by reason that Sir Christopher Hatton's countenance and credit' – Hatton was Keeper of Corfe Castle and Admiral of Purbeck and therefore interested in these parts – 'would work much against it, and surely would overthrow it when it should come to her Majesty's hands; and therefore would not cast away your money at this time in so [? doubtful] affairs. Worse than this, these wicked men – perhaps a local faction, patronized by Hatton – are so favoured and pitied as they had by parliament clean overthrown your former decree and quietness for ever, if I had not throughly laboured all my friends, and the Council also, for the stopping of the same.'[1]

These private bills, in which from the protagonists' point of view much was at stake, were 'followed' or 'solicited' with all the skill and energy possible. In 1584–5 the tanners, the curriers, and the shoemakers had rival bills in the House of Commons. Things went badly for the curriers, and one of them, a poor man, John Bland by name, got into trouble by rash talk with some shoemakers, asserting that 'the curriers could have no justice in this House'. The shoemakers' bill, he complained, was passed when only fifty members were present and the curriers' friends absent – a remark indicating that the bill was probably passed in the first hour of the morning before the House filled. It should not have been passed; and as for the tanners' bill, it had been only partially read, some leaves being left unread. For this libellous outburst, the wretched man was brought to answer at the bar of the House. Fortunately, a Privy Councillor, blessed with a sense of humour, set a merciful note: 'Good reason losers should have their words; he is a poor man and many children.' And so he got off with taking the Oath of Supremacy, making a humble submission, and paying his fee to the Serjeant: though alas! the Serjeant's fee, being outside mercy's jurisdiction, was twenty shillings – no small sum for a poor craftsman.[2]

In 1597 Lowestoft and Yarmouth had a battle royal over a bill promoted by the former. 'To speak without partiality', comments a diarist, 'a man might perceive most palpable wrong to Yarmouth offered by them that dealt for Lowestoft, for they openly in the House canvassed for voices and procured councillors to speak in the behalf of Lowestoft, which was much spoken of; neither tolerable nor sufferable in so equal and just an assembly.' But in spite of the lobbying, or perhaps because of it, the bill was defeated in a division on the third reading by one hundred and eight against ninety.[3]

Occasionally we hear of charges of bribery being made in the House itself. In 1571, 'there was much ado about such men of the House as were [sus]pected and burdened to have received fees ...

1. H.M.C. Rep. v, 579b.
2. D'Ewes, pp. 366–7; Lansdowne MS. 43, fol. 164.
3. I.H.R. Bull. xii, 22.

for the preferring or speaking to any bill'. The matter was committed
to certain of the House, including all the Privy Councillors, who in
their report declared that they could not 'learn of any that hath sold
his voice . . . or any way dealt unlawfully or indirectly in that behalf'.
The great Thomas Norton, who 'heard that some had him in suspicion that way', rose to justify himself, and was 'purged by the
voice of the whole House'.[1] At the end of the reign, in 1601, Sir
Robert Cecil, when vexed that he and his friends had been unable to
defeat a proviso to a bill, so far forgot himself as to make a charge of
bribery: 'This I know', he said, 'that good sums of money have been
proffered for the furtherance of this proviso.' He was contradicted
by a fellow-Councillor who pointed out that the land at issue was but
little and the cause both good and just. Probably it was mere spleen
with Cecil: even so, the fact remains that such a charge could be
made by so responsible a member.[2]

Whether crude bribery was employed or not, money had to be
spent on these bills. The city of Westminster was probably as favourably situated to keep its costs low as any promoter, for its bill in 1585
was virtually Lord Burghley's. All the same, the costs included 20s.
for 'a marchpain at Christmas in the name of the inhabitants' to its
two members, Robert Cecil and Thomas Knyvet, and to the Recorder
of London; 20s. 8d. for a dinner to the committee, including the
city's two members; 32s. for one 'perisse' and wafers for the Lords
of the Parliament when the bill was committed in that House; and
23s. 6d. for a breakfast to the Lord Treasurer's gentlemen and others
'in gratifying their pains'.[3]

Dinner to a committee may not have been unusual. It must have
served to ensure attendance at the meeting afterwards; for occasionally – and perhaps fairly often in the latter part of the reign, when
there were many committees and prominent members were over-
burdened with them – a committee was inadequately attended and
the House had to authorize a new meeting, thus incurring delay,
which was the deadly enemy of private bills. Certainly, dinner or no
dinner, the custom was growing by which, as a treatist wrote in 1610,
'the parties' to a private bill 'do commonly solicit the committees to

1. *C.J.* i, 93; *Trans. Devon Assoc.* xi, 488.
2. TOWNSHEND, p. 302.
3. *Local Government in Westminster*, pp. 24–5.

meet, and otherwise deal with them for their favours'. We inherit an excellent illustration of the practice in a document of 1576 that is best described as a private whip: 'The clothiers humbly desireth your honourable presence and assistance by two of the clock at the committee of the bill which Sir Henry Poole, knight, preferred unto the honourable House for Gloucestershire, Wiltshire, Somerset, and other counties; and that you will be well pleased to consider the equity therein desired, which is only to reform the common abuses and deceits used in wool and yarn, with some other things very necessary to the good state of clothing within this kingdom. The penalties therein contained are very small and the benefit of them only to the use of the poor, without any cheating or profit to any party ... The committee is in the Star Chamber.'[1]

One result of all this organized effort seems to have been an increasing demand by parties to private bills to be heard, along with their legal counsel, either in committee or in the House, or in both. In 1581 the committee on a bill against the Merchant Adventurers of London was authorized to hear any witnesses, both for and against the bill, who asked to come before them. Our Thomas Drurie, who tried to bribe members in 1589, complained to some peers that neither the Lower House nor its committee would hear him or his witnesses, though in fact he had 'been heard at large both in this House and also before the committees'. In 1597 'the counsel learned on both sides in the bill concerning ... Lowestoft and Yarmouth ... were this day heard at large in this House at the bar till the breaking up of this court'. One can only register an impression; it is that this practice was on the increase. However, it could not become automatic and general because sessions were short and time quite inadequate.[2]

The House grew increasingly sensitive about members being involved professionally in private suits. 'Private bills', says an early Stuart tract, 'are usually drawn by counsellors of law not being of the House, and sometimes by those of the House, and that for their fees; which, howsoever it hath by divers been held to be lawful, yet cannot be but very inconvenient, seeing afterwards they are to be judges in the same cause.' Arthur Hall put this sentiment more pungently — too pungently for the Commons, who expelled him

1. Stowe MS. 354, fol. 36; S.P. Dom. Eliz. 107, no. 48.
2. *C.J.* i, 130b; D'Ewes, pp. 448–9, 567a and cf. p. 505.

from the House for his slanderous tract in 1581: 'To turn the cat in the pan and to be a hireling, or a penny boy for any particular person, to have clients in matters of parliament, is token of too much vility . . . What should I write of this most filthy, unnatural, and servile vice, which shall for a few angels make you plead as partially in parliament as in any other court, not regarding your country but the jinks in your pocket?'[1]

Public bills could originate with the government or with individual members or with committees appointed by the House as the result of some motion. In 1554 and again prior to Elizabeth's first parliament, the Privy Council appointed a committee of its own to prepare the government's legislative programme.[2] Perhaps it did the same for later parliaments, though more likely, preparations were made in a less formal way. Whatever the procedure, the government certainly had its bills in each parliament; and in all likelihood the chief responsibility for such business rested on William Cecil. However, as the reign progressed, more and more public bills seem to have originated with ordinary members, and in consequence there was probably less need than formerly for the government to survey the whole field of general legislation to ensure that the needs of the Commonwealth were met. If we had the means of telling, we should probably find that the proportion of avowedly government bills decreased as time went on. An incident indicative of the new, the adult outlook of members may be cited from the parliament of 1601. Our very young lawyer-diarist, Hayward Townshend, introduced a bill to prevent perjury and unnecessary suits in law. 'Mr Speaker', said he, 'I take every man to be bound in conscience to remove a little mischief from the Commonwealth before it take head and grow to a great inconveniency . . . A gentleman, well-experienced, having found this grief common to the poorer sort . . . entreated me at my coming into this House this morning to offer unto your considerations this bill.' Similarly, in the previous parliament Sir Edward Hoby had moved for a committee to frame a bill for continuing any statutes that were lapsing: it was a responsibility which undoubtedly would have been left to the government in ealier days.[3]

1. Add. MS. 36856, fol. 30b; HALL, *Account of Quarrel*, p. 94.
2. *A.P.C.* iv, 398, vii, 28 TYTLER, *Reigns of Edward VI & Mary*, ii 345.
3. TOWNSHEND, p. 221; D'EWES, p. 555.

Members who had bills to introduce could either deliver them to the Speaker or the Clerk to be presented to the House at a convenient time, or alternatively could seize their opportunity and move them in the House themselves. 'Mr Speaker', said Francis Bacon in 1601, 'I am not of their minds that bring their bills into this House obscurely, by delivery only to yourself or the Clerk, delighting to have the bill to be *incerto authore*, as though they were either ashamed of their own work or afraid to father their own children. But I, Mr Speaker, have a bill here, which I know I shall be no sooner ready to offer, but you will be as ready to receive and approve. I liken this bill to that sentence of the poet, who set this as a paradox in the forefront of his book, *First water, then gold*; preferring necessity before pleasure ... This, Mr Speaker, is no bill of state, nor of novelty, like a stately gallery for pleasure but neither to dine in or sleep in; but this bill is a bill of repose, of quiet, of profit, and of true and just dealing; the title whereof is "An act for the better suppressing of abuses in weights and measures".'[1]

The Speaker determined the order in which bills were read, subject always to the over-riding will of the House and to the general principle that public matters took precedence of private. 'He hath to receive all the bills to be brought into the House. He ought to cause the Clerk to read them openly, plainly, and sensibly', said Hooker. When the Clerk had finished his reading, the Speaker – wrote Lambarde – 'taking the bill in one hand, and his cap in the other hand, may say, "You have heard the bill, the contents whereof be these ..."'[2] A more detailed description, written in the 1620s, is probably near enough to the procedure of late-Elizabethan days to be worth quoting: 'The Clerk, being usually directed by the Speaker, but sometimes by the House, what bill to read, with a loud and distinct voice first readeth the title of the bill, and then, after a little pause, the bill itself; which done, kissing his hand, he delivereth the same to the Speaker, who, standing up uncovered (whereas otherwise he sitteth with his hat on) and holding the bill in his hand, sayeth, "This bill is thus entitled", and then readeth the title; which done, he openeth to the House the substance of the bill, which he doth either trusting to his memory or using the help or altogether the reading of his breviate, which is filed to the bill, sometimes read-

---

1. TOWNSHEND, p. 189.   2. Hooker's tract; Add. MS. 5123, fol. 7.

ing the bill itself, especially upon the passage of a bill when it hath been much altered by the committees, so that thereby it differeth very much from the breviate . . . When he hath thus opened the effect of the bill, he declareth to the House that this is the first reading of the bill, and delivereth the same again to the Clerk.'[1]

Theoretically, it was the Speaker's duty to prepare the breviate or epitome, and he might refuse to allow the sudden reading of a bill on the plea that he needed time to do this.[2] But it is obvious that some or perhaps most promoters of bills prepared their own breviates, which might be read or used by a member when introducing the bill, and presumably might be used by the Speaker.[3] There are a number among the State Papers, sometimes with arguments, and answers to possible objections, compiled with a view to briefing supporters or securing the goodwill of Burghley or others.[4]

If our diaries convey the right impression, then the House seldom challenged the Speaker's choice of bills for reading, all-important though this was. In 1593 a member wanted a private bill read, whereas the Speaker very properly wished first to read a public bill from the Lords, commended by her Majesty. The issue went to a vote, and the House supported the Speaker. But in 1601 'the Speaker gave the Clerk a bill to read, and the House called for the Exchequer bill. Some said Yea, and some said No, and a great noise there was. At last Mr Lawrence Hyde said, "To end this controversy, because the time is very short, I would move the House to have a very short bill read, entitled, An act of explanation of the Common Law in certain cases of letters-patent". And all the House cried, I, I, I.' Mr Hyde's was quite another bill from the two in controversy! It was against monopolies, everyone's grievance. He united the House, and, illogically, his bill was read.[5]

There was a later occasion in that unruly session, when, according to an order of the day before, a certain bill was to be read; but the House called for the bill concerning ordnance. The Clerk fell to reading the former, 'but still the House cried upon the bill for ordnance'.

1. Add. MS. 36856, fol. 32.
2. *Bowyer's Diary*, p. 322; Stowe MS. 354, fol. 32.
3. Cf. S.P. Dom. Eliz. 107, no. 74.
4. Cf. ibid., 41, no. 24; 77, nos. 48, 76; 148, no. 7.
5. D'Ewes, p. 509; Townshend, pp. 229–30.

'At length, Mr Cary stood up and said: "In the Roman Senate the consul always appointed what should be read and what not. So may our Speaker, whose place is a consul's place. If he err or do not his duty fitting to his place, we may remove him; and there have been precedents for it. But to appoint what business should be handled, in my opinion we cannot." At which speech some hissed.

'Mr Wiseman said: "I reverence Mr Speaker in his place, but I make great difference between the old Roman consuls and him. Ours is a municipal government, and we know our own grievances better than Mr Speaker . . ." And all said, I, I, I.'

Finally, Sir Robert Cecil intervened. He preferred to have the first bill read, but to be rid of this spirit of contradiction besought the Speaker to proceed with the bill for ordnance. 'And that's the House's desire', he concluded. The bill for ordnance was read.[1]

There was obviously close collaboration between Privy Councillors and the Speaker over measures in which the government was interested, and as a rule such bills were favourably timed. On 6 June 1572, 'about the middle part of the sitting of the House, Hatton cometh in and whispereth with the Speaker. By the sequel it was guessed he brought a message from the Queen for the reading again of the Scottish Queen's bill, for presently after, the Speaker moved to have the bill read; whereat there was much sticking, for it was thought more haste than good speed that the matter, being of so great weight and having received a reading but the day before, it should now proceed to the second reading. Yet at length it was read, through the means of the Speaker especially.'[2]

The Speaker could also exercise much influence by the timing and framing of questions. In 1572 Robert Bell, an independent Speaker with puritan sympathies, seeing a puritan bill running into danger on the third reading, spoke at the end of the debate, being loth, as he said, that 'the bill should come to the question as it is'. In his opinion it would have safer passage if amended. The House took his advice and committed it.[3]

But Bell was exceptional. Most Speakers were more conscious of the government's wishes. They irritated rather than pleased independent members by their manoeuvres. In 1581, Mr Anthony Cope,

1. ibid., pp. 306–7. 2. Bodley, Tanner MS. 393, fol. 62.
3. T.C.D. MS. N. 2, no. 12.

member for Banbury and a leading Puritan, stood up at the end of one of the last sittings of the session and charged Mr Speaker – Solicitor General Popham – that 'in some such matters as he hath favoured, he hath without licence of this House spoken to the bill; and in some other cases, which he did not favour and like of, he would prejudice the speeches of the members of this House with the question'.[1] Then in 1593, our diarist, who though anonymous does not conceal his puritan sympathies, has several animadversions on the Speaker's conduct; which is not surprising, since the Speaker was Edward Coke. The following are examples: 'Beguiled with the question propounded by the Speaker' – who was following the lead of Privy Councillors; or on another occasion, when Cecil, Heneage, and Bacon were against a bill, 'the subtlety in propounding the question thus gained the casting away of the bill'. The diarist also notes that a proviso which the courtiers supported 'was much pressed': not content with putting the question three times, though each time the Noes prevailed, the Speaker allowed the courtiers to divide the House. The Noes still prevailed.[2]

In 1597 Speaker Yelverton wrote to Sir Robert Cecil about a bill: 'I did all the good I could for furthering of it, and made two questions; whether it should be committed, which being denied I moved whether it should be ingrossed, which was also denied; so as now no more questions be to be made of it. I did favour it as much as, with the dignity of my place, I could; and I am sorry, if you did anything affect it, that it succeeded no better.' There was nothing improper in the Speaker's behaviour this time, though his zeal to please the great was flagrant.[3]

The House voted orally. Hooker describes how the question was put for passing a bill. The Speaker says: ' "As many as will have this bill pass in manner and form as we have heard, say Yea." Then they which like the bill say Yea. "As many as will not have this bill pass, let them say No." Then they which like it not say No ... If the voices be doubtful, then shall he cause the House to be divided.' On a division the Ayes went out of the House into the lobby, while the Noes, because they were against a novelty, had the privilege of sitting still; though if the question were such as to make the Noes

1. *C.J.* i, 134.   2. Cotton MS. Titus F. II, fols, 58b, 66b, 95.
3. *Hatfield MSS.* vii, 482–3.

innovators, they and not the Ayes went into the lobby. The Speaker then chose one or two tellers from each side, who, after numbering those left in the House, numbered the others as they came back through the lobby door.[1]

There was an 'ancient order' that when a division resulted in the passing of a bill, the whole House, as well opponents as supporters, must go out with the bill and fetch it in again, presenting it to the Speaker and saying they affirm it.[2] The Clerk, for example, noted in his Journal in 1589: '... the bill was afterwards, according to the ancient orders of this House in such cases, carried out and brought in again by Mr Vice-Chamberlain with the bill in his hand, followed and attended on by all the members of this House then present, as well those that had first before given their voices against the passing ... as those ... with the passing.'[3] The practice clearly had its origin in the twin medieval ideas that law-making involved the consent of the whole community and that members were attorneys for their constituencies. Hooker in 1571 describes it as normal procedure. Probably at that date it was, and even Lambarde, as late as 1587, mentions it without qualification; but as the number of divisions increased and time became more pressing, this ritual tended to pass out of use, though not out of memory. Lovers of time's decorous precedents, of whom there were many then as now, or victors lusting to inflict the full humiliation of defeat on their opponents, occasionally moved for the ancient practice. Sometimes they had their way; sometimes Speaker and House wanted to get on with other business.[4]

Strange as it may seem, by late-Elizabethan days the method of dividing weighted the scales heavily against the Ayes. 'Observe', says our Jacobean tract, 'that though they that say Yea are most, yet many times when the House cometh to be divided, they are not found to be so, because many of them sit still, as loth to lose their places, and sometimes because they will not be observed to have said Yea; so that the division of them is a disadvantage to the side that goeth out.'[5]

1. Hooker's tract; Stowe MS. 354, fol. 31.
2. Hooker's tract; Stowe MS. 354, fol. 31.   3. D'EWES, p. 451a.
4. Add MS. 5123, fol. 8b; D'EWES, pp. 573b, 574b, 667b.
5. Stowe MS. 354, fol. 31b.

An incident in 1601 offers the perfect illustration. A proviso was 'put to the question twice, and in my conscience', says our diarist, 'the I, I, I were the greater number; but the Noes, Noes would needs have the House divided. So, the door being set open, no man offered to go forth'. Thereupon a member, Mr Martin, said, ' "Mr Speaker, I have observed it, that ever this parliament the Noes upon the division of the House have carried it; the reason whereof as I conceive it, is because divers are loth to go forth for fear of losing their places ... I therefore do but move this unto the House, that all those that have given their I, I, I, would according to their consciences go forth. And for my part, I'll begin." And so went forth.' The Ayes won by 178 to 134, much to the annoyance of Sir Robert Cecil and Sir Walter Raleigh. Cecil was for calling Mr Martin to the bar to answer for his speech; but the House would not have it, nor were Cecil's fellow-Councillors all with him.[1]

This amusing incident explains why the courtiers, with Mr Speaker's favour, carried a motion to a division in 1593, despite three emphatic negatives to the question. There was always a gambler's hope. However, our 1601 member, Mr Martin, overstated his case. Actually, two out of seven earlier divisions in that parliament were won by the side which went out of the House. Of the seventeen known divisions in 1601 they won only six – a disparity striking enough.

If the Commons Journals can be trusted, divisions were rare before Elizabeth's reign. There were only seven in the nine sessions from 1548 to 1558 – three in one session and one each in four others. It was another of the signs of immaturity. Between 1559 and 1581 there were twenty-five divisions in seven sessions, though oddly enough there was only one in 1581 – as there had been in 1572. Beyond 1581 the Commons Journals are lost, and the figures are perhaps incomplete; but such as they are, they agree with the general picture of a body reaching maturity in the last parliaments of the reign. From seven in 1593 – the same number as in 1589 – they jump to thirteen in 1597 and seventeen in 1601. Moreover, in 1593 there was an emphatic change. Before that parliament the odds in a division were slightly in favour of the Ayes, whereas from 1593 on they were heavily against. In 1593 the Ayes scored only one victory compared with six for the Noes.

1. TOWNSHEND, p. 301.

In these later years parliamentary tactics were rapidly developing, and men could speak of 'policies in parliament' – the actual title given to the first section in a Jacobean tract. This tract, written about 1610, opens with the three following paragraphs: 'If any man have a purpose to overthrow a bill, if he espy a manifest fault or inconvenience therein, the policy is to conceal it, until it be ingrossed and ready to be put to the question for passage.' ' 'Tis a common policy in parliament, if any man be against a bill but would not seem to be so, to speak for it and by way of objection to show such matter against it as may not be answered, which, notwithstanding, he must seem to answer himself.' 'If it be feared that a bill will be exhibited, it hath been a policy, in the beginning of a parliament, to prefer a bill to the same purpose . . ., but intricate, and clogged with other matters that may ask long disputation; also to insert some such clause as it may seem to carry closely some inconvenience, which being discovered when it cometh to question for the passage, if it come so far, may quash it.' [1]

True, this tract is Jacobean; but how similar in spirit are the following comments by a parliamentary diarist in 1585. 'If a man will stay a bill', it is 'good policy to say, "It toucheth corporations very near; therefore look well to it." They will cry, "Away with it", when they understand it not. So in bills for Justices of Peace', with penalties attached: 'a good policy to bid them look to it to bring that penalty upon themselves. So in a matter of commodation, as in the bill of wards: "It concerns you all that have manors holden of you, to be thus defeated of them" '. To clinch his argument from human nature, our diarist added a biblical allusion: 'So St Paul to get favour of the Sadducees, when he said, "I am accused of the hope of our fathers".' We have already seen how Serjeant Harris killed a bill stone dead on the first reading in 1601 by saying that it would enable ecclesiastical judges to determine laymen's inheritances.[2]

In 1593 there was sharp contest over a bill promoted by the City of London to prevent alien strangers from selling retail any foreign commodities – a bill, as it happens, of some interest in connection with the play of *Sir Thomas More*, ascribed to Shakespeare.[3] On the

1. Stowe MS. 354, fol. 30.
2. Lansdowne MS. 43, fol. 166b; above, pp. 360–1.
3. Cf. A. W. POLLARD and others, *Shakespeare's Hand in Sir Thomas More*.

report stage, legal counsel were heard at the bar of the House both on behalf of the City and of the alien strangers who opposed the bill. Counsel for the strangers had made the point that if this bill were passed, merchants would thereupon want to oust them from their trade, and shoemakers, tailors, and others from theirs. 'Upon this instant', says our diarist, the Speaker 'showed a bill requiring they might be debarred such trades as to be shoemakers and such like.' 'But', he adds – and here lies the reason for recounting the incident – 'this bill was thought to be put in by the strangers themselves of policy.' Of course the suspicion may have been unfounded; but that it existed is in itself revealing.[1]

Could 'policy' be more sophisticated than in the following cynical manoeuvre which helped to kill a bill in 1601? We are told that a proviso was offered, and the House divided on it. Though it was 'utterly misliked, yet divers that were minded to overthrow the bill went forth with the proviso, because they would have it joined with the bill to overthrow it'. They carried the proviso by 126 to 85, and then, after further debate, rejected the bill on another division by one vote, 106 to 105. The close voting caused much ado. Some of the defeated Ayes claimed that they could have Mr Speaker's voice. When it was ruled that he had no vote, a member disclosed what he termed a 'foul and great abuse', namely, that 'a gentleman that would willingly have gone forth – to vote Aye – according to his conscience, was pulled back'. 'Why!' interjected Sir Walter Raleigh, 'if it please you, it is a small matter to pull one by the sleeve, for so have I done myself often times.' At this, there was 'a great stir' in the House, and when silence was restored, Mr Comptroller and Secretary Cecil, with moral rectitude, reproved their reprobate. As a matter of fact, on this occasion two wrongs made a right, for, as our diarist tells us, 'there was another gentleman, a No, pulled out, as well as the other was kept in'.[2]

Members with bills to steer through the House or motions to make had to think of their timing; and as the Speaker largely controlled the order of business, this must often have called for his cooperation. There were two periods during a sitting when the unexpected might happen. The first was during the opening hour, before late-comers

1. Cotton MS. Titus F. II, fol. 68; cf. D'Ewes, pp. 505 ff.
2. Townshend, pp. 320–2; D'Ewes, pp. 683–4.

arrived. 'It hath at some times been ordered for the preventing of carrying of bills with few voices', says our tract of the 1620s, 'that no bill should be put to the passage until nine of the clock, which time the House is commonly full, or shortly after.' 'Private bills', says a rather earlier tract, 'are commonly read in the mornings when the House is not full.'[1] Some such policy obviously guided the Elizabethan parliament, but it was far from regular.

The second strategic period was towards the close of the sitting, when members' thoughts were on rising and dinner. 'A great advantage to the passing of a bill, or committing or ingrossing, to make the question when the House is desirous to rise, as at eleven or twelve a clock': so notes a diarist in 1585. And our anonymous member, bent on abating the length of the forthcoming session in 1581, and dealing with 'matters of long argument', not only told his Councillor-friend that the Speaker should not 'be too hasty with eftsoons reading of those bills that have been found upon a first or second reading to be so large walking-fields', but also added: 'Let them not be moved in the beginning or midst of the forenoon, but near toward the rising of the House.'[2]

Privy Councillors employed this stratagem with the bill against sectaries in 1593. It was a government measure which Burghley, apparently expecting stormy passage through a puritan House of Commons, first passed through the Lords, trusting to forcing tactics – rightly called by our diarist 'a strange course' – to get it through the Lower House before the approaching end of the session. It was given a first reading in the Commons on a Saturday. Then on the Monday, 'very late in the day and after eleven of the clock' – a palpable and unscrupulous manoeuvre – it was offered to be read again. A member objected, saying that 'the day was spent, it was a bill of great importance and would require much speaking to'; it should be deferred 'till better leisure and longer time might be spent on it'. However, it 'was pressed much to be read'. Many of the House rose, but 'the Privy Council and many others sat'; and so the issue was put to the question. The rebels won, and the Council's stratagem failed.

Later, at the report stage, the need for forceful methods again

1. Add. MS. 36856, fol. 36b; Stowe MS. 354, fol. 32.
2. Lansdowne MS. 43, fol. 167b; Harleian MS. 253, fol. 35.

arose. The bill had been drastically amended, but still its critics were dissatisfied and called for more amendments and another committing. 'The Council were more against' this, for the parliament was near its end and another leisurely committing would put the bill in jeopardy. At length, on Sir Robert Cecil's motion, the doors of the House were shut, while a committee, along with anyone taking exception to the bill, went to the Upper Chamber to add further amendments and bring the bill back for its third reading and passage that morning. The House was kept prisoner till past 3 p.m. – the record sitting of an Elizabethan parliament. 'We were content to yield to anything, so we might rise', wrote a member. 'I assure you, Sir, a great many of us caught such a faintness there, with so long fasting, having neither meat in our bellies nor wit in our heads, that we shall not, I doubt me, be able to make a wise speech there while we live.'[1]

1. Cotton MS. Titus F. II, fols, 92 ff.; *The Times*, 12 December 1929 (Nicholas Saunders's letter).

CHAPTER 21

Procedure: III

MUCH of the quality and success of our English parliament depends upon decorum – upon rules and conventions, some obviously essential to any large debating assembly, some archaic but pleasing little ceremonies or courtesies that maintain the dignity of the House and eventually cast the spell of ritual over the most combative and sceptical of newcomers.

Our knowledge of such matters virtually begins with Elizabeth's reign. No doubt there were rules of debate before Elizabeth came to the throne. No doubt also there were rules of conduct. Were not Court and society, and indeed the universe, ordered in their degrees, their cohesive principle deference? But the practical need for formal behaviour must have grown as the activity and liveliness of the Commons increased; and we are surely not wrong in thinking this growth one of the striking features of the Elizabethan period. Rulings and disputes on points of procedure were frequent. The House was hammering out its 'orders' and recording them in its Journals.

At the beginning of the 1571 parliament, 'certain things' were 'moved and agreed upon for orders of the House'. Alas! we are not told what they were, whether rules of procedure or of conduct. They may have arisen out of an hortatory address by the new Speaker. At any rate, the Speaker began the session of 1576 with a motion on procedure and in 1581 delivered a disquisition on conduct, asking members 'to use reverent and discreet speeches, to leave curiosities of form, to speak to the matter . . . and not to spend too much time in unnecessary motions or superfluous arguments'; moreover, they were to see that their attendant servants, pages, and lackeys were kept in good order. His speech prompted a motion which marks a stage in the etiquette of the House. It was, 'that Mr Speaker and the residue of the House of the better sort of calling would always, at the rising of the House, depart and go forth in comely and civil sort for the reverence of the House, in turning about with a low curtsy, like as they do make at their coming into the House; and not so unseemly and rudely to thrust and throng out as of late time hath been disorderly used'. The motion was welcomed by all. In 1601 the Speaker had to ask members to observe 'the ancient order' for putting off their spurs before they came in. Others wanted boots and rapiers taken away also, 'but nothing was done therein'.[1]

The simpler, basic rules of modern debate, though first described in Elizabeth's reign, and rightly praised by Sir Thomas Smith in his *De Republica Anglorum* as 'a marvellous good order', were clearly established before 1558. Members wore their hats in the House. If they wished to speak, they stood up bareheaded, and if more than one stood, the Speaker was to appoint him to speak first that first arose.[2] This was not always simple. In 1589 the Speaker had to admonish the House for great disorder, unbecoming its honour and gravity. Members stood up to speak, sometimes three or four together, and though knowing who rose first, would not give place one to another, counting on the acclamation of fellow-members, whose calls became 'a great confused noise and sound of senseless words', to win them a hearing. Furthermore, they many times in their motions and arguments uttered 'very sharp and bitter speeches'. When faced with a similar situation in 1593, Edward Coke invoked a refinement of the general rule: 'Then the Speaker propounded it as an order of the House in such a case for him to ask the parties ... on which side they would speak ... and the party who speaks against the last speaker is to be heard first. And so it was ruled.'[3]

No one could speak twice to one bill on one day, 'for else', as Sir Thomas Smith said, 'one or two with altercation would spend all the time'. As today, 'every man speaketh as to the Speaker and not as one to another'; 'neither may he name any other, but only by circumlocution, as by saying he that spake with the bill or he that made this or that reason'. 'No reviling or nipping words must be used; for then all the House will cry "It is against the order".' In consequence, says Sir Thomas Smith – writing, be it added, in the earlier half of the reign – 'there is the greatest modesty and tem-

1. Cotton MS. Titus F. I, fol. 135; T.C.D. MS. N. 2, no. 12; *C.J.* i, 118; TOWNSHEND p. 181.

2. SMITH, p. 54; Add. MS. 5123, fol. 8b.

3. D'EWES, p. 434; Cotton MS. Titus F. II, fol. 51b.

perance of speech that can be used' 'in such a multitude and in such diversity of minds and opinions'.[1] But as today, human nature was sometimes too much for rules. 'I delivered my reasons in the fall of the leaf, and he answers me again in the Spring, but yet it hath no fruit at all', said a lawyer-member in 1585, replying to a much delayed and cutting attack on his speech about the illegitimacy clause in the bill of vagabonds. 'There have been better bastards', he went on, 'are, and will be than ever he was.' Whether the House cried 'Order!' or the Speaker intervened, we are not told.[2]

'If any speak too long and speak within the matter, he may not be cut off. But if he be long and out of the matter, then may the Speaker gently admonish him of the time or the business of the House, and pray him to speak as short as he may.' So ran the rule, according to William Lambarde. But our less theoretical Jacobean commentator declared: 'A chief rule to speak well and commendably in the House is so to speak as it be *rara, vera, et ponderosa*; that is to say, not to delight to hear himself speak in every matter and upon light occasions. Secondly, when he speaketh, so to inform himself that his speech be grounded upon truth. Thirdly, that it be warranted upon good and sound reason.'[3]

The Elizabethan House of Commons had a short way with bores or with speeches that annoyed them. They hawked and they spat, they shuffled and they hissed. In 1572 when Arthur Hall made a speech favourable to Mary Queen of Scots and the Duke of Norfolk, 'the House misliked so much of his talk that with shuffling of feet and hawking they had well nigh barred him to be heard'. They dealt as drastically with a courtier-like speech in 1601 when Serjeant Hele declared that 'all we have is her Majesty's, and she may lawfully at her pleasure take it from us'. The House 'hummed, laughed, and talked'. 'Well,' quoth the Serjeant, 'all your humming shall not put me out of countenance.' The Speaker intervened: 'It is a great disorder that this should be used; for it is the ancient use of this House for every man to be silent when anyone speaketh.' Thus encouraged, the Serjeant proceeded, but soon 'the House hummed again and he

1. I use both Smith (op. cit., pp. 54–5) and Lambarde (Add MS. 5123), who clearly copied Smith.
2. Lansdowne MS. 43, fol. 170b.
3. Add. MS. 5123, fol. 9; Stowe MS. 354, fol. 33b.

sat down'. The same session 'an old doctor of the civil law spake, but because he spake too long and too low, the House hawked and spat to make him make an end'. On this occasion, the zealous and experienced Sir Francis Hastings, a lover of liberty and Puritanism, rebuked the offenders, as he had rebuked others in 1584 when by coughing and spitting they had tried to cut short arguments they did not like.[1]

It took courage for lesser folk to address the House. 'Mr Speaker, I pray you hear me', began a member in 1584; 'I speak but seldom.' In 1601 Mr Zachariah Locke, member for Southwark, 'began to speak, but for very fear shook, so that he could not proceed, but stood still awhile and at length sat down'.[2] Some made apologetic openings. Our 1584-5 diarist jotted down two as samples: 'Marcus Crassus would never speak after Hortensius, but I after many Crassi and Hortensii.' 'I had not thought to have spoken: I see so many apt and able men to speak.' Even 'the great parliament man' Thomas Norton, 'a man wise, bold, and eloquent', employed the same gambit, saying, in 1571, that 'he was not ignorant, but had long since learned what it was to speak on a sudden, or first, before other men in parliament'.[3] Speakers were not supposed to read their speeches, though it was held, probably then as later, that 'any man may in speaking help his memory with notes'. 'I will be bold to look in my tables', said Recorder Fleetwood; 'I see other men do it.'[4]

The standard of speaking in Elizabethan parliaments was very high: indeed, parliamentary oratory may be said to have begun its resplendent history in this reign. The set speeches were artificial in the purer sense of that word. George Puttenham, in his *Arte of English Poesie*, published in 1589, alludes to the speeches in the Parliament House and the Star Chamber of Sir Nicholas Bacon, the Lord Keeper, and of Lord Treasurer Burghley, 'from whose lips I have seen to proceed more grave and natural eloquence than from all the orators of Oxford or Cambridge'.[5] Bacon's speeches were

1. BODLEY, Tanner MS. 393, fol. 54; TOWNSHEND, pp. 205, 220; D'EWES, p. 335.

2. Lansdowne MS. 43, fol. 168; TOWNSHEND, p. 282.

3. Lansdowne MS. 43, fol. 172b; Cotton MS. Titus F. I, fol. 136.

4. Add. MS 36856, fol. 54; Lansdowne MS. 43, fol. 174.

5. Arber's ed. (1895), p. 152. Cf. PEACHAM'S *Compleat Gentleman* (1906 reprint), pp. 43-4.

preserved in collections made in the same spirit that prompted men of the Renaissance to collect the letters of famous humanists. Of speeches in the House of Commons, Sir Walter Mildmay's survive in such a collection.

Apart from the speeches of the Speaker, which were so exacting that Speakers-designate were given lengthy secret notice in order to prepare them, there were certain great speeches – in moving for a subsidy, or on such themes as Mary Queen of Scots, the Jesuit Mission, the Pope, or Philip of Spain – which Privy Councillors had to make. They stinted an audience of connoisseurs neither in length nor quality. In 1584, after the Throckmorton Plot, the Chancellor of the Exchequer, Mildmay, spoke 'for the space of one hour and more': the text of his speech survives. He was followed by the Vice-Chamberlain; 'and his speech was above two hours'. The Recorder of London, who was no mean judge, if loquacity breeds judgement, was mightily impressed: 'Before this time never [were] heard in parliament the like matters . . . They were *magnalia regni*.'[1]

It was this sense of the consuming interest of parliamentary affairs that caused some members to keep diaries; and it was the erection of speaking into an art, calling for wit, phrase, and quotation that led many to write out their more deliberate speeches, a fair number of which survive. Did not the irrepressible Peter Wentworth, bane of his beloved Queen, pace in his garden between sessions, ruminating on the speech with which he was to startle everyone when the new session opened; and did he not come to the parliament of 1593 armed with the speeches, as well as the bill and petitions, for his projected but ill-fated succession campaign?[2] The time was not far distant – it came with the early Stuarts – when the stationers, 'publishers' of manuscripts, sold copies of speeches – priced according to the repute of the member – and 'true relations' of the House of Commons' proceedings.[3]

Classical, historical, and biblical allusions abounded in these speeches. Latin quotations were looked for as adornment. A member in 1586 began his speech by saying that he would not 'speak Latin':

1. Lansdowne MS. 41, fol. 45.
2. Cf. my articles on Wentworth, *Eng. Hist. Rev.* xxxix, 36 ff., 175 ff.
3. NOTESTEIN and RELF, *Commons Debates, 1629*, introduction.

it was 'too scholar-like'.[1] Legal precedents or arguments also never came amiss to a body of men, so many of whom had been to the Inns of Court.

Already in the first half of the reign, when our diaries enable us to see what was going on, there was a group of prominent but independent members who were the core of the debating; members who became known as 'great' or 'old' parliament men and were sought after by the promoters of bills and motions and in demand for committees. Thomas Norton, joint-author of the play *Gorboduc*, who tacked a bill on to the main government measure in 1571, carrying it through the Commons past strenuous official opposition, and who led the independents in the attack on Mary Queen of Scots and the Duke of Norfolk in 1572, was probably the most outstanding. An idea of his activity may be gathered from his account of an after-supper talk at a friend and fellow-member's house at the end of the 1581 session, when he was rebutting the charge of being in the Queen's disfavour. ' "You have taken great pains this parliament", said one of the company, "and there be few of the acts which either you have not drawn, or travailled about penning them at committees." ' ' "It is true," said I, "but there is none of them that I did draw and offer of my own first device, but all that I have done I did by commandment of the House, and specially of the Queen's Council there . . . Besides these pains, [I have] written many a bill of articles that the House did not see." '[2]

A unique figure was William Fleetwood, Recorder of London. Not for him the injunction '*rara, vera, et ponderosa*'; though he could be weighty enough. With his wit and his fund of legal and historical lore he held a privileged position, playing on his audience as a skilled musician on his instrument. When the wit is abstracted from his frequent speeches, as happens in a diary of 1572, one is astonished at the capacity of the House to bear with such displays of largely irrelevant knowledge; but when the wit is captured, as in a delightful diary of 1584–5, his popularity – but not the irrelevance – is easily understood.

Criticizing a bill with restrospective provisions, he cited a number of old statutes, then smugly said: 'Ye would think I had studied this year, I am so ready and perfect . . . I could keep you here till two a

1. Harleian MS. 7188, fols, 88 ff.   2. *Archaeologia*, xxxvi, 109 ff.

clock with like cases, for I had a collection of them till my book was picked from me. But I have said thus much of old statutes that young men may note it in their tables.' Then he went off on a tale of the Bishop of Winchester's cook, who had 'spurge comfits' — purgative sweetmeats – given him. 'Do you laugh at it?' exclaimed Fleetwood, as the House responded to his skilful touch. 'I tell you it is no laughing matter, when you hear the end.' The cook in revenge made a pottage of which an old woman died: 'and so I think she would, though she had not eaten' it, 'for she was very old'. This story led him to 'the statute for poisoners, that they should be boiled to death in hot lead, let down by little and little'. This in turn brought on a recollection of childhood: 'I remember I saw one once when I was a little boy, sitting behind my grandfather upon a horse, and was taken away when I cried for fear, for I tell you, it was a terrible matter to behold.' With innocent complacency he added: 'I could tell you of others, and I think you would be content to hear me these two hours.' Probably he was right, though for our part we might sympathize with the Clerk of the House who once noted: 'Recorder of London, a long tedious talk, nothing touching the matter in question.'

The style was the man. Inveighing against 'long bills, full of tautology and cacophony, penned in barbarous English', his memory recalled 'Mr Temple, who was as noble a parliament man as ever was in the House', who 'would cry out of long bills. I remember him: he was a very honest gent and he was buried in the churchyard at — very honorably.' On another occasion: 'Mr Speaker, in the like bill heretofore, one Mr Browne did demand a question of the Speaker, which was this: "And please you, Mr Speaker, if a man do sup of my porridge, is it lawful for me to have a lick at his ladle?"' We may let our amusing Recorder sum himself up. As he entered upon a quite pointless antiquarian commentary on the names of courts, he declared: 'But now you will say, I am out of the matter; but yet the best is, I will come in again.'[1]

What a contrast was Thomas Digges, the mathematician, member for Southampton in 1584–5 on the Earl of Leicester's nomination, and a frequent speaker in that parliament! 'Digges', says our diarist, 'commonly doth speak last, and therefore saith, "Every

1. The excerpts are from Lansdowne MS. 43, fols. 164 ff.

matter must have an end, and therefore to draw this to a con-clusion" '.[1]

The impression left by our diaries is that in the latter part of the reign what may be termed quality-debating was more broadly based. There was no Thomas Norton, no William Fleetwood, and after 1593 no Peter Wentworth; but the total effect of more diffused activity is very striking. The government and Court benches pre-sented a trio of exceptionally able speakers wholly different from each other in style and character. There was the incomparable Francis Bacon, so wise, so sententious. Even the parliamentary diarist momentarily and involuntarily adapts his style to that of the author of the *Essays*. The other two were Sir Walter Raleigh, incalculable, superb; and Robert Cecil, the embodiment of efficiency. Cecil evidently had a favourite opening gambit for his speeches: 'As I re-member', he said in 1593, 'I have been of this House these five parlia-ments, and I have not determined to say anything in these assemblies further than my cogitations should concur with my conscience in saying bare I or No. Give me leave, I pray you, to rehearse an old saying, and it is in Latin, *Nec te collaudes, nec te vituperes ipse* [neither extol nor disparage thyself]; for me to do the one were ex-ceeding arrogancy, and to do the other, I do confess I hope you will pardon me.' Twice again that parliament, he began: 'I am unwill-ing to speak'; 'I promised myself silence'. And in 1601 we have it again: 'I am sorry and very loth to break a resolution that I had taken, which is, for some respects to have been silent, or very sparing of speech all this parliament.' If his protestations were more than mere form, his instinct for management made nonsense of them. He was an effective parliamentary leader, though inclined on occasions to be irritable and tactless.[2]

Bills often got through with little or no debate. Sometimes, con-trary to normal practice if not to the rules, they might be read twice in one day; while on rare occasions, either as a compliment to some person or to a beneficent purpose, or else in the rush of the last days of a session, a bill might be passed through all its stages in one morning. On the other hand, it was very rare for a debate on any reading to spill over into the next sitting, and seldom that any bill

1. ibid., fol. 169b.
2. D'EWES, pp. 471, 475, 509; TOWNSHEND, p. 182.

monopolized a morning. Consequently, in the normal debate there was not time for many speakers. From the Journals and diaries it would seem that seven or eight speeches were a goodly number at a single reading, and twelve, thirteen, or, as on an occasion in 1572, eighteen touched high-water mark.[1]

In spite of the theory of equality, there was probably a social convention about the order of sitting in the House, other than that which placed Councillors and high royal officials next to the Speaker. In 1601 Sir Edward Hoby entered the Chamber while Sir Robert Cecil was speaking, and, 'coming to sit near the Chair', no one gave place to him. He therefore went and 'sat next the door', evidently in a petulant mood, for Cecil interrupted his argument with the caustic remark: 'If any that sit next the door be desirous to sit next the Chair to give his opinion, I will not only give him my place, but thank him to take my charge. We that sit here, take your favours out of courtesy, not out of duty.' Clearly, 'next the door' was not the place for a member of Hoby's quality. Presumably, here sat the meaner and younger. Perhaps it was at this end, furthest away from authority, that there developed – as Townshend calls it in 1597 – 'the rebellious corner in the right hand of the House'. In 1584–5 Recorder Fleetwood had occasion to rebuke some such boisterous spirits: 'Do you laugh?' he said, in the midst of a speech. 'Laugh not at me, no more than I do at you. You deal uncivilly with me. It is you always, there in that corner of the House.' Fellow-countrymen may or may not have sat together, but they could certainly act together. In 1601 we are told that 'the Devonshire men made a faction' against a bill, managed to stop further discussion of it, and so killed it.[2]

Attendance was a constant problem. Theoretically, members were obliged to give full attendance from the beginning to the end of a parliament, unless authorized to be absent. Discipline belonged to the Crown, but in 1515 an act of parliament imposed upon the Speaker and Commons the task of licensing early departures and penalized unauthorized absence with loss of wages. The penalty of course shed its sting as constituencies ceased to pay wages. Many

1. *C.J.* i, 110; D'EWES, p. 432b; T.C.D. MS. N. 2, no. 12; fragment of a journal for 1572 in Lord Braye's possession.

2. TOWNSHEND, pp. 199, 298; *I.H.R. Bull.* xii, 20; Lansdowne MS. 43, fol. 174.

Elizabethan members obtained licence from the Speaker or from the Speaker and the House, when they had reasonable excuses to offer; but many just went off, though in doing so they were guilty of a misdemeanour which either the Crown or the House might punish. In 1559, when parliament was adjourned for a ten days' recess over Easter, the Council wrote to the Sheriffs of the several counties instructing them to admonish any members who had 'departed from this parliament without licence' and warn them to be back on the day parliament recommenced, 'as they will answer for the contrary'.[1]

If it was not easy to restrain members from going home, it was impossible to keep them in regular attendance six days a week. Their duty was plain. 'None ought to depart the House before the Speaker arise to go', says Lambarde. In 1566 anyone doing so was to pay fourpence to the poor-box, a penalty increased to sixpence in 1589.[2]

We can obtain some idea of attendances from division figures, though of course they only give the members present on particular occasions; and divisions were usually few before 1597. The maximum number at a division in the earlier parliaments of the reign was 276 in 1563, out of a total membership of 411. In the later parliaments it was 345 in 1593, out of a membership of 462. In 1566 the highest figure in the four recorded divisions was 160; quite exceptionally low, and perhaps partially explained by this being a second session, held on prorogation. Some members probably stayed at home this session, despite possible penalties. We have only one division figure for the comparable parliament of 1572, which lasted for three sessions. This is for 1581, when 215 voted. The minimum division figures range from 86 in 1589 – exceptionally low, the next lowest being 100 in 1601 – to 157 in 1593.

In 1585, Bland, the currier, complained that there were 'scantly fifty persons in the House' when a bill was passed; which is certainly a much lower attendance than any of our division figures show, and if not explained as the myopia of an embittered loser, must reflect the House before it filled in the early morning. However, even at 'the golden speech' of Queen Elizabeth in 1601, when the Commons

1. 6 Hen. VIII, c. xvi; *A.P.C.* vii, 74.
2. Add. MS. 5123, fol. 9b; *C.J.* i, 76; D'EWES, p. 439a.

clamoured for all to be admitted, the attendance was apparently only one hundred and forty.[1]

The device employed against absenteeism was 'calling the House', when members' names were read from 'the Clerk's book', each going out of the House as he was called. 'It is a common policy', says Lambarde, 'to say upon the Wednesday that the House shall be called on Saturday, and on Saturday to say it shall be called on Wednesday, and so from day to day, by fear thereof to keep the company together.' In 1566, after several roll-calls during the session, at the end the House was called on two successive days and on the next and final day the defaulters were called, and twelve allowed to make default. What happened to the rest, we are not told. In 1581 the policy of keeping members on tenterhooks, described by Lambarde, was practised; and then, at the end of the session came swingeing fines on those absent the whole session without licence; twenty pounds for county, and ten pounds for borough members. Others who had attended, but departed without licence, were to lose their wages – a nominal penalty for many, though for the future they were threatened with fines as well. How the fines were collected we are not told: presumably they were certified into the Exchequer and so enforced.[2]

In 1589 the problem of securing better attendance was remitted to a committe. Ultimately it was agreed to inflict fines and amercements on those who defaulted at the calling of the House or were 'much or long absent' without licence or reasonable cause. But there is no evidence that the resolution was implemented. Indeed, just as the Queen in 1584 had found fault with the negligence of members 'in coming to the Parliament House and departing before the rising of the House', so now in 1589, 'upon some intelligence given to her Highness' that 'one half at the least' were absent, she intervened again, ordering the House to be called and defaulters noted.[3]

The truth was, that calling the House took much time, and the device adopted earlier in the reign of holding a special afternoon meeting for the business ceased to work when committees became so numerous that free afternoons were rare. In 1601, less than three

1. D'EWES, p. 366b; TOWNSHEND, p. 262.
2. D'EWES, p. 429b; Add. MS. 5123, fol. 11; C.J. i, 81, 136b.
3. Lansdowne MS. 43, fol. 170b; D'EWES, p. 453a.

weeks before the end of the session, a member complained that contrary to custom the House had not yet been called.[1] Perhaps pressure of business was sufficient excuse; perhaps the generality of members did not like this self-discipline.

The House of course had its drones. Members who came up to town to see fashions or attend to their own business, were not likely to be assiduous in their parliamentary service. But lawyers, too, gave much trouble. Their presence was considered essential for the proper scrutiny of bills; yet they were always disappearing through the doors and down the stairs to the courts in Westminster Hall. In 1585 Recorder Fleetwoodd moved 'that those of this House towards the law, being the most part of them at the bars in her Majesty's courts, attending their clients' causes and neglecting the service of this House, be called by the Serjeant to repair unto this House presently'. This was done, and 'many of them' came back. Another time that session Fleetwood himself asked leave to go to the assizes, 'but was denied of the House'. Says our diarist: 'He did ask of glory, knowing they would not spare him.' And the diarist adds, 'Afterwards, when he would have gone out a doors, they cried, "No! No!" about twelve a clock and would not suffer him.'[2]

James I's parliaments had the same trouble with their lawyers. In that reign, the authorities had less success with the problem of attendance. At any rate, Elizabeth's parliaments never seem to have reached such depths as were then recorded: twenty members present besides the Speaker one afternoon, and seventeen when the House assembled next morning. Such negligence, reaching Elizabeth's ears, would have brought instant, vigorous reprimand. But other times, other ways. Under James I the House resented the Crown's interference. Having been first admitted to a junior partnership in this matter of discipline by the act of 1515, they were now for ejecting the senior partner, originally sole owner.[3]

It was symptomatic of the new age being fashioned in Elizabeth's reign that parliamentary affairs began to be discussed outside the House, at parties, in taverns, and ultimately in the streets. Parliament was a council. Its business, like that of the King's Council, was supposed to be secret. Indeed, the Clerk of the Parliament's oath

1. ibid., p. 661a.   2. ibid., p. 347; Lansdowne MS. 43, fol. 166b.
3. *Bowyer's Diary*, pp. 25, 363, 99–100.

contained – *mutatis mutandis* – the secrecy clause sworn to by all Councillors: 'Ye shall keep secret all such matters as shall be treated in his said parliaments and not disclose the same before they shall be published, but to such as it ought to be disclosed unto.'[1] When a group of protestant opposition members invited themselves to dine with Sir William Cecil in Mary's reign, Cecil managed to evade sharing their subsequent imprisonment by forbidding them to discuss parliamentary business – an injunction they ignored.[2]

But the Elizabethan period was an expansive age. Taverns and tavern-talk multiplied, and gentlemen walked in St Paul's to exchange news and gossip. 'There was one Robert Phillipson who in Lothbury in London kept a table of twelvepence a meal for gentlemen', one John Crokes, who kept a similar table in Whitecross Street, and one Wormes, beside Fleet Bridge 'in the late house of courtly and courteous Gilbert Walker'; as well as 'Mistress Arundel's, the old and honourable ordinary table, as I may term it, of England', where the parliamentary hotheads of Mary's reign foregathered. These were the haunts of the young and choleric Arthur Hall, member for Grantham and former ward of Lord Burghley, where he and his like ate, played cards, and talked in mid-Elizabethan times. Here began his notorious quarrel with Melchisedech Mallory, which, with his pathological obstinacy and indiscretion, landed him in serious trouble with the House of Commons. Incidentally, the quarrel showed that parliament matters were common table-talk, for Mallory called Hall a fool, who had had to eat his words in the last parliament.[3]

As well bid the tide stay as stifle conversation on so increasingly interesting a topic as parliament. The after-supper talk which Thomas Norton had with his friends in 1581, one of whom was not a member of parliament, was a detailed discussion of the proceedings in that session. There must have been many such, even though authority frowned on it all. In 1585 the Queen told the House 'that she heard how parliament matters was the common table-talk at ordinaries, which was a thing against the dignity of the House'.[4] In 1589 a member asked the Speaker to admonish the assembly 'that

1. John Brown's Commonplace Book in Lord Braye's MSS.
2. My article in *Tudor Studies*, p. 275.
3. *Account of a Quarrel*, pp. 4 ff.   4. Lansdowne MS. 43, fol. 170b.

speeches ... be not any of them made or used as table-talk'; which he did, reminding them that they were 'the Common Council of the Realm'. Finally, excitement over the monopolies campaign in 1601 provided that note of transition to early-Stuart times which is apparent in so many aspects of late-Elizabethan history. 'Then must I needs give you this for a future caution', said Sir Robert Cecil, revealing the gulf between his age and ours; 'that whatsoever is subject to a public exposition, cannot be good. Why! Parliament matters are ordinarily talked of in the streets. I have heard myself, being in my coach, these words spoken aloud: "God prosper those that further the overthrow of these monopolies. God send the prerogative touch not our liberty." '[1]

As today, no outsider was allowed on the floor of the House. From time to time an unauthorized individual strayed in. 'Mathew Jones, gentleman, being found sitting in this House – in 1593 – and no member of the same, was brought to the bar, and there being charged by Mr Speaker ... humbly excused himself by ignorance; and appearing unto the House to be a simple, ignorant old man, was upon his humble submission pardoned, to be discharged tomorrow, paying his fees, and ordered in the meantime to remain in the Serjeant's ward of this House'. The Commons' bark, which was terrifying enough on these occasions, was worse than their bite, though the Serjeant, with his fee, always took a good mouthful.[2]

There was one extraordinary occasion in June 1572, without parallel in Elizabeth's reign, when Catherine de Medici sent over the great French nobleman Francis de Montmorency and the diplomat de Foix to ratify the Treaty of Blois and make an offer of Alençon's hand to Elizabeth. Some members of the mission were allowed to be present in the House of Commons at the reading of a bill. 'One French lord – perhaps Montmorency himself – was permitted to enter the House and to sit by Mr Treasurer, certain others to stand at the bar; which [bill] was argued in their presence by Mr Yelverton against the bill and Mr Recorder with the bill.' It was evidently a show-piece put on for their benefit, with the two star-debaters speaking. We should not have known of this curious incident but for a private member's diary.[3]

---

1. D'EWES, p. 432b; TOWNSHEND, p. 251.
2. D'EWES, p. 511. 3. T.C.D. MS. N. 2, no. 12.

CHAPTER 22

The Close of the Session

SAID a member in 1601: 'The granting of the subsidy seemed to be the *alpha* and *omega* of this parliament.' And the subsequent speaker pleaded 'that seeing the subsidy was granted and they yet had done nothing, it would please her Majesty not to dissolve the parliament until some acts were passed'.[1] The sentiment was not novel. In 1566 the Commons deliberately held up the money bill while they conducted an agitation over the succession to the throne; and later, in 1589, some were for delaying the ingrossing of the bill, fearing that when it was passed, the session would soon end.[2] Nor did the point escape the attention of that member who gave advice to a Councillor in 1581: 'When the principal matter, as subsidy or such like, for which the session was assembled, is once understood, then it is by and by conceived that until such matter be ended, the session will hold; and then such as would prolong the session give as many delays to that matter as they may.' To minimize delays he suggested that the subsidy bill should be ready beforehand, both the paper draft and the ingrossed parchment text. 'If any alteration happen, a piece of parchment is soon cut out and a new put in amended.'[3]

The government usually managed, whatever the counter-manoeuvres of private members, to get its money bill and any other vital measures through more or less to time, and the closing ceremonies of the session followed as quickly as possible. These ceremonies were always held in the afternoon.[4] Normally, the two Houses spent the morning of the last day, or even the early afternoon as well, giving the Queen's bill of pardon its one reading, and passing through their last stages any bill or bills that could be got ready for

---

1. TOWNSHEND, pp. 203–4.
2. *Eng. Hist. Rev.* xxxvi, 503 ff.; D'EWES, pp. 440–1.
3. Harleian MS. 253, fol. 35.
4. D'EWES, p. 427, conjectures that in 1589 the ceremonies were held in the morning; but S.P. Dom. Eliz. 223, no. 34 proves that he was wrong.

the royal assent. Occasionally, however, they were left with nothing worth doing. In 1601 the Commons sat quietly talking with one another about 9 a.m., some hundred being present out of the membership of four hundred and sixty-two, when a member rose and to pass the time put a case to the House on one of the new statutes of rogues, in the manner of a moot-day at the Inns of Court. They spent a brief morning in this exercise, reminded the Speaker of a request that he was to make to the Queen in their name that afternoon – which, to their great annoyance, he omitted to do – and then adjourned till 1 p.m. In the afternoon, they reassembled rather dilatorily, waited till after 2 p.m., when no doubt they knew that the Queen had arrived, and then went up to the gallery-door of the House of Lords, where they stayed about half an hour before the door was opened.[1]

Elizabeth always attended these ceremonial sittings, except in 1586-7 when she tactfully stayed away from a parliament concerned with the death of Mary Queen of Scots, and had her functions performed by commissioners. There was no public procession as at the opening of a parliament. The Queen came by barge from the Palace of Whitehall, sometimes about 2 p.m., at other times about 3 or 4 p.m., and once as late as about 5 p.m. Landing 'on the backside of the Parliament Chamber', she proceeded to her Privy Chamber, a nobleman bearing the Sword before her and a noblewoman her train, with lords, ladies, and heralds in attendance. Here she put on her parliament robes, while the peers put on theirs and took their places, ready for her entry into the Parliament Chamber; preparations which seem to have taken from half an hour to an hour.[2]

The setting was similar to that of the opening days. As described in 1566, 'the Queen's Majesty, being apparalled in her parliament robes, with a caul on her head, came forth and proceeded up and took her seat; the Marquis of Northampton, carrying the Cap of Maintenance, ... stood on her right hand, and the Earl of Westmorland the Sword at her left hand, with the heralds and Serjeants-at-Arms before her; the Queen's mantle borne up on either side from her arms by the Earl of Leicester and the Lord of Hunsdon, who always stood still by her for the assisting thereof when she stood up;

1. TOWNSHEND, pp. 333-4.   2. I.H.R. Bull. xii, 24.

her train borne by the Lady Strange, assisted by the Lord Chamberlain and Vice-Chamberlain. At the left hand of the Queen and south side kneeled the ladies; and behind the Queen at the rail stood the Lord Keeper on the right hand, the Lord Treasurer on the left hand, with divers young lords and peers' eldest sons.'[1]

When all were set, the Commons were admitted, preceded by their Speaker carrying the subsidy bill in his hand and escorted by two Councillor-members. Bowing their way to the rail, the Speaker there made three more obeisances and then opened the proceedings with an oration.

Much was expected of him, and he usually gave much. 'Mr Speaker', notes the Commons' Clerk in his Journal for 1566, 'made an excellent oration of two hours long.' Mercifully, not all were so long, though one wonders whether it was indisposition or the Speaker's loquacity which caused Elizabeth in 1576 to adjourn the closing ceremonies after the Speaker's oration and conclude them the next afternoon – a unique happening.[2]

Speaker Yelverton's speech in 1597, about five thousand words in length, was more than twice as long as his main speech at the beginning of the parliament. According to Roger Wilbraham, a connoisseur in such matters, he 'made a most fine and well filed speech, very short – an interesting comment, since the speech probably took close on an hour to deliver – and many well-couched sentences, somewhat imitating but bettering Euphues.' 'This speech', he adds, after his report of it, 'was full of elegancies, sweetly delivered; but thought too full of flattery, too curious, and tedious.' In truth – for we possess Yelverton's own text and can judge for ourselves – its prose was rich and musical; it was imaginative in its conceits, mature in its wisdom; perhaps too obsequious to the younger ear, but in the high Elizabethan tradition. 'It is a wonder to other countries, amid the tempestuous storms they be tossed with', runs one typical passage, 'to behold the calm and halcyon days of England, that possesseth a princess in whom dwelleth such undaunted courage without all dismay of any womanish fear, such singular wisdom without insolency, and such sincere justice without rigour.'[3]

1. D'Ewes, p. 113b.   2. C.J. i, 81; T.C.D. MS. N. 2, no. 12.
3. Yelverton MS. 121, fol. 22 ff.; Wilbraham's Journal, Camden Soc. Misc. x, 10–12.

Usually, these orations had an exordium in which the Speaker displayed his classical or historical knowledge and developed some theme from the art of government, linked with England or its Queen. Speaker Williams in 1563 described Elizabeth as 'the fourth Queen, establisher of good laws', whose three predecessors were Palestina, 'reigning before the Deluge', Ceres, and 'Marc., wife of Bathilacus, mother to Stillicus'. Alexander the Great, Cyrus, and Croesus also came into it. Edward Coke, true to form, showed by a quotation from Ine that Parliament, complete with spiritual and lay peers, knights and burgesses, and Convocation, was a West-Saxon institution; which Lord Keeper Puckering in his reply confirmed by citing King Canute! 'This sweet Council of ours', said Coke, as he developed his theme, 'I would compare to that sweet commonwealth of the little bees'; or as Wilbraham summarized the passage, he 'desired leave to compare her Majesty to a bee' — *'rex sine aculeis*, the master bee without sting'.[1]

Sooner or later, the Speaker touched on the proceedings of the session. He might do little more than ask for the royal assent to bills; or he might enter into some detail. He might include a petition that the Commons had charged him to make. Both in 1563 and 1566 he asked Elizabeth to marry, and ten years later made a final, eleventh-hour request. In 1572, after the Ridolfi Plot, echoing the grave concern of the Commons that she had not agreed to put Mary Queen of Scots to death, he cited the examples of Mithradates King of Armenia and 'Rothrodistus', of Isaachius Emperor of Constantinople and his brother Alexius, and of David and Absalom, adding Aesop's fable of the man, the serpent, and the lion, as warning and a spur to execute Mary. In 1581 the Speaker had special thanks and certain requests to offer, and in 1597 he actually incorporated in his speech a petition on the subject of monopolies prepared by a committee of the House.[2]

There remained two further duties to perform: to thank the Queen for her Act of General Pardon, which was indeed a substantial benefit to people in a law-ridden age; and to offer the subsidy or money bill, with appropriate words of loyalty and devotion, making 'low congés'

1. D'EWES, pp. 74, 465; WILBRAHAM, p. 3.
2. D'EWES, pp. 75a, 115b, 232b; T.C.D. MS. N. 2. no. 12; ibid.; *C.J.* i, 137; *I.H.R. Bull.* xii, 24; Yelverton MS. 121, fols. 26 ff.

as he handed over the bill.[1] Occasionally he asked for the Queen's pardon if the Commons or he had given offence.

The oration ended, the Queen called the Lord Keeper to her, and while he knelt gave him instructions what to reply. Except for last-minute thoughts, it must have been idle ceremony. The Lord Keeper's speech was not *ex tempore*. All the same, it did embody the Queen's instructions, sometimes her very phrases. It also re-hearsed the points in the Speaker's speech; so much so that in 1593 our diarist described it as 'an answer *verbatim* almost', and forbore a proper report, 'though it was done very exactly and excellently well'. Perhaps an inkling of what happened may be obtained from a letter of Burghley's to Secretary Davison on 1 December 1586, when after sittings devoted mainly to the Babington Plot, there was a cere-monial adjournment by royal commission: 'I pray you remember her Majesty to send in writing the manner of the speeches that my Lord Chancellor shall use tomorrow at the prorogation of the parlia-ment. I know her Majesty meaneth to thank them for their pains, and especially for their care and continuance therein for her safety.' The occasion of course was quite extraordinary, and it would be rash to argue with any certainty from it. But the Lord Chancellor on 2 December, before delivering his speech, went through the dumb-show of receiving instructions from the Queens' commissioners, al-though he presumably possessed them already in Elizabeth's own hand.[2]

If we may judge from Sir Nicholas Bacon's speeches, which range from about three thousand to four thousand words in length, the Lord Keeper's reply, though not brief, was shorter than the Speaker's oration. It kept fairly well to pattern, first rehearsing the Speaker's points, and then conveying the Queen's instructions. It might include reprimands addressed to the Commons, for encroaching on the prero-gative, or for discourtesy to the Lords or to Privy Councillors. 'Her Majesty hath commanded me to say unto you', declared Bacon in 1571, 'that like as the greatest number of them of the Lower House have in the proceedings of this session showed themselves modest, discreet, and dutiful, as becomes good and loving subjects, and meet

1. WILBRAHAM, p. 42.
2. Cotton MS. Titus F. II, fol. 97b; S.P. Dom. Eliz. 195, no. 22; my note in *Eng. Hist. Rev.* xxxv, 113.

for the places that they be called unto; so there be certain of them, although not many in number, who ... have showed themselves audacious, arrogant, and presumptuous, calling her Majesty's grants and prerogatives also in question, contrary to their duty ... and contrary to the express admonition given in her Majesty's name in the beginning of this parliament.' In 1576 the Queen by contrast was in mellow mood: 'Her Majesty had considered the great pains taken in the making of those laws, their discreet proceeding and modest dealing in this session of parliament, which she did most thankfully accept; and though one member thereof – the redoubtable Peter Wentworth – had overslipped himself, yet upon his humble submission declared, she cannot but hope he will be a profitable member of his commonweal.' Truth to tell, even when she chastised, there were words of comfort to pluck up their dismayed spirits.[1]

When the Lord Keeper expressed the Queen's thanks for the subsidy bill, they were always in felicitous and endearing terms. It was common form for him to urge his listeners to show the same alacrity in collecting the taxes as they had done in granting them; and this part of the speech gave Elizabeth in 1576 the opening for one of her unconventional acts which, though disconcerting for her victim, must have charmed the company. Bacon had begun to dilate in rather long-winded fashion on this theme of payment, when the Queen interrupted and commanded him to cease. 'Lo! my Lords and masters', he concluded, 'her Majesty's pleasure is that I shall forbear any further to exhort you ... Her Majesty thinketh it needless and a vain matter to exhort men so willingly and lovingly disposed, and had rather hazard a part of the thing granted, than to breed any suspicion ... that she is doubtful of your faithful and diligent dealing ...' In his own text of the speech, which we possess and in which he inserted the interruption, Bacon whimsically added: 'Hereafter followeth that I intended to have said if I had not been countermanded.'[2]

His speech ended, the Lord Keeper commanded the Clerk of the Crown 'to read the acts'; whereupon the Clerk 'stood up before the little table set between the woolsacks, and after obeisance made began to read' the titles of the bills passed by both Houses. As each was read,

1. D'Ewes, p. 151; T.C.D. MS. N. 2, no. 12.
2. Cambridge, C.C.C. MS. 543, fols. 25 ff.; T.C.D. MS. N. 2, no. 12.

the Clerk of the Parliaments, standing up and consulting a paper signed by the Queen, gave the royal answer, both Clerks thereupon again making obeisance. The Queen herself had a paper in her hand, 'by which she examineth the bills as they be read'. In 1593, because the Clerk of the Crown 'could not well see nor read' – it was after 7 p.m. in early April, the Chamber was probably ill-lit and the clerk old – the Queen commanded the Attorney to read the titles.[1]

To public bills the royal assent was *La Royne le veult*, the Clerk making a short pause after the words *La Royne*; to private bills, it was *Soit faict comme il est désiré*.[2] Incidentally, the French ambassador, De Maisse, was very surprised to find his language used in these responses.[3] The lay and clerical subsidies and the act of general pardon received more elaborate answers. For the lay subsidy the response was: *La Royne remercie ses loyaulx subjects, accepte leur benevolence, et aussi le veult*. In 1597, when it was intoned, Elizabeth 'rose up and bended herself to the commonalty, opening her arms and hands; and then the commonalty kneeled, and then she sat down and they stood up again'. She did the like to the clergy, when the royal assent was given to their subsidy. Whether this charming and expressive ritual was new, we do not know: perhaps it sprang from the mellow and spontaneous affection of age. The act of pardon came last. Elizabeth rose and stood as the Clerk pronounced the thanks of her subjects, ending, *et prient à Dieu qu'il vous donne, en santé, bonne vie et longue*; at which the Commons 'gave a loud *Amen*'.[4]

On two occasions – if not on more, for one cannot but reflect that had certain diaries not survived, we should know nothing of these happenings – there were incidents which revealed that the formalism of the royal assent had not yet won its final victory over the sovereign. In 1571 during the antiphony of the Clerks, two of the bills were brought to Elizabeth who, after perusing them, called Lord Burghley to her. When they had talked awhile, the bills were delivered to the Clerk of the Parliaments, who returned to his place, and there the title of one – the bill of treasons – was read. Thereupon, before the royal assent was given, the Queen rose to explain her attitude to the

---

1. Cotton MSS. Titus F. I, fol. 81; F. II, fols. 99b ff.
2. Cf. *Lords Journals*, ii, 225; *I.H.R. Bull.* xii, 25.
3. DE MAISSE, *Journal*, p. 31.
4. *I.H.R. Bull.* xii, 26; *Lords Journals*, ii, 225.

409

bill and why she had taken exception to the second bill that had been tacked on by the Commons, but deleted by the Lords. She also appears to have commented on two bills: one for respite of homage, a Commons' bill which had languished in the Lords; and the other a bill to limit legal counsellors' fees, a Lords' bill which apparently passed the Lower House too late for any amendments to be passed by the Higher House. She promised 'in time' – a fugitive promise indeed! – to take order for reforming these evils herself: in other words, to employ the royal prerogative rather than parliament.[1]

The second incident was in 1572. The whole purpose of this session had been to deal with the problem of Mary Queen of Scots. Elizabeth had refused to let parliament put her to death. She was now unwilling to assent to the milder bill against her. But, either deceiving herself, or hoping to deceive parliament, she wished the formal words of rejection, *La Royne s'advisera*, to be interpreted literally – as a postponement and not a veto. When the title of the bill was read, she called Lord Keeper Bacon to her, and instructed him to explain her purpose and her reasons. 'The Queen's pleasure is', said Bacon, 'I wish you not to be moved though upon a strange occasion a strange answer have been made.' Here the precise Elizabeth interrupted him to point out that as yet no answer had been made. Correcting himself, Bacon proceeded with his task, and afterwards the royal veto – which was not meant as a veto, and nevertheless proved to be one – was pronounced.[2]

The veto was still a normal part of procedure. It was used by Elizabeth in every parliament, and there is no evidence that as an institution it caused comment or resentment. In fact, we must conclude that the Crown was constitutionally as free to quash a bill as either House was to quash the other's bills. After passing two such divergent bodies as Lords and Commons, there was of course less occasion to suppress measures at this stage; nor did the sovereign lack means of blocking obnoxious bills during their progress through the two Houses. Moreover, politics – the art of the possible – were not entirely divorced even from Tudor monarchy. Too drastic or ill-considered a use of the royal veto might have stirred up trouble.

The number of bills vetoed by Elizabeth in any session varied from one to twelve. In 1563 she vetoed six, in 1576 seven, in 1581 one,

1. *Trans. Devon Assoc.* xi, 490   2. T.C.D. MS. N. 2, no. 12.

410

in 1585 nine, in 1593 one, and in 1597 – not the forty-eight of our text-books, but twelve.[1] Curiously enough, in 1563 the Lords spent the early part of the last afternoon seeing through their final stages four bills that a few hours later were vetoed. Perhaps they were too late for the Queen's scrutiny and decision; but it was not so in other sessions.[2]

Occasionally the veto reflected a significant conflict of policy and will between Crown and Parliament. The bill against Mary Queen of Scots in 1572 is the most dramatic example. But there were others. A Commons' bill for coming to church and receiving the communion, passed by both Houses in 1571, and another for the more reverent observing of the Sabbath Day, passed in 1585, were both vetoed, clearly because the Queen objected to unofficial legislation on the Church. Then in 1571 she also vetoed a Commons' bill to relieve Sheriffs and Justices of the Peace of the cost of assize diets, on which subject there had been a bill in 1563, stopped in the Lords by Elizabeth, who then declared that she herself would take order in the matter, administratively.[3] Once more she was defending the prerogative.

But normally no real divergence of principle was involved. The measures vetoed were private bills or others of minor significance, which the Queen, free from the hazards of parliamentary tactics and lobbying, and perhaps better informed than either Commons or Lords, thought it inexpedient to pass. Here no doubt Burghley's advice was all-important. As we have seen, the Queen called him to her when in 1571 she wished to consider two bills during the actual ceremony of the royal assent. It was he who kept a close eye on proceedings and received from the Clerks during the session lists showing the stages of all bills in both Houses. There is such a list for 1576 entitled, 'A list of the acts passed in both Houses. Those that be crossed are such as her Majesty is thought will not assent unto'.[4] Both promoters and opponents of bills sent him statements of their case, which he could weigh at leisure.

1. Cotton MS. Titus F. I, fol. 81; S.P. Dom. Eliz. 107, no. 88; T.C.D. MS. N. 2, no. 12; ibid.; Cotton MS. Titus F. II, fol. 99b; my note, 'Q. Elizabeth's Quashing of Bills, 1597/8', *Eng Hist. Rev.* xxxiv, 586–8, xxxvi, 480; Lansdowne MS. 83, fols. 207–8.
2. *Lords Journals*, i, 618.   3. ibid., p. 605.
4. S.P. Dom. Eliz. 107, no. 88.

It so happens that a petition from the Bailiffs and burgesses of Conway survives to give us the perfect justification for the royal veto. Its date is 1585 and it asks Burghley to secure the Queen's veto of a bill to hold the county sessions at Carnarvon only, instead of Carnarvon and Conway. The bill had been promoted by the knight and burgess for the county and town of Carnarvon, the only representatives in parliament from that shire; and it passed both Houses without the corporation of Conway being aware of its existence. Even now, declared the Bailiffs, they could not prepare an answer to its argument, because they could not 'for any fee' procure a copy of the bill from the Clerk of the Higher House. The veto was the only remedy left, and whatever the intrinsic merits or demerits of the bill, justice obviously demanded its exercise. Vetoed the bill was.[1]

Other statesmen and courtiers than Burghley could reach the Queen's ear; and no doubt did. Did not Thomas Howard warn Weymouth that if he went forward with their bill, Sir Christopher Hatton's influence would overthrow it, 'when it should come to her Majesty's hands'?[2] But it was not easy to fool or persuade Elizabeth; and there can be little doubt that Burghley's responsible and dispassionate advice was paramount.

The number of acts to which the Queen gave her assent varied from ten in 1586–7 and seventeen in 1572, both extraordinary parliaments, to forty-eight in 1563 and forty-nine in 1585. In the whole reign, the total came to four hundred and twenty-nine, of which rather more than one-third were private acts. Both Houses quashed each other's bills, or let them lapse. The greater slaughter was done by the Lords; naturally, because fewer bills originated with them. Moreover, behind their own bills there was greater prestige, as the Commons were reminded when in 1585 the Queen instructed the Lord Chancellor to rebuke them for rejecting a Lords' bill without first asking for a conference with their Lordships. In 1585 nine bills passed the Commons but failed to pass the Lords: and as we have seen, the Queen vetoed another nine.[3]

Though the Lord Keeper was the Queen's mouthpiece, and she herself – or so she said in 1566 – did not love to speak 'in such open assemblies', nevertheless, 'remembering that commonly prince's own

---

1. ibid., 176, no. 49; T.C.D. MS. N. 2, no. 12   2. Above, p. 374.
3. T.C.D. MS. N. 2, no. 12.

words be better printed in the hearer's memory than those spoken by her command', she sometimes broke through the formality of these occasions to address her parliament. In 1566, after a troublesome session and before the Lord Keeper pronounced the dissolution of the parliament, she spoke winged words to the Commons: 'Who is so simple that doubts whether a prince that is head of all the body may not command the feet not to stray when they would slip? God forbid that your liberty should make my bondage, or that your lawful liberties should anyways have been infringed.' She ended as a mother over her children: 'Let this my discipline stand you in stead of sorer strokes never to tempt too far a prince's patience; and let my comfort pluck up your dismayed spirits and cause you think that, in hope that your following behaviour shall make amends for part of these errors, you return with your prince's grace, whose care for you, doubt you not, to be such as she shall not need a remembrancer for your weal'.[1]

In 1576 the Queen again spoke, though not till the prorogation had been pronounced and the greater part of the Commons had departed. Alas! our diarist could not hear the speech – 'scant one word of twenty, no one perfect sentence' – and no text survives. Nor could this same diarist hear when in 1585 Elizabeth again spoke, this time before the prorogation. Indeed, hearing could not have been easy in the packed crowd of Commons behind the bar, 'where – said Hayward Townshend in 1597 – was the greatest thrust and most disorder that ever I saw'. However, Stow the chronicler, though never a member of parliament, preserved the text of the 1585 speech. It was a declaration of affectionate thanks, in Elizabeth's most winning manner, coupled with comments on the state of the Church, which had been troubling the Commons. The Queen spoke again in 1589, probably answering a petition to declare war on Spain, made by the Speaker and agreed on that very day by both Lords and Commons. All we know about her speech is a single sentence quoted by Edward Coke in the next parliament, but it gives the tone and effect: 'Many come hither *ad consulendum qui nesciunt quid sit consulendum.*' 'A just reprehension to many', added Coke.[2]

In 1593, when the Lord Keeper had ended his speech, after a pause

---

1. D'Ewes, p. 116b; my article, *Eng. Hist. Rev.* xxxvi, 513–14.
2. T.C.D. MS. N. 2, no. 12; ibid.; *I.H.R. Bull.* xii, 24; Stowe, *Chronicle*, sub anno 1585.

the Queen rose and spoke 'in golden words'. 'A most princely speech', says the diarist, 'but ill fortune was I stood so as I could not hear but little of it.' It was a speech to England at war, worthy in its diction, its courage, its emotion to rank with the unsurpassed speeches to which we in our own day have listened. 'This kingdom', she said, 'hath had many noble and virtuous princes. I will not compare with any of them in wisdom, fortitude, and other virtues; but (saving the duty of a child, that is not to compare with her father) in love, care, sincerity, and justice, I will compare with any prince that ever you had or shall have.' 'For mine own part, I protest I never feared, and what fear was my heart never knew. For I knew that my cause was ever just, and it standeth upon a sure foundation . . . Glad might that king my greatest enemy be, to have the like advantage against me . . . Even our enemies hold our nature resolute and valiant'; and whensoever they shall make any attempt against us, 'I doubt not but we shall have the greater glory'.[1]

Finally, in 1601, her last parliament, though she had in the course of the session delivered her 'Golden Speech' to the Commons, long to remain in the memory of its hearers and of posterity, 'parliament being dissolved and each one ready to depart without further expectation, as the manner is, the Queen's Majesty raised herself out of her royal seat and made a short, pithy, eloquent, and comfortable speech'. Roger Wilbraham, who alone records it – Hayward Townshend, the parliamentary diarist, must, one suspects, have made a rapid exit and thus most lamentably failed us – explains that 'besides I could not well hear all she spake, the grace of pronunciation and of her apt and refined words, so learnedly composed, did ravish the sense of the hearers with such admiration, as every new sentence made me half forget the precedents'. The young Dudley Carleton, no flatterer, who was present, perhaps masquerading 'as a burgess', was also full of praise in a letter to his intimate friend, John Chamberlain: 'The Queen concluded all with a long speech – evidently Carleton was less patient than that connoisseur of speeches, Wilbraham – which was much commended by those who heard her: the Bishop of Durham told me he never heard her in a better vein.'

The speech was a review of her whole reign; a final accounting –

1. I cite from both Cotton MS. Titus F. II, fols. 98–9, and STOWE, *Chronicle*. There is a summary in Wilbraham's Journal, *Camden Misc.* x, 4.

who can doubt it? – to her people. 'Concerning our affection to our people', she concluded, 'it is our happiest felicity and most inward joy that no prince ever governed a more faithful, valiant, and loving people, whose peace and prosperity we evermore prefer before all temporal blessings; and be you well assured, whether we make peace or war, the good of our people shall be evermore preferred therein. We never attempted anything to damage or dishonour our people, and though we may not attribute merits to our own wit in choosing out the safest harbour for us all to anchor at, yet the finger of God, directing the actions of all princes that sincerely serve Him, and our long-lived experience (though in a mean wit) shall make us able to discern and embrace that which shall tend to the prosperity of our people; to whom I wish, that they that wish them best may never wish in vain.'[1]

Elizabeth may have spoken on other occasions. We cannot be sure; yet certain it is that there was no session of parliament but felt the impress of her personality.

Usually, the final act of a session was the prorogation or dissolution, spoken by the Lord Keeper on the Queen's command. 'It is her Majesty's pleasure that this parliament shall be dissolved; and she giveth licence to all knights, citizens, and burgesses to depart at their pleasure. And so, God save the Queen! And all the Commons said aloud, *Amen*!' 'And then the Queen rose and proceeded into her Privy Chamber, and shifted, and then to her barge, and so to the Court.' In 1601, as she left the Chamber, she spoke to the Speaker and the Comptroller, giving them 'particular thanks'.[2]

If the legal term was already over and the London season at an end, most members probably made their way speedily home; some from the boroughs to make report on the proceedings to their fellow-townsmen, others to tell their budget of news to friends and neighbours. An occasional member took home a diary or the text of a speech, to serve as a memorial of a rare and exhilarating experience. Alas! the accidents of time have taken their toll of these manuscripts, but enough remain, in the British Museum, the libraries of ancient universities, and the muniment rooms of country houses, to revive for us the spirit and deeds of our glorious past.

1. *Camden Misc.* x, 44–7; *Cal. S.P. Dom., 1601–3*, p. 134.
2. TOWNSHEND, p. 336; Cotton MS. Titus F. I, fol. 81; *Cal. S.P. Dom, 1601–3*, p. 134.

LIST OF
ELIZABETHAN PARLIAMENTS

	Year	Date of election writ		Dates of sessions
1	1559	5 Dec. 1558		25 Jan. to 8 May, 1559
2	1563–7	10 Nov. 1562	(i)	12 Jan. to 10 Apr. 1563
			(ii)	30 Sept. 1566 to 2 Jan. 1567
3	1571	unknown		2 Apr. to 29 May, 1571
4	1572	28 Mar. 1572	(i)	8 May to 30 June, 1572
			(ii)	8 Feb. to 15 Mar. 1576
			(iii)	16 Jan. to 18 Mar. 1581
5	1584–6	12 Oct. 1584		23 Nov. 1584 to 29 Mar. 1585
6	1586–7	15 Sept. 1586		29 Oct. 1586 to 23 Mar. 1587
7	1588–9	18 Sept. 1588		4 Feb. to 29 Mar. 1589
8	1593	4 Jan. 1593		19 Feb. to 10 Apr. 1593
9	1597–8	23 Aug. 1597		24 Oct. 1597 to 9 Feb. 1598
10	1601	11 Sept. 1601		27 Oct. to 19 Dec. 1601

NOTE. The year dates cover the period from the date for which the parliament was summoned to the date of dissolution, and do not always coincide with the sessional dates.

Index

Abingdon, borough of: enfranchised, 134 n.; elections and M.P.s, 203, 299; Steward, 202

Adams, Robert, Mayor of Chichester, 250, 255

Aldborough (Yorks), borough of: enfranchised, 134 n.; elections and M.P.s, 182 n., 217, 219, 220

Aldeburgh (Suffolk), borough of: enfranchised, 134 n.; election, 135 n.

Alençon, Francis of Valois, Duke of, 402

Alford, Francis, 153, 155

Alford, Roger, 215

Alleyn, Sir Christopher, 207 n.

Almer, William, of Pantyokin, 106-12

Altham, James, 372

Andover, borough of: enfranchised, 134 n., 137, 138, 139; elections and M.P.s, 229, 299; High Steward, 137, 139, 202, 228

Anglesey, 112; M.P., 144, 280

Anne of Cleves, Queen, 239

Appleby, borough of, elections and M.P.s, 260, 299

Armada, the, 40, 282, 304, 341

Arnold, Sir Nicholas, 261

Arundel's, Mistress, eating house, 401

Ashbie, William, 260

Ashby-de-la-Zouch, 37, 164

Ashley, John, 189, 219

Ashwell, 132

Association, Bond of, 210

Atkins, Thomas, Town Clerk of Gloucester, 262-9

Atkinson, Mr, 373

Attorney General, the, 73, 83, 92, 147, 168, 222

Atye, Arthur, 228-30, 299

Audley, Thomas, Speaker, 319

Awdeley, John, 217 n.

Aylesbury, borough of: enfranchised, 134 n., 175; elections and M.P.s, 174-6, 182

Babington Plot, the, 179, 278, 367, 407

Bacon, Lady Ann, 301

Bacon, Anthony, 160, 229 n., 301

Bacon, Edward, 192, 202

Bacon, Sir Francis, 55, 145, 160, 224; elections, 171, 174, 179, 190, 192, 230; as M.P., 289, 301, 363, 379, 382, 396; references to his Essays, 23, 131, 224, 396

Bacon, Nathaniel, 55-6, 301

Bacon, Sir Nicholas, Lord Keeper, 54-5, 199, 202, 302; speeches, 392, 407-8, 410

Baeshe, Edward, Surveyor of Victuals for the Navy, 220

Bagenall, Sir Henry, 143, 197, 280

Bagot, Richard, 56-7, 227

Bagworth Park, 167 n.

Baker, Sir John, Speaker and Privy Councillor, 273, 286

Baker, Richard, Town Clerk of Gloucester, 266-9

Banbury, borough of: enfranchised, 134 n.; elections and M.P.s, 286, 382; puritan ministers in district, 299

Banbury, Owen, yeoman, 108

Banister, Edward, 187 n.

Banister, Laurence, 187 n.

Barker, William, 186 n., 187 n.

Barlow, John of Slebech, 246

Barlow, Robert, of Barlow, 33

INDEX

Edmund Burke
On Government, Politics and Society

Selected and Edited by B. W. Hill

Quoted more frequently than almost any other political writer, Edmund Burke has been cast in many roles – as arch-defender of established authority, radical critic of traditional orthodoxies, exponent of liberal values. Yet the historical Burke is a much more complex and fascinating thinker than any of these views allows.

The aim of this new selection is to reveal the range of Burke's outlook as politician, imaginative writer, and philosopher by drawing upon the extensive speeches and pamphlets on the American Colonies, the Monarchy and the Party system, and the Government of India, as well as the more widely known *Reflections on the Revolution in France*.

In his long introduction and editorial comments, Dr Hill presents Burke as an eclectic thinker, but a consistent advocate of social morality, a friend of good caring government, and an opponent of extremist politics whether of the Right or the Left.

'Almost alone in England, he brings thought to bear upon politics, he saturates politics with thought.' *Matthew Arnold*

'Burke *is* an extraordinary man. His stream of mind is perpetual.' *Samuel Johnson*

'No English writer has received, or has deserved, more splendid panegyrics than Burke.' *Leslie Stephen*

'There is no wise man in politics, with an important decision to make, who would not do well to refresh his mind by discussion with Burke's mind.' *Harold Laski*

The Fontana History of Europe

Praised by academics, teachers and general readers alike, this series aims to provide an account, based on the latest research, that combines narrative and explanation. Each volume has been specially commissioned from a leading English, American or European scholar, and is complete in itself. The general editor of the series is J. H. Plumb, lately Professor of Modern History at Cambridge University, and Fellow of Christ's College, Cambridge.